W9-BKS-727

This work documents the history of techniques that statisticians use to manipulate economic, meteorological, biological, and physical data taken from observations recorded over time. The decomposition tools include index numbers, moving averages, relative time frameworks, and the use of differences (i.e., subtracting one observation from the previous value in the series). Professor Klein argues that nineteenth-century business journals, such as *The Economist* and the *Commercial and Financial Chronicle*, were as important to the development of time series analysis as Latin treatises on probability theory. While examining the roots of mathematical statistics in commercial practice, she traces changes in analytical forms from table to graph to equation. Klein cautions that we risk measurement without history in the mechanistic blending of the probability theory of stationary processes with the practical dynamics of commercial traders. This history is accessible to students with a basic knowledge of statistics, as well as financial analysts, statisticians, and historians of economic thought and science.

Statistical Visions in Time

Statistical Visions in Time

A History of Time Series Analysis, 1662–1938

JUDY L. KLEIN

CAMBRIDGE
UNIVERSITY PRESS

PUBLISHED BY THE PRESS SYNDICATE OF THE UNIVERSITY OF CAMBRIDGE
The Pitt Building, Trumpington Street, Cambridge CB2 1RP, United Kingdom

CAMBRIDGE UNIVERSITY PRESS
The Edinburgh Building, Cambridge CB2 2RU, United Kingdom
40 West 20th Street, New York, NY 10011-4211, USA
10 Stamford Road, Oakleigh, Melbourne 3166, Australia

First published 1997

Printed in the United States of America

Typeset in Photina

Library of Congress Cataloging-in-Publication Data
Klein, Judy L., 1951–
Statistical visions in time : a history of time series analysis,
    1662–1938 / Judy L. Klein.
      p.   cm.
    Includes bibliographical references (p. 315–334) and index.
    ISBN 0-521-42046-6 (hardback)
    1. Time-series analysis – History.   I. Title.
QA280.K59   1997
519.5'5'09 – dc21   96-36856
                                                              CIP

*A catalogue record for this book is available from
the British Library.*

ISBN 0-521-42046-6 hardback

To Polly and Leon Klein

Contents

Figures and Tables

Tables

Preface

In this study, history is not only an end in itself; history is also a means to understanding problems that persist with current applications of regression and correlation on time series data. Before I took up the history of statistics, I was a user and a teacher of statistics. Questions would run through my mind as I wrote equations on the blackboard. One was why do econometricians rely so heavily on regression analysis at the expense of other quantitative techniques?[1] I tried in different ways to articulate the inconsistencies that I saw in using regression, a technique of logical comparison, to explain and predict temporal processes. That led me to the question of how the early practitioners and theoreticians of time series analysis perceived the discrepancy that I thought was so blatant. Pursuing this history has provided me with a rich understanding of the contradiction: juxtaposing short-term and long-term focuses, distinguishing the problems of biometrics and econometrics, weaving the scientific propensity to decompose with the practical propensity to make profits, giving context to the first articulation of the concept of a trend, and generating a philosophical perspective of a variety of space–time notions that mathematicians have used to explain problems in the statistical analysis of temporal processes.

I was encouraged to come across a vision, remarkably similar to my own, of this paradox of logical and historical variation in Lucien March's 1904 study of the French money market (see Figures 1.4, 1.5, and 9.3). Similarly, I was heartened to learn that Udny Yule had spent twenty years pondering the cause of nonsensical correlations in time series data, and that his questioning eventually led to his pioneering specification of autoregressive processes. Besides positive reinforcement of our doubts, history also offers us "new" solutions. Concepts and techniques that were dead ends in their original context and thus forgotten within the mainstream practice sometimes have the capacity for generating viable new directions decades later. The important role of flexible intervals between observations in the earliest studies of autoregressive

---

[1]   An answer to this question came as much from my investigation into the history of graphs in economics (Klein 1995b) as from this present study.

stochastic processes has this potential. Similarly, a historical approach that crosses disciplines can rotate perspective and encourage new ways of thinking. The contrast, for example, between serial correlation with meteorological and economic data reveals the link between time and space that was so important to Yule's specification of statistical series or stochastic sequences. Likewise, connecting Herman Wold's articulation of types of motions that were equivalent to states of rests to that of Galileo or Newton allows one to have a richer grasp of stationary processes.

The focus of this history is on the origins of statistical time series analysis. Although more weight is given to applications in political economy, the breadth of this book, like that of the nineteenth-century work it highlights, is interdisciplinary. Statistical work in other social sciences and biology and meteorology is also included. I have assumed on the part of the reader a basic understanding of statistical terminology such as mean, standard deviation, normal distribution, and the gist of correlation and least squares regression. The first appendix provides technical demonstrations for most of the algorithms referred to in the text. This history is another way of comprehending these terms and could be of use to those who still feel uncomfortable with their grasp of statistical theory. As a student and as a teacher, I found that the theories and techniques of statistics are often more approachable as the "why" and "when" dimensions are added to the "how" and "what."

Acknowledgments

This history required access to scholarly works spanning several centuries and cultures. I am indebted to the libraries, archivists, and librarians of the Library of Congress, the Bank of England, the Royal Society, University College, London Guildhall University, Georgetown University, Mary Baldwin College, and to the many contacted through the interlibrary loan service. I especially thank Terry Bell, the former chief librarian at the Bank of England for his assistance in research.

Colleagues and friends from a variety of disciplines gave me constructive feedback on drafts of chapters, including Tim Alborn, Jeff Biddle, Sam Boestaph, Yana Mintoff Bland, Lis Chabot, Mary Hill Cole, Neil de Marchi, Mary Ann Dimand, Ruth Dudley Edwards, Jean Gilman, Andrew Harvey, James Henderson, Kevin Hoover, Thomas Humphrey, Leon Klein, Christopher Napier, Roderic Owen, Sandra Peart, Lundy Pentz, Andrew Pickering, Jane Pietrowski, Ingrid Rima, and Nancy Wulwick. Anne McGovern, Michelle Griffith, Nataliya Bondareva, and Sybila Jobin helped me with foreign language translations. Scott Parris at Cambridge University Press and Lydia Petersson provided sound editorial guidance. Many students encouraged me with their questions and suggestions, and I am particularly appreciative of the research assistance of Mary Alice Bomar, Marta Galopin, and Alison Martin. The interdisciplinary climate at Mary Baldwin furnished a superb atmosphere for writing this history; conversations with artists, mathematicians, historians, philosophers, art historians, anthropologists, and biologists fed into my work. My discussions with Jan Olsson and Nancy Dahlstrom over the years were especially inspiring. This book was originally intended to be a revision of my Ph.D. dissertation. Although it grew into something quite different, the advice I received from Mike Cowen, John Nankervis, and Len Stafford at London Guildhall University and Ron Smith, my external examiner, was invaluable in writing this book.

I am particularly grateful to Mary Morgan and Ted Porter for the example they set, their encouragement in pursuing a broader history of science, and their detailed critique of this project over several years.

A Travel to Collections grant from the National Endowment for the Humanities and a Mednick Fellowship enabled me to use the resources of several British archives in 1990. Given my heavy teaching load, this book would not have been completed before my children were grown had it not been for a grant from the National Science Foundation (SBR 9312693). The support from the Science and Technology Studies Program of the NSF was instrumental not only in terms of funding research but also in the direction provided by its thorough review process.

I am indebted to my family for its support and willingness to share in the opportunity cost of this lengthy project. My parents, to whom this book is dedicated, have always encouraged me to ask what has been and what ought to be. I began asking these questions of statistics before Justin and Heather were born and their patience and curiosity with my investigation has been a source of strength. Finally, I thank my husband, Brian Arthur, for enthusiastically pursuing esoteric questions of mathematics and etymology, skillfully mastering the software necessary for the graphics in this book, and shouldering some of the pain of the creative process.

Permissions

The author thanks the following societies and publishers for their permission to reprint diagrams and other materials used in this book: The Library, University College, London, and Dr. Sarah Pearson for permission to use Figure 1.3 (Udny Yule's sketch of the frequency distribution of 1,000 shots of a battery gun resolved into two chance distributions, Pearson Papers, Box 107), Figure 2.8 (Maria Sharpe Pearson's etching of the Bridge of Life, Pearson Papers, Box 95), Figure 7.6 (Karl Pearson's photographs of the bivariate frequency surface constructed by Lugio Perozzo, Pearson Papers, Box 230), Figure 8.2 (Karl Pearson's chart of the history of the definition of statistics, Pearson Papers, Box 49), a 400-word excerpt used in Chapter 7 (from Karl Pearson's lecture notes in "A Course in Chance Mortality Curves," Pearson Papers, Box 49), Figure 5.10 (Bowditch's composite photograph of American female college students, Galton Papers, Box 158/1A), and Figure 7.4 (Alfred Wallace's sketch in a letter to Francis Galton of a form "irregular deviations" might take if natural selection were at work, Galton Papers, Box 336); the International Statistical Institute for permission to use Figure 1.2 (Figure 1.6 in the International Statistical Institute, *Bibliography on Time Series and Stochastic Processes* [1965]); McGraw-Hill for permission to use Figure 7.2 (Figure 1-14 in Raymond C. Moore, Cecil G. Lalicker, and Alfred G. Fischer, *Invertebrate Fossils* [1952]); Johns Hopkins University Press for permission to use Figure 8.3 (Figure 2 in Pierre S. Du Pont de Nemours, *On Economic Curves*, translated by Henry W. Spiegel [(1792) 1955]); Basil Blackwell Publishers for permission to use Figures 10.2 and 10.3 (Figures 13, 14, 15, Table XIII, and Figure 19 in Udny Yule, "Why Do We Sometimes Get Nonsense-Correlations between Time-Series? – A Study in Sampling and the Nature of Time-Series," *Journal of the Royal Statistical Society*, 89 [1926]); the *Review of Economics and Statistics* for permission to use Table 9.3 (Table 1 in Edwin Frickey, "The Problem of Secular Trend," *Review of Economics and Statistics*, 16 [1934]); the Royal Society for permission to use Figure 10.1 (Table 1, Table III, and Diagram 1 in F. E. Cave-Browne-Cave, "On the Influence of the Time Factor on the Correlation between the Barometric Heights at Stations More Than 1000 Miles Apart," *Proceedings of the Royal Society of London*, 74 [1905]).

1

Introduction

History is moving statistics and statistics is frozen history.

Schlözer 1804, 86

We set ourselves a formidable challenge in the statistical analysis of time series data. We want to comprehend processes of change, but the analytical tools we often use were designed for making comparisons in cases where history was frozen. Probabilistic reasoning, deviations from a mean, frequency distributions, least squares regression, correlation, and hypothesis testing are methods by which we make static comparisons. Several historians of science have tracked the development of these tools through a history of probability theory. The probabilistic tradition of comparing deviations from expected values came out of studies in which time and the specific history of the phenomena were irrelevant. Throwing dice or drawing balls out of an urn might well take place over time, but the results of one person throwing a die and repeating that 100 times should be no different than the results of 100 people simultaneously casting dice. Such is not the case when we work with prices or temperatures recorded over time. What I want to concentrate on in this history are the tools for freezing history when time and sequence have influenced the raw data. Taking first and higher-order differences, smoothing with moving averages, and rearranging a time series into a grid of cross sections are tools for decomposing series until the process we are left with is equivalent to observations on a state of rest.

While the seventeenth-century philosophers Blaise Pascal and Pierre de Fermat were pondering stable probability ratios based on leisurely games of chance, John Graunt and other European merchants were using a different kind of quantitative reasoning to reckon their profits and losses in changing markets. These merchants and financiers did not borrow their mathematics from the natural philosophers or scholars cloistered in the universities; rather they popularized their own algorithms for analyzing fluctuations. It was nineteenth-century mathematicians who appropriated and used these monetary algorithms to freeze history in their investigation and modeling of temporal phenomena. That appropriation from commercial practice to a statistical theory of time series analysis is one of two major themes of this book and forms the basis of the stories in Part I.

The second major theme, which is particularly brought out in Part II, is that our ivory-tower blending of the static comparisons of probability theorists with the practical dynamics of commercial traders puts limitations on our capacity to understand changes around us. From as early as Udny Yule's work in the 1920s, some mathematicians have recognized that statistical procedure based on sampling theory can be a poor fit for data generated from temporal processes. In 1938, Herman Wold assuaged some concerns over the sampling problem in his identification of the stationary stochastic process. A stationary process is one in which the probability structure, including the mean and measurements of dispersion about the mean, does not change over time. As Wold demonstrated, once the data are in a stationary form, least squares regression analysis and spectral analysis can be used and all stationary time series can be decomposed into a few generic models. When we reduce our data to stationary time series in order to solve the sampling dilemma, however, we often create new problems by canceling out historical change and suppressing the long-term variation. Most of the techniques we use for decomposing time series data until the "corrected" series are stationary are the same tools that financiers and speculators used to track short-term fluctuations. Similarly, some of the algorithms we use to model or to reveal unobserved components of time series were originally used by politically savvy bankers to veil true fluctuations. In this book, I use the early commercial history of these algorithms to shed light on the limitations of conventional analysis of stationary time series.

A major source of problems and limitations in time series analysis is that it is sometimes difficult to reconcile *logical* variation with *historical* variation. In the English language, the word "variation" is used to describe how things differ from each other at one moment in time, as well how things change over time. Logical variation is the static comparison referred to in most statistical procedures. It is a question of how things at one moment in time compare or differ. The calculation of a deviation from the mean of a cross-section sample is a computation of logical variation. This static comparison with a mean value is the basis for frequency distributions, hypothesis testing, regression, and correlation. Historical variation, on the other hand, is fluctuation and process; it is a question of how things develop, evolve, or change over time.

To some extent this distinction between logical variation and historical variation corresponds to the distinction between algorithms used in probability theory and those used in commercial practice. Other distinctions arise when we look at subject context – the nature of the phenomena under analysis. In Part II of this book, I explore the importance of subject in the molding of notions of statistical processes. In this introductory chapter, I begin with one case that serves as a lead into a comparison of subject context and process. The comparative overview of juxtapositions of logical variation and statistical process sets the scene for understanding the significant input of commercial practice to time series analysis, which I introduce in the latter part of the chapter.

The Metaphor and Reality of Target Practice

This book is about men reasoning on the likes of target practice. From John Graunt onward, most of the natural philosophers and statisticians covered in this history paid homage to the aiming and firing of weapons and the gauging of the accuracy of marksmen. The philosophers used the image of shooting at targets to explain and defend their statistical way of thinking. Nineteenth- and twentieth-century mathematicians, including John Herschel, Karl Pearson, Udny Yule, and Frederick Mills, seriously studied target shooting and incorporated the results into reasoning on statistical theory. The traffic between ballistics and statistical theory was two-way; for example, in the late nineteenth century, the Russian government hired the mathematician Pafnuty Lvovich Chebyshev to introduce innovations in artillery strategy and practice in the Russian army. Several decades later, the Soviet government gave credit to Andrei Nikolaevich Kolmogorov for important contributions to the theory of ballistics that aided in the Soviet victory in World War II (Tikhomirov 1991, 112). Also during World War II, the Polish statistician Jerzy Neyman, who was instrumental in the development of hypothesis testing, was contracted by the U.S. National Defense Research Committee to study multiple bomb aiming. Neyman's applications of a statistical way of thinking to the study of bombing included calculations of the optimum spacing of bombs to destroy mines for a landing on Normandy beach; successful testing of his hypothesis that the optimal use of a group of bombers confronting the same number of enemy ships would be for all the bombers to aim at one ship; and the design of an optical device that measured the average coverage of multiple bombs and the probability that bombs would start a fire (Reid 1982, 186, 190, 196). The American mathematician Norbert Wiener, who contributed to the theory of random stochastic processes such as Brownian motion, channeled his investigations in World War II to the prediction of the future position of enemy aircraft based on observed past positions for the determination of optimal firing of anti-aircraft guns (Wiener 1964, 19).

Marksmen and targets were also the basis for metaphorical reasoning on statistical processes. Adolphe Quetelet used the bull's-eye of a target as a simile for his *l'homme moyen* as did Nathaniel Pickering Bowditch for his composite photographs (see Chapter 5). Karl Pearson relied almost solely on five imaginary marksmen of death to rationalize his decomposition of the curve of the age distribution of mortality into five chance distributions (see Chapter 2). In a similar vein, Irving Fisher justified the first model of a distributed lag with the image of a gunner shooting out each month's allocation of bullets – price changes – down a logged time road (see Chapter 9). If you take away the metaphor of the marksmen firing at their targets, there is little statistical reasoning left in their essays to support the theses of Pearson and Fisher. The metaphor of target practice persisted even as mathematicians transferred their sights from random error to random disturbance. As part of his explanation for what we now label the stationary autoregressive process, Udny Yule suggested the analogy of boys sneaking into a room and using a pendulum for target practice (see Chapter 10). This random disturbance of pea shots would cause changes in the amplitude and phase of the oscillation and would deter the tendency of the pendulum's oscillation to damp to a point of rest. Yule's notion of "flexible periodicity" was explained as a pendulum bearing the brunt of schoolboy target practice.

Given that target practice reappears as an analogy throughout the history of time series analysis, it will serve us well as a starting point for distinguishing different types of processes that contain an element of chance. A rough chronology distinguishing pioneering statistical investigations into statistical processes is highlighted in Table 1.1. We can see by its placement in the middle that the subject of target practice bridged the reasoning of the early probability theorists, who studied games of chance or measurement error, and the natural philosophers and mathematicians of the late nineteenth and early twentieth centuries who investigated gas diffusion, biological evolution, and economic change. To most of the early probabilists of the seventeenth and eighteenth centuries, chance was a human illusion, albeit one that could often be reasoned and quantified. Jakob Bernoulli, for example, spoke of the certain fate perfectly plain to an all-knowing God, but only sketched out in the imperfect human observation process. God saw and knew everything with certainty and his design was exact and purposeful. The natural order was deterministic; the stochastic element was in human comprehension. In the late nineteenth-century imagery of Karl Pearson, however, it was as if God were a marksman – but not a perfect shot. By the end of the nineteenth century, chance and error were treated not just as properties of human perception but also as integral parts of the divine or natural order. Target practice was one of the metaphorical bridges between the stochastic art of the way based on trials that Bernoulli described and models of active stochastic processes nested in twentieth-century theories of time series analysis.

There are at least two processes at work in the case of target practice: the active data generating process of taking aim and firing and the passive observation process of looking at the residue of the first process. In the first step of target practice, there is the design of a target with concentric circles emanating from a central point. Then comes the aim and the shot, followed by another aim and shot, and so on. "Stochastic" means to aim at a mark. No one is a perfect shot all of the time, so stochastic also implies the random missing that accompanies the aiming and firing. Although this missing follows no sequential pattern in time, if one examines the target cloth at the end of the practice session there usually is a recognizable pattern of logical variation around the bull's-eye. The density of holes near the center of aim is usually greater than that farther away. In his lectures on chance mortality curves, Karl Pearson demonstrated that the end results of target practice could be mapped as a normal distribution:

Table 1.1 *Subject contexts for statistical processes*

Process	Early examples	How historical variation is reconciled with logical variation
Observation process: games of chance (*Chapter 6*)	Pascal 1654 Fermat 1654 Huygens 1657 Bernoulli 1713	Numerous observations on chance trials yields clustering of observed values about expected values
Observation process: measurement of single object (*Chapter 6*)	Simpson 1755 Gauss 1809 Laplace 1810	Random errors of observation cause observed values to cluster about the mean true value
Observation process: measurement of similar objects (*Chapter 7*)	Poisson 1837 Quetelet 1835,1846	Myriad of accidental causes results in heights of individuals in a regiment displaying bell-curve frequency distribution
Target practice (*Chapter 1*)	Herschel 1850, 1867 Pearson 1891	Residues of random stationary active process can be mapped as bell-curve distribution
Diffusion of gases (*Chapter 7*)	Maxwell 1859, Boltzmann 1872	Distribution of velocities of individual particles will be a bell-curve; equilibrium = most probable state
Biological evolution (*Chapter 7*)	Weldon 1893 Pearson 1894	Logical variation across species carries the capacity for shifting the mean of the species via natural selection and inheritance
Fluctuations in temperature, pressure, sunspot activity, rainfall (*Chapters 5, 9, 10*)	Laplace 1827 Lubbock 1830, 1833 Buys Ballot 1847 Schuster 1906 Cave-Browne-Cave 1905	Rearrange data into relative time framework Decompose into sinusoids Split into equinox-to-equinox sets, use first differences
Fluctuations in trade, prices, production (*Chapters 5, 9, 10*)	MacKenzie 1829 Jevons 1862 Hooker 1901, 1905 Norton 1902 March 1905	Rearrange data into relative time framework Decompose data into stationary and nonstationary processes, model and estimate only stationary component

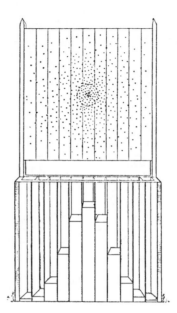

Figure 1.1   Pearson's hypothetical sketch of the results of target practice. In the top half of the sketch, the bullet holes are dispersed around the center target; if the shots fall directly to a receptacle beneath, they fill in the bell curve distribution shown in the bottom half. *Source:* Pearson 1897, 23.

> Now let me remind you of the manner in which a marksman puts shots into a target. They cluster close round the bullseye, are more scattered as we depart from it, and if we make a curve by plotting up the frequency to distance we get our friend the normal curve or rather a half of it. It balances about the *mean* deviation, whence we obtain the standard deviation, or a measure of the accuracy of aim.[1] (Pearson 1891, 6–7)

Pearson supported this with several diagrams. The top of Figure 1.1 is the frontal view of the target after a hypothetical practice; the bottom is the frequency distribution of the horizontal location of the holes about the target. Pearson's statistical reasoning on target practice is a like a mapping in projective geometry. The point of the bullet or the arrow, which starts in the shooter's weapon, maintains its integrity as a point on the target cloth. Distance between the points in each case (within the gun, within the cloth) changes. The points are then mapped onto a distribution plane. The residue of the active process of aiming and firing is geometrically projected onto a two-dimensional plane. After a certain point in the observation process, the individual measurements of horizontal displacement from the target, marshaled in a frequency distribution, take on a recognizable form that can be summarized by an equation. From this equation, one can work out, as John Herschel did in his 1867 essay on "Skill in Target Shooting," comparative measurements of skill for marksmen

---

[1]   In his essay on "The Chances of Death," Pearson went so far as to assert that any frequency distribution could be conceived as "due to a marksman of a certain skewness of aim using a weapon of a certain degree of precision" (Pearson 1897, 25).

aiming at targets with a variety of dimensions or the probability of missing, in any one shot, a circular area centered on the bull's-eye.[2]

The Russian probability theorists Boris Vladimirovich Gnedenko and Aleksandr Yakovlevich Khinchin used the dispersion from the target of the impact points of cannonballs to explain the relevance of Aleksandr Mikhailovich Lyapunov's central limit theorem to stochastic processes:

> Since the dispersion is the result of the action of an enormous number of independently acting factors (for example, the irregularities in the milling of the shell casing, the head of the shell, the variations in the density of the material of which the head of the shell is made, the minute variation in the quantity of explosive material in the various shells, the small errors, which are unnoticeable to the eye, in the aiming of the cannon, the minute variations in the composition of the atmosphere for the various firings, and many others), each of which influences only to an almost negligible degree the trajectory of the shell, then it follows from Lyapunov's theorem that it ought to be subject to a normal law. This situation is taken into consideration in the theory of artillery fire and is deemed fundamental in the evolution of firing rules. (Gnedenko & Khinchin 1962, 120)

According to Lyapunov's central limit theorem, as long as the active process is determined by a large number of stochastic causes that are mutually independent with relatively small influence, the observation process culminates in a geometric statement of logical variation such as a normal frequency distribution. Thus, we can say what the center of aim or expected value is and we can say how likely some deviation from that value is. We can find the conditions that meet Lyapunov's specifications in ideal target practice, urn drawing, coin tossing, and dice throwing. In these cases of random, stationary active processes, we essentially have little need for a distinct time series analysis to analyze the active process; time series data can be treated as cross-section data. Similarly, a measurement process that generates errors of measurement may take place over time but it does not require an analysis different from that used to handle measurements made simultaneously. Indeed, Christiaan Huygens, Jakob Bernoulli, Abraham de Moivre, Carl Friedrich Gauss, and others reasoning on games of chance and errors of observation did not perceive their acts of comprehension as observation *processes*. It was the Russian mathematicians, starting with Pafnuty Lvovich Chebyshev, Andrei Andreevich Markov, and Aleksandr Mikhailovich Lyapunov in the late nineteenth century, who articulated the law of large numbers and central limit theorems by treating observations as a *sequence* of independent random quantities.

---

[2] Ideally, the mapping of the residues of target practice leads to a normal bell curve, but human marksmen are human – they often have a bias in their aim that skews frequency distributions. Although some of the techniques that are applicable to cases of normal distributions may not hold, skewed distributions are still statements of logical variation and, as long as the probability structure does not change as the process continues, probabilistic reasoning and summary parameters can be used. Pearson and others even questioned whether errors in measurement strictly followed the normal distribution in practice. In a letter to Yule in September 1896, Pearson referred to the fact that the personal errors of measurement of his students, including Yule and Alice Lee, generated skewed curves and that Pearson's own curve was the only one approaching the normal type.

Process and Subject

The first stochastic process relevant to the development of statistical theory was what we can now perceive of as an observation process of counting (see first three entries in Table 1.1). In one of the earliest treatises on probability theory, Jakob Bernoulli described his art of conjecturing as the "stochastic art." It was guessing, after careful analysis of observations. If you observed enough throws of the dice or flips of the coin or deals of the cards, the mathematical law underlying that game of chance would be revealed. The challenge was to figure out how many constituted enough and how quickly you could reach near certainty in your conjecturing on the target. For example, one of the important tenets that the early probability theorists derived was that the certainty was proportional to the square root of the number of observations. In the observation process of games of chance, trials are the equivalent of time.

While the active process of shooting at the target or throwing dice might well be stationary, with a constant mean and constant variance, the passive process of observation often proceeds from wide to narrower dispersion as certainty is increased. Herman Wold illustrated this nonstationary observation process in the time plot reproduced in Figure 1.2. With regard to the object of observation, nothing changes except by chance. With regard to the observer, each new observation added to your sample brings you closer to certainty, albeit in a nonlinear fashion. In the cases of target practice and throwing dice, we assume that the active process of throwing or firing is random – where a shot hits does not depend on where the previous shot hit. We also assume the active process is stationary: data are generated from a constant probability structure with a constant mean (center of aim) and constant dispersion. There are important differences in the philosophies and historical contexts of statistical reasoning on games of chance, errors of measurement, and target practice that are explored in Part II of this book. The following notions, however are common to all:

- The data-generating process is stationary.
- Each action is independent of the previous one.
- Trials are the equivalent of time.
- The passive process of comprehending the underlying parameters by cumulative observations is nonlinear.

These common properties enabled investigators to use similar techniques of inference. John Herschel acknowledged the shared properties and algorithms of target practice and the observation process in his 1850 essay on probabilities:

> Suppose the rifle replaced by a telescope duly mounted; the wafer by a star on the concave surface of the heavens, always observed for a succession of days at the same sidereal time; the marks on the wall by the degrees, minutes, and seconds, read off on divided circles; and the marksman by an observer; and we have the case of all direct astronomical observation where the place

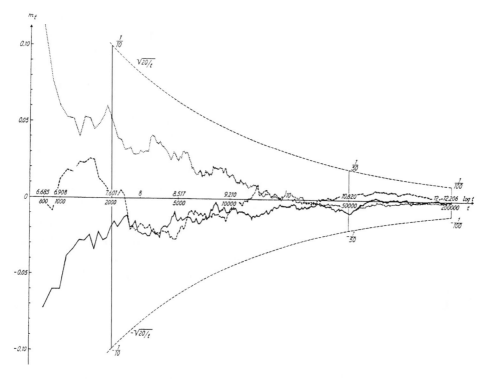

Figure 1.2   Wold's plot of the law of large numbers revealed through the observation process. The mean values for three realizations of a coin-tossing experiment
converge toward zero with the increase in the number of trials up to t = 200,000
(on a logarithmic time scale). *Source:* International Statistical Institute 1967, Figure 1.6.

of a heavenly body is the thing to be determined. Or we may substitute for
the wall the floor of a lofty building or deep mine, and for the marksman an
experimenter dropping, with all possible care, smooth and perfectly spherical
leaden balls from a fixed point at the summit of the building or the mouth
of the mine, with intent to determine, by the means of a great number of
trials, the true point of incidence of a falling body, – a physical experiment
of great interest. We might, if we pleased, instance more complicated cases,
in which the elements to be determined are numerous and not *directly* given
by observation, but with such we shall not trouble our readers: suffice it to
say that the rule above stated, or, as it is technically called, the "Principles
of Least Squares," furnishes, in all cases, a system of geometrical relations
characteristic of the *most probable* values of the magnitudes sought, and
which, duly handled, suffice for their numerical determination. (Herschel
[1850] 1857, 397)

But what if life is not like target practice or a crap shoot? What if sequential
observations are dependent on previous values? Can probability theory and
the mind-set of deviations from a mean value speak to nonstationary processes?
As we will see in Part II, there have been some innovative answers to those
questions. To take one example (explained in detail in Chapter 7), the late

nineteenth-century biometricians suggested an ingenious marriage of logical and historical variation. They saw the geometric snapshots of cross-section measurements of an organ of a species as both cause and evidence of biological evolution through natural selection. Charles Darwin, Alfred Russel Wallace, Francis Galton, Raphael Weldon, and Karl Pearson asserted that logical variation across the species was a necessary condition for evolution. The latter three saw the process of evolution as a shifting of the mean with each generation's distribution. According to the biometricians, variety and deviation from the mean carried the capacity for historical variation that took the form of an evolutive shifting of mean or mode.

Weldon, Pearson, and Galton also perceived double-humped (bimodal) distributions as evidence that natural selection was at work and the species was evolving – perhaps to the point that eventually there would be two separate species (see Weldon's study of Naples Crabs in Chapter 7). In trying to construct some formal rationalization of this double-humped distribution as evidence of an evolutive process, Pearson had his lab assistant, Udny Yule, plot a frequency curve for 1,000 shots from an artillery gun in American target practice (Figure 1.3). In his 1894 lectures on evolution and the geometry of chance, Pearson decomposed the curve connecting the observed frequencies into two chance distributions. Not only did the center of aim differ slightly from the center of the designed target, but there seemed to be two centers. Pearson reasoned that either the shooters were aiming for the boundaries of the target circle or there was a "shifting of the mean" in midfiring. The statistician's decomposition of empirical frequency distributions on organs of cross sections of species into geometric chance distributions could reveal the shifting of the mean that was the end result of the process of random variation confronting natural selection.

The weaving of logical variation and historical variation took quite different forms in the empirical investigations of meteorological and economic phenomena. In contrast to the biometricians who used cross-section data, these investigators had to use time series data on temperature, barometric pressure, sunspot activity, rainfall, prices, bank deposits, exports, marriages rates, and so forth. When marshaled into a frequency distribution, the data rarely took the form of a bell curve. Not only were distributions skewed, but particularly with economic data, there was the additional problem that the mean was not constant. There was often an evolutive quality to the phenomena under study when measurements were plotted against time.

Figures 1.4 and 1.5 illustrate one of the contradictions raised in the blending of logical and historical variation when time series data have an evolutive quality. In the scatterplot in Figure 1.4, two variables are inversely related in terms of change over time but positively related in term of the slope of the regression line or sign on the correlation coefficient. The slopes of the short lines sequentially connecting each point are opposite in sign to the slope of the least squares regression line that would best fit the data. In a point-to-point reality, if x increased, y decreased. The slope of the regression line (dy/dx), however, is positive; higher than average values of x are associated with higher than average values of y.

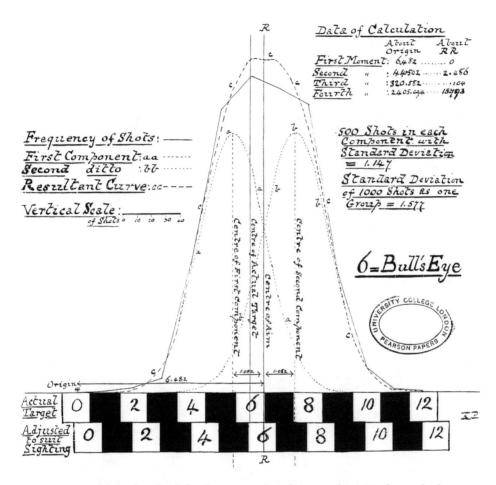

Figure 1.3   Yule's sketch of the frequency distribution of 1,000 shots of a battery gun resolved into two chance distributions. In his lectures on evolution and the geometry of chance, Pearson used this slide as an example of a "shifting of the mean." *Source:* Pearson Papers, Box 107, The Library University College London.

A technical way of explaining this contradiction is that it occurs when there is an inverse relationship in sequential change, yet both x and y show a positive trend over time (their increases are greater in value than their decreases). The trend and the inverse sequential co-relationship are evident in Figure 1.5.[3] As we will see, history provides us with an even richer understanding of this contradiction: juxtaposing short-term and long-term focuses, distinguishing the problems of biometrics and econometrics, weaving the scientific propensity to decompose with the practical propensity to make profits, giving context to the first articulation of the concept of a trend, and generating a philosophical perspective of a variety of space–time notions that

---

[3]   Further technical discussion of this example with a plot of first differences of x and y appears in Chapter 3.

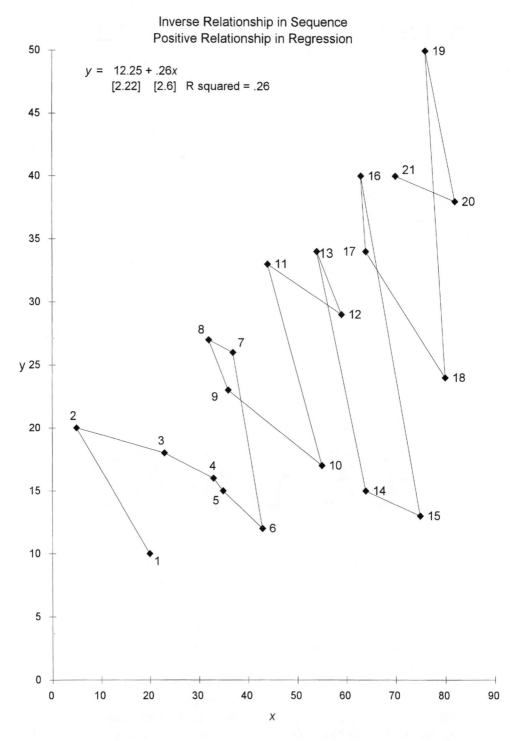

Figure 1.4   Scatterplot of hypothetical data on *x* and *y* illustrates a case in which there would be a positive slope on a regression line fitted to the data, even though *y* decreases with every increase in *x*, and *y* increases with every decrease in *x*.

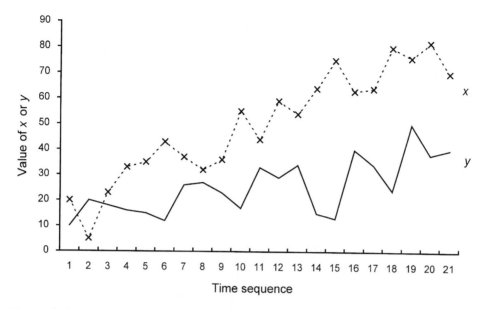

Figure 1.5   Time sequence plot of x and y values that had formed the coordinates for the scatterplot in Figure 1.4. For both variables there is an upward trend over time.

mathematicians have used to explain problems in the statistical analysis of temporal processes.

Decomposition

The question posed for many investigators, particularly those working with economic and social data, was how to use time-neutral statistical techniques to analyze processes of change. Deviation is a comparison by subtraction within a structure that targets one reference value. The typical or true value (usually the arithmetic mean) is subtracted from an actual value. The analytical framework of the law of deviation, frequency distributions in general, analysis of variance, correlation, and regressions analysis is one of timeless static comparison. Figure 1.6c illustrates the typical visual form of the law of deviation. The bell-curve frequency distribution is a summary pattern of many deviations from the same reference mean, quantified and arranged in a cross section of a population at one point in time. The problem for those trying to use statistical theory to explain or predict change over time is that the nearest thing they have to geometric structure in simple arrangements of raw time series data is fluctuations over time (Figure 1.6a). The trick for the statistician is to turn fluctuations into deviations. One of the easiest routes to the transformation of fluctuations into deviations is *decomposition* until one reaches oscillations (Figure 1.6b). As we will see in Chapter 10, Udny Yule, Gilbert Walker, Eugen Slutsky, and Aleksandr Yakovlevich Khinchin constructed the basic building blocks for modeling stationary stochastic processes by starting with theories of oscillations. In order to get a well-behaved oscillatory series out of

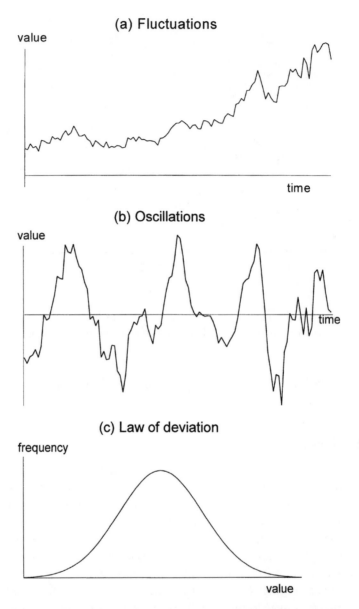

Figure 1.6   Statistical visions in time series analysis. Empirical investigators often have to go from fluctuations to deviations via oscillations.

the raw data, it is particularly important to eliminate any evolutive elements or secular trends. Detrending the data leaves one with the more manageable cyclical and random components of the series. The cyclical and random components can usually be classified as data generated from a stationary process – we can assume the observations have a constant mean and constant variance. The various data manipulation tools that practitioners of time series analysis use to satisfy the criteria of stationary oscillations are the subject of the chapters in Part I.

Mathematical philosophy and science had offered little guidance in matching statistical theory and change. As Nicholas Georgescu-Roegen has pointed out, "Process implies Change and Change is the most baffling concept in philosophy . . . to explain Change is the highest aim of any special science, even though we usually proclaim that science can study only what does not change" (Georgescu-Roegen [1971] 1976, 39).

There was, however, a group of nineteenth-century thinkers who did not let philosophy or science become a stumbling block to comprehending change. These "captains of finance," as Thorstein Veblen called them, measured and thrived on change. For them, change could mean corporate vitality or death, but no change was certain death, and ignorance of change reduced life expectancy. With money in their pockets, numbers at their fingertips, and rules from their thumbs, they processed quarterly, weekly, and daily time series to profitable advantage. These merchants, financiers, and speculators had a feel for averages, moving averages, and unusual deviations. They had simple, effective ways of manipulating time series data for easy comparisons. Their tricks of the trade and their focus on the short-term with a blind eye to the possibility of life cycles or evolution in economic systems enabled mathematicians to appropriate their techniques for the decomposition of time series and the identification and reconstruction of stationary time series.

The Pulling-Up versus the Trickle-Down Theory

In the beginning there was statistical theory, then there were applications to finance; or so the story of time series analysis would seem to go. The story is a good fit for some statistical tools. Correlation and regression analysis were first used by mathematicians such as Karl Pearson to quantify processes of inheritance and evolution. A century later, portfolio managers in financial centers around the world routinely use regression to estimate their *"betas,"* which quantify the risk involved in their stock holdings in relation to that of the market as a whole.

There are, however, many instances of mathematicians *pulling* analytical tools up from the depths of commerce to the heights of science. In several cases, the history of time series analysis indicates a chronological primacy of what I call "monetary arithmetic," algorithms developed to participate in or comprehend monetary exchanges. If we look at specific techniques, monetary algorithms often preceded the political arithmetic, which was later appropriated for statistical method and theory. Such categorizations can be slippery and the problem of classification is compounded by the fact that often landmark cases in the history of time series analysis are bridges between two of the categories. Nonetheless, there are some general characteristics, highlighted in Table 1.2, that serve to distinguish monetary algorithms, political arithmetic, empirical investigation, and mathematical statistics.

This pattern of development from the context of commerce to that of science and mathematics and back again is particularly apparent in techniques used to decompose time series and reconstruct statistical structures in time. The

Table 1.2 *Comparisons of arithmetic contexts in the development of time series techniques*

	Monetary algorithms	Political arithmetic	Empirical investigation	Mathematical statistics
Context	Ledgers, accounts weekly business journals	Parliamentary testimony, pamphlets on political economy, annual reports to Royal Statistical Society	Presentations to learned, scientific, and statistical societies	Academic journals
Purpose	*Profit* compute exchange, determine financial currents and movements	*Persuasion* investigate business cycles, policy issues	*Truth* decompose, equate fluctuation with deviation, search for empirical laws	*Beauty* search for mathematical laws, model processes
Form	*Tables* short series, absolute values, verbal comparisons	*Tables* long series, relative changes	*Graphs* decomposed series, regression and correlation	*Equations* hypothetical series, regression and correlation

roots of the Rule of Three, serial differences, relative time frameworks, index numbers, and moving averages tap the daily working habits of European merchants, financiers, and bankers. In the hands of these men of commerce – or "mechanical artists," as Thomas Sprat (1667, 67) labeled them – the algorithms were often techniques of composition used in the arrangement of quantities in a table form. In the hands of the empirical statisticians, the algorithms became techniques of decomposition in a geometric form. In the context of mathematical statistics, the algorithms became models of processes in an algebraic form.

In Inglis Palgrave's *Dictionary of Political Economy*, political arithmetic is described as the "mother science of both statistics and political economy" (Bourne 1894, 56). The stage of political arithmetic is particularly fascinating, since at that point persuasion was as great a stimulus, if not greater, than was investigation in the development of techniques. The interplay of deception and accountability in the public presentation of monetary accounts led to some ingenious forms of data manipulation. Algorithms used for composing deceptive data series in this stage later became tools of decomposition used to reveal laws and model reality.

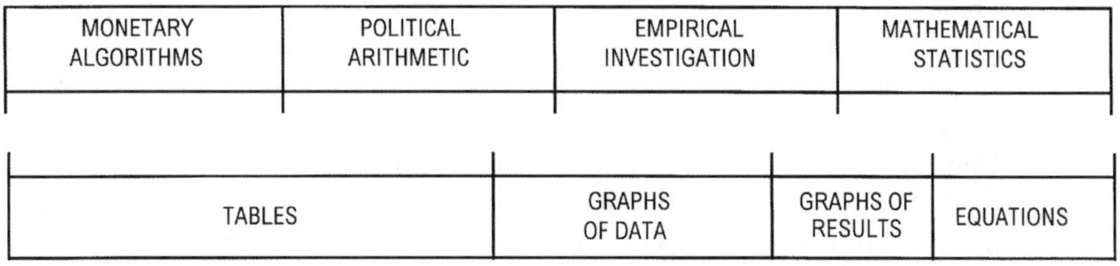

MONETARY ALGORITHMS	POLITICAL ARITHMETIC	EMPIRICAL INVESTIGATION	MATHEMATICAL STATISTICS

TABLES		GRAPHS OF DATA	GRAPHS OF RESULTS	EQUATIONS

Figure 1.7   Correspondence of arithmetic contexts with forms of output.

I have broken down the stage of scientific arithmetic even further into empirical investigation and mathematical statistics. The inputs of empirical investigation in the development of technique included recognition of statistical populations or samples, measurements of and focus on central tendency and deviation from the center, decomposition, and empirical laws manifested in geometric forms. With mathematical statistics, mathematicians often manufactured the data with, for example, a random number generator, and transformed the algorithms into algebraic equations to specify models of stochastic processes.

Transitions from the Table to the Graph to the Equation

The periodization from commercial to political to scientific arithmetic parallels a comparison of forms of statistical representation of temporal phenomena from the tabular to the graphical to the algebraic modes. As can be seen from the time lines in Figure 1.7, the qualitative changes in forms of representation did not exactly correspond to the breaks in the arithmetic contexts.

Tables were the chief form of quantitative analysis for both monetary and political arithmetic. For example, in his statistical textbook, written around 1901, but published posthumously in 1913, the political arithmetician Robert Giffen included an entire chapter on constructing tables but did not feature a single graph. Graphs were occasionally used for political arithmetic, for example, in the work of William Playfair, but the golden stage for graphs was that of empirical investigation in the late nineteenth and early twentieth centuries. In his 1891 lectures on the geometry of statistics at University College, Karl Pearson argued that graphs had been used earlier for "rhetorical statistics" or as mere means of representation. In the hands of the late nineteenth-century statisticians, Pearson explained, they had become means of investigation.

In advocating graphs as a means of investigation, Pearson cited the work the French statisticians, Émile Cheysson and Étienne Jules Marey. Cheysson had been the inspector general of the *Ponts et Chaussées* and president of the Paris Statistical Society. His admiration for the usefulness of geometric statistics is apparent in a speech on statistical method to French military officers:

When a law is contained in figures, it is buried like a metal in the ore; it is necessary to extract it. This is the work of graphical representation. It points out the coincidences, the relationships between phenomena, their anomalies, and we have seen earlier what a powerful means of control it put in the hands of the statistician to verify new data, discover and correct errors with which they may be stained. Old numerical statistics, treated by drawing, can suddenly show brilliantly the law that they contained within, unknown to everyone and which, similar to those tardigrades for whom a drop of water resuscitates, had been sleeping for centuries awaiting their awakening.

The graphical expression of statistics has become an art with processes as ingenious as they are varied. It has resources and solutions for all problems, and it is the task of the statistician to discover and apply those which best suit each particular case. (Translated from Cheysson, 1890, 34–35)

In a similar vein, Marey maintained,

Science has two obstacles in front of it which hinder its progress; there is first the defective power of our senses for discovering truths, and then the inefficiency of language to express and transmit those truths which we have acquired. The object of scientific methods is to surmount these obstacles; the graphical method reaches this double end better than any other. (Translated from Marey 1878, i)

This change in the use of graphs from representation to investigation coincided with a change in the purpose of geometry. While René Descartes had perceived arithmetic as the best mode of dealing with geometry, Pearson and his cohorts saw geometry as the best means of dealing with arithmetic:

Geometry originated as a science of measurement, and up to the days of Descartes, geometry was the chief mathematical means of investigation. But Descartes invaded the province of geometry and actually made algebra – a science of number – the means of reaching geometrical truth. Newton was nearly the last of the great geometrical investigators. But in the last few years geometry has been turning the tables on arithmetic and algebra. It has not only developed itself enormously, but to crush its old antagonist it has absolutely called machinery into its service, and now we have reached an epoch when geometry has become a mode of ascertaining numerical truth. (Pearson 1891, 11)

Expression in a geometric form was a precondition for a notion's inclusion in the canon of statistical theory.[4] During Pearson's time, diagrams and geometric forms were as important as equations in the use and development of statistical theory. For example, in his 1889 book review in *Nature*, Ysidro Edgeworth

---

[4]   This is particularly apparent in British works, and Joan Richards (1988) clearly documents the important role of geometry in British secondary and higher education; Euclid's *Elements* was a standard textbook in secondary schools, and the Mathematical Tripos, with a strong geometric component, was an integral part of Cambridge education. Richards explains that in nineteenth-century Britain, the descriptive and applied powers of geometry rather than its potential as a formal system of abstraction were emphasized and that the enthusiastic British response in Pearson's day to projective geometry was in keeping with this descriptive theme.

describes Francis Galton's *Natural Inheritance* as being based "on a foundation of geometrical reasoning." In looking at the letters exchanged between Edgeworth, Galton, Karl Pearson, Udny Yule, Alfred Wallace, and Raphael Weldon, I have been struck at the constant use of diagrams to explain and understand, even in the most informal communications.

One would be hard pressed to think of a key paper on time series statistics presented to the Royal Society or Royal Statistical Society from 1877 to 1927 that did not include a diagram as part of the analysis. There was, however, a change in the nature of the graphs around the turn of the century. Nineteenth-century statisticians plotted the raw data – for example, the price of wheat against time. Early twentieth-century statisticians were more likely to plot the results of their statistical analysis – for example, correlation coefficients against various time lags. As we get more into the realm of hypothetical models of stochastic processes, geometry gives way to sophisticated algebra, and journal articles contain many equations, but few, if any, graphs.[5]

Measurement without History

The periodization of the development of analytical tools from commercial to political to scientific arithmetic and the accompanying change in the discursive format from the table to the graph to the equation is treated in Part I. One of the chief purposes of Part I is to explore in depth the commercial and political history of methods of decomposition ultimately used in empirical investigations and mathematical statistics. Part II addresses the philosophical inquiries into the problems of reconciling methods based on static laws of deviation with dynamic fluctuations in the data. I am concerned in both parts to see how close we come in time series analysis to *measurement without history*. Adapting the algorithms of merchants and financiers, we decompose until we reach a stationary process to analyze. Along the way, however, we discard the evolutive qualities that speak to history. Also, we rarely use history in determining appropriate intervals between observations or in rearranging our data into reconstructed samples.

In coining the term "measurement without history," I have drawn on the phrases bantered about in the debate between members of the Cowles Commission and the National Bureau of Economic Research (NBER) in the late 1940s. In his review of *Measuring Business Cycles*, Tjalling Koopmans accused NBER economists Wesley Mitchell and Arthur Burns of using "measurement without theory." In reply, Rutledge Vining questioned whether the Cowles Commission was guilty of using economic theory that was incompatible with measurement.[6] This debate, minus the catchy phrases, had been going

[5]   From his study of past issues of *Biometrika* and the *Journal of the American Statistical Society*, Stephen Fienberg (1979) concluded that a major decline in the use of statistical graphs in these two journals after the 1920s coincided with the rise of mathematical statistics.

[6]   The spat between the Cowles Commission and the National Bureau of Economic Research in the 1940s did not lay to rest the debate on measurement without theory versus theory without measurement. For example, Lawrence Klein, an advocate of Keynesian simultaneous equations models used by the Cowles Commission, accused Thomas Sargent and Christopher Sims, advocates of Vector Autoregression

on long before the 1940s. It surfaced, for example, in a contentious round table session on "The Present Status and Future Prospects of Quantitative Economics" sponsored by the American Economic Association in December 1927. In her remarks at the session, Eveline Burns (no relation to the NBER's Arthur Burns) lamented the fact that the discussion between quantitative workers and economic theorists had been so acrimonious. Trying to patch up relationships, Burns stated,

> In calmer moments we are all willing to concede that there is a danger that the quantitative worker may concentrate too exclusively upon those things which are capable of measurement, and may even shape his concepts to the limited nature of his available data, while the qualitative worker – the pure theorist – may become so pure as to be unhelpful in a world where measurable quantities play an important role. Moreover in the last resort neither school will insist that it can progress without entering the domain of the other. (Burns 1927)

I would add that quantitative workers need history as well as theory as a guide in the measurement of changing phenomena. This book is an argument for the study of history in two senses: we can use a history of our analytical tools to clarify their potential and their limitations, and we can use a history of the phenomena under study in our time series analysis to reconcile logical and historical variation.

The story ends with Herman Wold's articulation of stationary processes in 1938. Although I am proposing a periodization of technique into monetary algorithms, political arithmetic, empirical investigation, and mathematical statistics, I do not see this development as progress from a crude beginning to a glorious present-day science. I am interested in comparing contexts for the development of analytical tools and in using history to shed light on the conditions and limits of their utility. For example, in the late nineteenth and early twentieth centuries there was an unusual correspondence of monetary, political, and scientific arithmetic that led to first differences being used not only to make a profit but also to unearth economic laws and model stochastic processes. It was usually the differences, not the absolute values, that corresponded with the gain–loss focus of the speculator, the short-term, static focus of the social scientist, the marginal focus of the theoretical economist, and the stationary focus of the statistician. The use of serial differences often takes us from a dynamic frame of reference of absolute values into a realm of timeless

Models, of measurement without theory in their business cycle modeling of macroeconomic time series (see L. Klein 1977; L. Klein 1985, 11). A more recent reincarnation of the theory/measurement debate was between Sims and fellow new empiricists on the one hand and, on the other hand, the advocates of the use of calibration or computational experiments to investigate questions of policy based on notions of the real business cycle. This debate was played out in the pages of the winter 1996 issue of the *Journal of Economics Perspectives*. Finn Kydland and Edward Prescott opened their arguments with a claim that their methods of calibration used both theory and measurement. As Kydland and Prescott explained it, their approach was to "pose a question; use a well-tested theory; construct a model economy; calibrate the model economy and run the experiment" (Kydland and Presscott 1996, 70). Sims questioned their form of "measurement" and claimed that his own data compression technique based on probabilistic inference from actual observations was more useful than highly restricted calibration.

increments or steady-state change, uniform motion, and frozen history. Stationary statistical analysis, however, like marginal economic analysis, is now being challenged. In confronting the limits of our economic and ecological systems and the limits of our social science, some economists and statisticians are searching for a type of analysis that is dynamic, has a long-term perspective, and can deal with ubiquitous nonstationary processes. We would do well to be aware of the biases and constraints inherent in data manipulation techniques grounded in the speculative reckoning of financiers.

Part I

Commercial Arithmetic and Practical Dynamics

2

Reckoning on Death and Chance with the Merchant's Rule

Mathematicks at that time, with us, were scarce looked upon as Academical Studies, but rather Mechanical; as the business of Traders, Merchants, Seamen, Carpenters, Surveyors of Lands, or the like, and perhaps some Almanack Makers in London. . . . For the Study of Mathematicks was at that time more cultivated in London than in the Universities.

John Wallis, seventeenth-century British mathematician, quoted in Taylor [1954] 1968, 4

In 1662, a London cloth merchant made several ingenious social comparisons that centuries later are considered the seeds of a science of quantitative observation. John Graunt's use of mathematics was not what we would call sophisticated; in fact he described it as the "Mathematiques of my Shop-Arithmetique" (Graunt [1662] 1975, 7). Graunt's mercantile analytical tools included comparison by division in the forms of ratios and percents, comparison by subtraction over time to follow increases and decreases, and the use of relative time frameworks to search for and predict seasonal and cyclical patterns. These arithmetic tools, socially distributed by merchants, became the basis for algorithms used in inductive studies from the seventeenth century onward. Although the data Graunt worked with were time series spanning twenty years, his chief arithmetic tool, the Rule of Three or the Merchant's Rule, is not usually associated with time series analysis. This comparison by division, however, is at the core of several types of data manipulation used in statistics, and I use it in this chapter to contrast the different contexts of quantitative reasoning.

The development from monetary to political to scientific arithmetic is the structure for this and all other chapters in Part I. We begin with an examination of Graunt's adaptation of his shop arithmetic into a policy tool applied to the bills of mortality. I then explore the leveling qualities of seventeenth-century urban labor markets and epidemics and their impact on political and statistical notions of population. In the last section of the chapter, I examine Karl Pearson's appropriation of Graunt's techniques and subject for his own scientific investigation into the age distribution of deaths.

The Merchant's Rule

The main tool of Graunt's mercantile-turned-political arithmetic was the Rule of Three. The Rule of Three is the simple arithmetic technique of using three knowns to solve for a fourth unknown factor in a ratio relationship. For example, solving for c in the expression

$$\frac{a}{b} = \frac{c}{d} \text{ or } a{:}b = c{:}d.$$

Graunt, for example, noted that from 1628 to 1662, 139,782 males and 130,866 females were christened. Using the Rule of Three, he simplified the gender comparisons by stating that there were fourteen men to every thirteen women. He carried this shop arithmetic into the realm of political arithmetic with the assertion that the value of the ratio served as proof that legislation against polygamy was consistent with the *"Law of Nature"* (Graunt [1662] 1975, 57–58).

In *Capitalism and Arithmetic: The New Math of the 15th Century,* Frank Swetz argues that for centuries the Rule of Three was the most esteemed mathematical technique in Europe. Swetz sees the Rule of Three as essential for all societies in which trade and exchange flourished. Although it can be traced to mathematical works from India and China as early as A.D. 250, its popularity and importance in Europe were due to its use in commercial practice, and it was often called the "Merchant's Rule" or the "Merchant's Key."[1] The earliest known printed mathematics books in the West are from late fifteenth-century Italy. These were texts for those engaged in commercial reckoning. The Rule of Three, *de regola del tre* or *la regula de le tre cose,* was the primary mathematical technique in these early texts and almost all of the illustrations given for the Rule of Three were of a mercantile nature.

In his book on *Painting and Experience in Fifteenth-Century Italy,* Michael Baxandall asserts the Rule of Three was such an important part of the training and work of merchants that they "played games and told jokes with it, bought luxurious books about it, and prided themselves on their prowess in it" (Baxandall 1988, 101). Baxandall reproduces several paintings that illustrate his premise that the universal commercial use of the Rule of Three, along with the technique of gauging volumes in the course of exchanging commodities, greatly influenced quattrocento Italian art. The commercial patron commanded art that visually played on the skills of comparing ratios and comparing volumes. Two centuries later, the merchant Graunt was flaunting his prowess

---

[1]   A distinguishing name for the algorithm is still used in some countries. An Argentinean student explained to me that she determined comparative advantage in international trade problems by using the Rule of Three. This was the first time I had heard the expression outside of pre–twentieth-century tomes. Another student from Bulgaria also spoke of the comparative advantage calculation as the Rule of Three. The episodes brought to my mind that the entire logic of nineteenth-century comparative advantage problems in international trade and of twentieth-century exchange rate calculations in international finance is an exercise in the Rule of Three.

with this rule and trying to persuade king and councilors of its effectiveness in simplifying comparisons of awkward quantities.

Although its popular origins were in commerce, the Merchant's Rule eventually became an important tool in the science of observation. Karl Pearson and Udny Yule, unlike John Graunt, were undoubtedly linked in their formal education and their research programs to the realm of science, mathematics, and statistical theory. One of the important vehicles for publishing their statistical research was the journal *Biometrika*. In a 1901 letter to Pearson, Yule suggested a quotation from Charles Darwin on quantitative methods as a motto for the new journal. Pearson agreed and used this passage, from Darwin's letter of May 23, 1855, in the first editorial of *Biometrika*: "I have no faith in anything short of actual measurement and the Rule of Three" (Darwin 1911, 411; Yule 1901b; Pearson 1901a, 4). The Rule of Three was the primary instrument of analysis in Graunt's seventeenth-century political arithmetic on the bills of mortality. By the nineteenth century, Darwin was far from alone in relying almost totally on the Rule of Three for quantitative analysis of observed natural and social phenomena.

The authors of the fifteenth-century Italian arithmetic books often used examples of the selling of cloth to illustrate the Rule of Three. It should, therefore, come as no surprise that a draper was to make the link between monetary and political arithmetic and introduce the Rule of Three to Charles II and his advisers for the purposes of quantitative decision making in public policy. In 1662, John Graunt's exhaustive and ingenious use of his "Shop-Arithmetique" ensured the unusual appointment of a cloth merchant to the newly formed Royal Society.[2] In his history of the Royal Society, Thomas Sprat used Graunt's appointment as an example of the king's, and thus the Royal Society's, regard for the "manual Arts" and "Mechanick Artists." In appointing Graunt as a charter member of the Royal Society, Charles II, according to Sprat, "gave this particular charge to His society, that if they found any more such Tradesmen, they should admit them all, without any more ado" (Sprat 1667, 67). It is no accident that the first foot in the door for the social sciences was that of a haberdasher.

Political Arithmetic with the Rule of Three

Why were the methods and conclusions of this merchant so well received by Charles II, his Privie Council, and the newly chartered Royal Society? In an essay on objectivity and authority, Ted Porter illustrated how statistics, in the realm of public policy, were used more to justify and rationalize than to discover and understand. Hereditary rulers who had absolute, unquestionable authority had no need for statistics (Porter 1991, 252). When Graunt presented his observations, the British royal family had only just come back into power following a civil war, the beheading of Charles I and Oliver Cromwell's rule (1649–1658). Charles II needed to reconstruct the crown's authority,

---

[2] A modern-day equivalent would be the election of a financial analyst on Wall Street to the National Academy of Science.

and Graunt in an obsequious way catered to that need. For example, one of Graunt's points was that 1660, the year of the restoration of throne, was a healthy and fruitful one and that, along with the evidence of health in 1648, "doth abundantly counterpoise the *Opinion* of those who think great *Plagues* come in with *King's* Reigns, because it happened so twice, *viz. Anno 1603* and 1625" (Graunt [1662] 1975, 51).

What had impressed Charles II was Graunt's skillful use of the Rule of Three to address such issues as population growth, age-specific mortality, the sustainability of a fighting army, the social futility of polygamy, the timing of plagues, and the age of the earth. Graunt noted the bills of mortality were made little use of other than to note weekly increases and decreases for general conversation, and in times of plague, "that so the rich might judge of the necessity of their removall, and Trades-men might conjecture what doings they were to have in their respective dealings" (Graunt [1662] 1975, 17). Graunt's achievement in bridging monetary and political arithmetic stemmed from his surmounting the boundaries of time in calculating ratios and making comparisons that could serve a state in justifying its actions and decrees. With over twenty years of data on cause of death and number of burials and christenings by sex, Graunt compared, through division and subtraction, one year, season, or parish with another, he calculated "mediums" to eliminate irregularities, and he reduced unwieldy raw proportions into percentages and other comprehensible forms. Graunt's calculations with the Merchant's Rule revealed the remarkable stability of some social mass phenomena over time and across parishes. Graunt's discovery of stable ratios has been recognized by many, but few have acknowledged Graunt's mercantile way of thinking and his insightful time series analysis.

In his ninety-page pamphlet, Graunt:

- reduced data from weekly bills from 1604–1660 into a few "Perspicuous Tables"
- examined inconsistencies, inaccuracies, biases, and limitations of data observed
- grouped observations into distinct categories, such as cause of death due to acute or to chronic diseases
- made comparisons between regions and over time
- calculated a life table
- patterned life cycles and seasonal variations of disease
- estimated the population, and death, birth, and growth rates for London

Three of the tables that Graunt constructed from the bills of mortality are reproduced in Tables 2.1 through 2.3. Most of Graunt's analysis on the data in the tables was comparison by division with the Rule of Three. The following passage, in which he compares the number of plague deaths with total deaths, illustrates his almost tortuous use of the Rule of Three:

Table 2.1 *Graunt's table of annual burials and christenings in London from 1604 to 1651. The first four columns of burials do not include deaths due to the plague, which are counted in the fifth data column. Graunt cautioned that from 1642 onward, the account of christenings was not an accurate recording of total births.*

The Table of Burials and Christnings in London.

Anno Dom.	97 Pari-shes.	16 Pari-shes.	Out-Pari-shes.	Buried in all.	Besides of the Plague	Christ-ned
1604	1518	2097	708	4843	896	5458
1605	1014	1974	960	5948	444	6504
1606	1941	2920	935	5796	2124	6614
1607	1879	2772	1019	5670	2352	6582
1608	2391	3218	1149	6758	2262	6845
1609	2494	3610	1441	7545	4240	6388
1610	2316	3791	1369	7486	1803	6785
1611	2152	3398	1166	6716	617	7014
	16715	14780	8747	50142	14752	52190
1612	2473	3843	1461	7778	64	6986
1613	2406	3679	1418	7503	16	6846
1614	2369	3504	1494	7367	22	7208
1615	2446	3791	1613	7850	37	7682
1616	2490	3876	1697	8063	9	7985
1617	2397	4109	1774	8180	6	7747
1618	2815	4715	2066	9596	18	7735
1619	2339	3857	1804	7999	9	8127
	19735	31374	13328	64436	171	60316
1620	2726	4819	2146	9691	21	7845
1621	2438	3759	1915	8112	11	8039
1622	2811	4217	2392	8943	16	7894
1623	3591	4721	2783	11095	17	7945
1624	3385	5919	2805	12199	11	8199
1625	5143	9819	3886	18848	35417	6983
1626	2150	3285	1965	7401	134	6701
1627	2315	3400	1988	7711	4	8408
	24569	39940	19970	84000	35631	62114

The Table of Burials, and Christnings, in London.

Anno Dom.	97 Pari-shes.	16 Pari-shes.	Out-Pari-shes.	Buried in all	Besides of the Plague	Christ-ned
1628	2412	3311	2017	7740	3	8564
1629	2536	3992	2243	8771	0	9901
1630	2506	4101	1521	9237	1317	9315
1631	2459	3697	1132	8288	274	8524
1632	2704	4412	1411	9527	8	9584
1633	2378	3936	2078	8393	0	9997
1634	2937	4980	1982	10399	1	9855
1635	2742	4966	2943	10651	0	10034
	20694	33495	19327	73505	1603	75774
1636	2815	6924	3210	12959	10400	9522
1637	2188	4265	2818	8681	3082	9160
1638	3584	5926	3751	13261	363	10311
1639	2592	4344	2612	9548	314	10150
1640	1919	5156	3246	11321	1450	10850
1641	3148	5092	3417	11167	1375	10670
1642	3176	5245	3578	11999	1274	10370
1643	3395	5552	3269	12216	996	9410
	23987	42544	25221	91752	19244	80443
1644	2593	4174	2574	9441	1492	8104
1645	2524	4639	2445	9608	1871	7966
1646	2746	4872	2797	10415	2365	7163
1647	2672	4749	3041	10462	3597	7332
1648	2480	4288	2515	9283	611	6544
1649	1865	4714	2910	10499	67	5825
1650	2301	4138	2310	8749	15	5612
1651	2845	5002	2597	10804	23	6071
	21026	36676	21199	78896	10041	54617

Source: Graunt [1662] 1665, 174–175.

In the year 1592, and 1636 we finde the proportion of those dying of the *Plague* in the whole to be near alike, that is about 10 to 23. or 11 to 25. or as about two to five.

In the year 1625. we finde the *Plague* to bear unto the whole in proportion as 35 to 51. or 7 to 10. that is almost the triplicate of the former proportion, for the *Cube* of 7. being 343. and the *Cube* of 10. being 1000. the said 343. is not 2/5 of 1000.

In *Anno* 1603. the proportion of the *Plague* to the whole was as 30 to 37. viz. as 4. to 5. which is yet greater then that last of 7 to 20. For if the Year 1625. had been as great a *Plague*-Year as 1603. there must have died not onely 7 to 10. but 8 to 10. which in those great numbers makes a vast difference.

We must therefore conclude the Year 1603. to have been the greatest *Plague*-year of this age. (Graunt [1662] 1975, 45–46)

Table 2.2 *Graunt's table of burials and christenings by sex for London from 1629 to 1664. The distinction of sex was initiated in the London bills of mortality in 1629. Graunt took a subtotal at the year 1640, because he thought that after that year the accounts, particularly for christenings, were not exact. He asserted, however, that the neglect after 1640 affected both sexes equally, so comparisons with ratios or proportions would still be accurate.*

(180)

The *TABLE* of *Males, and Females,* for LONDON.

(181)

An.Dom.	Buried Males	Buried Females	Christened Males	Christened Females
1629	4668	4103	5218	4683
1630	5660	4894	4858	4457
1631	4549	4013	4422	4102
1632	4932	4603	4994	4590
1633	4369	4023	5158	4839
1634	5676	5224	5035	4820
1635	5548	5103	5106	4928
1636	12377	10982	4917	4605
	47779	43945	39708	37024
1637	6392	5371	4703	4457
1638	7168	6456	5359	4952
1639	5351	4511	5366	4784
1640	6761	6010	5518	5332
Total	73451	65293	60664	56549
1641	6872	6270	5470	5200
1642	7049	6224	5460	4910
1643	6842	6360	4793	4617
1644	5659	5274	4107	3997
1645	6014	5465	4047	3919
1646	6683	6097	3768	3395
1647	7313	6746	3796	3536
1648	5145	4749	3363	3181
	51577	47185	34804	32755

An.Dom.	Buried Males	Buried Females	Christened Males	Christened Females
1649	5454	5112	3079	2746
1650	4548	4216	2850	2722
1651	5680	5147	3231	2840
1652	6543	6026	3220	2908
1653	5416	4671	3196	2959
1654	6972	6275	3441	3179
1655	6027	5330	3655	3349
1656	7365	6556	3668	3382
	44005	41333	26380	24085
1657	6578	5856	3396	3289
1658	7936	7057	3157	3013
1659	7451	7305	3209	2781
1660	7960	7158	3724	3247
1661	10448	9287	4748'	4107
1662	8623	7931	5216	4803
1663	8035	7321	5411	4881
1664	9369	8928	6041	5681
	66400	60843	34902	3180
Total	235427	214658	156750	14623

Source: Graunt [1662] 1665, 180–181.

Graunt's comparison by division resulted in various final forms that are summarized in Table 2.4. Proportions were Graunt's most common form of comparison, and the data set used for most of his proportions comprised annual observations on death due to different causes in London from 1629 to 1636 and from 1647 to 1659. Graunt calculated chance of death due to different causes by taking deaths due to one cause, summed over twenty years, and dividing that by total deaths summed over twenty years. With these proportions, Graunt constructed tables of notorious diseases and casualties so that "persons may the better understand the hazard they are in" (Graunt [1662] 1975, 31).[3] Graunt wrote that one of the chief goals of his analysis was "to

---

[3] Philip Kreager (1988) places Graunt's use of proportions in the context of the role of proportional checks in monitoring "accompts" in the typical bookkeeping practices of seventeenth-century London. Kreager also sees Graunt's inconsistencies in sums and his informal attitude toward totals as typical mercantile accounting.

Table 2.3 Data from Graunt's "Table of Casualties" displaying the annual number of deaths in London by cause from 1647 to 1660 and from 1629 to 1636. Given the "Incapacity of a Sheet," Graunt limited his table to twenty-two years, omitting the years between 1636 and 1647 because "nothing Extraordinary" happened in those years. In many of his calculations, Graunt used the twenty-year (1629–1636 and 1647–1658) total for burials, which is in the next to last column. Given the incapacity of my sheet, I omitted six columns of subtotals of annual groupings and aggregated twenty-five causes of death that resulted in less than sixty-five burials in twenty years into a row labeled "sum of the others." I also appended the last column that recalculates the row totals and illustrates some printing or calculation errors in Graunt's totals.

	1647	1648	1649	1650	1651	1652	1653	1654	1655	1656	1657	1658	1659	1660	1629	1630	1631	1632	1633	1634	1635	1636	In 20 Years	Corrected
Abortive and Stil-born	335	329	327	351	389	381	384	433	483	419	463	467	421	544	499	439	410	445	500	475	507	523	8559	8559
Aged	916	835	889	696	780	864	804	974	743	892	869	1176	909	1095	579	712	661	671	704	623	794	714	15759	15896
Ague and Fever	1260	884	751	970	1038	1212	1282	1317	689	875	999	1800	2303	2148	956	1091	1115	1108	953	1279	1622	2360	23784	23561
Apoplex, and Suddenly	69	74	64	74	106	111	118	86	92	102	113	138	91	67	85	95	37	79	82	97	104	34	1760	1760
Blasted	4	1			6				4		5	3	9	8	13		10	13	6	4			99	89
Bloody flux, Scouring and Flux	155	176	802	289	833	762	200	386	168	368	362	233	346	251	449	438	352	348	278	512	346	330	7818	7787
Burnt, and Scalded	3	6	10	5	11	8	5	7	10	5	7	4	6	6	3	10	7	5	1	3	12	3	125	125
Cancer, Gangrene and Fistula	26	29	31	19	31	53	36	37	73	31	24	35	63	52	20	14	23	28	27	30	24	30	609	621
Canker, Sore-mouth and Thrush	66	28	54	42	68	51	53	72	44	81	76	93	73	68	21	27	21	41	28	31	39	74	689	1010
Child-bed	161	106	114	117	206	213	158	192	177	201	236	225	226	194	150	157	112	171	132	143	163	230	3364	3364
Chrisomes, and Infants	1369	1254	1065	990	1237	1280	1050	1343	1089	1393	1162	1144	858	1123	2596	2378	2035	2268	2130	2315	2113	1895	32106	32106
Colick, and Wind	103	71	85	82	76	102	80	101	85	120	113	179	116	167	48	57	51	55	45	54	37	50	1389	1389
Cold, and Cough							41	36	21	58	30	31	33	24	10	58	51	55	45	54	50	57	598	597
Consumption, and Cough	2423	2200	2388	1988	2350	2410	2286	2868	2606	3184	2757	3610	2982	3414	1827	1910	1713	1797	1754	1955	2080	2477	44487	46583
Convulsion	684	491	530	493	569	653	606	828	702	1027	807	841	742	1031	52	87	18	241	221	386	418	709	9073	10363
Dropsie and Typany	185	434	421	508	444	556	617	704	660	706	631	931	646	872	235	252	279	280	266	250	329	389	9623	9077
Drowned	47	40	30	27	49	50	53	30	43	49	63	60	57	48	43	33	29	34	37	32	32	45	827	826
Executed	8	17	29	43	24	12	19	21	19	22	20	18	7	18	19	13	12	18	13	13	13	13	384	366
Flox, and small Pox	139	400	1190	184	525	1279	139	812	1294	823	835	409	1523	354	72	40	58	531	72	1354	293	127	10576	10576
Found dead in the Streets	6	6	9	8	7	9	14	4	3	4	9	11	3	6	18	33	20	6	13	8	24	24	243	236
French-Pox	18	29	15	18	21	20	20	20	29	23	25	53	51	31	17	12	12	12	7	17	12	22	392	402
Gout	9	5	12	9	7	7	5	6	8	7	8	13	14	2	2	5	3	4	4	5	7	8	134	134
Grief	12	13	16	7	17	14	11	17	10	13	8	13	14	4	18	20	22	11	14	17	5	20	279	279
Hanged, and made-away themselves	11	10	13	14	9	14	15	9	14	16	24	18	11	36	8	8	6	15	3	8	7		221	222
Jaundice	57	35	39	49	41	43	57	71	61	41	46	77	102	76	47	59	35	43	35	45	54	63	998	998

Table 2.3 (cont.)

	1647	1648	1649	1650	1651	1652	1653	1654	1655	1656	1657	1658	1659	1660	1629	1630	1631	1632	1633	1634	1635	1636	In 20 Years	Corrected
Jaw-faln	1	1						2	2		3	1			10	16	13	8	10	10	4	11	95	95
Impostume	75	61	65	59	80	105	79	90	92	122	80	134	105	96	58	76	73	74	50	62	73	130	1639	1638
Killed by several Accidents	27	57	39	94	47	45	57	58	52	43	52	47	55	47	54	55	47	46	49	41	51	60	1021	1021
King's Evil	27	26	22	19	22	20	26	26	27	24	23	28	28	54	16	25	18	38	35	20	20	69	537	531
Livergrown, Spleen, and Rickets	53	46	56	59	65	72	67	65	52	50	38	51	8	15	94	112	99	87	82	77	98	99	1421	1422
Lunatick	12	18	6	11	7	11	9	12	6	7	13	5	14	14	6	11			4	2	2	5	158	158
Meagrom	12	13		5	8	6	6	14	3	6	7	6	5	4		24	24		4			22	132	132
Measles	5	92	3	33	33	62	8	52	11	153	15	80	6	74	42	2	3	80	21	33	27	12	757	767
Murdered	3	2	7	5	4	3	3	3	9	6	5	7				2	3	7		6	5	8	86	86
Overlaid and starved at Nurse	25	22	36	28	28	29	30	36	58	53	44	50	46	43	4	10	13	7	8	14	10	14	529	519
Palsie	27	21	19	20	23	20	29	18	22	23	20	22	17	21	17	23	17	25	14	21	25	17	423	423
Plague	3597	611	67	15	23	16	6	16	9	6	4	14	36	14		1317	274	8	1	1		10400	16384	16384
Plague in the Guts				1	23	110	32	23	87	315	446	253	402										991	991
Pleurisie	30	26	13	20	23	19	17	23	10	9	17	16	12	10	26	24	26	36	21		45	24	415	425
Purples and Spotted Fever	145	47	43	65	54	60	75	89	56	52	56	126	368	146	32	58	58	38	24	125	245	397	1845	1845
Quinsie and Sore-throat	14	11	12	17	24	20	18	9	15	13	7	10	21	14	1	8	6	7	24	4	5	22	247	247
Rickets	150	224	216	190	260	329	229	372	347	458	317	476	441	521									3681	3681
Mother, rising of the Lights	150	92	115	120	134	138	135	178	166	212	203	228	210	249	44	72	99	98	60	84	72	104	2700	2504
Rupture	16	7	7	6	7	16	7	15	11	20	19	18	12	28	2	6	4	9	4	3	10	13	201	200
Scurvy	32	20	21	21	29	43	41	44	103	71	82	82	95	12	5	7	9	25	9	00	10	25	593	644
Sores, Ulcers, broken & bruised Limbs	15	17	17	16	26	32	25	32	23	34	40	47	61	48	23	24	20	48	19	19	22	29	504	528
Spleen	12	17				13	13	13		6	2	5	7	7									68	68
Stone and Strangury	45	42	29	28	50	41	44	38	49	57	72	69	22	30	35	39	58	50	58	49	33	45	937	931
Stopping of the Stomach	29	29	30	33	55	67	66	107	94	145	129	277	186	214		6			6		6	6	669	1067
Surfet	217	137	136	123	104	177	178	212	128	161	137	218	202	192	63	157	149	86	104	114	132	371	3094	3104
Teeth and Worms	767	597	540	598	709	905	691	1131	803	1198	878	1036	839	1008	440	506	335	470	432	454	539	1207	14236	14236
Tissick	62	47													8	12	14	34	23	15	27		242	242
Vomiting	1	6	3	7	4	6	9	14	7	27	16	19	8	10	1	4	1	1	2	5	6	3	136	136
Worms	147	107	105	65	85	86	53								19	31	28	27	19	28	27		830	827
Sum of the Others	23	27	41	40	22	23	23	29	40	21	27	29	77	97	18	20	20	26	33	13	28	31	601	534
Graunt's Total																							229250	
Recalculated Total																							232312	

Source: Graunt [1662] 1665. foldout.

Table 2.4 *Final forms of Graunt's comparison by division:* $\frac{a}{b} = \frac{c}{d}$

Type	Numerical form	Example
Ratio	c & d are integers, small and close in value	14 males to 13 females
Rate of occurrence	c is equal to 1	1 in 32 die yearly in London
Proportion	c is equal to 1 or d is equal to 229,250 (total deaths) or c/d in simple form	Of total deaths, 1 of 1,500 "dies Lunatick," 51 of 229,250 starve
Percentage	d is equal to 100	7 percent die of old age

understand the Land, and the hands of the Territory to be governed, according to all their intrinsick, and accidental differences." He also admitted however, "That there is much pleasure in deducing so many abstruse, and unexpected inferences out of the poor despised Bills of *Mortality*" (Graunt [1662] 1975, 72).

Graunt's investigation led to several interesting conclusions:

- The practice by English women of maintaining a straight, horizontal posture during childbirth resulted in a higher maternal death rate than in countries where this was not the fashion (Graunt [1662] 1975, 43).
- Mental work, typical of businesses in London, produced "*Anxieties* of the minde," which hindered breeding compared with the "*corporal Labour and Exercizes*" of the country (56).
- Polygamy should not be allowed since the sex ratio at birth of males to females was greater than one, and where it is allowed "Wives can be no other then Servants" (13, 57–60).
- During the great plagues, one-fifth of the population of London died while two-fifths fled to the countryside; but the "City is fully re-peopled within two years"; the plague that began in 1603 lasted eight years, the one that began in 1636, twelve years, but the plague of 1625 lasted only one year (11, 47).
- Wars could easily be waged and colonies settled without destroying the due proportion of males to females (59).
- The population of England and Wales was 6,500,000, and the population of London represented one-fifteenth of the total (11, 54).
- The population of London doubled in 70 years compared with 280 years in the country parishes (12, 53–54).
- Not including great plagues, the death rate for London was 1 in 32, which was higher than that of the country, which was 1 in 50 (76).
- There are four children for every marriage (14).

- The world was not more than 5,610 years old, "which is the *age* of the world according to the *Scriptures*" (70).

Graunt's Epidemiology

The link between the shop arithmetic and the political arithmetic also comes out clearly in Graunt's analysis of seasonal and annual variations. In addition to his extensive use of the Merchant's Rule, Graunt employed comparison by subtraction, "medium" (average) annual values, and relative time frameworks to identify unhealthy years and seasons and to search for cyclical patterns in illness.[4] For example, Graunt labeled a year as "sickly" if the number of burials in that year was greater than the numbers in the previous year and the subsequent year.

Graunt's search for temporal patterns included a study of the progress of some diseases in absolute time. Graunt tried to determine whether rickets, a disease that appeared on the bills for the first time in 1634, was a new disease or merely a new name for an existing disease. Graunt concluded that the former was the case. He used the image of "backstarting" (what contemporary consumption theorists would call the "ratchet" effect) to visualize a typical temporal pattern of the annual progression in the mortality of a new disease such as rickets:

> Now, such backstartings seem to be universal in all things; for we do not onely see in the progressive motion of the wheels of *Watches*, and in the rowing of *Boats*, that there is a little starting, or jerking backwards between every step forwards, but also (if I am not much deceived) there appeared the like in the motion of the *Moon*, which in the long *Telescopes* at *Gresham-College* one may sensibly discern. (Graunt [1662] 1975, 39)

Using a relative-time framework, Graunt determined that, "the unhealthful Season is the *Autumn*" (Graunt [1662] 1975, 51). This was particularly true during epidemics of bubonic plague. The number of plague deaths generally peaked in late August or September. If mortality could be tracked on a weekly basis, then a marked increase in deaths in late summer would signal a visitation of pestilence.

The emerging urban markets in seventeenth-century London, in addition to providing Graunt the analytical tools, called forth the data for his observations. Throughout the seventeenth century, every week, in every parish of London, state-appointed searchers visited the homes of the recently deceased to determine the cause of death. The searchers, older women by decree, reported their findings to the parish clerks, and every Thursday, the numbers of parish christenings and burials and the causes of death were published and sent to those who had paid four shillings per year for the bills of mortality (a portion

---

[4]   In Chapters 3 and 5, I examine in more detail the monetary algorithms of first differences and relative time frameworks respectively.

of the annual bill of mortality for 1665 is reproduced in Table 2.5). The subscribers included merchants anxious about the future of their trade and the wealthy, who could afford to leave town at the first hint of pestilence.

Great Plagues

Graunt applied his "shop-arithmetique" to numbers gleaned from the searchers' data, which had been tabulated on a weekly basis from as early as 1532.[5] These parish bills, regularly posted to monitor the course of plagues, were products of a modern way of perceiving and accounting the human creatures that inhabited the British Isles. The bubonic plagues were mass phenomena, and visitations brought home the numerical equivalence of the dead, whether they were rich or poor while they lived.[6] The breakdown of the sense of the individual was vividly described in Daniel Defoe's account of the mass burial pits in which thousands of corpses were put during the 1665 London plague:[7]

> The Cart had in it sixteen or seventeen Bodies; some were wrapt up in Linen Sheets, some in Rugs, some a little other than naked, or so loose, that what Covering they had fell from them in the shooting out of the Cart, and they fell quite naked among the rest; but the Matter was not much to them, or the Indecency much to any one else, seeing they were all dead, and were huddled together into the common Grave of Mankind, as we may call it, for here no Difference made, but Poor and Rich went together, there was no other way of Burials. . . .
>
> It was reported by way of Scandle upon the Buriers that if any Corpse was delivered to them decently wound up, as we call'd it then, in a Winding Sheet Ty'd over the Head and Feet, which some did, and which was generally of good Linen; I say, it was reported, that the Buriers were so wicked as to strip them in the Cart and carry them quite naked to the Ground. (Defoe [1722] 1968, 69–70)

Thomas Dekker's description of mass burial during the 1603 visitation in London is similar:

---

[5] Charles Hull (1899, lxxx–xci) draws on many historical sources to try to determine the dates and forms of the earliest bills of mortality. The fire of 1666 apparently destroyed all sets of London bills before 1658, but Graunt's tables, John Bell's *London's Remembrancer*, and assorted manuscripts enable a reconstruction of some of the earlier years. The distinction of births and deaths by sex and the designation of cause of death were introduced in the London bills in 1629. Graunt therefore chose that year as the start of his data analysis. Following suggestions by Graunt and William Petty, the London bills eventually included number of marriages and age of death.

[6] As one can see in Table 2.3, the leveling qualities of the London bills of mortality are also evident in the number of executions. For the year 1649, King Charles I and commoners are presumably added together to calculate the total of 29 deaths.

[7] Although Defoe's account was published in 1722 as an eyewitness account of a London saddler in 1665, historians doubt that Defoe was more than four years of age during that year of the plague. The narrative was supposedly based on a journal of H.F., which, as James Sutherland points out in his introduction to *The Journal*, are the initials of Daniel Defoe's uncle. Unlike in his other works, Defoe makes extensive use of data and documentation in *The Journal*, and it is very possible that Graunt's observations (from later editions) or John Bell's *London's Remembrancer* was one among the sources Defoe used.

Table 2.5 *A portion of a London bill of mortality for the plague year of 1665. This was a year-end bill that totaled deaths by cause for the entire year. Not included in this reproduction are the total deaths by Parish.*

1665.

A General BILL for this prefent Year,

Ending the 19th Day of December 1665.

According to the Report made to the Kings moft excellent Majefty,

By the Company of Parifh Clerks of LONDON, &c.

DISEASES and CASUALTIES.

Disease	No.	Disease	No.	Disease	No.
Abortive and Stillborn	617	Executed	21	Overlaid and Starved	45
Aged	1545	Flox and Small Pox	655	Palfy	30
Ague and Fever	5257	Found dead in the Streets, Fields, &c.	20	Plague	68596
Apoplexy and Suddenly	116			Planet	6
Bedrid	10	French Pox	86	Plurify	15
Blafted	5	Frighted	23	Poifoned	1
Bleeding	16	Gout and Sciatica	27	Quinfy	35
Bloody Flux, Scowring, and Flux	185	Grief	46	Rickets	557
		Griping in the Guts	1288	Rifing of the Lights	397
Burnt and Scalded	8	Hang'd and made away themfelves	7	Rupture	34
Calenture	3			Scurvy	105
Cancer, Gangrene, and Fiftula	56	Headmouldfhot and Mouldfallen	14	Shingles and Swine Pox	2
Canker and Thrufh	111	Jaundies	110	Sores, Ulcers, broken and bruifed Limbs	82
Childbed	625	Impofthume	227	Spleen	14
Chrifomes and Infants	1258	Kill'd by feveral Accidents	46	Spotted Fever and Purples	1929
Cold and Cough	68	King's Evil	86	Stopping of the Stomach	332
Colick and Wind	134	Leprofy	2	Stone and Strangury	98
Confumption and Tiffick	4808	Lethargy	14	Surfeit	1251
Convulfion and Mother	2036	Livergrown	20	Teeth and Worms	2614
Diftracted	5	Megrims and Head-ach	12	Vomiting	51
Dropfy and Tympany	1478	Meafles	7	Wen	1
Drowned	50	Murdered and Shot	9		

CHRISTENED { Males — 5114 | Females 4853 | In all — 9967 }   BURIED { Males — 48569 | Females 48737 | In all — 97306 } Of the Plague 68596

Increafed in the Burials in the 130 Parifhes and at the Peft-houfe this Year 79009

Increafed of the Plague in the 130 Parifhes and at the Peft-houfe this Year 68590

Source: A Collection of the Yearly Bills of Mortality from 1657 to 1758 Inclusive [1758] 1759.

> All ceremonial due to them was taken away, they were launched ten in one heap, twenty in another, the gallant and the beggar together, the husband saw his wife and his deadly enemy whom he hated within a pair of sheets. What rotten stenches and contagious damps would strike up into thy nostrils. (From Dekker's *Seven Deadly Sins of London*, 1606, quoted in Creighton [1891] 1965, 482)

Plague epidemics definitely qualify for the label of mass phenomena, and the weekly mortality during plague years was structured through time in a symmetrical, formal pattern. Graunt and his contemporaries saw this pattern in comparisons of weekly mortality tables. In all major and minor plague years in London in the seventeenth century the peak mortality was in the last weeks of August and the first weeks of September. Linked with the seasonal pattern, there was also a change in the typical symptoms of the disease during the course of an epidemic. The changing severity of the symptoms was one of the determining causes of the seasonal symmetry in the mortality curve. The symptoms at the prime of the life of the visitation were very different from those experienced at the birth and death of the epidemic. Creighton quotes William Boghurst, an apothecary who treated hundreds of cases of the plague in 1665:

> It fell not very thick upon old people till about the middle or slake of the disease, and most in the decreases and declining of the disease. . . . In summer about one-half that were sick, died; but towards winter, three of four lived. (Boghurst quoted in Creighton [1891] 1965, 675)

Defoe also remarked on the change of the rate of mortality of those infected:

> few people that were touch'd with it in its height about *August* and *September*, escap'd; And, which is very particular, contrary to its ordinary Operation in *June* and *July*, and the beginning of *August*, when, as I have observ'd many were infected, and continued so many Days, and then went off, after having had the Poison in the Blood a long time; but not on the contrary, most of the People who were taken during the two last Weeks in *August*, and in the three first Weeks in *September*, generally died in two or three Days at farthest, and many the very same Day they were taken. (Defoe [1722] 1968, 191–192).

Indeed, Defoe mentions rumors of a specific turning point in the mortality: the peak was apparently one September morning when 3,000 died in London between the hours of one and three o'clock in the morning.

An indication that the disease had lost its fatal strength was when the swellings (the buboes) in the lymph nodes discharged pus (suppurated). This was much more common in those who were smitten after the early autumn peak of the epidemic. Hardened buboes characterized the more fatal form of the disease that was common around the August–September peak. Creighton did not publish graphs of seasonal variation in his nineteenth-century study of the history of epidemics in Britain, but his description of the temporal change in the bubonic symptoms evokes a visual image of the seasonal

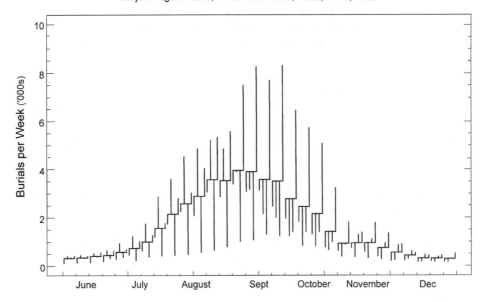

Figure 2.1   This plot is based on data in the fifth edition of Graunt's *Observations* ([1662] [1676] 1899). The height of a horizontal line measures the number of deaths for that week averaged over four plague years.

epidemic "curve" or "law" that must have entered into the minds of those like Creighton and Graunt who constructed tables of the weekly deaths from the bills of mortality:

> an epidemic of plague declined as a whole in malignity towards the end, so that the buboes suppurated, and three out of four, or three out of five, patients recovered. If that were the case in the descent of the curve, why should there not have been something corresponding in the ascent? (Creighton [1891] 1965, 655)

Graunt in the seventeenth century, Defoe in the eighteenth century, and even Creighton in the nineteenth century worked with tables to get a sense of the process of plague mortality. I have taken the liberty of using some of the raw material Graunt worked with to construct graphs that will give those of us less attuned to tabular reasoning a sense of the temporal patterns of epidemics of bubonic plague. If one plots typical seasonal variation of deaths per week in seventeenth-century London during plague years, one constructs a bell curve with a peak in mortality in early autumn (see Figures 2.1, 2.2). There is no similar seasonal ordering patterns of mortality in the nonplague years of the sixteenth or eighteenth century, even in cases of other epidemics (see Figures 2.3, 2.4,). There was no periodic pattern to the appearance of plagues in London that would enable one to predict which year would be a plague year. Once a plague arrived, however, it took on an incredible weekly

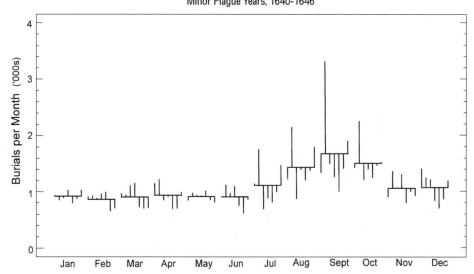

Figure 2.2   This plot is based on data in J. Bell 1665. The height of a horizontal line measures the number of deaths for that month averaged over seven years.

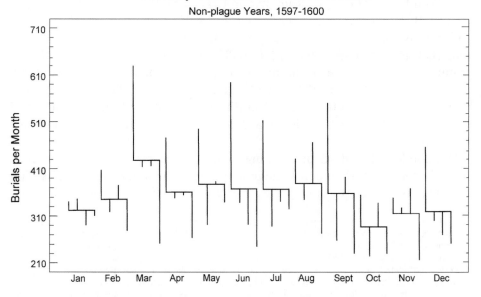

Figure 2.3   Plot based on data from Hull [1899] 1986.

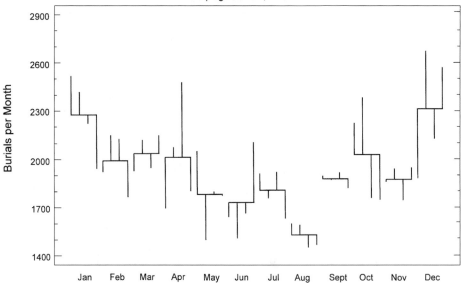

Figure 2.4   Plot based on data in Heberden [1801] 1973.

pattern in late August: first exponential growth, a turning point, then rapid decline.[8]

The parish clerks, responding to decrees by the lord mayor and financed by the merchants and the rich, tracked the mortality pattern week to week in the form of tables of absolute counts (deaths or deaths due to the plague in the past week). Unfortunately, few of the weekly bills survived the great fire of London in 1666, but from data in Graunt's fifth edition of *Observations* (1676), Bell's *London's Remembrancer* (1665), W. Heberden ([1801] 1973), and manuscripts that Hull (1899, 426–428) investigated, it is possible to construct graphs of seasonal variation. The graphs used in Figures 2.1–2.4 group weekly (in the case of Figure 2.1) or monthly data (in the case of Figures 2.2–2.4) in a relative time framework of an annual cycle. For Figure 2.1, the horizontal axis orders the weekly data from the first week in June until the last week in December; for Figures 2.2–2.4, the months go from January to December.

What follows is a description of Figure 2.1, but a substitution of the word "month" for "week" will adapt the description to the other three figures. The vertical axis measures deaths per week in London parishes. The height of the

[8] I did not come across any reference to this historical seasonal pattern in the accounts I read of the outbreak of bubonic and pneumonic plague in India in the fall of 1994. There were reports in late August of a visitation of bubonic plague in the Maharashtra State in western India. By late September, thousands of cases of bubonic and pneumonic plague had been reported in neighboring states, particularly in the city of Surat in the state of Gujurat. By late October, public health officials were saying they had the epidemic under control. Even in the great epidemic of 1665, mortality was "under control" by the end of October in London. A historical awareness of previous trackings of the predictable seasonal pattern of the plague would have aided health workers, reporters, and medical journalists covering this recent outbreak. Some scientists are using an awareness of the seasonal pattern of the Ebola virus to determine which animal carriers would be consistent with a November peak in human mortality.

horizontal line for each week measures the number of deaths for that week averaged over the four great plague years. The height of the end of a vertical line perpendicular to a horizontal line plots the number of deaths in that week for a specific year, and the length and direction of the vertical line indicates each year's deviation from the average for that week.

Figure 2.1 illustrates the weekly variation in total deaths for the years of major plague visitations in London, 1603, 1625, 1636, 1665. One can see the peak of average mortality in the fourteenth week after the beginning of June, which would be the last week in August or first week in September. The average number of deaths for the four great plagues years for that week was 4,000. One can see by the upward reaching vertical lines on the far right of each horizontal bar that the deaths in 1665 were above average for almost every week and greater than any of the preceding years. In the first week in September 1665, parish clerks in London recorded 8,252 deaths.[9]

Even for minor plague years in the seventeenth century, in which total annual plague deaths were 3,000 or less, and in which diseases such as typhus (spotted fever) claimed more lives, the remarkable seasonal pattern persists. This is true for weekly and monthly variation. Figure 2.2 plots the variation in deaths per month over an entire year for the years of relatively minor pestilence from 1640 to 1646. The symmetrical pattern centered around a peak of deaths in September is not evident in the monthly variation plotted from the bills of mortality recording deaths from 1597 to 1600 (Figure 2.3). Likewise the seasonal pattern of mortality for 1764–1767 (Figure 2.4), with declining deaths as the summer proceeds and a peak of monthly mortality in early winter, is remarkably different from that in the preceding two centuries.[10]

The weekly, numerical tracking of the ascent and descent of the curve and the sudden, indiscriminate elimination of over a sixth of the urban population no doubt helped to lay the seeds for a statistical way of thinking. In seventeenth-century London, a person could be just a corpse and a corpse could be a number. As Graunt illustrated, the numbers could be manipulated to quantify population and the rate of change in population. The acknowledgment of equivalence and the summation of many individuals led to a recognition of social mass phenomena. The whole was different from the sum of the parts and displayed a stability and certainty in stark contrast to the attributes of individual constituents. Populations could thus be characterized by summary parameters and analytical images.

Population

The significance to statistical theory of Graunt's observations on the bills of mortality stems from three important insights: the applicability of mercantile arithmetic to a social and political science of observation; the importance of

[9]   There were more people living in London in 1665 compared with the other years, but even the proportionate mortality appears to be higher in 1665. Based on estimates of London population by Charles Creighton ([1891] 1965, 660) and the number of deaths recorded in the bills of mortality, 17 percent of the population died in 1603, 16 percent died in 1625, and 21 percent died in 1665.

[10]   The high autumn mortality in the seventeenth century might have been as much a background cause of the relatively high frequency of bubonic plague epidemics as an effect of the epidemics.

population to the state; and the stability of social proportions and ratios over time and across parishes. Population is a key concept in the logic of statistical method. The act of defining a population is premised with the assumptions of an equivalence of individual constituents, of an order and relationship binding the constituents, and of a manifestation of the whole.[11] The historical context in which these assumptions were first relevant to nation-states is also the context in which statistics had its origins.

Equivalence of all inhabitants, like equivalence of outcomes in a game of chance, is a relatively modern notion. For example, Karl Marx in volume one of *Capital* argued that Aristotle failed to fully understand the economic relationship of value in exchange because his ideas were the product of a slave society where equivalence between laborers had no meaning (Marx [1867] 1976, 152).[12] Rigid social inequality bound in a system of tradition prohibited notions of equivalent exchange values and of population in feudal as well as slave societies.

Geoffrey Kay and J. Mott (1982) argue that, in Britain at least, the feudal order was replaced by the order of equivalence, which gave rise to the notion of population. Kay and Mott point out that the Doomsday Book of the eleventh century did not count people, but instead, listed fiscal units to which groups of people of varying status were attached and emphasized the extent and use of property rather than the number of people. The counting of John Graunt and William Petty six centuries later assumed political and fiscal equivalence of citizens and their labor as a source of value.[13]

By the seventeenth century, commodity exchange in London was becoming what Marx would describe as a "very Eden of the innate rights of man" (Marx [1867] 1976, 280). The sphere of circulation of commodities between people appeared to be an exclusive realm of freedom and equality, and within this sphere what counted was not the specific nature of concrete labor, but simply abstract labor time embodied in goods produced for exchange. With the market's reduction of the essence of all value to human labor in the abstract, and with the political creation of an "order of equivalence," a population way of thinking became a necessity for the state. Joseph Schumpeter described this dawn of the era of equivalence: "A numerous and increasing population was the most important *symptom* of wealth, it was the chief *cause* of wealth; it *was* wealth itself – the greatest asset for any nation to have. Utterances of this

[11]   For example, in the course of explaining the "science of means" in his article on the "Method of Statistics" for the *Jubilee Volume of the Royal Statistical Society*, Ysidro Edgeworth commented, "The term 'Means' of course implies the correlative conception: members of a class, or terms of a 'Series' (in Mr. Venn's phrase) of which the mean is to be taken: 'Massenerscheinungen' in the language of Professor Lexis" (Edgeworth 1885, 182).

[12]   In Marx's words: "However, Aristotle himself was unable to extract this fact, that, in the form of commodity-values, all labour is expressed as equal human labor and therefore as labour of equal quality, by inspection from the form of value, because Greek society was founded on the labour of slaves, hence had as its natural basis the inequality of men and of their labour-powers. The secret of the expression of value, namely the equality and equivalence of all kinds of labour because and in so far as they are human labour in general could not be deciphered until the concept of human equality had already acquired the permanence of a fixed popular opinion" (Marx [1867] 1976, 151–152).

[13]   William Petty not only equated one person to another but even land and people through calculation of the monetary value of each. He considered the latter equation the most important consideration in "political oeconomies" because it was a condition for allocation of the proportionate and thus fair share of the tax burden (see Hull 1899, lxxi).

kind were so numerous as to render quotations superfluous" (Schumpeter 1954, 251).

In his observations on the bills of mortality, Graunt noted that "Princes are not only Powerfull but Rich, according to the number of their People (Hands being the Father, as Lands are the Mother, and Womb of Wealth)" (Graunt [1662] 1975, 61).[14] Eighteenth-century philosophers considered population one of the most important social issues, and by the end of the nineteenth century the concept of population was an integral part of statistical theory. John Graunt's observations inspired Johann Peter Sussmilch's work on population. That in turn inspired Thomas Malthus, and the latter was a source of inspiration to Charles Darwin.[15] The "Divine Order" that became Sussmilch's theme was initiated in Graunt's revelation of the stability of the ratios he calculated over time. Graunt's declaration of stability, in phenomena as diverse as the ratio of male to female births or the proportion of accidental deaths to total deaths, meshed well with the goal of the scholars of the Enlightenment to find uniformity amid variety and order amid chaos.

Graunt's Statistical Structure in Time: The Life Table

Graunt's confidence in the stability of the ratios that he had constructed spanning twenty years of data is evident in his construction of the first life table. This statistical structure in relative time is now a staple in actuarial practice. The relative time is the human life cycle marked by decades of age. Examining the numbers dying by each cause over twenty years, Graunt estimated how many deaths were those of infants, and how many were elderly. For these decades of the life cycle and the ones interpolated in between, Graunt determined out of 100 live births how many died at each decade, and therefore what percentage was alive above each age.

Graunt calculated that in twenty years 71,124 people, out of a total death count of 229,250, died of causes that he surmised affected only children. His next step was to use the Merchant's Rule to put this into a proportional form that readers could easily grasp: "that is to say, that about ⅓ of the whole died of those diseases, which we guess did all light upon children under four or five Years old" (Graunt [1662] 1975, 29–30). Graunt guessed that one-half of deaths due to certain other causes (e.g., small-pox) were also children under six and concluded that "thirty six *per centum* of all quick conceptions, died before six years old" (Graunt [1662] 1975, 30).[16]

Graunt estimated that 1 in 15 of all deaths, 7 percent, were attributed to old age by the searchers, and concluded that "if in any other Country more

---

[14] Although Graunt spoke of the people of a land, Philip Kreager (1988) points out that he never actually used the word "population."

[15] James Bonar ([1929] 1966) discussed the links between Graunt and Sussmilch.

[16] The Rule of Three was an act of commerce and percent was an act of finance. If money had been borrowed or lent then the phrase "per cent" or "per centum" was in the vocabulary. "Per cent" was a type of proportion, an offspring of the "Rule of Three"; it was a statement of the rate of interest (for word origins see the *Oxford English Dictionary*, 2nd ed., 1989, vol. 11, 1031). It was in the life-table construction, when he wanted a common denominator for each decade of life, that Graunt reduced proportions to percents. Although Graunt used first differences and expressed some proportions in the form of percents, he never combined the comparison by subtraction with comparison by division in a

Table 2.6 *The first life table, constructed by John Graunt.*

Viz. Of an·hundred there dies within the first fix years ————36 The next ten years, or *Decad*————24 The fecond *Decad*-15	The ⸱third *Decad*--------9 The fourth----6 The next————4 The next-----3 The next-----2 The next-----1

Source: Graunt [1662] 1665, 125.

then seven of the 100 live beyond 70, such Country is to be esteemed more healthfull then this of our City" (Graunt [1662] 1975, 32). Graunt interpolated percents between the extremes of infancy and old age and crudely estimated the number of deaths for each decade of life for a cohort of 100 live births.[17] Graunt's life table is reproduced in Table 2.6. True to his aim of *political* arithmetic, Graunt's first use of the life table was to estimate the number of fighting men from London the king could rely on for future wars. From his table, Graunt calculated that 34 percent of all males were between the ages of sixteen and fifty-six; he translated that into approximately 70,000 men of fighting age in London proper.

In a footnote in his 1899 edited version of Graunt's observations, Charles Hull lists Edouard Mallet's estimates of relative frequency of death by age based on recordings of age of death in Geneva from 1601 to 1700. Mallet's data showed 42.6 percent of all deaths were of those aged six or less, and 5.8 percent of those who died were over seventy-six years of age. Neither Graunt nor Mallet constructed graphs from their tables, but Figure 2.5 graphically compares Graunt's estimates of the relative frequency of age of death to those of Mallet's. The former, being an arithmetical interpolation between the two end-point ages, is obviously a smoother graduation, but the images are similar.

Graunt's work inspired not only the construction of life tables (e.g., by Edmund Halley), but also the inclusion of age of death in the London bills of mortality. In 1758, Corbyn Morris summarized death by age based on the London bills for various years in the eighteenth century. Figure 2.6 illustrates the stark contrast between the age distribution of deaths in London in 1728–30 and in the United States in 1991.[18] What is striking in the plots of Graunt's,

---

calculation of a *percent change*. *Percent change*, as opposed to just *percent*, was not a common monetary algorithm until the nineteenth century. When Graunt examined growth or change over time he used expressions such as "doubled" or "encreased from one to four."

[17] Karl Pearson (1978) and Anders Hald (1990), among others, discuss Graunt's interpolation in the construction of a life table.

[18] With both Figures 2.5 and 2.6, one must keep in mind that the age distribution of the population influenced the age distribution of death and vice versa.

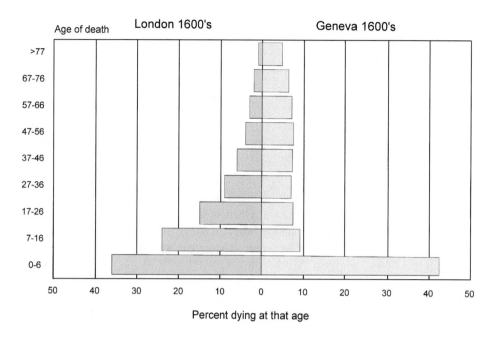

Figure 2.5   Age distribution of death in seventeenth-century London and Geneva. *Source:* Graunt ([1662] [1676] 1899).

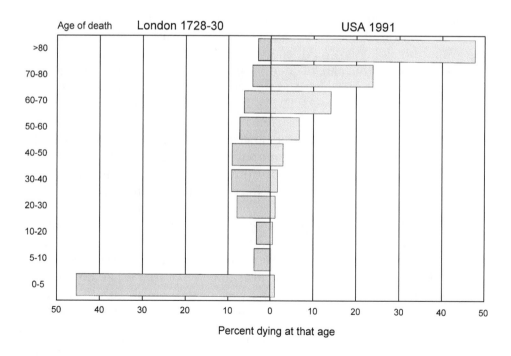

Figure 2.6   Age distribution of death in eighteenth-century London and twentieth-century USA. *Source:* Morris [1758] 1759, U.S. National Center for Health Statistics 1995.

Mallet's, and Morris's data is the high level of child mortality. Even in the U.S. data, the first few years of life appear more precarious than those that immediately follow.

Graunt's observations on the bills of mortality earned him membership in the Royal Society and posthumous fame as the "father of statistics." Graunt's original contribution to the construction of life tables is well recognized as is his observation that year after year, parish after parish, there were more males born than females (Graunt reduced the ratio for London to fourteen males to every thirteen females). Even his observation that "Physicians *have two* Women *Patients to one* Man, *and yet more Men die then Women*" (Graunt [1662] 1975, 12) is still referred to in the popular press of the late twentieth century.

Karl Pearson and others have seen Graunt's main contribution to statistics as the implicit recognition of the stability of statistical ratios over time and space (Pearson 1978, 30). For example, Graunt noted with "Chronical" diseases, such as consumption (tuberculosis), suicide, and even in the case of some types of accidents, such as drowning, over the years the deaths due to particular casualties bore a constant proportion to the whole number of burials.

Although Graunt's contribution in the area of stable ratios is well recognized, far less attention has been paid to the link between Graunt's arithmetic and his occupation. Only a merchant would have analyzed the data from the bills of mortality in the way that Graunt did, and it was merchants, anxious to predict the future course of their trade, who paid the four shillings for the results of the work of the searchers and parish clerks on the bills of mortality. Also, out of past experience or wishful thinking, merchants had confidence in the overall stability of the numbers they worked with through thick and thin markets. Graunt not only demonstrated the stability of ratios, but he also hoped that his analysis would lead to even greater commercial and social stability. He argued that careful quantification of "the People" would engender "the knowledge wherof Trade, and Government may be made more certain, and Regular" (Graunt [1662] 1975, 79). The merchants' desire for, and confidence in, stability proved instrumental in Graunt's calculation of ratios spanning two decades and in later nineteenth-century commercial practice that fed into the construction and modeling of stationary time series.

Graunt was a retailer and his shop arithmetic consisted of using comparison by division to simplify relationships, using comparison by subtraction to determine the temporal patterns of illness and mortality, calculating "mediums" (averages) over time to eliminate irregularities, presenting the data in the form of spread-sheet-style tables, and reorganizing the values into relative time frameworks for comparisons between seasons and between ages.[19] In adapting his shop arithmetic to political arithmetic, Graunt expanded the time horizon, addressed issues of policy, and used his analytical tools to persuade and justify. In their reckoning of the chance of death, nineteenth-century

[19]   While replicating Graunt's work, I realized that the obvious choice of software was not a statistical package, but rather a spreadsheet program, which is more associated with financiers and retailers than with scientists or econometricians. The formulas commonly used with spreadsheet software are very similar to Graunt's shop arithmetic. I also noticed in my spreadsheet replication that Graunt had made several errors, some quite significant, in his arithmetic.

scientists and applied mathematicians built on the monetary and political layers, but embellished the storytelling with symbols embedded in equations and laws embodied in smoothed curves. Karl Pearson's work on the age distribution of the chance of death serves as an excellent illustration of how the shop-*cum*-political arithmetic of Graunt was modified for the purposes of scientific investigation and the development of a mathematical theory of statistics.

Pearson's Statistical Structures in Time: Mortality Curves

> To the Royal Society
>> which fostered the many lines of inquiry set in train by John Graunt through his 1662 publication, *Natural and Political Observations on the London Bills of Mortality*

Thus read the dedication of Egon Pearson's edition of his father's lectures on the history of statistics (Pearson 1978). Karl Pearson was one of many Royal Society fellows who was inspired by Graunt's political (shop) arithmetic, and Graunt was one of the major actors in Pearson's history.

In his essay "The Chances of Death," Pearson addressed a question similar to that of Graunt's: Out of a cohort of 1,000 people born alive at the same time, how many die at each age? In contrast to the table that Graunt constructed, Pearson answered with a mortality curve (Figure 2.7). The graph included the frequency of death by age plotted from data collected from 1871 to 1880 by the registrar-general.[20] Pearson decomposed the curve connecting the data points into five smooth curves mapped out from mathematical functions of chance frequency distributions centered on the ages of 72, 42, 23, and 3 years and 1 month before birth.

Pearson's essay was an argument for adopting a modern, more mature notion of chance and death. The medieval notion of chance was that of chaotic, random incident; the modern notion of chance was that of mathematical law and geometric order. Similarly, the medieval metaphor of death was the random action of the "dance of death."[21] In contrast with the medieval image of the dance of death, Pearson saw death as "a marksman with a certain skewness of aim and a certain precision of weapon" (Pearson 1897, 25). To metaphorically explain his decomposition of a mortality curve into five chance distributions, Pearson had his wife paint his stochastic view of the chances of death as that of five marksmen of death aiming their deadly weapons at humans traveling over the bridge of life (Figure 2.8).[22] To compare his view of death – that is, a regiment of marksmen maintaining law and order in mass

---

[20]   In London in 1824, the state took over from the church the regular publication of mortality data.

[21]   The image of the "dance of death" may have had a more orderly, deterministic flavor in the Middle Ages than Pearson gives credit for. Historian Mary Hill Cole pointed out to me that medieval dances were often very defined, formal, and scripted rituals.

[22]   In his essay Pearson mentions that he had asked two artists to draw his image of the bridge of life. The one trained in "the modern impressionist school" failed, but his wife "reared among the creations of Holbein, Flaxman, and Blake" came closer to realizing his image. Karl Pearson's rough sketch and Maria Sharpe Pearson's prints and large painting of the bridge of life are in the Pearson Papers at The Library, University College, London.

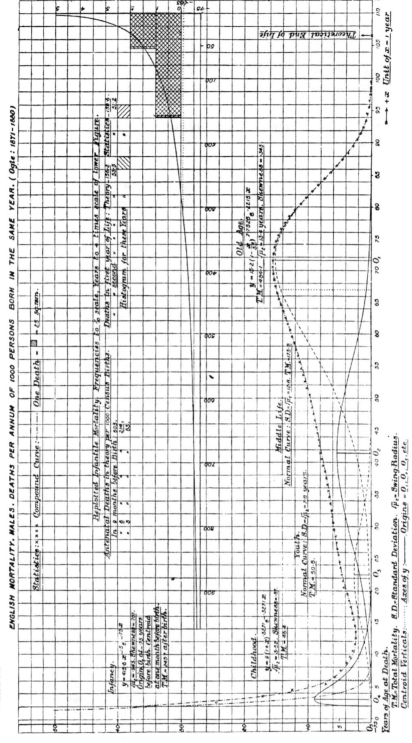

Figure 2.7 Pearson's plot of the age distribution of death in England 1871–1880 (curve with x's), broken down into five component chance distributions. *Source*: Pearson 1897, plate IV.

Figure 2.8 Maria Sharpe Pearson's etching of the Bridge of Life. Each marksman represents a component curve on Figure 2.7. *Source:* Pearson 1897, frontispiece.

PLATE II.

GROSS-BASEL.

Figure 2.9   Fifteenth-century images of the "Dance of Death" at the church at Gross-Basel. *Source:* Pearson 1897, plate II.

phenomena – with the medieval image, Pearson reproduced examples of the older notion of the "dance of death." These reproductions included fifteenth-century images from a cemetery in Gross-Basel (Figure 2.9) and sixteenth-century prints of Holbein.

Pearson's marksmen aimed their weapons at the mode years of the five frequency distributions. The type of weapon gave a sense of the maximum mortality in the mode year and the standard deviation of the distribution. For example, the weapon of the mortality of childhood was centered on the third year of life, more people died at this mode than at the mode of youth or middle-age mortality, and the standard deviation of childhood mortality was less than any other except that of infancy. The precision and deadliness of the marksman of childhood was thus conveyed with the weapon of a "maxim gun." In middle-age mortality, centered on the forty-second year of life, the fire of the marksmen is "slow and scattered, and his curve of destruction a very flat-topped one. His work might by typified by a blunderbus as compared with the rifle-fire of old age death" (Pearson 1897, 31).

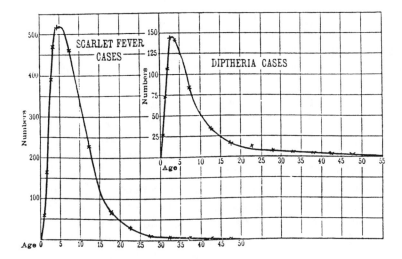

Figure 2.10   Pearson's plots of the frequency of illness by age. *Source:* Pearson 1897, 33.

Table 2.7 *Properties of Pearson's mortality curves in "The Chances of Death"*

	Mode in years of age	Standard deviation in years	Skewness	Total mortality out of 1,000	Weapon of death in "Bridge of Life"
Infancy	−0.08	.94	0.71	245.7	Bones of ancestry
Childhood	3	3.52	0.87	46.4	Maxim gun
Youth	23	7.8	0	50.8	Bow and arrow
Middle age	42	12.8	0	173.2	Blunderbus
Old age	72	13.4	0.34	484.1	Rifle

It is obvious from the overlapping component frequency curves in Figure 2.7 that a person dying at age fifteen could have been struck by either the marksman of childhood, middle age, or youth, though most likely that of youth. Pearson did not fully explain how this translated into reality, but he linked the five distributions to different causes. He plotted the age distribution for cases of various illnesses including enteric fever, scarlet fever, and diphtheria. The latter two are obviously childhood killers; they are rarely the cause of death in the first year of life (infancy) and relatively few people catch or die of these diseases after the age of 10 (see Pearson's graph reproduced in Figure 2.10).

Pearson reasoned that the laws of frequency, deduced from coin tossing and dice throwing, were the laws of all large numbers, including the age distribution of the frequency of death. The five law curves he saw in operation for age-determined mortality were frequency distributions that could be described with equations (noted on Figure 2.7) from which values for a mode, mean, standard deviation, coefficient of skewness, maximum mortality in mode year, and total mortality covered by entire distribution could be determined (see Table 2.7). The skewed distribution of old age gave a theoretical limit to life that would not exist if the distribution were a normal one. Although only the curves for youth and middle age were strictly bell curves, all five curves were chance distributions.

The most interesting curve – and marksman of death – is that of infancy. For one thing, Pearson's equation for infantile mortality predicts the deaths before birth of 605 fetuses for every 1,000 live births, with most of these occurring within the first three months of conception.[23] Pearson had not intended to go into this antenatal region, but the only equation that would fit the postnatal data took him there. The second striking feature of Pearson's analysis of infant mortality was his linking it to heredity. Pearson's commitment to the eugenic cause is blatant in his choice of a human skull as the weapon to typify the human encounter on the bridge of life with the most deadly marksmen of all, the marksmen for fetuses and infants. Pearson lay the blame for the "unremitting destructiveness" of infantile and fetal mortality with "bad parentage": "The marksman Death strikes down the young life with the bones of its ancestry" (Pearson 1897, 36). This choice is inconsistent not only with the visual metaphors of the other marksmen, but also with Pearson's literal analysis of causes of death at other ages. Pearson was unable to perceive ways for reducing infant mortality other than state control of who should be allowed to prosper and multiply.[24]

With regards to the issue of biological evolution and the "numerical measures of the processes described by Darwin," Pearson saw his work on the age distribution of mortality as helping to "localise the time and manner of selection" (Pearson 1897, 41). Pearson's main theme, however, was illustrating the scientific reconstruction of the notion of chance. As Pearson saw it, "Our conception of chance is one of law and order in large numbers; it is not that idea of chaotic incidence which vexed the medieval mind" (Pearson 1897, 15). The data and hypothetical curves of mortality (Figure 2.7) drawn by Karl Pearson and the print of the "Bridge of Life" (Figure 2.8) etched by Maria Sharpe Pearson are both images of Pearson's vision of "law and order in large numbers." They are the visions of an applied mathematician schooled in geometry and the leisurely arts of gambling and archery; the visions of a well-

---

[23] Note that the comparison by division of 605 fetuses with 1,000 live births is a ratio. The postnatal deaths at each age compared with 1,000 live births are proportions.

[24] In Chapter 7 there are more details on the link between the eugenics movement and the development of statistical theory, including Pearson's admiration of Adolph Hitler's "experiment." Suffice to say here, the dramatic decrease in the infant mortality rate over the past century has not been due to a state-controlled change in the gene pool. In 1994 only 6 out of 1,000 infants died in Britain compared with the 152 deaths out of 1,000 infants Pearson recorded for the 1870s. That decline is due to changes in the environment in which the unborn and the newly born are nurtured – changes that stem from popular awareness of nutrition and hygiene, new medicines, a higher standard of living, and a more equitable distribution of prenatal and postnatal health care. The policy prescriptions implied by Pearson's naming of the cause as bad ancestry would have been much less effective and caused far more strife than the adopted public health policies that have emphasized nurture rather than nature.

to-do, white, male, British professional schooled in the fine arts; the visions of a eugenist schooled in the Darwinian theory of evolution.

Pearson, with his mortality curve decomposed into mathematical laws associated with games of chance and target practice, and Graunt, with his percent table of an age distribution of deaths, constructed statistical structures in time. Pearson's five distributions are parallel to time, and his conception of the chances of death resembles a moving average. The chance of dying at age fifteen is like a weighted average of the chance of dying at the ages of three, twenty-three, and forty-two. The structures in time of Graunt and Pearson do not, however, describe any process of change through time. The structures are not, for example, tales of the development of a typical individual, as Adolphe Quetelet's structures in relative time were (see Chapter 5). Although those whose deaths are recorded are at different ages of the life cycle, the data are taken at one moment in time and the laws depicted are out of time. Graunt's table and Pearson's curve are means for static comparisons; one can compare the chance of death at age twenty with the chance of death at age fifty. Similarly, Graunt's and Pearson's structures in time are descriptions of societies. Individuals are unlikely to identify with the age-specific chances of death unless they forsake a subjective notion of probability for a frequency approach. To the individual, a disorderly "dance of death" might still be a more appropriate image of the fatal moment.

To Graunt's shop arithmetic, Pearson and other applied mathematicians added the academic regalia of laws: smooth lines, uniform shapes, and algebraic equations. Empirical paths plotted through ages were decomposed into age-specific functions in relative time. Summary parameters economized on information, and the formal laws were generalized to and from other mass phenomena. Death and chance could be reckoned not only with the Merchant's Rule and tabular "accompts" but also with equations and geometry. Roots for the mathematical structuring of temporal statistics, however, lie with the *Mechanick Artists*, demanding discipline and control of commercial processes, tracking the course of future demand, and reckoning on the accumulation of their capital.

3

Commercial Currents and First Differences

This practice of studying the residues is perhaps most common in the business world. A glance by our leading journals will convince the reader how familiar this method is outside the text-books. The mill owner and the speculator are constantly watching the net changes, the differences, and these become the motives of their actions. The economist may profitably study these differences for the verification of his laws.

John Norton 1902, 34

Forecasting is the essential aim of both the economic scientist and the man of affairs. According to the most approved doctrine, economic profit has its origin in economic changes. Other forms of income – interest, wages and rent – would exist in a purely stationary state, but there would be no profit. The talent of the director of industry in the modern state consists in his capacity to foresee and to exploit economic changes, and his profit is proportionate to the accuracy with which his forecasts are made. The economic scientist is likewise concerned with changes. His talent consists in his capacity to separate the general from the accidental, to detect the routine in the multitudinous details. His success is proportionate to the simplicity and generality of the routing that he may discover and the accuracy with which he is able to foretell the size and direction of future changes.

Henry L. Moore 1917, 164

Since the fifteenth century, the quantitative methods of merchants and financiers have influenced the type of mathematics taught and used in Europe. In the latter half of the nineteenth century, capitalist enterprise made its mark on statistical theory with its emphasis on changes or first differences of time series data. In 1902, John Norton encouraged fellow economic statisticians, who were searching for empirical laws, to employ the differencing algorithms that the millowner and speculator had found so useful. That appropriation proved effective not only for empirical investigators but also for those working on a mathematical theory of statistics. By the 1920s and 1930s, statisticians were exploring the statistical properties of differenced series in order to decompose time series, to classify series based on performance with repeated differencing, and to identify and isolate the "dangerous" or "evolutive" components of nonstationary series.[1]

Nowadays, differencing is one of the most popular and powerful tools in an econometrician's kit. Investigators who use Autoregressive Integrated Moving Averages difference their observations until the series are stationary and then estimate a univariate model of a stationary process with least squares regression (see, e.g., Box & Jenkins 1970 or Harvey 1993). Similarly, advocates of cointegration analysis (see, e.g., Perman 1991 or Rao 1994) classify series and models based on the behavior of the residuals at various stages of differencing. In both approaches, the order of "integration" of a series refers to the number of times a series must be differenced before it becomes a stationary series.

The flow from monetary to political to empirical to mathematical arithmetic is very evident in the structure of this chapter on differencing. We begin with a look at the importance of comparison by subtraction in the commercial arithmetic of nineteenth-century financial periodicals like the London *Economist*. Financial journalists, such as Robert Giffen and William Newmarch, bridged the commercial and political realms. Giffen and Newmarch used differenced series to present data for "public men" who discussed and decided on political policy. The exploration of the use of first differences in this political arithmetic leads into its use in empirical investigations in economics and meteorology. Finally, we take on early twentieth-century mathematicians' use of differences in debates on the sources of nonsense in the correlation of time series. This culminates in Udny Yule's suggestion that the coefficient of autocorrelation of serial differences could indicate "dangerous series" and Oskar Anderson's suggestion that successive differencing could be used to classify series and to separate the systematic from the random components.

Monetary Algorithms: The Net Changes of Speculators

Similar to the Rule of Three, serial differences (formed by sequentially subtracting previous values from present values) have a history in commercial practice. In his observations on the bills of mortality, Graunt used first differences to search for temporal patterns in morbidity and mortality. In his attempt to make trade and government "more certain and Regular," Graunt searched for seasonal and other periodic patterns in the numbers and quantities he had access to. With the bills of mortality, he used a relative time framework to determine seasonal mortality, and he used comparison by subtraction to determine the temporal pattern of "sickliness" (other than that due to the plague) that would enable him to predict "by what spaces, and intervals we may hereafter expect such times again" (Graunt [1662] 1975, 50). He labeled a year as "sickly" if the burials in that year were greater that in the previous and subsequent years. His method revealed that the intervals between the sickly years varied between two and eight years.

---

[1] Appendix 1 includes a technical discussion of the construction and properties of differenced series.

Graunt examined the pattern of serial differences to show that the years in which births were less than in the preceding or following years were also likely to be "sickly" years as he defined it.[2] Graunt's comparison by subtraction, however, played second fiddle to his use of comparison by division, and it was really within the context of nineteenth-century financial speculation that the full potential of first differences was realized.

In his seventeenth-century history of the Royal Society, Thomas Sprat had described John Graunt as an artist who used his hands. Graunt used his hands for passing cloth and money to other people and for recording these transactions with pencil and paper. When it came to numbers and quantities, Graunt was a manual worker. The Rule of Three was a rule of thumb. The merchants' use of this rule was the material source of comparison by division, and that source fed into the science of observation. By the nineteenth century, however, both European commerce and the science of observation had generated needs for additional algorithms more suited to comprehend change over time. In his 1850 essay on "Quetelet on Probabilities," John Herschel argued that the "high temperature and pressure of modern civilization," manifested in commercial gluts and financial panics, commanded a more dynamic way of thinking. Herschel wrote, "The Rule of Three has ceased to be the sheet anchor of the political arithmetician, nor is a problem resolved by making arbitrary and purely gratuitous assumptions to facilitate its reduction under the domain of that time-honoured canon" (Herschel [1850] 1857, 436–437).

By the mid-nineteenth century, merchant capital in Britain and North America had given way to industrial capital. It was in turn being eclipsed by finance capital. In the words of Thorstein Veblen, by 1870 the "captains of finance" controlled industrial output (Veblen 1919, 13). These manual artists were still number manipulators, paper pushers, and pencil holders, but only money, and rarely cloth or any other physical commodity, passed directly through their hands. An archetypal image of capitalism in the fifteenth-century Venetian Republic was the merchant folding cloth, counting coins, and reckoning with the Rule of Three. The analogous image of capitalism in late nineteenth-century London was the financier digesting pages of *The Economist* and calculating and comparing increases and decreases in values and volumes.[3]

The "leading journals" that John Norton referred to (see the quotation at the start of this chapter) in his advocacy for the study of residues or differences were the *Commercial and Financial Chronicle*, *The Economist*, and *The Statist*.[4] Each issue of these weekly journals had pages of tables that enabled swift comparisons over time regarding prices of commodities and securities, value

---

[2] Although Graunt calculated "mediums," to determine the average number of burials or christenings over, for example, a seven-year period, his method of determining sickly years for London was not subtraction (deviation) from an average, but comparison with the previous and subsequent years (serial differences).

[3] One wonders what the analogous image would be for late twentieth-century capitalism – the financial analyst studying the candlestick plots of an index options market on her computer screen?

[4] In her *Guide to Business History*, Henrietta Larson (1948, 440) describes the *Commercial and Financial Chronicle* as the "leading" American business periodical of the latter half of the nineteenth century, directed primarily at finance and modeled on the London *Economist*.

and volume of imports and exports, railway traffic, government revenues and bank returns. With the early issues of *The Economist*, which began in 1843, most tables displayed only absolute values, but in such a way that the reader could easily determine how that week's or month's value compared with previous ones. The text summarizing the table usually referred to the increases and decreases from one period to the next. Beginning with the editorship of Walter Bagehot in 1860, many tables in *The Economist* included columns showing the increases or decreases over the previous week, month, or year. Rather than listing all changes in one column with a plus or minus sign preceding the value, the tables were often constructed with a column for increases and a separate column for decreases. Sample tables from various issues of *The Economist* are reproduced in Figure 3.1.

Increases and decreases tabulated in a single column, percent changes, and price indices were common features of the annual *Commercial History Supplement* of *The Economist*, which was first compiled by William Newmarch in February 1864.[5] Similarly, under the editorship of Robert Giffen, *The Statist*, first published in 1878, made use of empirical averages, percent changes, and eventually the price index designed by Augustus Sauerbeck. The *Commercial and Financial Chronicle*, which began publication in New York in 1865, showed a pattern of development similar to that of its London model, *The Economist*: in the first issues the tables displayed absolute values for comparable dates with textual discussions of increases and decreases, then columns for absolute increases and decreases became more prevalent, and eventually relative (percent) changes were included in a separate column. By the late 1880s all three journals frequently tabulated percent changes of volumes and values. The staple, however, of the numerical and verbal comparisons in these journals was the absolute increase or decrease from a previous period, what we with econometric hindsight call first differences.[6]

Movements in capital and commerce were the subject of the statistical comparison in these journals, and first differences were the primary means of tracking change. According to the leader in the first issue of the *Commercial and Financial Chronicle*, the aim of the journal was "to give readers a classified, accurate, trustworthy record of all the movements in commercial and financial affairs" (*Commercial and Financial Chronicle*, June 30, 1866, 1). Similarly, the

---

[5] The pioneering role of *The Economist* in constructing price indices and terms of trade statistics is discussed in *The Economist 1843–1943: A Centenary Volume* (1943, 138–151). The entire volume, Scott Gordon's (1955) essay, "The London *Economist* and the High Tide of Laissez-Faire," and Ruth Dudley Edwards's *The Pursuit of Reason* (1993) provide interesting histories of that journal.

[6] The trade journals were not alone in publishing first differences of financial data. The New York Associated Banks announced each Saturday morning the increases or decreases, from the preceding week, of loans, deposits, and reserves of member banks. These weekly statements, which were first made in 1853, had held, according to John Norton, "for over forty years a well recognized place of importance in the financial world. These statements have been again and again for weeks at a time the absorbing 'feature' of the security market" (Norton 1902, 22). Internal communications within the Bank of England also illustrate the importance of first differences in the analysis of periodic fluctuations and financial panics. Columns for increases and decreases of notes, reserve, and bullion are found throughout the statistics used by the governors of the Bank of England from the 1860s to the 1890s (Bank of England 1890).

1850.] THE ECONOMIST. **1357**

FRIDAY NIGHT.

The preceding accounts, compared with those of last week, exhibit,—

A decrease of Circulation of	£4,218
An increase of Public Deposits of	358,171
An increase of Other Deposits of	230,975
An increase of Securities of	741,998
A decrease of Bullion of	210,572
A decrease of Rest of	53,502
A decrease of Reserve of	216,257

The *circulation*, by the present returns, following very nearly the same course as last year at this period, has *decreased* 4,218*l*: the *public deposits* have *increased* 358,171*l*; *private deposits* have *increased* 230,975*l*; the *securities* have *increased* 741,998*l*, the increase being of private securities; the *bullion* has *decreased* 210,572*l*, the decrease being wholly of gold coin and bullion in the Issue Department, the silver has remained unchanged, and the gold and silver coin in the Banking Department has increased 4,513*l*. The *rest* has *decreased* 53,502*l*; and the *reserve* has *decreased* 216,257*l*. The great increase of private securities, and the decrease of bullion, are the features most worthy of notice.

	March 30. dols	June 30. dols	September 28. dols
Loans and discounts	91,118,163	95,992,872	90,728,282
Stocks	12,113,205	12,627,494	13,177,944
Specie	7,729,946	11,653,339	10,045,380
Cash items	9,259,681	9,181,481	10,498,874
Bank notes	2,451,729	3,071,749	3,631,957
Due from banks	10,112,530	11,881,966	10,982,530
Capital	47,361,325	47,779,727	48,418,762
Circulation	24,634,461	24,214,341	26 615,556
Deposits	42,050,384	46,191,466	48,407,553
Due to banks	17,975,618	22,961,786	22,644,087

While the capital has been increased 839,035 dols, the discounts show a falling off, compared with the June report, of 5,264,590 dols. The special capital has decreased 1,608,069 dols, while the circulation of notes have been increased 2,401,215 dols. The most extraordinary feature in this comparative statement is the decrease in the amount of specie in the vaults of the banks. It is a matter of considerable curiosity to know where all the receipts of California gold dust goes to. It is pretty certain the banks get very little of it.

July 1, 1865.] THE ECONOMIST. **787**

II.—Increase and Decrease in the periods ended June 30, 1865, as compared with the corresponding periods of the preceding year.

	Quarter ended June 30, 1865.				Year ended June 30, 1865.	
	Increase.	Decrease.	Increase.	Decrease.	Increase.	Decrease.
	£	£	£	£	£	£
Customs	...	268,000	...	...	...	517,000
Excise	1,000	...	...	...	833,060	...
Stamps	...	49,000	...	...	19,000	...
Taxes	...	25,000	...	...	7,000	...
Property Tax	...	259,000	...	...	290,000	936,000
Post Office	10,000	...	...	...	5,500	...
Crown Lands	1,000	...	...	...	...	165,700
Miscellaneous	...	135,680	...	...	...	...
Totals	12,000	736,680	...	...	1,214 500	1,618,703

£724,680 Net Decrease.

£404,203 Net Decrease.

Annexed are the traffic returns of some of the American railways for May :—

	Miles open.	1865. dols.	1864. dols.	Increase. dols.	Decr. dols.
Chicago and Alton	220	312,316	158,939	153,377	...
Chicago and North-Western	607	568,903	466,830	102,073	...
Cleveland and Pittsburg	218	215,568	203,514	12,054	...
Illinois Central	706	454,745	414,372	40,373	...
Michigan Central	329	401,455	271,552	129,902	...
Michigan Southern	484	358,194	267,126	86,068	...
Pittsburgh, Fort Wayne, & Chicago	467	601,237	525,751	75,486	...
Toledo and Wabash	242	138,738	127,000	11,719	...
New York Central	489	1,204,435	1,004,435	200,000	...
Chicago and Rock Island	182	227,260	188,695	38,565	...

Jan. 13, 1883.] MONTHLY TRADE SUPPLEMENT. **3**

I.—QUANTITIES of ARTICLES IMPORTED for MANUFACTURE.

	Quantities, Dec., 1882.	Inc. or Dec. % Compared with Dec., 1881.	Quantities, Twelve Months, 1882.	Inc. or Dec. % Compared with 1881.
Cotton, raw ......cwts	1,998,100	+ 40·9	15,794,600	+ 5·6
Flax —	85,400	— 22·1	1,354,400	— 8·2
Hemp —	103,300	+ 55·4	1,190,000	+ 18·7
Hides, raw —	6,650	+ 38·3	95,500	+ 17·5
Indigo —	543,600	+ 72·2	5,964,300	+ 20·5
Jute —	210,000	+ 6·3	3,375,300	+ 16·1
Silk, raw ......lbs	313,500	— 23·9	6,195,100	+ 11·9
Wood, hewn and sawn ...loads	21,889,700	+ 34·9	483,954,300	+ 8·2
Wool ......lbs	241,800	+ 66·8	3,282,500	+ 34·0
Iron Ore ......tons	7,400	— 4·1	37,700	— 6·1
Lead —	51,700	+ 21·5	626,900	+ 15·7
Pyrites —	36,100	— 6·6	487,600	+ 19·8
Tin ......cwts	264,000	— 15·0	2,437,900	+ 33·2
Flaxseed and Linseed ...qrs	87,900	+ 92·0	1,113,800	— 6·2
Tallow ......cwts	1,806,500	— 18·3	35,800,500	— 24·3
Tobacco (unmanufactured) lbs				

year, yet in summing up the values of the food imports, the combined total is found hardly to differ from 1881.

IV.—IMPORTS of ARTICLES of Food.

	Values, Dec., 1882.	Inc. or Dec. Compared with Dec., 1881.	Values, Twelve Months, 1882.	Inc. or Dec. Compared with 1881.
(Eatables.)	£	£	£	£
Living animals	418,900	+ 27,500	9,272,000	+ 746,600
Bacon	612,000	— 189,200	6,224,900	— 2,623,700
Beef—Salted or fresh	198,600	+ 3,100	1,773,500	— 870,600
Butter	931,900	+ 89,700	11,339,200	+ 477,600
Cheese	362,300	+ 2,900	4,742,400	— 486,800
Wheat	2,252,300	+ 610,400	34,237,100	+ 2,570,200
Flour	1,226,700	+ 568,300	10,631,900	— 1,526,100
Indian corn	330,000	— 169,600	6,522,100	— 3,870,400
Oats	627,100	+ 296,700	4,604,000	+ 823,000
Barley	917,500	+ 342,800	5,541,500	+ 1,472,100
Eggs	206,600	+ 45,400	2,381,900	+ 59,300
Fish—Cured or salted	141,000	— 73,200	1,659,400	— 168,700
Hams	115,100	— 16,600	1,523,300	— 308,200
Meat—Various	229,100	+ 22,100	2,378,300	+ 223,600
Potatoes	119,100	+ 33,500	998,900	— 98,600
Rice	347,100	+ 136,800	3,297,400	— 368,900
Lard	125,000	— 96,000	1,862,400	— 340,200
(For Drinking Purposes.)				
Coffee	169,900	— 125,900	5,188,900	+ 215,600
Tea	891,400	— 193,900	11,363,300	+ 13,500
Sugar (raw)	1,703,800	— 138,700	20,915,100	+ 669,500
Ditto (refined)	468,000	+ 107,200	3,969,300	— 58,000
Wine	474,900	— 6,900	6,463,500	— 196,700
Spirits	182,400	— 23,900	1,874,900	+ 198,900
	13,050,700	+ 46,700	157,765,200	— 289,300
	Increase = 0·4 %		Decrease = 0·2 %	

Figure 3.1 Financial tables of first differences. *Source: The Economist.*

Table 3.1 *Quantitative reasoning in nineteenth-century journals*

Quantitative emphasis	Title	First date and place
Tabulated weekly, monthly data for trade, finance, commerce	*The Economist*	1843, London
	The Statist	1878, London
	Commercial and Financial Chronicle	1865, New York
Practical algorithms for handling vital statistics	*Journal of the Institute of Actuaries*	1852, London
Descriptive statistics, empirical, social science, statistical technique	*Journal of the Royal Statistical Society*	1839, London
Natural science, mathematical philosophy, statistical theory	*Philosophical Transactions of the Royal Society*	1665, London
	Biometrika	1901, London

table of contents in *The Economist* referred to tables of values, not as "current prices," but either as "price current" or "the movement in prices."[7]

Political Arithmetic: The Statistics of Public Men

If we look closely at the publications of the commercial, the political, the empirical, and the mathematical realms of quantitative reasoning in the late nineteenth and early twentieth centuries we can see links. For example, we can take the journals listed in Table 3.1 as representative of distinct types of quantitative reasoning addressed to separate audiences, and roughly ranked from the use of simple concrete comparisons to descriptive statistics to mathematical statistical theory. Yet, strong connections existed between the journals and respective readers. Robert Giffen, known for his recognition of "Giffen Goods," was, at various times, president of the Royal Statistical Society, editor of the *Journal of the Royal Statistical Society*, assistant editor of *The Economist*, and founding editor of *The Statist*. The latter magazine regularly published proceedings of the Royal Statistical Society, which in turn published excerpts from supplements to *The Statist* on financial and commercial history. William Newmarch served not only as editor of the *Journal of the Royal Statistical Society*, but also as an assistant to Walter Bagehot, editor of *The Economist*. In the latter capacity, Newmarch wrote the magazine's commercial history and statistical review supplements.

Stanley Jevons, who considerably advanced the use of index numbers (along with Newmarch), the geometric mean, and semi-log graphs, was a fellow of

---

[7] Even today *The Economist* emphasizes changes over levels. A majority of the graphs are plots of index numbers and the key columns in the few tables at the back usually contain percent change calculations.

both the Royal Society and the Royal Statistical Society and read and corresponded with *The Economist* and other trade journals.[8] George Udny Yule, also
a fellow of both societies, published papers not only in the *Journal of the Royal
Statistical Society* and *Philosophical Transactions*, but also in the *Journal of the
Institute of Actuaries*. For several years, the latter carried an opening quotation
from Francis Bacon on each issue that called to mind the scientific duties of
professional businessmen: "I hold every man a debtor to his profession, from
the which as men of course do seek to receive countenance and profit, so
ought they of duty to endeavor themselves by way of amends to be a help
and an ornament thereunte."

Financial journalists, such as William Newmarch and Robert Giffen carried
the rude comparisons of financial movements a step further in their work for
the Royal Statistical Society. This was the transition from monetary to political
arithmetic. In moving from the speculative context of monetary arithmetic to
the policy orientation of political arithmetic, Newmarch, Giffen, and others
retained the tabular method of presenting first differences, but they aggregated
values across sectors of the economy, extended the time period covered (and
thus the length of the data series), searched for cyclical patterns of change
in the series, and directed their investigations to matters of policy.

Giffen, for example, distinguished between the specific short-term data used
by merchants in their particular trade and the more general statistics needed
by "public men" to see "the general variation in the average price of the class
to which the goods belong, in other words, what the change in price is upon
a great scale" (Giffen 1913, 67).[9] The first use of the data was for financiers
to compare one week's values with another, but the same variables, aggregated
and connected in a longer series, could also be used by "public men" to give
clues to the causes of economic fluctuations: "The statistics, again, become
useful after a series of years in showing the ups and downs of trade, and the
tendency for good years to follow each other in succession, and for bad years
also to succeed each other, so that there have come to be what are called
'cycles of trade'" (Giffen 1913, 68).

William Newmarch was another bridge between the quantitative reasoning
of financiers and of "public men." At an 1882 meeting of the Royal Statistical
Society following Newmarch's death, Giffen praised Newmarch's bridging of
these realms, particularly with regard to his use of first differences and percent changes:

> He was remarkable not merely as a statistician, but as a man of business
> and as an economist, and his special *forte* as statistician was to throw light
> on problems connected with the theory of business – especially banking –

---

[8] See, for example, Jevons's letter to the editor of *The Economist* published May 8, 1869. In that letter
Jevons used data from past issues of the journal to construct index numbers that indicated a general
depreciation in the value of gold and an appreciation in commodity prices since the gold discoveries of
1849. Jevons praised Newmarch's statistical work and the "invaluable annual review" of *The Economist*
(Jevons 1869, 530).

[9] These quotations on the adaptation of statistics for "public men" are from Giffen's textbook on statistics
written in the 1890s but not published until after his death in 1913.

and on the applications of political economy to the real world by means of statistics. . . .

Mr. Newmarch, in fact, popularized the idea that the daily changes in the movement of business can be generalized and referred to the working of the laws of human nature, and in a thousand ways the idea has been worked out and made useful to the world. (Giffen 1904, 2, 3)

One medium for Newmarch's and Giffen's generalization of daily changes in movements of series was the historical supplements of economic data published jointly by the financial press and the Royal Statistical Society. Giffen's interest in developing descriptive statistics for "public men" is also evident in his employment as the chief of the statistical department of the British Board of Trade and in his testimony to several royal commissions investigating financial matters. Giffen referred to annual changes in commercial, economic, and demographic data in his evidence in the 1870s and 1880s before commissions investigating silver and gold standards, taxation, and securities trading and the London Stock Exchange.

Even in presentations to the Royal Statistical Society, the British Association, or the Royal Economics Society, however, Giffen and Newmarch relied only on descriptive statistics and tables and avoided mathematical theory, diagrams, and graphs. Likewise, in his handbook, *Statistics*, written in the 1890s and edited posthumously by Henry Higgs and Udny Yule, Giffen did not include diagrams, equations, or geometric figures. There is, however, an entire chapter on the art of constructing tables.

There was a considerable gulf between the statistical approach of political arithmeticians like Giffen and mathematical statisticians like Udny Yule. This is illustrated in Giffen's discussion as chairman of a session of the Royal Statistical Society in which Yule used the very novel technique of least squares multiple regression to quantify the effect of changes in government policy on the changes in pauperism:

They were all much obliged to a gentleman of his mathematical attainments for bringing his powers to bear on some of the questions which many of them were accustomed to discuss without much use of that science. It was very interesting to see mathematicians so much interested in the handling of statistical material, and he should hope in the course of times that a great many valuable results might be obtained by that means. It would be very desirable if this cold light of science could be brought to bear on the discussion of a great many subjects which excited passion in the public mind, and caused contradictory and violent statements of the most remarkable character. . . . (Giffen's discussion in Yule 1899, 291–292)

Although Giffen thought Yule's work was "useful to those who were practical students of the subject, and who had not an equipment of mathematics," he cautioned on the power of mathematics to fathom economic causation:

He should doubt extremely whether any application of the mathematical method would enable one to say that when a given effect of an economic kind was produced in the community, it was possible to affirm that so much of that effect was due to one cause and so much to another. . . . He thought that those accustomed to the complexity of economic causes and effects must recognise that that was hardly the right way to work. (Giffen's discussion in Yule 1899, 292)

Giffen thought in terms of comparison by division or comparison by subtraction. He was unable to go beyond the Rule of Three to comprehend the equation Yule had estimated by least squares regression. Yule pointed out in his rebuttal that with his technique of splitting up an effect into portions due to several causes, the splits were

> not fractional but algebraic parts of whole change. In some cases the change he ascribed to a change in out-relief was greater than the whole change that had taken place, but against that there would be something to set off due to some other cause, which had brought about a change in the opposite direction. . . . The change due to either factor separately need not be a fractional part of the whole changes. (Yule 1899, 294–295)

Although the numerical comparisons of the financial periodicals from Britain and the United States in the late nineteenth century inspired new statistical techniques, their form places them in the realm of monetary and political arithmetic, not in the realm of "scientific arithmetic." The high math and science characterized by statistical theory, such as Yule's, involved geometric reasoning, abstract visual queues, algebraic modeling of relationships, and a recognition of statistical population in which the mean and deviation from the mean had significance. The comparisons in the financial journals rarely covered more than six time periods, they usually did not include a calculation for an average and never for deviations from the average, and they only took the form of tables or textual descriptions. But like the Merchant's Rule, the speculator's net changes were adopted and adapted by those engaged in the science of observation.

Scientific Arithmetic: The Serial Differences of the Statisticians

For both financiers and economic statisticians, changes were more the analytical reality than levels. For the financier, the increases and decreases were the source of gains and losses; for the social scientist, the taking of first differences sculpted out the short-term fluctuations that political economy had come to emphasize at the expense of studying long-term, systematic changes.[10] Similarly, for statisticians there were advantages in emphasizing changes over

---

[10]   A typical twentieth-century justification for using first differences rather than absolute levels to get closer to the truth in financial analysis can be found in the work of Harry Roberts: "At least, it is safe to say that the close resemblance between market behavior over relatively long time periods and that of simple chance devices has escaped general attention, though the role of chance variation in very short time periods has often been recognized. One possible explanation is that the usual method of graphing stock prices gives a picture of successive *levels* rather than of *changes*, and levels can give an artificial appearance of 'pattern' or 'trend' " (Roberts 1959, 2).

levels; although the absolute values of different commodities could not be meaningfully grouped in a sample or a series, the changes in values could. Also, as Arthur Bowley, Reginald Hooker, and others were to discover, absolute or relative changes could be used to patch up short, unconnected series into a single, long, consistent series.

In statistical analysis, changes are usually more manageable than levels of times series; they are more likely to oscillate in a fixed range about a constant mean, yielding a stationary series. Figures 3.2a and 3.2b illustrate some of the effects of manipulating raw time series data with first differences. The top graph is a time sequence plot of the hypothetical data I regressed and plotted out in Figure 1.4. The absolute values show an upward trend in both series and the tendency for y to decrease from sequence to sequence when x increases. The regression equation, as noted in Chapter 1, yields a statistically significant positive slope coefficient on x, even though sequentially there is an inverse relationship between x and y. This is the long-term, more–more or less–less relationship evident in a broad sweep of the top graph, but not apparent in the bottom graph. The bottom plot is of the first differences of each series. With constantly oscillating series, the analogy of repeatable sampling can be assumed and the tools of frequency distributions, correlation, and regression analysis used. In the differenced series, no trend is present, both series oscillate about a similar mean, and regression yields a statistically significant negative slope coefficient on x. This highlights the short-term, more–less relationship.[11] Nineteenth-century political economists and pursuers of profit usually took the short-term view.

The tendency for differenced series to oscillate about a constant mean evokes Alfred Marshall's notion that, more often than not, stocks are dynamic and flows are static.[12] Reconstructed series of changes display eternal, inorganic motion without a life cycle. With differences, there is often no birth, growth, or depletion as there might be with the original levels or stocks; there are just oscillations which can be treated as values sampled from a cross section of a population or generated from stationary processes.

Maurice Kendall justified his use of first differences in analyzing commodity prices in a similar way: "The decision to use first differences instead of the original series was not an arbitrary one. When a price is fixed on a free market both parties know what was the price of the previous transactions and use that price as a starting point for negotiation. It is the change, not the absolute value, which constitutes the fundamental element in price determination" (Kendall 1953, 13; Roberts's and Kendall's articles are reprinted in Cootner 1964).

[11]   Eugen Slutsky recognized a short-term emphasis inherent in differencing with reference to sinusoids: "If a curve is represented by a sum of sinusoids, then the differences of all orders are sums of sinusoids having waves of the same periods as the curve. The higher the order of the difference, the more pronounced are the shorter periods, since the differencing process weights the shorter periods as against the longer ones" (Slutsky [1927] 1937, 125).

[12]   Marshall wrote:

I hold that the essential distinction between statics and dynamics, if the terms must be used, is not the same as, nor even closely related to that between stocks and flows. In fact the most perfect instances of statical problems are those which deal with "steady flows" of labour capital and goods, of wages, interest and prices in a stationary country: in which each year is just like the past, in which each generation is like that which went before.

It may be noted, as an incidental confirmation of this opinion, that our choicest illustrations of the statical or stationary state relate to agricultural and not to mineral prices. Now the annual output of a farm is a true flow: but the annual output of a mine is not a true flow, it comes out

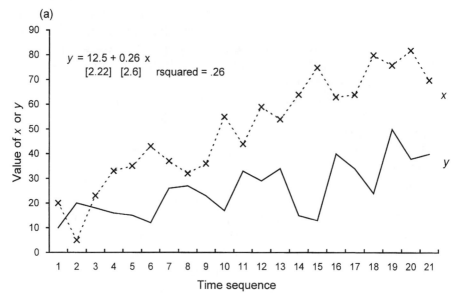

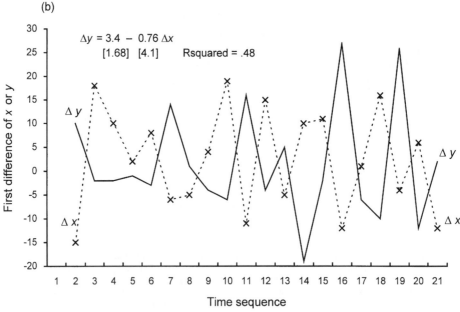

Figure 3.2   Time sequence plots of (a) x and y and (b) first differences of x and y.

As John Norton had predicted, studies of first differences proved to be extremely profitable in the determination of economic laws from time series data. Table 3.2 highlights some of the key studies in the early applications of first differences in the correlation of economic and meteorological data.[13] In

of stock: and, if the mineral veins are not practically unlimited, the exhaustion of the stock will disrupt the statical rest. (Marshall 1898, 46)

[13]   This table does not include Yule's 1899 regression of the decennial "changes" in pauperism on the decennial "changes" in out-relief and "changes" in other variables. Although this was the first published

the early studies, the primary purpose of differencing series before correlating them was to highlight short-term fluctuations and reduce the influence of the trend or secular changes. The advocates of the variate-difference method, including Oskar Anderson and Student, took differencing several steps further, in a literal and figurative manner. They argued that in order to eliminate the causal distortion of the time factor, series should be differenced until the correlation coefficient of the nth differences was the same as that of the nth -1 differences. In his attempt to refute the idea of time as a causal factor and yet still account for spurious correlations with time series, Yule used the autocorrelation of first differences as the criteria by which "dangerous series" were identified. The "dangerous series" were to be classified a decade later as nonstationary series.

What follows is a detailed discussion of those investigations listed in Table 3.2. That discussion illustrates the transition in the use of first differences from the empirical studies of Norton and Hooker to the more mathematical and theoretical studies of Anderson and Yule. That chronology also traces out the gradual construction of the notion of a stationary time series.

Norton's Study of the New York Money Market

As can be seen from Table 3.2, Norton was one of the first to use serial differences in statistical analysis. His Ph.D. dissertation at Yale and the book based on his thesis were attempts to subject data from the New York money market to the frequency distribution and correlation analysis that Karl Pearson had applied in biology. Norton believed that his efforts, and similar investigations that he hoped would follow, would "reduce all this field of finance to an exact science" (Norton 1902, 86).

Norton's use of first differences in the study of the seasonal variation of reserves, deposits, and loans based on weekly data from 1879 to 1900 was quite sophisticated. His starting point was taking first differences in deviations from a trend, and rearranging these into fifty-two cross-section samples in a annual cycle-time framework.[14] He processed the data through several other algebraic manipulations before correlating the seasonal pattern of loans and reserves.

Although the use of first differences was common in business periodicals, such as the *Commercial and Financial Chronicle*, Norton thought the most appropriate financial calculations were first differences of deviations from the growth axis. He argued that the journals should remove the "growth element"

---

application of least squares multiple regression to economic data, Yule measured the changes not by taking first differences but by calculating the percentage ratio of one year's value to the value ten years earlier. Yule did this to avoid dealing with the combination of positive and negative numbers, but his use of a percentage ratio laid him open to criticisms that the appropriate specification should be nonlinear. Also, first differences might have yielded normal distributions of the variables. Yet, as Yule himself pointed out in response to criticism by Ysidro Edgeworth, percentage ratios led inevitably to skewed distributions if the variations were great or values approached the physical limit of 0 percent (Yule 1899, 288, 291, 293). Also, as we will see in the more detailed discussion of Yule's study on pauperism in Chapter 9, Yule's raw data were cross sections, not time series.

[14] Norton's procedure and conclusions are described in greater detail in Chapter 5.

Table 3.2 *Early uses of differences in regression and correlation of time series data*

Date	Example	Characteristics	Purpose
1902	Norton's study of the seasonal variation in reserves and loans on New York money market	First differences of percent deviations week to week	To describe and correlate annual paths in relative time
1904	Cave-Browne-Cave's correlation of barometric pressure at pairs of stations	First differences day to day	To determine time lag for weather prediction
1905	March's study of serial dependency with French banking and vital statistics	First differences year to year	To decompose, to correlate annual changes, to determine time lag
1905	Hooker's correlation of corn prices on markets in Berlin, Chicago, and Liverpool	First differences day to day	To correlate smaller rapid changes, to determine time lag, to construct continuous series
1914	Anderson's and Student's variate-difference method applied to prices, wages, death rates	1 to n differences year to year	To eliminate time factor and correlate residual variations
1926	Yule's study of serial correlation in time series	First differences term to term	To identify dangerous series (ones that yield nonsense bivariate correlations) by the positive serial correlation of first differences
1927	Anderson's decomposition of series into function-of-time and random components	1 to n differences term to term	To model the systematic component by order of differencing needed for stable variance
1927	Hotelling's study of differential equations subject to error	Second differences term to term	To determine periodicity by significant negative correlation between a series and its second differences

from the weekly clearing house statistics (in modern lingo, detrend the series), and should calculate the increases or decreases in the percentage deviations from a growth axis. His call to business journals to present statistics in forms that would be of more service to statisticians and economists – what we would now call detrended stationary series – were not heeded.

Cave-Browne-Cave's Use of Differences in Weather Prediction

Within three years of Norton's study, F. E. Cave-Browne-Cave (1905) used first differences in her investigation of the correlation of daily readings of barometric pressure at pairs of meteorological stations in different parts of the globe. The purpose of her study was to use the criteria of the highest positive value of a correlation coefficient to determine the appropriate space and time intervals for weather prediction. The time series data covered twenty years of two readings a day of the barometer at various stations. Cave concluded, for example, that given present reading schedules, the best predictor of barometric pressure at Halifax, Nova Scotia, was the barometric reading taken twenty-six hours earlier at Wilmington, North Carolina.

Her thorough investigation of this relationship included: dealing with seasonal variation by splitting the data into equinox-to-equinox sets; interpolating a curve of correlation coefficients by time lags to give meteorologists an estimate of the best intervals for readings in the case of a totally flexible schedule; and verifying her findings with correlations of the daily rise at pairs of stations. To reduce the tedious labor involved in the correlation of the daily rise (first differences), Cave performed the first published example of serial or autocorrelation on time series data. The correlation of daily rise at Halifax and Wilmington demonstrated, more vividly than the correlation of absolute values had, that the best prediction interval was twenty-six hours. Although first differences and autocorrelation were only supplementary to her primary investigation, the study, which was presented to the Royal Society by Karl Pearson, was remarkable in its early use of these techniques.[15]

March's Study of the French Banking System

In a paper presented to the Société de statistique de Paris in 1905, Lucien March measured the interdependencies of several pairs of financial series – for example, bullion and deposits of the Bank of France from 1885 to 1903. March focused on the correspondence of the signs of the first differences of the series. Using annual data, he subtracted the number of years the signs of the annual changes did not correspond for a pair of series from the number of years that they did correspond and divided the net occurrences of correspondence by the number of years in the series. March attributed this "indice de

---

[15]   Cave's contribution to the development of the notion of autoregressive processes is discussed in Chapter 10. Her diagram of the correlation coefficients plotted by time lag (reproduced in Figure 10.1) illustrates the change in the use of geometric vision from graphing raw data to graphing results.

dépendance" to the psychophysicist Gustav Theodor Fechner.[16] March put the use of differences into the context of statistical investigations that focused on short-term, in particular, annual changes.[17]

Hooker Introduces Differences to the Royal Statistical Society

Four years after using a moving average in the statistical investigation of social phenomena (see Chapter 4), Reginald Hooker introduced to the Royal Statistical Society another "method of a very simple character" to deal with problems of correlating time series data (Hooker 1905, 697). Using data on corn (wheat) prices in Berlin, Chicago, and Liverpool, Hooker correlated the differences between successive daily values in each series. He obtained correlation coefficients for the changes in daily values for each of the years from 1892 to 1899. From a comparison of these, Hooker concluded that the spot price of grain in Berlin was just as dependent on other world markets during the two years in which futures transactions in Berlin were suspended as it had been in the years in which the market operated.

Although Hooker thought that differencing could prove useful in any branch of science where time was involved, he thought it most serviceable in economic inquiries. The use of differences isolated "the usually smaller and more rapid alterations between successive observations" from the "slower 'secular' changes" (Hooker 1905, 696). In his 1901 investigation, Hooker had used a nine-year "instantaneous average" (moving average) to eliminate the nine-year trade cycle from the data and reveal the "trend" or secular movement. He then correlated deviations from the moving average for each pair of series. In 1905, however, Hooker recognized that the instantaneous average method of eliminating trend and highlighting cycles only worked in series that displayed periodic cycles, and would be of little use with his annual samples of daily values.

In his 1905 study, Hooker concluded:

> in examining the relationship between two series of observations extending over a considerable period of time, correlation of absolute values (deviations from the arithmetic mean) is the most suitable test of "secular" interdependence, and may also be the best guide when the observations tend to deviate from an average that may be regarded as constant. Correlation of the deviations from an instantaneous average (or *trend*) may be adopted to test the similarity of more or less marked periodic influences. Correlation of the difference between successive values will probably prove most useful in cases where the similarity of the shorter rapid changes (with no apparent periodicity) are the subject of investigation, or where the normal level of one or both series of observations does not remain constant. (Hooker 1905, 703)

[16]   It is interesting that Fechner's use of "just notable differences" between two sensations, to measure the intensity of a sensation (which he argued was a function of the logarithm of the stimuli), influenced not only the statistical studies of March and Ysidro Edgeworth, but also the calculus of pain and pleasure pursued by the marginalists in theoretical economics.

[17]   March's visual demonstration of the need for decomposing time series when co-relationships in the short term differed from those in the long term is reproduced in Figure 9.3 and discussed in Chapter 9.

With the exception of Hooker's probable awareness of Cave's study, it seems that the first applications of differences in correlation studies in the United States, Britain, and France were all independent of each other.[18] This is indicative of the widespread use of daily and weekly changes to track short-term movements in the financial world and of the growing interest in the social sciences on changes rather than absolute values. Most of the earliest uses of first differences were with very short-term movements in daily or weekly data. The wide acceptance, after 1905, of first differences in the correlation of time series is reflected in "Student's" (William Gosset's) remark : "Since Mr. Hooker published his paper, the method has been in constant use among those who have to deal statistically with economic or social problems" (Student 1914, 179).

The Variate Difference Method of the Mathematicians

In the same 1914 issue of *Biometrika* in which he commented on the popularity of first differences, Student, along with Oscar Anderson, introduced a more elaborate method of differencing for correlating time series. They argued that correlating first differences was valid only when the connection between the variables and time was linear, and they presented a new technique in "an effort to extend Mr. Hooker's method so as to make it applicable in a rather more general way" (Student 1914, 179). Student and Anderson suggested that the variables be differenced until the correlation of the nth difference of x and y was the same as the correlation of the $(n + 1)$ difference. The effect of this would be "to eliminate variability due to position in time or space and to determine whether there is any correlation between the residual variations" (Student 1914, 180).

Student had titled his method and essay "The Elimination of Spurious Correlation Due to Position in Time or Space," but Beatrice Cave and Karl Pearson in an article published a few months after those of Anderson and Student labeled it the variate difference correlation method. Cave and Pearson applied the method to several Italian economic series and concluded that it was successful in eliminating the distortion of time in correlation:

> If we turn as in the present paper to the actual correlations of the indices themselves, we find in every case an arid and scarcely undulating waste of high correlation. No one can obtain any nourishment whatever from the statement that the *Tobacco Index* is correlated with the *Revenue Index* to the amount of .983 and with the *Savings Bank Index* to the extent of .984! The organic relationship between these variates is wholly obscured by the

---

18 Hooker had suggested the correlation of first differences in a paper presented to the Royal Statistical Society in 1901. Using the same data on corn prices in the three markets, Hooker had tried to determine whether the suspension of the futures markets in commodities by the German Parliament from 1897 to 1899 affected the average price of grain, the stability of the price, and the influence of the markets of Liverpool and Chicago on the Berlin spot market. For investigation of the latter, Hooker calculated the correlation coefficients for each year from the daily absolute values. They were unusually high, and Hooker realized this was due to the influences of trends. He suggested in an appendix that a more appropriate measure of the connection of fluctuations in two markets would be the correlation of *differences* between the prices on consecutive days. It was, however, not until four years later that he followed up on his own suggestion.

continuous increase of all three of them with the time. But when we proceed to the sixth differences and see that the consumption of tobacco has little, if any relation to revenue, and is associated substantially but *negatively* with savings, we seem to touch realities, and realities of some worth. . . .

But there can be small doubt that to proceed from the actual correlation of such indices to the correlations of their higher differences gives the feeling of clearing away the sand of desert, and reaching all the ordered arrangements of an excavated town below; the slight undulations of the waste above are really fallacious, and enable us to appreciate nothing of the actual topography of the city. (Cave & Pearson 1914, 354)

Despite the eloquent metaphor used by Cave and Pearson, there were and are questions about the reality unearthed by repeated differencing. The variate difference method appears to launder the data until all that is left is white noise. It is debatable whether the bleaching reveals or destroys the interesting features of the series. Udny Yule (1921), for example, questioned the usefulness of isolating random residuals and demonstrated that in some cases the variate difference method tended to give correlations due to two-year oscillations. Warren Persons (1917) was also critical of the variate difference method and concluded that correlating deviations from a trend was the preferable method of time series analysis.[19]

Yule's Study of Nonstationary Processes

The advocates of the variate difference method had argued that the time-correlation problem was that time itself was a causal factor; the variables were functions of time and thus correlated with time. Yule disagreed with this and eventually came to the conclusion that the source of many problems in regressing time series was not that variables were correlated with time, but that observations were correlated with previous values in the same series, and that the changes in the observations were also correlated with previous values of changes. Starting with a pair of random series, Yule (1926) derived new pairs of series, and at each stage of derivation calculated the paired correlation coefficients. He demonstrated that a nonsensical, high positive correlation coefficient for a pair of series that were in essence not correlated was likely if the series being compared were comprised of successive terms and successive first differences that were both positively autocorrelated. Thus, the trademark of a dangerous time series that yielded nonsensical estimates of parameters was the positive relationship between differences from one observation to the next.[20]

[19]   In a Cowles Commission monograph of 1940, Gerhard Tintner reviewed the early literature and controversies on the variate difference method. The debate between Warren Persons and Oskar Anderson has several parallels with the more recent discussion of whether macroeconomic times series are "trend-stationary" or "difference-stationary" (see Chapter 9).

[20]   Harold Hotelling took this a step further in his study of stochastic differential equations, when he suggested that a significant negative correlation between a nonrandom series and its second differences would indicate a tendency toward periodicity (Hotelling 1927, 290–291).

Partly in response to Yule's work, Oskar Anderson (1927) adapted his variate difference approach to a system for specifying univariate models. Anderson argued that studying the behavior of the standard deviation of a single series through successive differencing could indicate the presence and nature of systematic and random components. He also used this scheme to decompose time series into deterministic and random components. The order of differencing necessary for the standard deviations to converge on a stable value indicated the order of the polynomial that could be used to model the component that was a function of time (see Chapter 9). The residual series was the random component. Anderson thus laid the groundwork for the approach of differencing until the series became stationary with a constant mean and constant variance.

Summary and Conclusion

First differences, like several other tools of time series analysis, were first popularized as monetary algorithms used by merchants, financiers, and speculators in their ways of observing significant movements in prices and volumes. Although John Graunt in his 1662 observations on the bills of mortality used first differences in a minor way in his transformation of monetary arithmetic into political arithmetic, it was with nineteenth-century finance capital that first differences came into widespread use.

In Britain and the United States in the latter half of the nineteenth century, speculators and financiers closely watched the increases and decreases tabulated in *The Economist*, *The Statist*, and the *Commercial and Financial Chronicle* to detect movements in prices and output and to plan their next course of action. The nineteenth-century bridge between monetary and political arithmetic was constructed by the likes of Robert Giffen and William Newmarch, both of whom worked as writers and editors for weekly financial journals as well as the more scholarly *Journal of the Royal Statistical Society*. The differenced series constructed for the "public man" covered longer periods of time and were more aggregated than those intended for merchants or financiers. The series were used to illustrate cyclical fluctuations in the economy and for persuasion and investigation on issues of public policy.

John Norton, Reginald Hooker, and other statisticians consciously appropriated first differences and other tools of finance for the purposes of scientific investigation. This third stage of development, empirical investigation, was characterized by the use of graphs and geometry and by the estimation of quantitative relationships. Near the turn of the century, differencing time series data before applying correlation and regression analysis became a technique for eliminating trends and generating series that could be treated as stationary. Differencing had an advantage over calculating deviations from a moving average in that the former could be useful even if there were nonperiodic fluctuations.

Mathematical statisticians did not stop with first differences. In 1914 the variate difference method was introduced. The advocates of using higher differences argued that series should be differenced as many times as was necessary to eliminate any correlation between a value in a series and the previous value. This was to rid the series of any functional relationship with time. In his review of the variate difference method, Yule (1921) pointed out the large gap between, on the one hand Cave-Browne-Cave, March, and Hooker, and on the other, Anderson, Student, Cave, and Pearson. Yule argued that the view of the earlier group of writers was that the essential difficulty of correlation of time series was "the isolation, for separate study, of oscillations of different durations" (see the section on decomposition in Chapter 9). In contrast, the advocates of the variate difference method saw the problem as "spurious correlation" due to variables being functions of time. The solution of the variate difference method was to eliminate all components that were functions of time and to correlate the serially independent residuals.

In trying to discredit the variate difference method and to form his own view of the cause of nonsensical results in the correlation of time series data, Udny Yule came to the conclusion that the problem was not values being correlated with time but values being correlated with previous values and the differences being correlated with previous differences. Positively autocorrelated first differences became a model of a "dangerous series" – a nonstationary process or an "evolutive" process, as Herman Wold was to label it twelve years later. Switching his attention from multivariate to univariate models, Oscar Anderson in 1927 suggested that differencing until the variance of a series stopped changing could be used to specify the model for the systematic component and to decompose the series until you were left with just the random component. With the work of Yule and Anderson, the differences that were the manifestation of commercial currents and the motives for speculators' actions became a means for both identifying and eliminating the nonstationary component of time series and for reconciling rest and motion in time series analysis.

4

The Interplay of Deception and Accountability in the Index Numbers and Moving Averages of the Bank of England

The documents which they [the Secret Committee] have withheld appear to have been drawn up at the Bank in such a manner as to puzzle rather than to inform, the understanding; and therefore that they were probably framed with the view of concealing the truth, not only from the public, but even from the committees themselves. – Instead of a plain and direct statement of particulars, the amounts of the cash and the discounts, have been given in a set of cabalistical numbers, which without the aid of other information would require an *Oedipus* to decypher them.

"On the Finances of the Bank" 1797, 248

Historically, it [publicity of cash and bullion accounts] would have been very valuable, enabling the Public to form a decision upon the mode in which the Bank had been conducted; and I cannot conceive upon what grounds that detailed information was withheld in 1819. The Directors gave to the Committee a sort of mystical scale of cash, bullion and discounts, but the amount that the scale represented was withheld. Now I cannot conceive why the Public is not entitled to know how the currency has been administered, and supposing the state of its treasure had been published down to within a year of the time at which the Committee sat, I cannot see what possible injury could have arisen.

Testimony of Thomas Tooke in Great Britain, Parliament 1832, 279

In stating your objection to the publication of the Accounts, do you contemplate a continued publication of the State of the Bank, or a periodical fixed publication from time to time, or a retrospective Statement of the nature of its transactions for an interval gone by; should you object equally to both sorts of publicity? – It would depend upon the mode in which the publication might be ordered; I presume it would be a periodical publication, in order to exhibit the fluctuation between succeeding periods. . . . I should think that the average of a preceding period would be a preferable mode for publication. . . .

Is the amount of bullion that the Bank hold, the only secret which you think it of importance to preserve in the affairs of the Bank? – Yes, so far as regards the Public; that is my individual opinion.

Testimony of J. Horsley Palmer, Governor of the Bank of England, in Great Britain, Parliament 1832, 57, 59

Money and time are intimately connected. Time is money, usury was a medieval sin because only God had mastery over time, and time series analysis has its origins in monetary exchange. This chapter seeks the development of index numbers and moving averages in the monetary and political arithmetic of the Bank of England. Both techniques were devised by the Bank in its response to parliamentary pressure, in 1797, 1810, 1819, and 1832, to reveal the amount of gold and silver backing the Bank's promissory notes. Scaled series and moving averages enabled the Bank to give publicity on the temporal pattern of the change in bullion, without revealing the actual value, and thus the absolute depths to which bullion dropped in times of panic. These tools of deception were eventually used by statisticians in the late nineteenth century and twentieth century to empirically reveal and mathematically model processes of change.

This history is not a strictly linear one. The algorithms used by the Bank were countered by the quantitative manipulations used by financial journalists attempting to tear back the veil and reconstruct the actual series. An analogy that came to mind while I perused the Bank of England ledgers and yellowed pages of the financial press was the ambiguity inherent in the coins minted by states before Archimedes' discovery in the third century B.C. of a means of measuring relative density. Until that discovery, it was impossible to figure out the metallic composition of coins without destroying them. For example, the first Western coins ever minted, those of Lydia in the seventh century B.C., were neither pure gold nor pure silver, but rather they were made from an amalgam of the two metals. Lydian traders and foreign merchants exchanging gold for coin had no means of determining the gold content of the coins they received. Over two thousand years later, London traders faced a similar dilemma determining the amount of precious metal backing their chief medium of exchange, Bank of England promissory notes.

Financial commentators, such as William Morgan, Thomas Tooke, David Ricardo, and James Wilson, took on the role of Archimedes in their attempts to determine the value of the gold and silver veiled by the manipulated series. The question that propelled Archimedes was how much gold was in the shiny metal shaped into a crown? The question that propelled Morgan, Tooke, Ricardo, and Wilson was how much gold backed the notes of the Bank of England? Thus, the fertility for statistical theory lay not only with the stately institution of the Bank of England, but also with the anti–status-quo press. An examination of this dialectical process yields insights to the separate contributions of finance, politics, and science to time series analysis used presently in the pursuits of profit in finance and truth in science.

Index numbers and moving averages were designed through compromises forged between British parliamentary committees, pushing for accountability to serve as a check on the management of a powerful institution, and a private bank insistent that secrecy was the key to maintaining confidence in its promissory notes. The interplay between deception and accountability and the popularization of the codes and keys to the codes by the financial press laid the foundation for two important elements of the canon of time series analysis.

This chapter begins with a narrative on the scaled series used by the Bank of England from 1797 to 1819 to give Parliament an account of the state of the Bank's treasure compared with its state in earlier times. When it became clear in 1832 that legislation requiring regular publication of its accounts was imminent, the Bank devised a moving-average algorithm. After discussing the publicity debate and its outcome, I link the Bank's use of scaled series and moving averages with the pioneering work of William Stanley Jevons and other empirical arithmeticians. This chapter closes with a discussion of Udny Yule's, Eugen Slutsky's, and Herman Wold's use of moving averages of random disturbances to model stationary stochastic processes.[1]

The Accountability of the Bank and the Secret of Its Treasure

The Bank in the eighteenth and nineteenth centuries was in a unique position to command quantitative innovation, whether by its employees or its owners or by the traders and bankers who were dependent upon its stability while fearing its power and competition. First chartered in 1694, the Bank of England was a private, joint-stock bank whose main function was lending money to the government. Stockholders expected the institution to maximize profits and dividends. The rulers of state expected loans to be given in times of excess expenditure and revenue shortfalls. The London trading community expected the Bank of England to extend short-term credit, be lender of last resort, and control money without impeding commercial growth or causing inflation. Parliament expected Bank lending to the public and private sectors to be prudent and stabilizing. Pressure came from all these quarters for quantitative summaries extracted from the daily accounts and the weekly, quarterly, semi-annual, and yearly balances. The list that follows, starting with the data the Bank was most willing to share with those holding it accountable, illustrates the spectrum of secrecy in the accounts of the Bank:

- advances to the government
- notes circulated
- commercial Bills discounted (credit extended to London merchants)
- cash (specie) and bullion

The last item on the secrecy spectrum was the Bank's treasure. It was the real money that enabled the paper money to circulate with confidence and stability because bearers of the notes of promise could at any time demand gold or silver coin from the Bank, in exchange for the notes. Until the mid-nineteenth century, governors of the Bank insisted that confidence in the paper money required confidentiality of the amount of metallic money held in the vaults. Stockholders, however, wanted to know the value of the treasure to judge whether they had been paid their just dividend. Those who argued for a strict ratio of cash to liabilities wanted to know if a prudent ratio was

---

[1] Technical descriptions of index numbers and moving averages can be found in Appendix 1.

being maintained.[2] Everyone in times of panic wanted to know if there really was any treasure left to back the notes circulating, and when the Bank suspended all cash payments after the drain of 1797, Parliament wanted proof that such drastic action was justified. The Bank needed to present the data in such a way that the relative severity of the 1797 drain would be evident without enabling quantitative comparisons to be made between the values of the reserves and the notes circulating. The Bank's invention of a scaled series that allowed for relative comparisons over time within a series, but prohibited comparisons between absolute values of different series eventually became a useful statistical tool for adding apples and oranges by adding the percent change in the price of apples and oranges.

Index Numbers and Scaled Series

Commerce and monetary exchange have been readily accepted as the historical source of index numbers. In his history of index numbers, Maurice Kendall (1969) argues that the earliest examples are calculations to determine to what extent prices, and thus the value of money, had changed over several decades or centuries. These examples include Bishop Fleetwood's calculation in 1707 regarding the value of money for Oxford dons and Dutot's calculations in 1738 questioning whether Louis XV was better off than Louis XII.[3] Kendall sees these examples as isolated incidents and considers the real pioneer of index numbers to be Sir George Shuckburgh Evelyn. In an essay published in *Philosophical Transactions* in 1798, Evelyn presented a "Table of Appreciation" illustrating the average levels of prices, relative to those of 1550, from the years 1050 to 1795.

The histories of Kendall, Irving Fisher (1922), and C. M Walsh (1901) deal exclusively with attempts to construct and use composite price indices and particular attention is paid to whether the earliest cases weighted price components and whether services were included as well as commodities. Index numbers, however, need not be composites or confined to prices. As Frederick Mills explained in his section on the nature of index numbers in his classic text on *Statistical Methods Applied to Economics and Business*, "In its simplest form this name is applied to a term in a time series expressed as a relative" (Mills 1924, 169). In general, an indexed series is a scaled series used to make relative comparisons, usually percent difference from the base or from another location in the indexed series. The values of the indexed series are not measured in units and their numerical values are meaningless unless one knows the base standard of the index and/or compares one observation with another.

---

[2]   Calls for full publicity of cash and bullion holdings came from both sides of the debate on whether the banks of issue should be forced to adhere to a minimum cash ratio. Samuel Jones Loyd and George Wade Norman, supporters of the "currency theory" and a strict ratio, as well as James Wilson and Thomas Tooke, associated with the "banking school," all called for complete, regular publication of the accounts.

[3]   Similar calculations can be found in the attempts by the Massachusetts government in 1780 to devise a tabular standard in order to justly compensate soldiers during the high inflation of the American war of independence (see Fisher 1913).

The scaled series of values of bullion and discounted commercial bills constructed by the Bank of England matches the general criteria of useful relative comparisons and meaningless absolute terms. It is interesting to note that the date of the first publication of the Bank's scaled series was 1797, one year before Evelyn's Table of Appreciation. Evelyn's calculations and those examples of price indices that preceded and succeeded him were necessary because the value of money had decreased, particularly in times of war. The Bank's scaled series were also related to the value of money, but in terms of how much precious metal backed Bank of England notes rather than the purchasing power of those notes.

The Bank's Response to the Panic of 1797

With only patches of respite, Britain and France engaged in war from 1793 to 1815. In late 1796 and early 1797, British subjects feared invasion by France and residents of London increasingly insisted on payment of specie from the Bank of England in return for bank notes. The gold and silver that formed the Bank's stock of cash was rapidly depleted. Minutes of the Committee of the Treasury of the Bank for 1797 reveal the concern of the directors of the Bank. During the month of January the store of cash was depleted by £409,000, and in the first three weeks of February there was a further drop of £213,000 leaving the Bank with only £1,500,000 in store on February, 21, 1797. The next day, the Bank sent an armed frigate to Hamburg to purchase gold and the depletion of cash continued with £90,000 paid on the 23rd and £130,000 on Friday the 24th. On Monday, February 27, the Bank suspended all cash payments and asked William Pitt, the prime minister and lord of the treasury, to give parliamentary security for Bank notes.

This suspension of cash payments and thus the Bank's circulation of purely paper money was to last until 1821. In 1797, it was a very unusual step for the Bank to take and Parliament immediately began committee hearings on the action. Whenever the Bank's accounts were examined by Parliament, a committee of secrecy was established to do so. Data released to such a committee was not intended to be shared with the rest of Parliament nor, of course, the public. The House of Commons Committee of Secrecy on the Outstanding Demands of the Bank of England and a Secret Committee with a similar mission in the House of Lords began to hear testimony on the affairs of the Bank of England in March 1797.

The Secret Committee of the House of Lords questioned the relative magnitude of the diminution of the Bank's specie and whether the financial panic of 1796 and 1797 had been precipitated either by the Bank decreasing the circulation of bank notes in times of increased wartime commerce, or by the Bank increasing advances to the government at the expense of lending to the commercial sector of London. In the course of testimony, directors of the Bank of England provided the Secret Committees with actual values of bank notes issued and advances made to the government. Even in the confines of parliamentary "secrecy," however, directors of the Bank were loathe to give the

Table 4.1 *The Bank of England's scale of cash and bullion (1797) given to a parliamentary Secret Committee and leaked to the public by William Morgan.*

1797.] *Important Tables relative to the Finances of the Bank.* 249

TABLE I. *Showing the Scale of Cash and Bullion in the Bank, from 1782 to 1797.*

	No.		No.	1789.	No		No.	1796.	No.
1782.		Dec. 31	1226	March 28	1462	Sept. 28	1032	January	558
March	602	1786.		June 27	1634	Dec. 29	868	March	490
June	586	March 24	1178	Sept. 26	1764	1793.		May	438
September	382	June 30	1220	Dec. 24	1756	March 30	580	July	414
December	352	Sept. 30	1256	1790.		June 29	728	Sept.	418
1783.		Dec. 30	1190	March 26	1712	Sept. 28	1128	Dec.	414
March	209	1787.		June 25	1652	Dec. 30	1274	1797.	
June	136	March 21	1098	Sept. 24	1684	1794.		January	338
October	78	June 30	1140	Dec. 31	1616	March 29	1420	February 4	340
December	116	Sept. 28	1270	1791.		June 28	1354	—— 11	356
1784.		Dec. 29	1186	March 26	1516	Sept 27	1336	—— 18	314
June	224	1788.		June 25	1552	Dec. 24	1282	—— 21	298
Sept. 25	3?6	March 29	1124	Sept. 24	1582	1795.		—— 22	284
Dec. 31	445	June 28	1240	Dec. 31	1420	March	1310	—— 23	268
1785.		Sept. 27	1404	1792.		June	1214	—— 24 }	
March 19	582	Dec. 24	1438	March 31	1236	Sept.	956	—— 25 }	210
June 25	884			June 30	1132	Dec.	*660		
Sept. 24	1174								

* **This number has been stated to represent** *fair cash.*

Source: "On the Finances of the Bank," 1797, 249.

actual values of specie held by the Bank or of bills discounted to London merchants. In place of actual values, they presented a scale of quarterly values of cash and bullion and a scale of monthly values of bills discounted over the previous four years.

Keys to the Mystical Scales

The Parliamentary oath of secrecy was broken with leaks to the financial world. In October 1797, the *Monthly Magazine and Register* published the scales of bullion and bills discounted in an article entitled "On the Finances of the Bank" (that table of the scaled series of cash and bullion is reproduced in Table 4.1). Just as significant, the anonymous author who carried the leak from the confines of Parliament to the literate public also made an educated guess at the actual values and published a reconstructed series parallel to the scaled series. The scaled and reconstructed values were quoted in other newspapers of the time. In 1798, Alexander Allardyce sent a reproduction of the entire *Monthly Magazine* article to major shareholders in the Bank of England as a quantitative assessment of Bank affairs.[4] For the next thirty-five years, the data and what Thomas Tooke called the "key" from "On the Finances

---

[4] Clapham ([1944] 1966, 1: 286) reported that in 1791 there were 2,465 voting shareholders of Bank of England stock. One-fifth of those had foreign addresses.

of the Bank" were used in various pamphlets in the debates on money and banking. Advocates of various positions – including the "bullionists" who supported the *Bullion Report* of 1810 calling for swift resumption of specie payment, those who thought the depression and deflation of the 1820s was caused by resumption, and those who thought it caused by other factors – all shared a common desire to know the amount of bullion held and bills discounted by the Bank over time. The scaled series and the estimated series were used by David Ricardo in his 1818 *Proposals for an Economical and Secure Currency* and his 1824 *Plan for a National Bank* (both reprinted in Ricardo 1962). Thomas Tooke also used the scaled and reconstructed values in his *Considerations on the State of the Currency* (1826) and in his *A Letter to Lord Grenville on the Effects Ascribed to the Resumption of Cash Payments on the Value of the Currency* (1829). This period was the primordial stew for the development of monetary theory. As Joseph Schumpeter described it,

> It is the common opinion that the foundations of the monetary science of today (or yesterday) were laid by the writers who discussed the issues of English monetary and banking policy from the Restriction Act (1797) to the gold inflation of the 1850's. This neglects indeed the French and Italian work of the eighteenth century but nevertheless comes nearer to the truth than such sweeping statements usually do. Many of those writers moved on an unusually high level. They soared with ease into the sphere of abstract generalization and were possessed of a genuine will to analyze. This is the more remarkable because most of them were men of practical affairs and primarily interested in practical measures. . . . it was the practitioners who were in the van of *analytic* advance, and research workers of different types were in most cases content to take their clues from them. (Schumpeter 1954, 688)

The Bank of England's scaled series and a key to breaking its code were publicized by a man of practical affairs. As Allardyce described it, the scaled accounts "have fallen into the hands of a gentleman, eminent for financial knowledge and acuteness" (Allardyce 1798, 32). Ricardo's description was similar, "an ingenious calculator discovered the whole secret which the Bank wished to conceal" (Ricardo 1962, 99). "On the Finances of the Bank" was signed by M. N., and the true identity of the author was never made public. Using good archival detective work, Piero Sraffa concluded that the author was William Morgan.[5] Morgan was a mathematical practitioner par excellence. He was chief actuary to the Society for Equitable Assurances on Lives and Survivorships from 1775 to 1830 and was elected to the Royal Society for his work on probability.[6]

---

[5] Sraffa reveals this in an appendix to volume 4 of *The Works and Correspondence of David Ricardo*, titled the "Ingenious Calculator." Sraffa deduced from a note in a manuscript of Alexander Allardyce's and from correspondence from Ricardo to Pascoe Grenfell that the author was William Morgan. Sraffa was clear in his labeling of the scaled series as "index numbers."

[6] Lorraine Daston (1988) argues that although Morgan brought considerable mathematical expertise to the position of actuary, his "almost pathological prudence" led to unusual surpluses for the Equitable as well as criticism of his wariness. Maurice Ogborn (1962) provides a full account of Morgan's life

In his 1797 article, Morgan anonymously explained how he broke what he called the "cabalistical numbers" and what Tooke later referred to it as the "mystical scale" of the Bank of England. Based on leaked testimony, Morgan gathered that one of the directors of the Bank had said that from the 18th to the 25th of February £600,000 was paid out in cash. The scaled values for that same time period decreased from 314 to 210 (see Table 4.1). The Bank had said that in its scale of cash and bullion, the value 660 represented the "fair cash," in other words the mean or typical level. Using a Rule of Three algorithm, Morgan concluded that this was actually £4,000,000 and he multiplied all scaled values by 6,060, then rounded to the nearest £10,000 to get the reconstructed values.[7] Given actual values for notes circulating and advances to the government and his reconstructed values for cash and bullion, Morgan was then able to break the code of the discounted bills by multiplying the scaled values by 2,220 and rounding off to the nearest £10,000.

Morgan used his tables of reconstructed values to note the very low value of cash at the time of the suspension of all cash payments and also to prove that the Bank of England had been far more generous in its lending to the government than to the merchants of London:

> I think the preceding statements incontestibly prove that neither our foreign trade nor our commercial intercourse at home have derived much advantage from the operations of this bank. Its chief energies have been unequivocally directed to another quarter. The advances to government have generally been four or five times greater than the private discounts. It must appear as if its principal had been to enable a minister to lavish the public revenue much faster than it could ever be collected; and to furnish him with the means of engaging in the most extravagant and ruinous expence, before his prodigality could be submitted to the deliberation of Parliament.[8] ("On the Finance of the Bank" 1797, 251)

Such conclusions were exactly what the Bank and the Secret Committees were hoping to avoid with the use of scaled series. The Bank had to indicate with the data the relative severity of the drain of 1797. Comparisons were needed within each series between one time period and another. The Bank,

---

including his medical training, reputation as a professional consultant on annuities, and his liberal contacts with John Horne Tooke and Thomas Paine. Ogborn also speculates that Morgan was the first person to produce X-rays through scientific experiment.

[7] It is puzzling why Morgan, who was so precise in his other calculations on the scale, assumed that since the 104 (the difference between 314 and 210) represented £600,000, 660 represented £4,000,000 rather than £3,808,000. Morgan's relative imprecision in this calculation and his incredibly low average error in computing the true values of discounted bills led me to wonder whether Morgan might have been working with more information than he disclosed. Were actual values of discounted bills leaked to William Morgan in 1797 before he published the key to the scaled series? If so, was Alexander Allardyce the one who gave him the actual figures? Allardyce was a shareholder in the Bank who was committed to publicity of the accounts. He circulated the scales that were published in the *Monthly Chronicle* to other shareholders and he knew the identity of the anonymous author. It would be difficult to investigate this suspicion two centuries after the fact.

[8] This sentiment supports Sraffa's deduction that William Morgan was the author of "On the Finances of the Bank." In his history of the Equitable Life Assurance Society, Ogborn (1962, 130) describes Morgan as opposed to the war, the method of financing war expenses, and Pitt's administration. Ogborn quotes Morgan in blaming the inconvertibility of Bank notes, not on public alarm, but on the gradual evil of increasing government debt.

however, did not want the data to be in a form that allowed for comparisons between series, such as the amount of notes compared with the amount of cash and bullion (the cash ratio), or the amount of credit extended to the government compared with the credit extended to private commerce.

Despite Morgan's publication of a key, the Bank of England used the same algorithm to update the scale of cash and bullion in testimony to Parliament in 1810 and 1819. The cat-and-mouse game continued when a letter to the editor of the *Morning Chronicle*, published on October 15, 1810, and signed A. B., leaked the scale of discounts. Ricardo made use of this in his *Notes on the Bullion Report*. Similarly, updated scales were leaked to Tooke in 1819. Tooke (1829), using Morgan's key, published reconstructed series for these new scales. One explanation for the Bank's persistent use of the same scale could be that Morgan's formula was incorrect and overestimated the value of specie.

Although I have yet to come across a direct citation to the formula for the scale in the archives of the Bank of England, one ledger[9] did include a table of the scaled values presented to Parliament in 1819 next to the table of the actual values on which the scale was constructed (see Table 4.2). With the two parallel series in front of me, I was able to break the code:

CASH AND BULLION

Steps for Scale Construction	Example: £2,192,813
truncate the last 4 digits	219
subtract 1	218
multiply by 2	436

The method for constructing the scale for discounted bills was more elaborate. I found the actual values of credits and debits of discounted bills in the *General Ledger*,[10] and compared these with the scaled series printed in Morgan's piece (see Table 4.3). I realized that credits and debits were balanced only after truncation. Division and subtraction were then used to construct the scale:[11]

COMMERCIAL BILLS DISCOUNTED

	Example:	
Steps for Scale Construction	Credits=£11,350,580	Debits=£8,056,698
truncate the last 4 digits	1135	805
subtract debits from credits	330	
divide by 2	165	
subtract first two digits	149	
(approximately 10%)		

---

9   Bank of England, *Memorials, Contracts, Accounts for Parliament*, vol. I, 1819–1843, Bank of England Archives, C66/1, pp. 24–25.
10 Bank of England, *General Ledger*, no. 17, began 1 March 1794, ended 28 February 1802, Bank of England Archives, ADM 7 32.
11 I had fun playing Sherlock Holmes in trying to break the code of the Bank's scaled series by comparing it with actual values in the ledgers, and I tried to share that adventure through a brainteaser in the biannual bulletin from the Bank of England Archives. One Bank employee succeeded in deriving the algorithm for the cash and bullion series, but there were no takers on the code for the discounted bills (Klein 1992, 1993)

Table 4.2 *The scale drawn up for the Lords Committee on Secrecy, April 1819, and the actual totals for gold and silver in possession of the Bank of England, 1814–1843*

Date	Scale	Actual (£)
29/ 01/ 1814	436	2,192,813
30/ 04/ 1814	476	2,391,881
30/ 07/ 1814	432	2,173,170
29/ 10/ 1814	430	2,166,383
28/ 01/ 1815	408	2,049,679
29/ 04/ 1815	416	2,091,689
29/ 07/ 1815	696	3,492,281
28/ 10/ 1815	798	4,002,838
27/ 01/ 1816	892	4,474,028
27/ 04/ 1816	1066	5,346,745
27/ 07/ 1816	1326	6,645,973
26/ 10/ 1816	1752	8,779,749
25/ 01/ 1817	1982	9,922,034
26/ 04/ 1817	2006	10,047,279
26/ 07/ 1817	2294	11,483,701
25/ 10/ 1817	2358	11,803,941
31/ 01/ 1818	2166	10,848,808
25/ 04/ 1818	1746	8,743,371
25/ 07/ 1818	1430	7,159,998
31/ 10/ 1818	1080	5,417,850
30/ 01/ 1819	910	4,562,946
02/ 04/ 1819	772	3,870,685

Source: Bank of England, *Memorials, Contracts, Accounts for Parliament*, vol. 1, 1819–1843, Bank of England Archives C66/1, pp. 24–25.

Morgan's average error in overestimating the original values of cash and bullion was £968,625. This error is 18 percent of the actual value (note the gap between the line representing actual values and the line representing Morgan's values in Figure 4.1). His error in estimating the original values of discounted bills was much smaller, £11,359, which is only .63 percent of the actual value. Morgan's method seems more "modern" and more useful than that of the Bank. The Bank of England had truncated and used a combination of additive and multiplicative steps. The truncation was useful in an age before mechanical calculators, but it is unclear why subtraction as well as multiplication or division was used, other than to make the trail back to the original a more complicated one. Morgan rounded off rather than truncated

Table 4.3 *The Bank of England's scaled series of discounted bills given to Parliament and the actual values, 1794–1797*

Date	Scale	Credits-£	Debits-£
05/ 07/ 1794	149	11,350,580	8,056,698
02/ 08/ 1794	120	12,506,879	9,845,390
06/ 09/ 1794	90	13,842,831	11,851,520
04/ 10/ 1794	92	15018,709	12,976,321
08/ 11/ 1794	85 *	16,327,418	14,437,664
01/ 12/ 1794	85 *	17,077,569	15,272,289
04/ 01/ 1795	104	18,842,275	16,548,786
07/ 02/ 1795	107 *	20,398,299	18,024,700
07/ 03/ 1795	103	2,650,566	376,464
11/ 04/ 1795	187 *	6,345,365	2,336,396
02/ 05/ 1795	176	8,079,050	4,179,576
06/ 06/ 1795	157	10,727,731	7,259,155
04/ 07/ 1795	220 *	14,400,101	9,543,037
01/ 08/ 1795	151	15,818,533	12,488,370
05/ 09/ 1795	85	16,996,322	15,115,098
03/ 10/ 1795	79	17,999,785	16,250,723
07/ 11/ 1795	96	19,797,019	17,671,526
05/ 12/ 1795	140	22,009,048	18,911,929
02/ 01/ 1796	179	24,812,097	20,852,197
06/ 02/ 1796	152	27,301,119	23,948,276
05/ 03/ 1796	127	3,300,537	483,569
02/ 04/ 1796	131	5,170,719	2,271,373
07/ 05/ 1796	129	7,604,684	4,750,475
03/ 06/ 1796	168	10,312,085	6,604,935
02/ 07/ 1796	165	12,446,860	8,793,182
06/ 08/ 1796	163 *	15,472,703	11,880,583
03/ 09/ 1796	151	17,480,889	14,141,287
01/ 10/ 1796	189	20,650,103	16489,526
03/ 11/ 1796	178	23,514,244	19,575,606
03/ 12/ 1796	171	26,054,200	22,269,559

Note: An (*) denotes scaled values that did not exactly match with the solutions to my algorithm.

Source: "On the Finances of the Bank 1797," 250; Bank of England, *General Ledger, No. 17, Began 1 March 1794, Ended 28 February 1805*, Bank of England Archives, ADM 7/32

and he assumed a Rule of Three, a ratio relationship.[12] The Bank's algorithm was never made public before this present investigation; it was Morgan's key that Tooke, Ricardo, and others adopted, and rounding off and the Rule of Three remain the basic ingredients in present-day index number construction.

[12] I consider Morgan's key to be the more modern, because of its consistent treatment of percent change. The modernity of Morgan's key might also be indicated by the fact that I could easily reconstruct

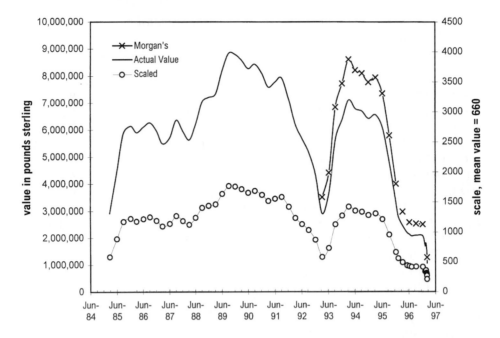

Figure 4.1   Plot to illustrate the relationships between the Bank of England's holdings of cash and bullion from February 1785 to February 1797, the scaled series that the Bank presented to Parliament, and William Morgan's estimates. The scaled series, measured on the right vertical axis, follows the same pattern as the actual values. Morgan's estimates, measured along with the actual values on the left axis, always overestimated the actual values. The scaled series and Morgan's estimates were published in "On the Finances of the Bank," 1797.

The financial situation in Britain during and after the Napoleonic Wars continued to provide a rich soil for the growth of tables of scaled series. The suspension of specie payment lasted from 1797 to 1821. The wars lasted until 1815, and during that time there was inflation. Deflation occurred as the war ended and the Bank tried, in steps, to return to full cash payment. George Shuckburgh Evelyn in 1798, Arthur Young in 1812, Joseph Lowe in 1822, and probably several others unknown to us constructed index number algorithms to assess the effects of the war and of paper money circulation on prices.[13]

Indexed series combine first differences with comparison by division, and the kernel of all index numbers is percent change. For example, John Taylor, in presenting evidence on monetary policy and commercial distress in 1844 – once again to a House of Commons Secret Committee – titled his tabular standard "Table of the comparative prices of ninety of the principal articles

Morgan's estimates from a formula copied cell to cell in a spreadsheet computer program. A spreadsheet was of no advantage in reproducing the Bank's scale-construction steps, which included truncations and the subtraction of the first two digits.

[13]   These works are discussed in Lowe 1822, Walsh 1901, Fisher 1922, and Kendall 1969. The latter three also discuss further theoretical and practical developments in composite price indices, due to the work of William Stanley Jevons, Augustus Sauerbeck, Etienne Laspeyres, Hermann Paasche, Ysidro Edgeworth, and Wesley Mitchell.

of commerce, expressed in centesimal proportions."[14] "Centesimal proportions" was the percent language of loans and inflation.

The history of index numbers as told by Maurice Kendall and Irving Fisher is a history of composite price indices reaching back to the inflation and then deflation connected to the Napoleonic Wars and the suspension of a notes-convertible-to-gold standard by the Bank of England.[15] There is another root, however, maybe even the tap root, of index numbers in the political arithmetic used to rationalize the suspension. The Bank of England's scale for cash and bullion yielded a pattern over time close enough to the actual pattern of change to persuade Parliament of the seriousness of the relative diminution of specie (see scale line in Figure 4.1). The scaled series, however, never indicated the actual values. The Bank of England's contribution to the development of index numbers was a table of a scaled time series that totally ignored absolute value, but gave a good indication of relative difference with a reference base (fair cash). The Bank's contribution was grounded in the need to reveal while simultaneously deceiving. The irony of the Bank's "mystical scale" was that it was designed to make comparisons between series impossible, and yet it became a way of connecting incomparable absolutes through their relative changes. Morgan's contribution was a rational, simple algorithm for moving from scaled to original series or vice versa while preserving the consistency of percent change. The irony of Morgan's attempt to destroy the veil was that his guess was incorrect – but it was fit and fertile, and its progeny thrived.

Restless Money and Moving Averages

The Bank of England's data manipulations to reveal patterns of change while masking actual values led not only to the first publication of a scaled series of index numbers in 1797, but also to the first publication of a moving average series in 1832. Since 1694, Parliament had periodically used the renewal of the Charter of the Bank of England to bring about changes in the privileges

[14] Norman Siberling (1919) used Taylor's index numbers of the price changes in ninety commodities from 1784 to 1833 to study price changes during the Napoleonic Wars. He demonstrated that in general prices rose from 1793 to 1814 and that prices in 1814 were 70 percent above the prices in the decade before the war. There was a considerable decrease in prices in 1815, when the war ended, and in 1816. By the time of the return to full specie payment in 1821, prices were at their prewar level. Siberling compared Taylor's price index with that of Stanley Jevons and concluded that Taylor's was more reliable.

[15] The narrow interpretation of the history of index numbers has stressed the controversies associated with the weights that are used to calculate a weighted average of price changes in composite indices: How should the weights be determined? Do the weights remain constant over time? Do the weights change with changes in prices? What method of calculating a price index should be used if the weights do not remain constant? Can an empirical investigation using composite price indices tell us whether inflation was due to a change in the value of money or a change the demand and/or supply of particular commodities? Is there really such a thing as the general price level? The explorations of these questions by William Stanley Jevons, Ysidro Edgeworth, Alfred Marshall, and John Maynard Keynes touched not only on empirical technique but also on monetary theory. Ragnar Frisch (1936) surveyed the theoretical issues connected with early twentieth-century attempts to construct price indices, and Joseph Schumpeter (1954) stressed the links between theoretical and statistical research in the work of Keynes, Gottfried von Harberler, and François Divisia. More recently, John Aldrich (1992) documented the "stochastic" approach to index numbers and its link to monetary theory in the work of Jevons, Edgeworth, and Keynes.

and responsibilities of the Bank.[16] In 1832, the House of Commons appointed a Secret Committee to inquire once again into the expediency of renewing the Charter of the Bank of England. One of the major questions addressed in its inquiry was, "What check can be provided to secure for the Public a proper management of Banks of Issue, and especially whether it would be expedient and safe to compel them periodically to publish their Accounts" (Great Britain, Parliament 1832, 3).

The actual amount of bullion held by the Bank of England had never before been made public; even the owners of the Bank of England (the Court of Proprietors) had never seen the accounts of actual values (Great Britain, Parliament 1832, 20). The only accounts made public had been the scaled series in 1797, 1810, and 1819, and Morgan's and Tooke's reconstructions from these series. In fact, the Bank's actual holdings of bullion at different dates was made public for the first time in the evidence published by the Secret Committee in 1832. The committee made clear, however, that the retrospective publication of the accounts of the Bank for the purpose of an occasional parliamentary debate on the renewal of the charter was very different from the "periodical publication during the course of its ordinary transactions" (Great Britain, Parliament 1832, 4).

In the course of the inquiry, the Secret Committee took evidence from the governor and directors of the Bank of England, directors of country banks, merchants, and capitalists that dealt on the exchanges. Most agreed that some publicity would serve as a check on the management of the Bank, but there was disagreement on whether the cash and bullion holdings of the Bank, the amount of its "treasure" backing the notes it issued, should be published. At one extreme were those who advocated total secrecy to avoid speculative panic, hoarding, and profiteering. Those advocating the opposite saw the regular publication of all accounts leading to increased public confidence, more cautious Bank management, and less speculative damage.

One of those who argued for total secrecy of the accounts was Nathan Meyer Rothschild, the "large capitalist" to whom the Bank of England was obliged to turn for "replenishing its coffers" in the panic and bullion drain of 1825 (Great Britain, Parliament 1832, 196). Rothschild argued that publication of the amount of bullion held by the Bank would be a "dangerous plan." Publication of accounts read only by intelligent people would do no harm, but the danger lay with "lower classes of people, that would read wrong statements in the newspapers" (Great Britain, Parliament 1832, 391). The problem with periodical publication of bullion holdings, according to Rothschild, was that people, particularly "little people," would compare one month's value to the next and panic if there were a decrease:

> I think it is much better that the Bank shall keep secret what gold and silver they hold, than to let it be known, because if people know that there is a

[16]   Although none mention the scaled series or moving averages of the Bank of England, Viner 1937, Clapham [1944] 1966, Fetter 1965, and Mathias 1983 serve as good sources for the general history of the Bank and British monetary policy during this time.

diminution in their stock of gold and silver, people will get frightened, and be induced to hoard; at last the Bank itself will feel alarm, and curtail its issues to such a degree as to cause a great deal of mischief to commerce.[17] (Great Britain, Parliament 1832, 392)

Similarly, Samuel Gurney, a bill broker connected with a Norwich bank, argued that the publication of bullion would be "very injurious" and cautioned against any publication because "credit is ticklish in its nature, and is by no means improved or protected by exposure" (Great Britain, Parliament 1832, 261).

Several others giving evidence, such as country bankers Vincent Stuckey and George Glyn, and the governor of the Bank of England, John Horsley Palmer, were in favor of publication of all accounts, except that of bullion. Stuckey agreed with the committee that the chief concern of the country bankers was "that the Bank of England's affairs should be conducted with steadiness, that there should not be contractions at one time and expansions at another" and that publication of the amount of bullion "might cramp the action of the Bank, so as to produce the unsteadiness" (Great Britain, Parliament 1832, 79). When asked "Is the amount of bullion that the Bank hold, the only secret which you think it of importance to preserve in the affairs of the Bank?" the Governor of the Bank answered "yes" (Great Britain, Parliament 1832, 59).

The directors of the Bank of England were divided on the opinion of periodically publishing the value of bullion, according to George Wade Norman, one of the directors giving evidence. Norman was in favor of publication of all accounts, including that of bullion; it would encourage good management of the Bank. Norman also argued that there was greater speculation with secrecy than would be the case with publicity, and that there was a danger in times of panic of public underestimation of the bullion holdings (Great Britain, Parliament 1832, 194–96).

Through its questioning, the committee expressed concern that in times of unfavorable foreign exchange, overissue of Country Bank paper, or political attempts to discredit the government, that publicity might increase the chances of "large capitalists" taking advantage of the Bank and of the public "exhausting the treasure of the bank" (Great Britain, Parliament 1832, 358). In particular it questioned whether the drain on bullion in the panic of 1825 might have been worse if the low state of the Bank's treasure had been known. Norman and two London bankers, Samuel Jones Loyd (Lord Overstone) and George Grote, all pointed out that even under the present system of secrecy, the public knew when the Bank's bullion was unusually low. According to Loyd, for example, the low state of the Bank's treasure in 1825 was, "in the money world of London, of perfect notoriety" (Great Britain, Parliament 1832, 243).

---

[17] Rothschild knew the profitable advantage of being privy to inside information that was not accessible to others. According to the entry for him in the *Dictionary of National Biography*, Rothschild organized a web of couriers and pigeon post on the continent so that he could gain news of political and commercial

Grote stated that the advantage of publicity would be to compel the Bank to "lay down some uniform, definite, and intelligible rule for determining the fluctuations in the amount of the circulating medium, and to adhere to that rule without deviation" (Great Britain, Parliament 1832, 357). Loyd saw "full and regular publication" of the Bank's accounts, including that of bullion, to be the "first great essential alteration which I conceive to be absolutely requisite" to improving the banking system. Loyd argued that information "systematically communicated . . . at frequently recurring periods set forth to the Public" would increase confidence in the Bank and make it more cautious in the face of questionable transactions (Great Britain, Parliament 1832, 241).

The governor of the Bank of England was the first person to give evidence to the Secret Committee, and his authority and testimony set the scene for the queries and compromises that followed. On the issue of publicity, Palmer "presumed it would be a periodical publication, in order to exhibit the fluctuation between succeeding periods." He was reluctant to publish any figures on bullion, but if publicity were required he urged that "the average of a preceding period would be a preferable mode for publication" (Great Britain, Parliament 1832, 57). Each advocate of publicity was asked about the possibility of publishing the bullion amounts retrospectively. Loyd thought "it would scarcely be sufficient" (Great Britain, Parliament 1832, 241). Tooke argued that there would be some historical value in even a retrospective publication (Great Britain, Parliament 1832, 279), and all advocates agreed that it would be preferable to total secrecy.

Faced with diverse testimonies, the members of Parliament searched for a way of presenting the accounts that would serve as a check on Bank management, yet not be so timely as to give advantage to those profiting from or attempting to discredit the Bank, nor so accurate as to let the public know the extremes to which bullion fluctuated. In accordance with Parliament's 1833 act on the Bank of England Charter (3rd & 4th WMIV cap. 98), the value of the Bank's holding of bullion and coin to be published in the *London Gazette* each month was to be the average of the three preceding months (Great Britain, Parliament 1833, 1276).[18] The value of the Bank's treasure published monthly from 1833 to 1844 thus formed a moving-average series. Smoothing was born.

The resolution of the publicity debate was the periodic publication of a value for bullion that was retrospective, exaggerated steadiness, and overestimated the value of the Bank's coin and bullion in times of drains. The compromise Parliament legislated gave the published accounts the "mystical" qualities one would expect from a powerful institution forced to take the first steps to open its books after 140 years of secrecy. The possible effects of the form of publicity are illustrated in Figure 4.2. The light line with unfilled square

events before others in London. His network was such that he was able to inform an incredulous British government of its victory at Waterloo a day before they heard of it from their own troops.

[18] While the public was treated to a monthly moving-average value, by the same legislation, the Bank was required each week to report the *actual* value of cash and bullion to the chancellor of the exchequer. This indicates the political and manipulative dimensions of the algorithm enforced by parliamentary legislation on the publicity of the accounts.

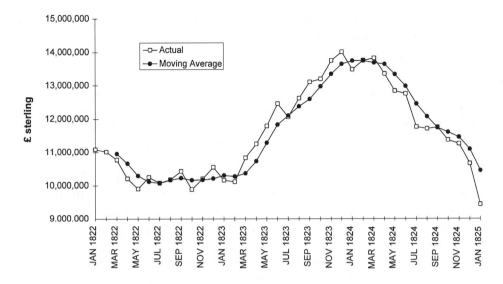

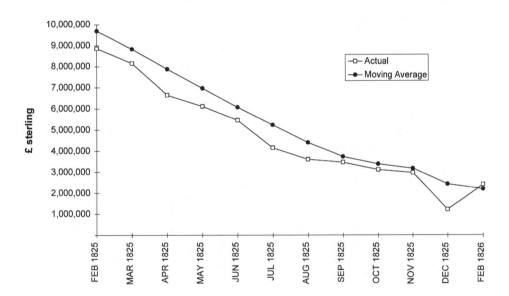

Figure 4.2   Actual values and three-month moving-average values of cash and bullion at the Bank of England from 1822 to 1826. The top chart illustrates the smoothing properties of a moving average over a time period of three years and the bottom chart illustrates the moving-average bias toward overestimation in a financial panic and drain, such as that of 1825. The actual values were tabulated in Great Britain, Parliament 1832, appendix 6.

markers connects actual values for bullion, at the end of each month, as published in evidence to the Secret Committee in Appendix 6. The dark line with filled circle markers connects monthly values that are the average of the three preceding months. The Bank only used the moving average on data after 1832 and, of course, the values were published in the form of tabular accounts, not graphs. Figure 4.2, however, illustrates the properties of the moving average and highlights its advantages in panics such as 1825. The dark moving average line is smoother than the lighter actual value line, never goes to the extremes that are displayed by the actual values, and always displays a higher value than the actual one in times of persistent decreases. In December 1825, when the Bank's treasure reached its lowest value for decades, the moving-average value is double the actual value.[19]

From 1833 onward, the movements of bullion became one of the most closely watched and discussed items on the British financial scene. The mystical qualities of the monthly Bank returns were not lost on observers of the London money market. For example, James Wilson in an 1840 pamphlet constructed a table of bullion values from 1832 to 1839[20] and commented,

> The fluctuations shown in this table, however great, are less than those which have actually taken place, owing to the mode in which the Bank's returns are made; being made once in each month of the average of the three preceding months. In the case of a diminishing amount, it is evident that at the moment when it is at the lowest point, that month has the advantage of being mingled with the two preceding months of larger amounts, and therefore showing a larger stock than is actually on hand. ... Thus the smallest and largest amounts of bullion in possession of the Bank is never shown. (Wilson 1840, 3, 4)

From that same pamphlet, titled *Fluctuations of Currency, Commerce and Manufactures Referable to the Corn Laws*, one can also gather why the Bank might want to be less than forthcoming about the extremes of bullion fluctuations:

> For some years past, during the exciting and ruinous changes which have taken place in the *money market*, as it is termed, men have eagerly sought for reasons and cures; but, as is too frequently the case, mistaking effect for cause, mere symptoms for the disease, the extent of that inquiry has seldom proceeded further than all agreeing in denouncing the Bank of England and the caprice of its management (expanding and contracting the currency at pleasure) as the groundwork and base of all the mischief. (Wilson 1840, 4, 5)

Unlike the London money market participants he described, Wilson did not hold the Bank responsible for the periodic fluctuations in the economy. On the contrary, he tried to demonstrate, with the Bank returns and the prices of imported and domestic wheat, that the cause of the "frequent recurrence of periods of excitement and depression in the monetarial and commercial interests of the country" lay in fluctuations in the price of wheat made more

---

[19]   The value of bullion and coin bottomed out on December 24, 1825, at £1,027,000. By February 28, 1826, it had risen to £2,459,510 (Great Britain, Parliament 1832, Appendix 28).

[20]   The construction of the table itself was remarkable. Wilson had to glean his data from individual issues of the *London Gazette* covering eight years. He only included, however, the moving-average values for every third month. As the Bank of England librarian Terry Bell pointed out to me, there are a few errors in Wilson's table.

severe by the barriers to trade embodied in the Corn Laws (Wilson 1840, i).[21] Wilson's dislike of the Corn Laws and his desire for free trade was eventually channeled into a weekly publication entitled *The Economist*. This journal contained editorial leaders advocating free trade, and numerous tables of data on trade and finance, on which, Wilson argued, all opinion and actions must be based (*The Economist*, September 2, 1843, 15).

In May 1844, a few months after the first issue of *The Economist*, Sir Robert Peel laid before Parliament eleven resolutions regarding a renewal of the Charter of the Bank of England. Peel's act called for the Bank to adhere to a strict cash ratio. This adherence to a currency principle would require careful monitoring of the amount of cash and bullion, and Peel's resolution number four called for the weekly publication of the true accounts of the Bank. Although he disagreed with Peel's insistence on a rigid cash ratio, Wilson strongly supported "the returns of the bank being made of its actual condition weekly instead of the average of the preceding three months, monthly" (*The Economist*, May 11, 1844, 771). That resolution was also supported by a majority in Parliament, and the moving average disappeared from the published accounts of the Bank of England in 1844. Although the moving average algorithm has been used by banks for similar purposes since then, it is to empirical investigations and mathematical statistics that our story now turns.[22]

Jevons's Use of Index Numbers and Moving Averages

Stanley Jevons was one of the key investigators that bridged the Bank of England's monetary/political arithmetic with the social science applications of index numbers and moving averages. The Bank of England had developed these algorithms in order to reveal a realistic mapping of change over time while simultaneously guarding the true value of the treasure in the vault. In the early nineteenth century, Arthur Young, Joseph Lowe, and John Taylor continued in the vein of political arithmetic, constructing price indices to support their interpretations of the effect of the Bank's suspension of cash payments. Jevons, however, took index number construction a step further, investigating and rationalizing the statistical properties of composite price

[21]   More details on statisticians' recognition of and reaction to the extreme fluctuations in the price of wheat in the nineteenth century can be found in Chapter 5 and in Klein 1995b.

[22]   In the latter half of the nineteenth century, banks continued to use and develop "systems of averaging." That was, for example, the term used by the New York Associated Banks to describe its practice of preparing statements. For the weekly statements, each bank, on Saturday, added up the values of loans, deposits, specie, and currency for the past six days and divided each total by six. These averages were of course not moving averages, but it does seem that banking practice is the source for the terms "process of averaging" or "systems of averaging" that John Poynting, Reginald Hooker, and others referred to in their statistical studies of time series analysis.

The Bank of England's use of ambiguity to quantify its reserves was refreshed during World War I. John Maynard Keynes remarked on this in describing the testimony of the governor of the Bank of England to a royal commission. According to Keynes, Lord Walter Cunliff "would only say that the Bank of England reserves were 'very, very considerable.' When pressed to give an even approximate figure, he replied that he would be 'very, very reluctant to add to what he had said' " (Keynes, quoted in *The Oxford Book of Money* 1945).

Also, Christopher Napier pointed out to me that twentieth-century rulings on the publicity of bank accounts in Britain have echoed the issues raised in the late seventeenth and eighteenth centuries. In the interest of maintaining stability, the Cohen Committee on Company Law Amendment of 1945

indices. The statistical legacy of the Bank's tabular code and Morgan's key to the scaled series was the rotation of perspective from absolute level to relative change. The adaptation of this tool allowed investigators to aggregate or group changes in cases where aggregation of absolutes would be impossible. Stanley Jevons explained this quality when he presented his composite price index in an 1863 study of the changing value of gold: "there is no such relation or similarity between a ton of iron and a quarter of corn as can warrant us in drawing an average between six pounds and three pounds." If one, however, measures the relative change in prices, then "the ratios 100:150 and 100:120 are things of the same kind, but of different amounts, between which we can take an average" (Jevons [1863b] 1884, 23). Thus, with rates of change, Jevons created a statistical grouping of similar but variable (in the logical, static sense) observations for which a mean had significance.

The focus on rates of change enabled Jevons and others to treat percent changes in each year as a statistical grouping of observations and to compare movement in one series with that of another. This latter capacity was fully developed by Arthur Bowley in his famous study of wages (Bowley 1895). Working with a large variety of data on wages from different places, occupations, and times, Bowley constructed a consistent index series from fragmented pieces. The links of the chain were rates of change. The irony here is that one reason the Bank constructed the scale was to insure that the value of cash could not be directly compared with the value of notes in circulation. Yet, one of the main uses of index numbers nowadays is to allow for easy joining or comparisons of percent changes in one series with percent changes in another.

In addition to constructing indexed series and laying the foundation for a stochastic understanding of composite price indices, Jevons was one of the first investigators to use moving averages of time series to search for empirical regularities. Key developments in the use of the moving-average algorithms are outlined in Table 4.4. The links from the Bank of England to James Wilson to Stanley Jevons are clear. Stanley Jevons carefully studied Wilson's 1840 pamphlet that tabulated the moving averages announced monthly by the Bank of England. In a presentation to the Dublin meeting of the Section F of the British Association in 1878, Jevons made reference to Wilson's pamphlet and distributed a semi-log graph plotting a three-year moving average of exports of merchandise from England to India (Figure 4.3b). In this study, as in several others, Jevons constructed useful bridges from monetary and political arithmetic to scientific investigation. From the world of commerce and finance, he adapted algorithms, data, and techniques of comparisons. He lengthened series, calculated reference means and deviations from means, decomposed series, and plotted series on two-dimensional graphs. In his search for seasonal and cyclical laws he pioneered the use of semi-log graphs, cycle-time frameworks, index numbers, geometric means, and moving averages in time series analysis.

In his 1878 presentation on commercial fluctuations, Jevons argued, as Wilson had done, that the demand for manufactured products was high only

granted banks the unusual privilege of not fully disclosing their reserves. Under the operation of this amendment, the disclosure of bad debt positions often took the form of a five-year moving average.

Table 4.4 *Key developments in the use of moving averages*

Date	Example	Context	Type	Form	Purpose
1832	Bank of England bullion value	Financial reporting	Retrospective 3-month time series	Number	Smoothing to eliminate extreme values
1840	Wilson's study of bullion over several years	Commercial fluctuations	Retrospective 3-month time series	Table	Smoothing
1877	Poynting's study of drunkenness	Social policy	Centered 20-town ranked cross section	Graph	Smoothing to neutralize differences
1878	Jevons's study of exports from England to India	Meteorology and commercial fluctuations	Centered 3-year time series	Semi-log graph	Smoothing to highlight decennial cycles
1883	Stewart's study of terrestrial magnetism	Meteorology	Centered 4-week time series	Table	Smoothing to eliminate irregularities
1884	Poynting's study of crop prices	Meteorology and commercial fluctuations	Centered 4-year as % of 10-year, time series	Graph	Correlation of deviations, highlight cycles
1901	Hooker's study of trade cycles and marriages	Political economy	Centered 9-year time series	Equation	Correlation of deviations, eliminate trend
1926	Yule's search for dangerous series	Time series	Retrospective 11-item random series	Graph, equation	Simulation to create series with correlated differences
1927	Slutsky's generation of cycles from random series	Cyclic processes	Retrospective 10-item, etc. random series	Graph, equation	Simulation to create cycles
1938	Wold's study of wheat prices, hypothetical correlograms	Temporal processes	Retrospective 5-year, etc. time series	Equation	Modeling of stationary processes

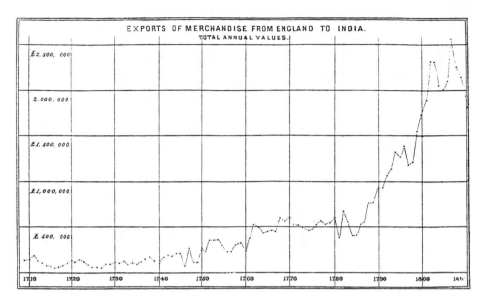

Figure 4.3a   Jevons's plot of exports with absolute values and linear scale. *Source:*
Jevons [1878b] 1884, diagram facing 218.

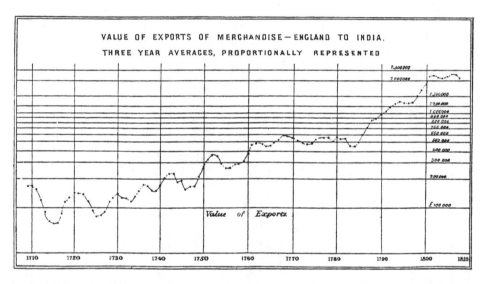

Figure 4.3b   Jevons's plot of exports with moving averages and semi-log scale.
Source: Jevons [1878b] 1884, diagram facing 219.

when food was cheap. Jevons was trying to highlight the decennial periodicity
of commercial crises, and his 1878 study suggested a link with sunspot variation. Solar activity influenced harvests in India, which in turn influenced
demand for British exports. The viewer does not get the sense of a strong
decennial period in the plot of the absolute values of English exports (Figure
4.3a), but it is more apparent in the moving-average plot (Figure 4.3b). For
Jevons, as for the Bank of England, the moving average was a smoothing device.

Terrestrial Magnetism and the Practice of Smoothing

Although the Bank of England's publicity on bullion in 1833 is the earliest example I have come across of a moving average, similar algorithms might well have been used by statistical cartographers and lab technicians to smooth curves and deal with errors in measurement without recourse to probability theory. The moving average is often perceived and used as a method of graduation for mapping data points into functional form. Smoothing curves by methods of graduation, like fitting lines by a least squares rule, has been a tradition closely connected with the mechanical practice of plotting or constructing.[23] An illustrative example is the progressive interpolation method used to investigate temporal and global variation in terrestrial magnetism. Jevons, as well as John Poynting and Balfour Stewart, studied the techniques of observation in terrestrial magnetism; all three of these men were pioneer users of moving-average algorithms in the 1870s and 1880s and all were employed at some point during that time at Owens College in Manchester.[24]

A method of progressive interpolation of time series data that is very similar to a moving average was included in the instructions by Friedrich Gauss and Wilhelm Weber in 1836 to those who had agreed to participate in the international project on terrestrial magnetism, the *magnetischen Vereins*.[25] Gauss, Weber, and the scores of other observers worked with "term observations," time series data. The participants in the international network were meant to take observations on magnetic declination every five minutes at the same exact time from noon to noon Göttingen mean time, on the last Saturday of January, March, May, July, September, and November.[26] The new organization of simultaneous observations and the new-style magnetometers created a need for a method of interpolating within times series. The less sensitive

[23] In mapping out the history of moving averages, I have explored the Bank of England root that influenced Jevons and perhaps John Poynting. I think there is an additional root in rules of thumb used by natural philosophers who frequently plotted data. Such a root is suggested in Udny Yule's note in a 1920 issue of the *Journal of the Institute of Actuaries*. Yule stated that the method of graduation suggested by George King (1909) for mortality tables was closely related to the graphic method published by John Strutt, Lord Rayleigh, in 1871 to correct curves representing the connection between two physical magnitudes.

[24] At Owens College, Jevons was professor of political economy and professor of logic, mental and moral philosophy from 1866 to 1876, Stewart was professor of natural philosophy from 1870 to 1887, and Poynting was a demonstrator in the Stewart's physical laboratory from 1876 to 1878.

[25] It is unlikely that the Bank of England's method of publicity had any bearing on the work of Gauss and Weber, and there might have been some earlier precedent for smoothing algorithms in terrestrial magnetism that I am unaware of. It seems, however, that the necessity for an algorithm like a moving average for time series data in the sciences only appeared in the 1830s with the peculiar features of the global magnetic association project.

[26] James Clerk Maxwell saw the Magnetic Union as an important step in the progress of science:
Numbers of scientific men joined the magnetic Union, learned the use of the new instruments and the new methods of reducing the observations; and in every city of Europe you might see them, at certain stated times, sitting, each in his cold wooden shed, with his eye fixed at the telescope, his ear attentive to the clock and his pencil recording in his note-book the instantaneous position of the suspended magnet.
Bacon's conception of "experiments in concert" was thus realized, the scattered forces of science were converted into a regular army, and emulation and jealousy became out of place, for the results obtained by any one observer were of no value till they were combined with those of the others. . . . It is to Gauss, to the magnetic union, and to magnetic observers in general, that we owe our deliverance from that absurd method of estimating forces by a variable standard which prevailed so long even among men of science. (Maxwell [1871] 1965, 2:245, 246)

more inaccurate needles of old had usually come to rest easily, and outside of a network an observer could patiently wait until the moment of rest to record the measurement. Vibratory motion, however, seemed to be an inevitable feature of the best instruments of the 1830s. As Gauss and Weber put it:

> It is not in our power so completely to quiet the needle of the magnetometer that it shall have no visible vibration; at least, it cannot be done with certainty, without some expense of time, and not for long; therefore, instead of an immediate observation, we must substitute such indirect modes of determination as to not require the entire absence of vibratory motion. (Gauss and Weber [1837] 1841, 43)

In their explanation of the result of observations made by the association for 1836, they addressed the problem of a lack of correspondence of the moment of observation with the equilibrium position of the magnetic needle. Gauss and Weber recommended interpolating between measurements observed before and after the appointed time. They gave as an example the way in which Dr. Wappäus derived the measurement of 867.16 for 15 hours 30 minutes on the August, 17, 1836:

15 hours/29 minutes/10 seconds		865 ° 2		
			866 ° 35	
	30	867 ° 5		
			866 ° 85	
	50	866 ° 3		
			867 ° 10	867 ° 16
30	10	868 ° 0		
			867 ° 65	
	30	867 ° 3		
			867 ° 90	
	50	868 ° 5		

The first column contained the times of observation in hours, minutes, and seconds, and the second column was the observed position of the magnetic needle every twenty seconds. The third column contained what Gauss and Weber called the "partial results," the means between each pair of actual measurements, and the single quantity in the last column was the final result, which was the mean of the means in the third column (Gauss and Weber [1837] 1841, 45).

There are several things that distinguish the algorithm used to construct the third column from a typical moving-average application: each average was an interpolation between a past and future, but not a present, observation; the intervals of time between the observations are established not by the dictates of the central organization, but by the period of the vibration of the needle there and then; therefore each of the progressive averages is thought to be a midpoint between the maximum and minimum positions of vibration and, while the original series oscillates and goes up and down, the series of progressive averages will generally map out the trend; the series of progressive averages is an intermediate step and it is the last derivation, the mean of the means, that matters; only two-period moving averages would be used; and the times of the partial and final results do not correspond to the times of any actual observation. Dr. Wappäus never observed the position of the needle at the appointed time of 15 hours 30 minutes, but, as Gauss and Weber saw it, his indirect route of measuring on either side of the appointed time yielded the true value in a way that direct observation could not:

> The position of the needle to be determined for any instant of time is not that position which the suspended magnet bar actually has at the instant, but that which it would have were its magnetic axis at that instant exactly in the magnetic meridian. (Gauss and Weber [1837] 1841, 42)

An 1883 entry by Balfour Stewart in the eighth edition of the *Encyclopedia Britannica* illustrates a continuity in the practice of using methods of graduation on time series observations in terrestrial magnetism. The intent of Stewart's moving-average algorithm, however, was not to eliminate the effects of second-to-second vibratory motion. Stewart tabulated the mean monthly values of the declination range at Kew Observatory that corresponded with forty-eight points of the year. The monthly mean range that corresponded with the first week in February, for example, was the mean of the ranges from four weeks on either side of that date (Stewart [1883] 1889, 169).

Poynting's Studies of Drunkenness and Crop Fluctuations

Another pioneer in the use of moving averages was John Poynting, who was interested in magnetism and who worked with Stewart at Owens College. Poynting's first published use of what might loosely be labeled a moving average was not, however, with meteorological time series. Poynting applied the algorithm to cross-section observations on social data and reached the conclusion that fewer pubs in a town led to greater drunkenness. Poynting's 1877 study on drunkenness statistics was presented to the Manchester Literary and Philosophical Society. Without the benefit of correlation or regression coefficients, Poynting used a visual comparison of curves to search for positive or inverse relationships between several variables. He used observations taken at one point in time, 1875, on a cross section of seventy-one towns in England and Wales. Poynting's three variables were the proportion of public houses to population, the proportion of persons prosecuted for drunkenness to population, and the percentage increase in population over the previous decade. For the latter two variables, Poynting ranked the towns from smallest to largest proportion of public houses and then constructed curves using a method of graduation based on what we now call a moving average:

> I took the mean of the numbers of persons to each apprehension for drunkenness for the first twenty towns, and put a mark on the diagram opposite the

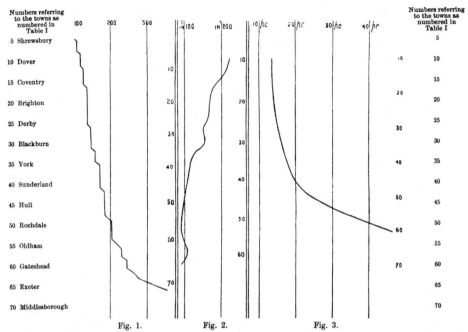

Fig. 1.   Table showing the proportion of public-houses to population in all towns of 20,000 and upwards in England and Wales (*Fortnightly Review*, Feb. 1877).   Year ending September, 1875.

Fig. 2.   Table showing the proportion of persons proceeded against in year ending September 29, 1875.

Fig. 3.   Table showing percentage increase of population in the towns from 1861 to 1871.   The curve obtained by grouping the towns in twenties.

Figure 4.4   Poynting's smoothed lines illustrating an inverse relationship between number of pubs and arrests for drunkenness. *Source:* Poynting [1877] 1920, 213.

> middle town of the twenty at a height representing this mean; then the mean
> for the twenty towns from the second to the twenty-first, and put a mark
> opposite the middle town of the twenty to represent this mean; then the
> mean for the twenty towns from the third to the twenty-second, and so on.
> (Poynting [1877] 1920, 499)

The curves for Poynting's three variables are shown in Figure 4.4. The curves that Poynting labeled Fig. 2 and Fig. 3 were constructed from the method of averaging described previously. From a visual examination of Fig. 1 and Fig. 2, he concluded that "the fewer public-houses there are the greater on the average the number of apprehensions for drunkenness" (Poynting [1877] 1920, 498–499). Poynting's rationale for smoothing was to "neutralise" the differences in police regulations and other circumstances between the various cities.

In his 1877 study of drunkenness, Poynting did not describe his method as a "process" of averaging nor did he refer to the averages as "instantaneous averages" (he was to use both terms in his 1884 work), nor indeed, were they really "moving averages."[27] All three terms imply time and sequence. It

[27]   The earliest reference to the term "moving average" cited in the 1989 edition of *The Oxford English Dictionary* is King 1912.

is also interesting to note that Jevons and Poynting himself described Poynting's 1877 figures as tables, not as graphs (Jevons [1882] 1977, 165).

In contrast, Poynting's 1884 investigation of prices and imports focused on time series plots and on the deviations from the instantaneous averages. In the 1884 study, Poynting joined the smoothing algorithms used in laboratories and observatories to the manipulation of data over time that had its origin in banking. In their brief histories of time series analysis, both Udny Yule (1921) and Harold Davis (1941) credit John Poynting's 1884 presentation to the Royal Statistical Society as the first statistical investigation of relationships between time series as well as the earliest application of moving averages. Both of these histories are based almost exclusively on works presented to the Royal Society or Royal Statistical Society. This institutionalized starting point ignores a rich history of technique and practice. Even within a broader history, however, Poynting's use of moving averages remains significant. Poynting made the moving average a mean reference, from which to calculate deviation, and used it as a tool of decomposition.

Poynting used what he called "a process of averaging" in his investigation of the possibility of a common meteorological phenomena causing simultaneous changes in crop production throughout the world. For example, in place of the observations for the average price of wheat for each year, Poynting computed a new average: taken in turn, each year in question became the fifth year in a group of ten years used to calculate the new average. The averaging continued until the supply of data was sequentially exhausted. The end result of this process was a new series of what Poynting called "instantaneous averages" that served as a linear standard with which to compare fluctuations in prices and imports.

Poynting's study of serial relationships was based on a graphical comparison of reconstructed curves illustrating the oscillations of wheat prices and British imports of cotton and silk (Figure 4.5). The purpose of constructing new series by using four-year moving averages taken as a percentage of ten-year moving averages was to manipulate the statistics so "as to show the true fluctuations, whatever they may be, with the effects of wars, increase of commerce, etc., as far as possible eliminated" (Poynting 1884, 35). As he described it, his curves were "submitted to a smoothing down process" (Poynting 1884, 43). Poynting compared the curves of prices and imports that had been "freed to some extent at least from accidental irregularities" and concluded that the fluctuations were similar enough to have been the effects of a common, global meteorological cause.

John Poynting's use of what he called an "instantaneous average" had a rough reception at the Royal Statistical Society. Some criticized Poynting for using mathematics that was too sophisticated, others argued that he had strayed too far from mathematics and had come perilously close to black magic in his manipulation of data. Almost all discussants recognized that his "process of averaging" was a tool of political economy.[28]

---

[28] One discussant to Poynting's paper asked, "What is an average?" and commented that "The system of averaging therefore for the purposes of economical practice was as far as he could see totally different from the system of averaging bases which commended itself to the mathematical mind" (Poynting

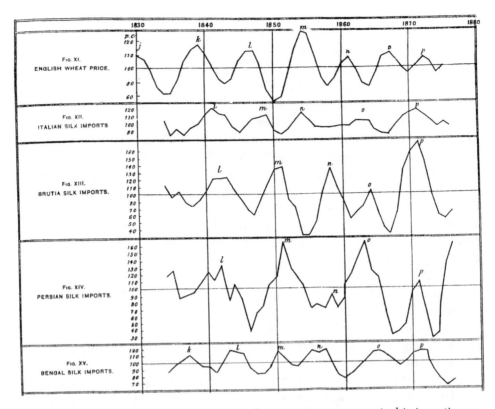

Figure 4.5 Poynting's plots of deviations from moving averages in his investigation of crop fluctuations. *Source:* Poynting 1884, 49.

From Fluctuations to Deviations via Smoothing

The method of averaging adopted by the Bank of England in publishing bullion values from 1832 to 1844, by Jevons in his study of periodic commercial fluctuations, by Poynting in his 1877 study of drunkenness, and by Stewart in his 1883 investigation of terrestrial magnetism was a method of smoothing (see Table 4.4). It was manipulation of data to eliminate irregularities or extreme fluctuations. The result was the elimination of some, if not all, geometric form. For example, Poynting observed in his 1884 study that if there were ten-year cycles in his price or import data, the plotting of a ten-year moving average would yield a nearly straight line (Poynting 1884, 36).

The geometrical reasoning of statistical method in the late nineteenth century involved a search for form and a celebration of deviations. It would seem, therefore, that smoothing techniques had no place in the science of means and variation. However, Poynting (1884) and Reginald Hooker (1901) demonstrated to the Royal Statistical Society that the smoothing process could be

1884, 73). Poynting did not use bullion values in his statistical study of agricultural prices, but he did use other Bank of England data taken from the same period. He would most certainly have been aware of the Bank's method used to report the value of bullion and of Jevons's use of a moving average in 1878. Although Poynting never mentions Jevons in his paper, Jevons's work came up in the discussion at the Royal Statistical Society following his presentation.

seen not just as an end in itself, but also as a means to reconstructing form consistent with the science of means. In particular, they used a moving average to change fluctuations into deviations through a process of what became known as "decomposition."

In his 1877 study on drunkenness, Poynting compared the smoothed curves to determine correlation. In his 1884 investigation of a common meteorological influence on agriculture, however, correlation was determined by comparing variations from the smoothed curves; the ten-year "instantaneous average" was a standard that allowed Poynting to determine whether an actual price was "above or below the average *for that time*" (Poynting 1884, 36). The moving-average value, like a statistical mean, is rarely, if ever observed, but in the perception of the statisticians it can be considered the "true" or at least the "expected" value. What had been a technique of deception for the Bank of England became a way at getting at the truth for fellows of the Royal Statistical Society.

Hooker, in his study of the correlation of the marriage rate with trade, argued that the chief difficulty of applying the theory of correlation to economic phenomena was that the "element of time is involved" and "the actual behaviour of any one set of variables is thus usually compounded of several movements due to as many causes" (Hooker 1901, 485). The correlation coefficient Hooker had first calculated for the raw data of the marriage rate and various series on British and Irish trade showed no significant relationship. He then used the moving average as a means to decompose time series data into separate movements determined by distinct causes. The "regular periodic movements" of trade and marriage yielded a significant correlation coefficient of 0.80.[29]

As a first step in decomposing the series in order to highlight the periodic movements, Hooker determined that his data on British exports and imports from 1857 to 1900 displayed a local maximum in trade approximately every nine years. He thus calculated each "instantaneous average" over nine-year intervals, and called the line representing the successive averages a "trend."[30] The trend line, according to Hooker, represented "the direction in which the variable is really moving when the oscillations are disregarded" (Hooker 1901, 486). Hooker's interest, however, lay with oscillations about the trend line. He thus subtracted the instantaneous average from the actual value for each year and correlated the deviations from the trend.

Thus, smoothing became a mere step in the process of constructing analytical form. Investigators took care to choose an averaging interval that rendered the series into one with the least shape possible. The comparison of the actual values with the relatively formless linear standard revealed the oscillations that often had "stationary" characteristics, which allowed them to be treated as if they represented deviations within static mass phenomena. Thus, the "process of averaging" transformed fluctuations into oscillations and deviations. This important technical solution to what Udny Yule called the "time-

[29] See Appendix 1 for an explanation of correlation coefficients.
[30] Udny Yule (1944, 75) attributed the origin of the concept of "trend" in time series data to Hooker's 1901 study.

correlation problem" had its origins in graphical and tabular algorithms and financial reporting. It is interesting to note that Hooker insisted that his use of an "instantaneous average" was not from "higher mathematics" but was rather "an elementary method" (Hooker 1901, 486). It was more a case of finance being applied to science than vice versa.

From a Tool of Deception to a Model of Reality

There are other ironies, as can be seen in Table 4.4, in the history of the moving average, besides it being a smoothing technique used to generate rough, stationary form. With regard, for example, to its use in the analysis of cyclical fluctuations, there were somersaults; the moving average was, on different occasions, used to eliminate, highlight, or create cycles. As a smoothing technique, the moving average was used to eliminate cycles and produce a trend line. Deviations calculated from the trend brought the cycles back *sans* trend.[31] The moving average was also used to create cycles in time series, where none existed before in the raw data. Simulations by Eugen Slutsky (1927) and Udny Yule (1921, 1926) demonstrated that new series characterized by cycles or correlated differences could be constructed, with the use of a moving average, from a series that originally displayed purely random variation.[32]

Yule's and Slutsky's simulations laid the foundation for the greatest irony of all. The moving average, which had first been used by the Bank of England to make it impossible for the public to ever know the actual value of its treasure, served, in the hands of Herman Wold (1938), as a hypothetical model of real processes. Life was a moving average, at least in cases of what Wold called "discrete stationary random processes." Wold, following the suggestion of Harold Cramér, constructed correlograms (time plots of autocorrelation coefficients) from simulated moving-average schemes of random variables (see Figure 10.5). He found that the hypothetical correlograms of moving averages resembled those based on economic empirical series, such as William Beveridge's trend-free index of yearly wheat prices in western Europe. Under the stimulus of Slutsky's and Wold's work, econometricians used moving averages not just to manipulate data but to also specify models of stochastic economic oscillations. Thus, the financial subterfuge constructed by the Bank of England and the Secret Committee became, a century later, a theoretical model of how things really work in a capitalist economy.

---

[31]   *Business Conditions Digest* published by the U.S. Department of Commerce in the latter half of the twentieth century used a moving average to eliminate random fluctuations and highlight cycles. Its choice of the time interval for averaging each series was based on a measurement they called MCD – months for cyclical dominance. The MCD is the minimum interval for which the average change in the value of the cyclical component is greater than that for random oscillations.

[32]   While Yule used a moving average of random disturbances to demonstrate that the variate difference method could generate spurious cycles, Slutsky saw moving summations of random disturbances as true models of cyclic economic processes. These different perceptions are further explored in Chapter 10.

5

Seasons, Tides, and Structures in Cycle Time

Merchants and manufacturers are of necessity intimately acquainted, by experience or by tradition, with such periodic fluctuations as occur in their own branches of industry. By the skill and rule-of-thumb knowledge which each one acquires in his own pursuits, they make allowance for such variations, and thus very rude comparisons of prices, stocks, and sales enable them to detect irregular changes in their own market, which is all that they require.

But this unwritten knowledge of commercial fluctuations is not available for scientific purposes, and it is always of a very limited extent.

Jevons [1862] 1884, 3–4

Stanley Jevons's reflection on merchants' rule-of-thumb methods introduced his investigations of periodic commercial fluctuations in a study presented to the British Association at Cambridge in 1862. Jevons saw his task as transforming "rude" business comparisons into scientific methods of comprehending fluctuations. The mercantile analytical tool that Jevons borrowed for this task was a relative time framework for ordering time series data. Merchants and financiers had a sense of the average price or volume of trade for a particular week or month in the year and they had a sense of the seasonal variation of the average value within the year. There were various levels of formality in the "rude comparisons" of merchants, but the forms of data presentation in weekly nineteenth-century business journals, such as *The Economist*, give indications of how comparisons were made. The data tables were often constructed for seasonal comparisons. The current week's prices and volumes of output were compared with the values for the same week in the previous year. In the more elaborate tables, a long time series would be rearranged into a matrix whose rows were months and whose columns were years. A financier glancing at the table could easily determine the typical value for March based on several years' data. This reshaping of a long time series vector into a matrix of cross-section observations was a precursor of Jevons's and Norton's statistical studies of seasonal and cyclical variation.

Compared with techniques covered in earlier chapters, the case for a chronological primacy of monetary algorithms is weaker with the relative time framework. It is clear even as early as John Graunt's *Observations on the Bills of*

Mortality that merchants mentally rearranged figures to capture seasonal variation. The published tabular rearrangement, however, also appeared early on in the sciences with, for example, Pierre Simon Laplace's 1827 study of the daily change in barometric pressure through the months of the year or the lunar cycle. Although it is not a strictly chronological progression, I have maintained a chapter structure of monetary, political, empirical, and finally scientific arithmetic. Following an explanation of what I mean by relative time framework, the first examples I address of statistical structures in cycle time are from nineteenth-century commercial practice. Jevons's appropriation of the tool for his study of seasonal variation is examined as well as the financial seasonal structures of James William Gilbart, Dionysius Lardner, John William Lubbock, and John Norton. The cycle time framework is one of several ties binding nineteenth-century economics and meteorology. The theoretical and methodological links between these two subjects are explored, and the reshaping of time series data in meteorology and economics is compared to cross-sectional relative time frameworks used by Adolphe Quetelet, Henry Pickering Bowditch, and Francis Galton. The relative time structure implicit in the regression analysis of Galton and Karl Pearson was not cycle time, but experiment time; control, as much as storytelling, became the investigative goal. The chapter ends with a discussion of experiment and model time and the limitations of connecting means in relative time as a method of summarizing processes.

In keeping with the flavor of earlier chapters, I contrast the elements of practical dynamics used by financiers and almanac makers with the geometric reasoning arising from more "scientific" statistical investigations. As with other statistical techniques, a major contribution of mathematics and science to the development of the relative-time tool was the substitution of graphs for tables. Other manipulations that distinguish the high theory from the low practice were the referencing to a mean and the use of decomposition. The latter was used to separate the artificial from the natural and the periodic from the irregular. In the hands of early biometricians and econometricians, the relative time framework became one way of transforming fluctuations into deviations and cycle time into the logical time of the experiment.

Relative Time Frameworks

With *absolute time*, every data point is associated with a unique date – e.g. January 1998. With *relative time*, every data point is associated with a place in a sequence.[1] In most of the statistical work examined in the this book, the time framework is evident from the units measured on the horizontal axis. With monthly data plotted against absolute time, values on the horizontal axis proceed, for example, from January 1997 to February 1997 to March 1997, and so forth. In the earliest statistical studies employing a relative time framework, sequence in a cycle is measured on the horizontal axis. For example, in Figure 5.3, Jevons's horizontal axis proceeds from January to February

---

[1]   The technique of rearranging a time series into a relative time framework is illustrated in Appendix 1.

to March or from the first quarter to the second quarter to the third quarter. The January is not attached to any one year. It is a typical January, connected to a typical February as a place in a sequence. The repeated sequence is a cycle of twelve months in a year. The absolute calendar time or the historical time of the observation is not a factor in the final analysis. Time matters only in the sense of sequence within a cycle, whether that cycle be an annual, diurnal, decennial, lunar, life, or business cycle. Time becomes a place one can visit again and again. Figure 5.1 illustrates examples of cycle time used in nineteenth-century and early twentieth-century statistical studies.

The logical time framework of most regression models and economic equilibrium models can also be seen as a type of relative time.[2] The horizontal axis of a simple regression diagram proceeds from low values of x to high values of x. In many scientific experiments the logical time can coincide with historical time. For example, if one is investigating the relationship between pressure and volume of a gas, with temperature held constant, one can gradually increase the pressure and note the corresponding value for volume. The values for pressure, from low to high, become the time framework for the study. I have labeled this type *experiment time*. In cases where the investigator cannot control the smooth procession from low x to high x, a scatterplot of observed coordinates is used. A regression line fitted to the scatter enables a viewer scanning from left to right to mark time with the sequence from low x to high x. I have called this type of logical time framework *model time*.

In an absolute time framework, processes are irreversible and nonrepeatable; in a cycle time framework, processes are irreversible but repeatable; in a model time framework, the generation of a pattern of y's in the sequencing of x's is reversible and repeatable. It is tempting in a model time framework to conclude that as x increases, y decreases (as one might do in the case of a negative slope on the regression line). The temporal process of comprehension and the construction of the line lull us into imagining process. As Joan Robinson (1980), however, has pointed out, there are dangers in falling into this trap. We would be wise to limit our conclusions to: high values of x are associated with low values of y.

In most of the diagrams reproduced in this chapter, relative time is indicated on the horizontal axis and the mean value of a sample is measured on the vertical axis.[3] The average point for each stage of the cycle was usually calculated from a cross section of observations corresponding to that stage. For example, Adolphe Quetelet used a group of several two-year-olds to calculate the height of *l'homme moyen* (the average man) at age two of the human life cycle (Figure 5.8).

The importance of the relative time frameworks used by financiers and almanac makers lies in the restructuring of time series data into samples that

---

[2] The term "logical time" was used by Joan Robinson (1980) to distinguish models and diagrams used to compare static positions (e.g., values of y for given values of x) from diagrams in historical time, which pattern processes of change (see Appendix 1).

[3] The diagrams I constructed to illustrate the seasonal pattern of deaths in London (Figures 2.1–2.4) plot out means in a cycle time framework. Karl Pearson's graph of age-specific mortality (reproduced in Figure 2.7), matches the relative time criteria of sequence of a human life cycle plotted on the

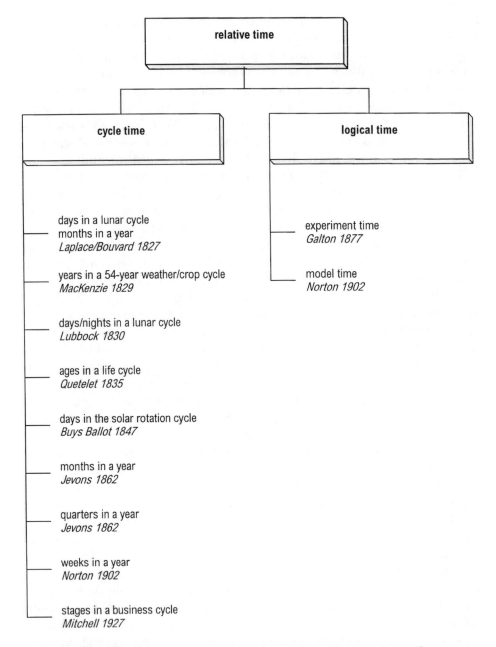

Figure 5.1   Relative time frameworks in nineteenth- and early twentieth-century statistical studies.

could be treated as cross sections. In Quetelet's studies of *l'homme moyen*, one of the most well known of the early statistical applications of relative time frameworks, the raw data were cross-section observations. It was with meteo-rological studies, such as John William Lubbock's, and economic studies, such

horizontal axis. Pearson's analysis, however, differs from the studies investigated in this chapter in his use of the vertical axis to measure frequency of death rather than a mean value.

as Dionysius Lardner's or Stanley Jevons's, that rearranged time series data were plotted in a relative time framework. All three of these Royal Society fellows were inspired by quantitative reasoning in commercial practice.

Reshaping Time Series in Commercial Practice

There is evidence of the use of a cycle time framework in merchant arithmetic as early as John Graunt's seventeenth-century observations on the bills of mortality. The arrangement of data in tables in business journals and in evidence given to parliamentary committees indicates the importance of and common use of relative time frameworks to commercial quantitative reasoning by the mid-nineteenth century. A selection of tables from nineteenth-century parliamentary testimony and from issues of *The Economist* and *The Statist* is reproduced in Figure 5.2.

The values for one week, one month, or one quarter were displayed in comparison with that same week, month, or quarter in previous years. Such a layout enabled financiers to get a feel for seasonal variation. Tables for seasonal comparison were used particularly in the display of banking and railway statistics. In his study of seasonal variation in the discount rate and other commercial data, Jevons referred to earlier works on fluctuations in credit markets by Gilbart (1854) and Charles Babbage (1856).[4]

Gilbart's testimony to the House of Commons in 1841 (reproduced in Bell 1842) serves as one of the earliest examples of economic analysis of seasonal variation. By organizing his monthly time series data on the circulation of bank notes into an annual relative time framework, Gilbart illustrated that the seasonal pattern of circulation for the country banks was quite different than that for the Bank of England. Critical of both the "Currency School" of Samuel Jones Loyd and J. R. McCulloch, and the "Banking School" of Thomas Tooke and John Fullarton, Gilbart was an advocate of what Lawrence White (1984) has called the "Free Banking School."[5] Free bankers argued in favor of unrestricted competition in the issue of notes. According to Gilbart and other spokesmen for free banking, only the Bank of England could overissue notes at will and cause monetary disturbances. Circulation of country bank notes, however, was completely dependent on the demands arising from trade. The onus was on Gilbart to demonstrate empirically that the country bank note circulation followed a natural, seasonal pattern, dictated by the annual agricultural cycle, and that the pattern differed from that of Bank of England notes.

---

[4] The work of Gilbart, Babbage, and Jevons on seasonal variation is also discussed in Nerlove, Grether, and Carvalho 1995.

[5] The "Currency School" was of the opinion that trade fluctuations and crises were often due to overissue of notes by the Bank of England and/or by country banks. The solution to this problem was to make the Bank of England the sole issuer of bank notes and force the Bank to adhere to a strict ratio of cash (gold and silver coin) and bullion to notes circulating. The "Banking School," while generally in favor of the Bank of England having a monopoly on note issue, thought that business fluctuations were nonmonetary in origin and that sustained overissue by either the Bank of England or the country banks was not possible. The money stock was self-regulating and a strict cash ratio was neither needed nor helpful.

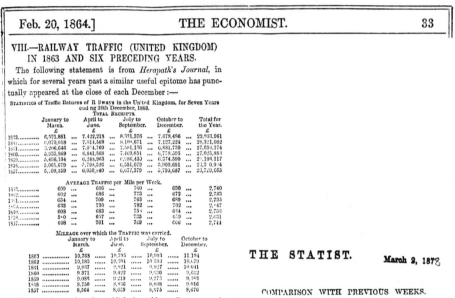

(No. 2.)—A Table of the Circulation of the Bank of England on the first and third Tuesdays in the Months of January, April, July, and October, in the years 1834 to 1839; showing the effects of the payment of the Public Dividends.—(Appendix, No. 16.)

	1834.	1835.	1836.	1837.	1838.	1839.
	£	£	£	£	£	£
January 1 ..	17,422,000	17,005,000	16,714,000	17,097,000	17,092,000	17,529,000
" 3 ..	20,089,000	19,100,000	18,416,000	19,033,000	19,693,000	19,478,000
April 1	18,544,000	18,092,000	17,727,000	17,964,000	18,578,000	18,111,000
" 3	19,194,000	19,146,000	18,773,000	19,375,000	12,789,000	18,869,000
July 1	18,689,000	17,410,000	17,310,000	16,884,000	18,737,000	17,611,000
" 3	20,249,000	19,490,000	19,108,000	20,036,000	20,807,000	18,850,000
October 1 ..	18,326,000	17,111,000	17,190,000	18,104,000	18,616,000	16,857,000
" 3 ..	19,398,000	18,055,000	18,247,000	18,764,000	19,308,000	17,646,000

Feb. 20, 1864.]   THE ECONOMIST.   33

VIII.—RAILWAY TRAFFIC (UNITED KINGDOM) IN 1863 AND SIX PRECEDING YEARS.

The following statement is from *Herapath's Journal*, in which for several years past a similar useful epitome has punctually appeared at the close of each December :—

STATISTICS of Traffic Returns of Railways in the United Kingdom, for Seven Years ending 26th December, 1863.

TOTAL RECEIPTS.

	January to March.	April to June.	July to September.	October to December.	Total for the Year.
	£	£	£	£	£
1863	6,521,881	7,422,218	8,331,376	7,678,486	29,953,961
1862	6,070,618	7,014,569	8,194,671	7,127,224	28,351,082
1861	5,206,646	7,004,760	7,581,186	6,881,730	27,694,274
1860	5,955,869	6,841,568	7,469,851	6,778,595	27,025,883
1859	5,436,134	6,245,963	6,986,433	6,374,590	25,106,117
1858	5,061,679	5,798,526	6,554,075	5,909,681	23,300,964
1857	5,109,359	6,050,840	6,077,379	5,795,687	23,729,665

AVERAGE TRAFFIC per Mile per Week.

1863	609	686	760	690	2,740
1862	602	686	773	672	2,733
1861	634	709	763	689	2,795
1860	633	730	782	702	2,747
1859	608	683	754	684	2,732
1858	580	657	735	659	2,631
1857	608	701	769	666	2,744

MILEAGE over which the TRAFFIC was carried.

	January to March.	April to June.	July to September.	October to December.
	£	£	£	£
1863	10,763	10,795	10,993	11,194
1862	10,183	10,204	10,501	10,679
1861	9,817	9,921	9,927	10,011
1860	9,371	9,422	9,530	9,622
1859	9,086	9,219	9,273	9,383
1858	8,750	8,836	8,838	9,016
1857	8,564	8,659	8,675	8,676

This table shows that the published weekly traffic returns of railways for the United Kingdom for the year 1863 amounted to 29,953,961*l*, being an increase of 1,632,878*l* over the returns for the year 1862, which increase is much more than the average increase for the past seven years.

THE STATIST.   March 2, 1878

COMPARISON WITH PREVIOUS WEEKS.

The following shows the Receipts from Customs, Excise, and Stamps in each of the last eight weeks, compared with the corresponding period of the previous years :—

	Customs		Excise		Stamps	
	1878.	1877.	1878.	1877.	1878.	1877.
	£	£	£	£	£	£
January 5..	277	314	196	392	178	206
12..	508	509	626	529	223	223
19..	388	358	705	620	179	193
26..	405	397	726	716	185	202
February 2..	375	327	799	803	228	232
9..	410	436	868	827	226	224
16..	387	369	585	542	232	190
23..	351	357	383	356	204	217

Figure 5.2   Financial tables in cycle-time framework. *Source:* Top – Gilbart's Table 2 in Bell 1842; Middle – *The Economist* 1864, 33; Bottom – *The Statist*, March 2, 1878, 17.

Gilbart's table illustrating the seasonal circulation of Bank of England notes is reproduced at the top of Figure 5.2. Gilbart argued that through such tables he had discovered "laws" in the uniformity of the seasonal patterns:

> The general law is, that the circulation [of the country bank notes] always makes one circuit in the year, being at its lowest point in August, and advancing to December, and continuing to advance to its highest point in the month of April, and then descending to its lowest point in August. . . .

>Another law which regulates the circulation of the Bank of England is some cause by which the circulation of the Bank of England is always at its lowest point in December. The circulation of the Bank of England ebbs and flows four times in the year; it is high in January, and descends to March; it rises again in April, and descends to June; it rises again in July, and descends to September; it rises again in October, and descends to December; but the December point is always the lowest point throughout the year, and this is the case in every year. (Gilbart, quoted in Bell 1842, 45)

The relative time framework also proved useful for the tabulation and analysis of railway statistics. This is evident in tables in *Herapath's Railway Magazine* and *The Economist* (see middle table in Figure 5.2) and in the tables and graphs in Dionysius Lardner's treatise on the *Railway Economy* published in 1850. Lardner's work was an inspiration to Jevons, and Lardner's graph on the variation of the daily traffic with the change of the seasons (Lardner 1850, 360) is an early example of connecting means in a relative time framework.

Jevons's Charts of Seasonal Variation

The relative time format used by traders and bankers for making "rude comparisons" was adopted by Jevons in his 1862 study of weekly, monthly, and quarterly fluctuations in the accounts of the Bank of England.[6]

>Taking the weekly accounts of the seventeen complete years, 1845 to 1861 inclusive, I have simply ranged them under each other in their numerical order within the year, and drawn the averages with all suitable precautions against error. All non-periodic variations seem to be nearly eliminated, and the seasonal variations remain. (Jevons [1862] 1884, 5)

Jevons argued that "facts carefully marshaled" were essential to the inductive investigation of the "intricate phenomena of trade and industry" (Jevons 1884, xxiv). The tabular marshaling of a long time series into a weekly, monthly, or quarterly arrangement was common financial practice, but Jevons embellished the analysis with the calculation and reference to means, the representation of laws with the plotted connection of the means, and the analysis of deviation from the path of the connected means.

These were the inputs of scientific practice: recognition of statistical population or sample, measurements of and focus on central tendency and deviation from the center, and laws manifested in lines or curves. Jevons was conscious of his scientific seal on the investigation of commercial phenomena, and he appealed to financial writers to adopt his practices. He expressed surprise that

---

[6] Jevons's presentation was summarized in *British Association, Notes & Abstracts* (Report of the 32nd Meeting, October 1862), published in 1863. Jevons's table of weekly averages of the Bank of England accounts was first published in *Journal of the Royal Statistical Society* in 1866 and reproduced in *Investigations in Currency and Finance* (1884). Jevons's complete paper on periodic commercial fluctuations and the tables and graphs of monthly and quarterly means were not published until they appeared in *Investigations in Currency and Finance.* Jevons's graphs of the monthly and quarterly means are reproduced in Figure 5.3.

financial writers did not calculate averages for referencing each week in the year, and he argued for the adoption of comparisons with reference means. In retrospect, he saw one of the main contributions of his 1862 study as providing tables of weekly means of the Bank of England accounts. Jevons was disappointed that his own calculation of averages got little distribution in the commercial world. Although his paper was presented to the British Association in 1862, the tables were printed only in 1866 (in an academic journal), and Inglis Palgrave (1873) stands alone among contemporary financial writers to refer to Jevons's tables (Jevons 1884, xxviii).[7]

In each of Jevons's charts of monthly fluctuations reproduced in Figure 5.3, his lines connect the means of twelve monthly cross-section samples that had been formed from one time series. For example, the point of 3.9 plotted for the January value of the average rate of discount was the mean discount rate for all the Januarys from 1845 to 1861.[8] These seventeen January values were treated as independent of each other and as random selections.

The graphs of quarterly seasonal variation were also constructed from time series rearranged into cross-section groups. Jevons's adjacent maps of monthly and quarterly paths through relative time serve as excellent examples of complementary time framework analysis. The monthly and quarterly patterns depicted by the lines connecting means of the cross-section samples are similar but by no means identical. The motion is different and the stories used to explain such motions are different. For example, Jevons looked, unsuccessfully, to the socially imposed quarterly time table of account settlements for an explanation of monthly fluctuations in bankruptcies.

In his 1862 study of seasonal variation, Jevons compared monthly or quarterly means to draw conclusions about typical, temporal, local maximums and minimums. Jevons noted, for example, the maximum of bankruptcies in the fourth quarter, which he thought was caused by the high rate of discount in the third quarter. With the evidence presented in the monthly chart, he argued that the occurrence of panics in October and November was due to "a periodic tendency of commercial distress and difficulty during these months" (Jevons [1862] 1884, 8).[9] The stories conveyed in Jevons's graphs were not historically accurate ones, in the sense that the processes mapped out were never identically observed. Jevons's story was meant to be a myth of typical experience that was repeated year after year if one could ignore the noise.

[7]   Stephen Stigler (1982) sees Jevons's main contribution to statistics as his advocacy for aggregating social data and ignoring the myriad of the specific influences that would cancel each other out. Stigler argues, however, that Jevons failed to take the "next logical step" to a probabilistic approach that would give a measure of confidence in his aggregates.

[8]   The dotted line in the top chart is based on thirty-seven observations for each month from 1825 to 1861. Jevons was thus able to illustrate structural change in seasonal variation in the mid-nineteenth century by comparing the solid line with the dotted line.

[9]   Jevons would not have been surprised that the two major crashes of the New York stock exchange in 1929 and 1987 and the liquidity crisis in 1907 that eventually led to the founding of the Federal Reserve were in October (see Klein 1995a). His theme of the tendency toward financial crisis in the fall was amplified in "On the Frequent Autumnal Pressure in the Money Market and the Action of the Bank of England," presented to the Statistical Society of London in 1866. It was in this paper that Jevons first printed the tables of the weekly averages of the Bank of England accounts. The paper, tables,

The cycle time format to track seasonal variation was not an end in itself for Jevons; it was the means for determining the unusual, irregular variations via comparison by subtraction. The goal of his analysis in 1862 was to mimic the merchants' reasoning and net out the typical course of commerce in order to identify the irregular or nonperiodic changes, which Jevons argued were "probably of more interest and importance" (Jevons [1862] 1884, 4). Jevons's method of calculating and connecting mean values to reveal the periodic variation, then subtracting the mean value from the actual values to focus on the instantaneous deviation, is a method of decomposition of time series. In this sense, Jevons's procedure of locating, then eliminating, the seasonal component is similar to John Poynting's and Reginald Hooker's use of moving averages to first reveal then eliminate the trend component of time series data. The raw data plotted in absolute time yielded fluctuations. Scientific chefs, such as Jevons and Hooker, prepared and cooked the raw data and transformed the fluctuations into oscillations and deviations. In the science of means, all laws had to be compatible with the law of deviation in its exponential form.

Jevons also decomposed the series of weekly averages into the "artificial" fluctuations of months and quarters, which were socially dictated by the timing of dividend payments and other claims, and the "natural" fluctuations of the year, which were driven by harvest and crop cycles. The netting out of the "artificial" movements was achieved by subtracting the average for the week in a typical quarter from the average weekly value in the year (Jevons 1863a, 158; [1862] 1884, 6).

Commercial practice was not the only input into Jevons's method of analyzing commercial fluctuations. He also argued for the adoption of the scientific methods of investigating fluctuations that had been employed in meteorology and terrestrial magnetism (Jevons [1862] 1884, 4). Jevons had shown a keen interest in meteorology in his earlier days in Australia. He had made daily recordings of the weather and had written essays on clouds and the Australian climate.[10] With seasonal variation, as well as with eleven-year trade cycles, Jevons sought explanations for commercial fluctuations in meteorological cycles. The applicability of relative time analysis was one of many features common to both meteorology and economics, and Jevons was not alone in connecting the two.

Economy and Weather; Economics and Meteorology

In the nineteenth century, there were close links between economics and meteorology in terms of phenomena, theory of phenomena, the practice of quantitative observation of the phenomena, and the observers themselves.

---

and diagrams, which an editor of *The Statist* plotted from the tables, were reproduced in *Investigations in Currency and Finance.*

[10] A good biographical essay that includes a description of Jevons's work in Australia can be found in chapter 2 of Margaret Schabas's book on Jevons's mathematical analysis (Schabas 1990). The first two volumes of Collison Black's collection of the papers and correspondence of Jevons also include references to his meteorological interests. Two articles by Jevons on the forms of clouds were published in the *London, Edinburgh and Dublin Philosophical Magazine and Journal of Science*, July 1857 and April 1858.

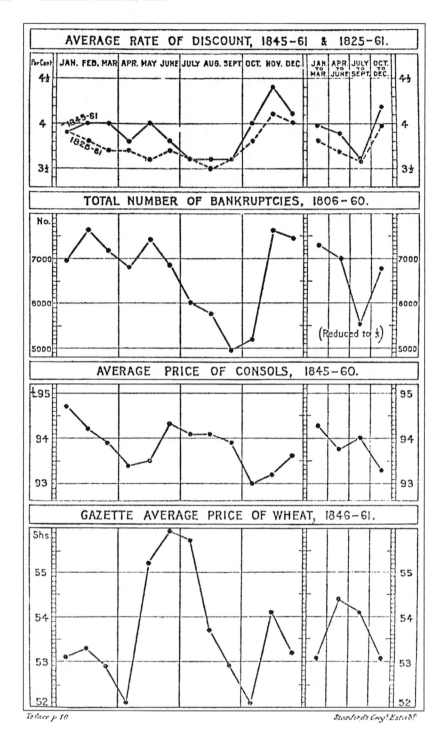

Figure 5.3   Jevons's plots of seasonal variation using a cycle-time framework.
Source: Jevons [1862] 1884, 192.

The price of wheat was the most graphed economic variable of this time; this was symptomatic of both its importance to European economies and its great variation from month to month and year to year.[11] In a similar vein to Quetelet's observation that the price of wheat was the most extreme case of variation he had studied, Jevons perceived the gathering of the harvest to be a cause of some of the most striking fluctuations in the monthly and quarterly charts (Jevons [1862] 1884, 8). Jevons was one of several nineteenth-century quantitative workers to connect economic tides with meteorological fluctuations via changes in the price of wheat.

As early as 1829, George MacKenzie used a relative time framework to explore long cycles in the weather and the economy. MacKenzie's hypothesis was that the preponderance of either solar east winds, solar west winds, lunar east winds, or lunar west winds in Britain determined the fate of the wheat crop for that season and that the nature of the winds and the price of wheat moved in a fifty-four-year cycle. MacKenzie had detailed data on the winds only for the period from 1803 to 1828, but he did possess a continuous series of annual observations on the price of wheat from 1594 to 1827 and occasional observations going back to the year 1202. MacKenzie rearranged the extensive time series of annual average wheat prices into fifty-four cross sections, from which he calculated the average price for that cycle stage (see Table 5.1 and Figure 5.4). MacKenzie argued that the average price of wheat in the first twenty-seven years of the cycle was considerably higher than in latter twenty-seven years of the cycle, and that this difference was related to differences in the nature and direction of the winds and in the quantity of rainfall. Through arithmetic reasoning that was echoed by Christoph Hendrik Diedrik Buys Ballot in 1847, MacKenzie argued that the lack of remarkable differences in the first and second half of the cycle of wheat prices when the data were arranged into a fifty-three-year or fifty-five-year period served as further proof of the fifty-four-year period.

In 1847, Hyde Clarke claimed that before he was aware of MacKenzie's work, he too had noted a fifty-four year cycle in the "physical economy." Clarke tested MacKenzie's old averages against the actual price of wheat from 1827 to 1844, and found support for MacKenzie's "circle" of wheat prices. Clarke speculated that the "cyclar period of famine" was related to fluctuations in the earth's electromagnetic field. Jevons picked up on Clarke's work in searching for cycles in the economy that could be related to meteorological cycles. This is evident not only in Jevons's 1862 study of seasonal commercial fluctuations, but also his 1878 study of trade cycles, which he linked to commercial moods influenced by tropical harvests and sunspot activity.

Many of the ground-breaking late nineteenth-century statistical time series studies that coupled causes with effects coupled the weather or celestial events with the economy. John Poynting (1884), while eschewing any cyclical analysis, reasoned that fluctuations in commodity prices in Europe were connected with those of India through common meteorological changes. John Norton

---

[11] In "The Method of Diagrams and the Black Arts of Inductive Economics" (Klein 1995b), I look at the history of economic graphs including graphs of the price of wheat.

Table 5.1 *George MacKenzie's table illustrating the fifty-four-year cycle of British wheat prices, rainfall, and wind patterns. In columns 4 to 15, MacKenzie rearranged a lengthy time series of wheat prices collected from 1202 to 1827 into fifty-four-year cross sections. The values in column 16 are the average for each cross section. He smoothed the average values to get the "circle" of prices in column 17 (see Figure 5.4). MacKenzie had data on rainfall and wind force (columns 18 to 20) only for the years 1803–1828.*

TABLE I.—*Physical Year, or Cycles of the Winds, Rains, and Prices of Wheat.*

1. General character of the Divisions of Cycle	2. Years	3. Cycle of Lots. East Wind	West Wind	4. 1200 to 1253.	5. 1254 to 1307.	6. 1308 to 1361.	7. 1362 to 1415.	8. 1416 to 1469.	9. 1470 to 1523.	10. 1524 to 1577.	11. 1578 to 1631.	12. 1632 to 1685.	13. 1686 to 1739.	14. 1740 to 1793.	15. 1794 to 1847.	16. Yearly aver. Price of Cycle.	17. CIRCLE OF THE PRICES.	18. No. days of Rain.	19. Sum or No. of Mean Rains.	20. Sum force of the Winds.	21. Periods of Increment and Decrement, &c. of the 54 Year Cycle of the Winds.
Division of 27 years of prevailing Lunar East Winds, of Invariable Winds; of dark Clouds, of durable Cloudiness, of high Winds; and of long Rains, or wet, windy years; and of high Prices of Corn.	1794	L +	L					32				53	34	51	51	44	46				Average Phenomena, &c. Increasing.
	95	L	L			21	35					58	25	47	73	43	48				
	96		S	L	36							56	46	34	76	49	50				
	97		S	S								56	30	25	52	47	52				
	98	L		L	72							56	35	25	50	43	54				
	99	L		L	40	51						53	34	27	67	44	55				
	1800	L	S									57	47	39	110	62	56				
	1	L	S			60	49	16				45	68	35	116	56	57				
	2		S	S		91						45	64	37	68	61	57				
	3	L	L			118		8			64	48	53	37	57	55	58	169	85	82	
	4		S	S								71	32	60	54	58		197	123	86	
	5		S	S								60	38	87	62	59		110	66	72	
	6		S	L								68	42	77	62	59		147	79	77	Extreme Increase of Phenomena, and of the Prices of Wheat, &c.
	7	L		L								64	45	73	61	60		191	106	86	
	8	L		L							48	40	35	79	50	60		176	94	141	
	9		S	L							74	38	34	94	60	59		170	103	167	
	1810		S	S	336				37		56	85	29	45	103	99	59	161	93	86	
	11	L		L			9				53	80	36	60	92	55	58	214	111	119	
	12	L		L				53			80	77	46	50	123	72	58	193	95	128	
	13	L		L							92	73	30	40	107	68	57	187	106	103	
	14		S	S							56	49	26	36	72	48	57	183	82	132	
	15	L	S					22			40	35	28	30	64	37	56	220	113	70	
	16	L	S	-							38	26	41	39	76	44	55	208	106	92	
	17	L		L	36		46				35	33	78	41	94	52	54	199	91	81	
	18	L		L			48	6			29	43	78	47	84	48	52	196	82	84	
	19		S	S			5		5		35	47	54	54	72	39	50	181	89	66	
	1820		S	S							31	65	46	43	66	50	48	175	68	53	
Division of 27 years of prevailing Solar East Winds; of variable Winds; of comminuted Clouds, Winds, and Rains, or dry, clear years; and of low Prices of Corn.	1821		S	L				51	8	36	66	51	57	54	43	46	186	80	65	Average Phenomena, &c. Decreasing.
	22	L		S		6	33	8			33	56	50	58	43	35	44	229	98	74	
	23		S	L				9	6	8	36	70	43	40	52	33	42	214	86	60	
	24		S	L		10				8	57	74	48	43	62	43	40	220	88	85	
	25	L		L		27		16		8	50	57	46	50	67	40	38	213	97	111	
	26	L		L	38			13		8	36	40	39	58	57	36	36	222	71	96	
	27		S	S	10			10		17	38	49	35	59	53	31	35	234	82	85	
	28	L		S	9				8	8	42	36	37	55		28	34	230	89	74	
	29	L		S	30			16		8	48	36	37	51		32	33				
	1830	L		L	48					8	41	40	36	42		36	32				
	31		S	L	10			10		8	38	44	35	45		27	32				
	32		S	L						8	40	42	37	42		34	31				
	33		S	S		37	2				48	42	48	34		35	31				
	34	L	S								46	41	46	36		43	30				Extreme Decrease of Phenomena and of the Prices of Wheat, &c.
	35	L		L	5	15					35	47	42	45		32	30				
	36	L		L							30	69	54	48		50	31				
	37	L	S		6		10				30	65	47	53		35	31				
	38		S	L	6		16				58	38	36	49		34	32				
	39		S	L		9					52	42	33	52		38	32				
	1840	L	S	48							48	59	27	39		44	33				
	41		S	S	40			3			52	60	28	41		37	34				
	42	L		L	12			10			49	45	39	45		33	35				
	43	L		L							36	47	43	51		44	36				
	44		S	L					40	28	44	40	53			41	38				
	45		S	L	62		30				42	40	38	47		43	40				
	46		S	S							55	44	35	42		44	42				
	47	L		S	4						68	47	38	48		41	44				Average Phenomena, &c. Increasing.

† *The Solar and Lunar winds are exactly equal in amount on the average, the rate of each being 175 days wind by the year; the remaining days of the year forming the amount of the calms by the average rate.*

Source: MacKenzie 1829, table I.

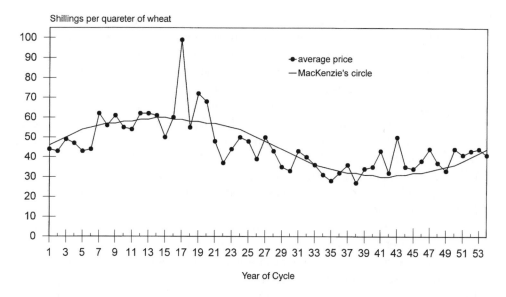

Figure 5.4   My plot of George MacKenzie's data illustrating the fifty-four-year cycle in the price of wheat based on data from 1200 to 1827. The serrated line with the dot markers plots the average annual price of wheat for each of the fifty-four-year cross sections from MacKenzie's column 16 of Table 5.1. The smooth line is MacKenzie's "circle of prices" given in column 17 of Table 5.1. MacKenzie used a geometric form of smoothing (not a moving average) to obtain his circle of prices. The diagram illustrates MacKenzie's assertion that the price of wheat was considerably higher in the first twenty-seven years of the cycle than in the remaining half. The year 1997 would be the forty-second year of MacKenzie's cycle. *Source:* MacKenzie 1829, table I.

(1902) examined the seasonal relationship between credit flows in the New York money market and temperature in New York. Henry Moore (1914, 1923) sought an explanation of business cycles in rainfall or the transit of the planet Venus.

John Norton's statistical study of the New York money market serves as a good illustration of the linking of the weather and the economy in a relative time framework. Norton wanted to quantify the seasonal variation of reserves, deposits, and loans based on weekly data from 1879 to 1900.[12] Norton in essence fitted a trend line to his time series data with the use of a geometric curve, which he labeled as a "growth axis."[13] Norton calculated the percentage deviation from the trend line as the ratio of the algebraic difference of the actual value and the growth axis, to the growth axis value for a given week. Having calculated the percentage deviation, he then took first differences of the percentage variation for each week.[14]

---

[12]   Norton took care in choosing the intervals between his observations. For constructing a time series of financial data, he reasoned, "the week is much nearer the ideal unit; for it combines the practicability of handling with an approximate continuity" (Norton 1902, 15). He urged editors of government publications to consider reporting weekly series.

[13]   Unlike Reginald Hooker (whose work is discussed in Chapters 3, 4, and 9), Norton did not use the word "trend" nor did he represent the growth axis with a moving-average series.

[14]   Norton's pioneering use of first differences is discussed in Chapter 3 and his approach to the decomposition of time series is discussed in Chapter 9.

Norton's first step in using differences to comprehend what he called the "annual period" of reserves (seasonal pattern week-to-week) was to construct tables and frequency polygons to show for each of the fifty-two weeks of the year, the number of years out of twenty-two that there were increases in reserve deviations and the number of years that there were decreases. He also calculated the average weekly changes in reserve deviations and the probable error of these mean values for each of the fifty-two weeks in a typical year. Finally, Norton eliminated data from four years of extreme volatility, took into account the fact that the sum of the advances slightly exceeded the sum of the declines, and sequentially added the changes to obtain a curve showing the "annual period of the reserves" (Norton 1902, 54). He did likewise for loans and temperature.

For the determination of the annual cycle by weeks Norton thus began with time series in absolute time – consecutive weekly observations spanning twenty-two years. He took deviations from the growth axis, calculated first differences of the deviations, and finally analyzed the first differences in relative time. On his relative time graphs, the horizontal axis sequentially ordered the fifty-two weeks of a typical year. The vertical axis measured, for example, the number of occurrences of increases and decreases or the net value of the changes for the relative week. He thus marshaled the single time series of 1,144 observations of first differences into fifty-two cross sections for each week; there were twenty-two values in the sample of week one of the typical year, twenty-two values in the sample for week two, and so on. The steps he took eliminated the influences of trends and business cycles and highlighted the typical seasonal changes. Norton was quite clear about the role of this elaborate analysis in bridging the intuition of the business world with the methodology of the science of observation: "the annual period of the reserve deviations, long known to bankers by experience but hitherto unmeasured, is clearly revealed" (Norton 1902, 102–103).

For the analysis of reserves and loans there were numerous tables and graphs. Norton's Diagram 18 is reproduced at the top of Figure 5.5. The bold line represents the typical annual paths of reserves, the line broken by solid dots tracks loans. Temperature is mapped with the dotted line broken by circles. The numbers on the horizontal axis refer to weeks in a typical two-year stretch. From this diagram, Norton concluded that there was a strong relationship between the three variables, and that with respect to reserves and loans, changes in the former preceded the latter by three weeks. Norton confirmed this time lag with an analysis of the correlation coefficients of the loan period and the lagged reserve period (Diagram 19 in Figure 5.5).

Norton described the relationship between the average temperature and average reserve periods as a "shuttle-cock correlation": there was a positive relationship between the two when the temperature was above the annual average and an inverse correlation when the line of the temperature period was below average (Norton 1902, 95). For Norton, temperature was unquestionably the primary cause of general seasonal variation in the changes in the reserve deviations. Like Stanley Jevons, John Poynting, and Henry Moore,

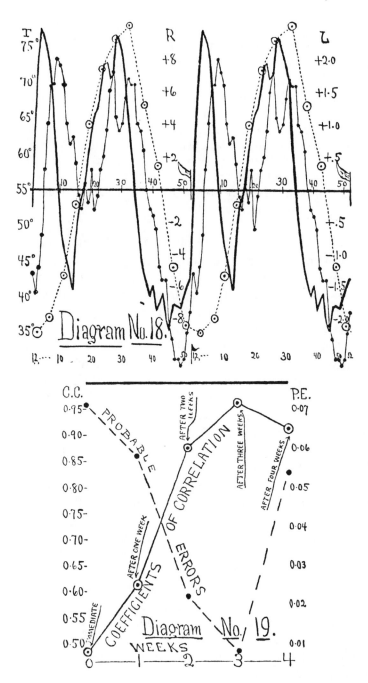

Figure 5.5   Norton's Diagram 18 of the weekly patterns of deviations from the average loan (line broken by solid dots), reserves (bold line), and temperature (dotted line broken by circles) and his Diagram 19 of the correlation coefficient for loan deviations against various lags of reserve deviations. *Source:* Norton 1902, 92.

Norton linked meteorological and economic fluctuations. Norton, however did not look to the heavens – sunspots or the transit of Venus – for cause, but rather to earthly temperature to explain the seasonal, commercial cycles:

> Laws may change, theories may change, local changes of vast importance may come to pass, but the primary facts on which this period rests are not ruled by laws of men, nor modified by theories of reformers, nor escaped by local shifting. It rests on the facts of nature, on the temperature of hemispheres, on the very twistings of the earth upon its axis, and as long as summer follows winter and we obtain our foods from the soil of the earth by the growth processes of nature, somewhere ceaselessly responding will be found this banking rhythm. (Norton 1902, 59)

Nowadays, banking rhythms are rarely, if ever, linked with natural rhythms. Nor is much attention given to seasonal patterns within the year except to eliminate them, behind closed doors, for the presentation of seasonally adjusted data. The loss of seasonality, the separation of credit flows from natural rhythms, and a totally socially constructed reality might be seen by some as indications of economic development and the progress of human civilization. Many critics have scorned Jevons's, Moore's, and Norton's inclusion of meteorological phenomena as exogenous variables in economic functions. The last laugh could be on these "modern" critics and the painful irony facing us in the future might well be that the main fault of the economic models of Jevons, Poynting, Hooker, Moore, and Norton is not that temperature and rainfall were considered as variables, but that they were not treated as endogenous variables in a simultaneous system: climate is now influenced by economic development as well as vice versa.[15]

Parallel to the cause–effect connection of the economy and the weather in the nineteenth-century statistical models was the similarity of the quantitative methods of nineteenth-century economics and meteorology. Statisticians working with commercial data were just as at home with meteorological data. For example, Reginald Hooker, who was one of the first to apply the correlation of deviations from moving averages and the correlation of first differences to commercial data, went on to apply statistics to "agricultural meteorology" and served as president of the Royal Meteorological Society. The raw material in statistical studies of meteorology and economics was also similar: it was usually time series data that yielded skewed distributions and cyclical and seasonal patterns. These characteristics of the phenomena and of the quantitative observations of the phenomena of meteorology and economics stand

---

[15] Despite the ridicule, contemporary and since, given to theses theories linking trade cycles with meteorological and astronomical phenomena, the studies of Jevons and Moore continue to receive serious attention by historians of economics. Among recent examples, Mary Morgan (1990) focuses on the statistical innovations and failings of Jevons's and Moore's work in the context of econometric studies of business cycles; Sandra Peart (1991) examines the importance that Jevons attached to commercial moods as the link between solar activity and industrial production; and Philip Mirowski (1984, 1990) explores the reasons for the ridicule of Jevons and Moore in the context of the neoclassical paradigm that eschewed notions of systematic instability, extraterrestrial shocks, and anything that might hint of astrology.

in contrast to the cross-section observations and normal distributions more commonly found in biology and psychology.

In addition to theory and method, metaphor was a link between meteorology and economics. The economists searched for measurable variables that could be "barometers" of commercial fluctuations, and the metaphor of "tides" was a common allusion in nineteenth-century tracts on seasonal and trade cycles.[16] Jevons, Gilbart, and many nineteenth-century financial commentators spoke in terms of the ebbs, flows, and tides of credit. The tracking of tides, like the tracking of credit, lent itself to a cycle time analysis.

Lubbock's Study of Tides and Lunar Phases

The life and work of John William Lubbock captures the nineteenth-century nexus between meteorology and economics. Lubbock was a working partner in the Lubbock & Co. banking firm and also investigated tides, eclipses, the orbits of comets, and planetary perturbations. He was a fellow of and his work was published by the Royal Society, the Royal Astronomical Society, the British Association, and the Society for the Diffusion of Useful Knowledge. Lubbock also published tracts on money and banking, and his diagrams of credit flows and tidal progressions are remarkably similar.

Lubbock was one of the first investigators to graph empirical and hypothetical commercial processes, and Jevons paid tribute to Lubbock's stimulus to his own work on fluctuations. In his book *On Currency*, published anonymously in 1840, Lubbock used fact curves in absolute time to display co-relationships between the observed values of bullion and bank note circulation. He also used law curves to hypothesize the lagged co-relationships in a relative time framework of intervals after an initial policy change.[17]

Whether he was wearing the hat of the banker or the hat of the almanac maker, Lubbock was a *practitioner* of mathematics. He was a principal contributor to the *British Almanac* published by the Society for the Diffusion of Useful Knowledge (SDUK). The similarity of the meteorological tables in the *Almanac* to the tables published in financial journals is striking. Meteorological tables, like commercial tables, were a marshaling of observations taken over time into a serial or cross-section format. Many of the tables constructed for the almanacs and the financial press assumed seasonal or cyclical variations had priority over other types of variation. Figure 5.6 shows the page for the month of January in the *British Almanac* of 1830.

The meteorological almanac tables differed in some respects from the commercial tables. The numbers in the former were often forecasts derived from mathematical equations. The forecasts were of the timing of events such as

---

[16] Regarding nineteenth-century economists' appropriation of metaphors from other sciences, Tim Alborn (1994) has illustrated the appropriation of the circulation metaphor from physicians and Philip Mirowski (1990) has examined the appropriation of the energetics metaphor from physics.

[17] Fact curves are curves plotted from empirically observed data; law curves are plots of hypothesized relationships. This distinction in economic graphs and the historical importance of Lubbock's graphs are discussed in "The Method of Diagrams and the Black Arts of Inductive Economics" (Klein 1995b). Lubbock's path-breaking work in monetary theory is discussed in Henderson 1986.

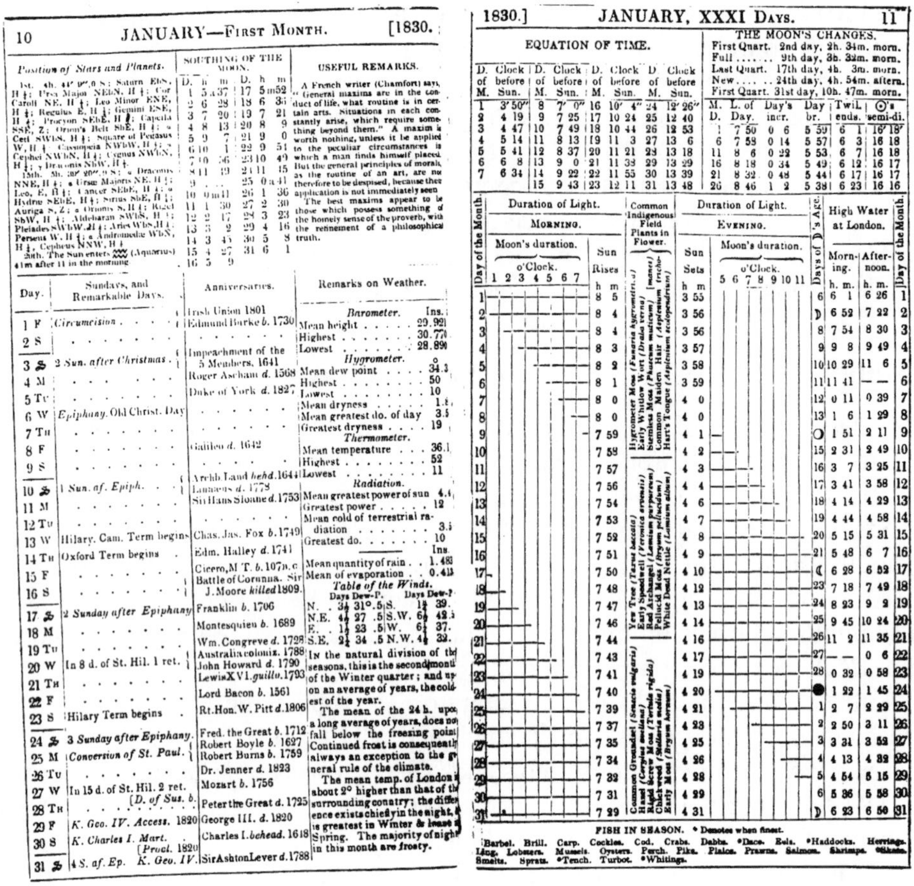

Figure 5.6   The entry for January 1830 in the *British Almanac* published by the Society for the Diffusion of Useful Knowledge.

the time of the moon's rise or the moment of high water. In contrast, the numbers in the commercial tables were always observations from the past (e.g., yesterday's price); there was no forecasting based on mathematical equations in the nineteenth-century financial journals. Another distinguishing feature of the meteorological tables was their focus on measurements of central tendency (e.g., mean monthly temperature) or dispersion (highest and lowest temperatures for that month) as key references. Also the graphic quality of the relative time tables (e.g., the "table" on the duration of lunar light in Figure 5.6) is unique. Measurements of central tendency and dispersion and the use of functional lines and equations were part of the erudition that the Society for the Diffusion of Useful Knowledge hoped would trickle down.

The investigation of lunar phenomena in particular called forth relative, cycle time analysis. In the 1830 *Companion to the British Almanac* and in his 1833 study of the "semi-menstrual inequality" of the time of high water, Lubbock used the relative time framework of phases of the moon (as measured

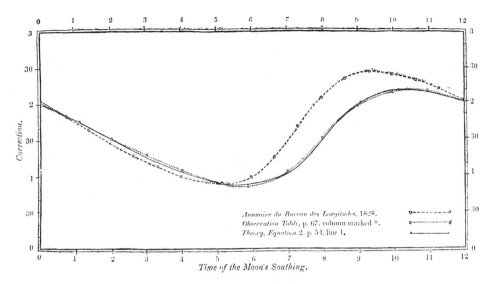

Figure 5.7   Lubbock's plot of the timing of high water in the lunar cycle. *Source:* Lubbock 1830, 65.

by the time of the moon's transit across the meridian) to rearrange 13,073 time series observations on the daily difference between the time of high water at the London docks and the time of the moon's southing (the moon's transit across the meridian). He plotted a curve connecting the means of the eleven constructed cross sections and visually compared this with curves based on his equation for prediction of the establishment of ports (the time of high water) and the predictions from the French *Annuaire du Bureau des Longitudes* (see Figure 5.7).

Lubbock's connecting-means-in-cycle-time analysis was directed toward interval information as a step toward answering a larger question. In his investigations of tides, the intermediate question was, What was the interval of time between the southing of the moon and the time of high water? The answers could be used as an empirical check on the predictions deduced from trigonometric equations. This was useful in the construction of more accurate tide tables. Lubbock, however, also saw the interval determination as a step toward predictions of gravitational pull and determination of the mass of the moon relative to that of the earth. With his relative time graphs on currency, Lubbock attempted to answer the question, What was the interval of time between a policy change at the Bank of England and its effect on circulation? Speculation on this led to the question of just how major a factor was the length of the interval in causing policy overshooting. Lubbock in effect asked, What was the relative mass, and thus the gravitational effect, of bullion or Bank of England notes on country bank circulation?

Lubbock the banker and almanac maker observed and reshaped time series into cross sections. Lubbock the mathematician produced laws by calculating and then visually connecting means of these synthetic cross sections.

Quetelet's Study of *l'Homme Moyen*

Adolphe Quetelet, who was, like Lubbock, an astronomer and mathematician, was another pioneer in the graphing of processes in a relative time framework. In a study presented to the Brussels Royal Academy in 1827, Quetelet included a diagram plotting the average temperature, number of births, and number of deaths for each month of a typical year in Brussels.[18] Quetelet also used plots of connected means in relative time to summarize human development over a life cycle, but these data originated as cross-section observations. The relative time plots of human development were studies in what Quetelet called "social physics." Quetelet adapted the physical concepts of equilibrium, motion, and center of gravity and the law of observational error to mass social phenomena.

Subjects for Quetelet's investigations into equilibrium and motion included:

- population growth and social prosperity
- development of human stature, weight, and strength
- development of moral and intellectual faculties
- development of the social system

After establishing the importance of looking at the social body and asserting his confidence in the law of large numbers, Quetelet focused on the average person, *l'homme moyen*. In 1835 he published *Sur l'homme et le développement de ses facultés, ou Essai de physique sociale* (the English translation, *A Treatise on Man and the Development of His Faculties*, was published in 1842).[19] Quetelet's treatise brought together various studies on human development that had been presented to the Brussels Royal Academy. Quetelet calculated the means of height, weight, intelligence, and the like for cross sections of the population of the same age. For Quetelet, the mean was more than an empirical average; it was the "target" of a divine shooter, who displayed "admirable economy" in creating human civilization. No one individual may have had the characteristics of the average man, the target may not have been hit a single time, but with numerous observations it became "so well pointed out by the marks around it, that they would aid at once in rediscovering it, if it should chance to be lost sight of" (Quetelet [1835] 1842, x). The target of *l'homme moyen*,

---

[18]   In the same year, Pierre Simon Laplace and his colleague A. Bouvard published their studies on the within-day changes of barometric pressure over the months of the year. This was a follow-up to Laplace's 1823 test of the hypothesis that the moon caused tides in the atmosphere analogous to those in the oceans. In the earlier study Laplace took the difference of the mean diurnal change for the days immediately near the new and full moon. In 1827, they rearranged a single time series of diurnal changes into cross sections for each month of the year. Stephen Stigler (1986) discusses the "right" and "wrong" details of Laplace's two studies in light of current statistical theory.

Christoph Hendrik Diedrik Buys Ballot also made use the relative time framework in his 1847 inquiry into the effect of the solar rotation cycle on temperature. Buys Ballot's table, which many consider a precursor to Schuster's periodogram, is discussed in Chapter 9.

[19]   Quetelet's concepts of *l'homme moyen* and *méchanique sociale*, his connection of liberal politics and statistical laws, and his legacy of applying the law of error to social mass phenomena are discussed in Porter 1986, Stigler 1986, Hilts 1973, and Hankins 1908.

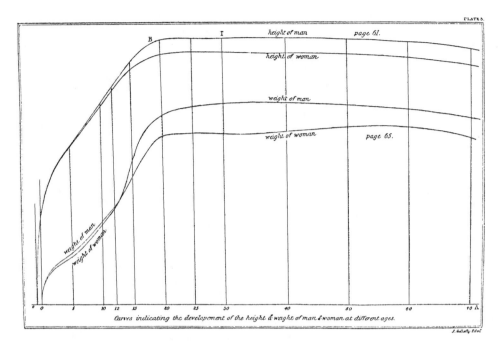

Figure 5.8   Quetelet's growth curves for Belgian males and females. *Source:* Quetelet [1835] 1842, plate 3.

Quetelet argued, should be recognized as society's center of gravity. The latter concept was held in high regard by Quetelet, who often mentioned the usefulness of assuming a singular point in studying the physical forces.[20]

Quetelet's studies of human developmental variation focused on the growth of the average individual from birth to death. This process of change is repeated in every individual. Quetelet assumed constant conditions and was thus able to use cross-section data and logic to look at developmental variation. Figure 5.8 reproduces Quetelet's curves showing the growth patterns of the average man and average women by age. The plotted point for each age represents the mean height or weight calculated from a cross section of Belgians of each age. The growth curves are lines connecting means in the relative time of the human life cycle.

The arrangement of data by age was repeated with several other characteristics including number of crimes detected, number of literary works published, number of deaths, pulse rate, and strength of grip. Figure 5.9 reproduces Quetelet's curves of connected means in relative time for the first two. The following passage is typical of Quetelet's interpretations of the patterns observed

[20] That singular point need not even reside in a physical mass. In his *British Almanac* essay on tides, Lubbock (1830, 50) praises the approach of the seventeenth-century mathematician John Wallis, who assumed a common center of gravity between the moon and the earth. The reduction of the relationship between the earth and the moon into a single fictitious mass with one center, rotating on its own axis, and revolving around the sun, enabled Wallis to explain and predict tidal phenomena.

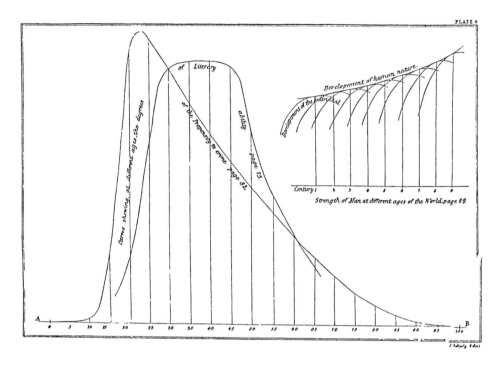

Figure 5.9   Quetelet's plots of the propensity to crime and literary ability by age and his hypothetical curve of the development of human strength by generations. *Source:* Quetelet [1835] 1842, plate 4.

when he put the cross-sectional data into a relative time framework of age in the human life cycle:

> Towards the age of 24, there is a peculiar circumstance connected with men; namely, a maximum which is not observed in the curve of mortality of women. The period of this maximum coincides with that when man shows the greatest inclination to crime; it is the stormy age of passion, which occupies a most conspicuous place in the moral life of man. (Quetelet [1835] 1842, 32)

Empirical investigations in which one of the variables under examination is age have unusual qualities. An analysis of change over time can be done with an individual at different stages of her or his life cycle, or people of different ages, at one point in time, can be a mass surrogate for one person. If one is trying to determine the relationship between height and age of people, does one take a sample of different aged people and for one moment observe various heights and ages? Or does one need observations on one person over an entire life? The former is usually the most convenient since the study can be completed in a much shorter time period, but there are other considerations. In the cross-section study, one risks the possibility that the relationship has not been the same for all historical time periods covered by the ages of the sample. A period of famine might have affected one age group, short people might live longer. The latter consideration was put forward by Quetelet to explain the decline in height as the growth curves for men and women approach the end of the life cycle.[21]

A longitudinal study can highlight historical influences – for example, recent longitudinal studies on U.S. females who are in their thirties and of those who are in their fifties show remarkable differences in relation of age to labor force participation, first marriage, birth of first child, and other factors. A cross-section study of the relationships of any one of these characteristics to age would describe a pattern that no women from any generation has experienced or will experience.

One of the first investigators to construct a longitudinal check on Quetelet's cross-section methods of quantifying human development was Henry Pickering Bowditch. In a study of twelve American children presented to the Massachusetts State Board of Health in 1872, Bowditch derived growth curves similar to those of Quetelet's with the exception that near age twelve, the height of females exceeded that of males. The board commissioned Bowditch to conduct a more thorough study of the growth of children in Boston. Bowditch's 1877 and 1891 investigations, based on cross-sectional data on over 24,000 school children, also produced growth curves in which the curve of females overtook that of males between the ages of twelve and fifteen. Bowditch's longitudinal and cross-section studies on human development, which included not only the mapping of means, but also the mapping of percentiles, were the precursors of growth curves commonly used by pediatricians today.[22] In addition to the growth curves, composite photography was another method by which Bowditch adapted the tool of connected means to look at the aging process. Influenced by Francis Galton's interest in composite photography, Bowditch photographed many different groups of people and for each group constructed a composite portrait that was meant to represent the typical, the mean of that group.[23] Composite photography was a method for determining average values from "unmeasurable anatomical peculiarities" (Bowditch 1894, 331). This technique was used by Bowditch, Galton, and others in mental institutions to capture the typical portrait of those suffering from specific mental illnesses, in prisons to capture the portrait of a typical criminal, and at colleges to capture the portrait of a typical student for a graduating class. Figure 5.10 reproduces Bowditch's composite portrait of the typical American female

---

[21] The theme of an inverse correlation between life expectancy and height has been recently taken up in an article in *Challenge* magazine. Dennis Miller (1990) argued that the difference in average life expectancy between women and men was possibly due to the fact that short people lived longer than tall people. Osteoporosis as a process of "shortening" the spine with aging could also serve as a modern explanation for the shape of Quetelet's curves.

[22] In his fascinating book *On Growth and Form*, D'Arcy Wentworth Thompson discusses and illustrates the work in cycle time of Quetelet, Bowditch, and many other nineteenth- and twentieth-century investigators.

[23] Galton first wrote on composite photography in the 1870s. One of his several descriptions of the technique and equipment needed appears in an appendix to *Inquiries into Human Faculty and Its Development*. Bowditch argued that his approach (described in Bowditch 1894, 342) was much simpler than Galton's.

Figure 5.10   Bowditch's composite photograph of 287 American female college students. *Source:* Galton Papers 158/1A, The Library, University College, London.

college student. The portrait was based on 287 individual photographs taken during the late 1880s.[24]

In 1894, the popular *McClures Magazine* published an article by Bowditch entitled "Are Composite Photographs Typical Pictures?"[25] To support his affirmative answer to this question, Bowditch included individual and composite portraits of Boston physicians and portraits of the same group five years later (reproduced in Figure 5.11). The left group forms one cross section, the right another cross section, and the composites in the center are the means for each sample. The viewer's process of glancing at the left central portrait then the right, is a process of connecting means to capture the aging process.[26]

Like Quetelet and Karl Pearson, Bowditch justified the significance of focusing on possibly nonobserved centers with the metaphor of the target:

> From the relation which these dimensions bear to each other, typical forms may be deduced, which though not accurately representing any individual in the group, are yet more truly *representative* of the group than any individual can be, for they are ideal forms round which individuals group themselves in accordance with the law of accidental variation, as shots group themselves round the bull's-eye of a target. (Bowditch 1894, 331–332)

[24] The composite photograph of the female American college student, scores of other composite photographs, and Bowditch's correspondence with Galton are in the Galton Papers at the archives of the University College, London. Using a composite portrait to capture the typical individual of a group was not just a late nineteenth-century fad. On September 11, 1995, Rebecca Quick reported in the *Wall Street Journal* that General Mills was planning to digitally "morph" photos of seventy-five women into one image of the Betty Crocker of the nineties. The contest, to have your photo form a part of the composite that would grace cake boxes around the world, was open to women of all races between the ages of 18 and 118 who had a love of baking, family, and community. Computer technology has also enabled researchers to take composite faces to a three-dimensional level. In the December 1995 issue of *Scientific American*, Mahusree Mukerjee reported on a study that should enable burn victims to use three-dimensional plastic masks painlessly created from two-dimensional photographs using a "meanhead" and several "eigenhead" variations. Joseph Atick, Paul Griffin, and Norman Redlich of Rockefeller University derived a mean shape from scans of 347 air force pilots. They combined the mean with up to 40 standardized variations derived from eigenfunctions to form a database of generic facial shapes from which shading in two dimensions could be translated into three-dimensional form.

[25] In this article Bowditch compared the composite photographs of horse-car drivers, horse-car conductors, and Boston physicians to illustrate that the composites captured the different degrees of intellectual expression of countenance in the three groups. Like Galton, Bowditch saw the construction of a composite as a "beautifying" process that eliminated individual irregularities, and he argued for its use in ethnography and the study of racial physiognomy. In an article entitled "Mean Looking," *The Economist* (May 5, 1990) reported on a study by Judith Langlois and Lori Roggman that claimed verification of Galton's notion that composites were more beautiful and appealing that the originals from which they were formed. These two psychologists from the University of Texas at Austin formed several composites from the digitized photographs of ninety-six women and ninety-six men and reported that people found the composites more attractive and that the more faces that went into making the composite, the more appealing the composites were. Langlois and Roggman linked the appeal of the typical to a human comfort with simple recognition and the notion that the mean value was the end result of the survival of the fittest in natural selection.

[26] Artist and photographer Nancy Dahlstrom pointed out to me that with regards to several features of the Boston physicians – the shape of the face, for example – the composite photograph is not a good average of the individual portraits. It is also interesting to note that composite photography would not be so successful in capturing the typical American female college student or Boston physician in the late twentieth century. The variations for these groups are now considerable. A sample of Boston physicians, for example, would include females and people from diverse races and nationalities with disparate hair styles. This increase in diversity in the United States stands in contrast to Quetelet's supposition that variation would decrease with the progress of civilization. On the other hand, Bowditch chose a group of physicians that dined at the same club; there might still be considerable homogeneity in a sample determined by who eats with whom.

Figure 5.11   Bowditch's portraits and composites of Boston physicians at one point in time and five years later. *Source:* Bowditch 1894, plates 1, 2.

The image of the target is reinforced in the arrangement of the individual portraits around the bull's-eye of the composite photograph.

The mean points of cross sections connected by lines in relative time are more like moving targets than moving averages are. It is ironic that stochastic processes[27] are often contrasted with deterministic processes. The two notions

27   According to the *Oxford English Dictionary* (2nd ed., 1989, vol. 16, 730), stochastic is derived from the Greek expression meaning "to aim at a mark."

are as similar as they are different. The process of shooting at a target seems closely associated with determination. There is a purposeful, teleological quality to the rifle range that is rarely acknowledged in the joining of the image of aiming and firing to the those of dice-throwing Gods or urn-picking populaces.

It is also ironic that if the divine shooters hit the target of *l'homme moyen* at every age, the result could be a nonviable process. Many have criticized Quetelet's static image of *l'homme moyen*. The combination of average length legs, arms, torso, and organs could very possibly be a dysfunctional, impossible form. Similar criticism can be applied to Quetelet's dynamic image of human development. The "law" displayed by the path connecting means in the human life cycle could envision a highly improbable process of growth. Bridging through cycle time is misleading if there is a significant organic relationship to values that are less time-distance away than the interval of a complete cycle. This is the risk of connecting cross-section means in cycle time.

Quetelet was very sensitive to the choice of time interval in constructing his samples and the choice of time framework in structuring his stories. He examined the diurnal cycle by hour, the monthly cycle by day, the annual cycle by month, the human life cycle by year, and the secular trend of human civilization by generations. The latter was obviously a hypothetical rather than an empirical inquiry. Quetelet entertained the possibility that with regards to some characteristics, the evolutionary variation of the species over many generations could well mimic the developmental variation exhibited by humans:

> I have said that, although the laws of the development of human nature were not generally the same as those of the average man of any one period, yet these laws might in certain circumstances, be identically the same; and that human nature, under certain circumstances might be developed in a manner similar to a single individual.[28] (Quetelet [1835] 1842, 100)

For Quetelet, the key to understanding the principles of social physics (the true mechanics of human history) was to follow the changes in the average man in many nations from one generation to the next. Quetelet's theory of human evolutionary variation involved hypotheses on both changes in the measurement of central tendency (*l'homme moyen*) and in the measurement of dispersion (the range of the cross section of the population). In some cases, such as that of scientific knowledge, the capacity of the average person would increase with succeeding generations. Quetelet illustrated this hypothesis of an increase in the value of human strength through the passing ages of the world with a hypothetical connected-means graph, which is reproduced in the upper right corner of Figure 5.9.

Quetelet's theory of the social physics of the "civilizing" process also included an hypothesis of a progressive decrease in the magnitude of dispersion as society became more perfectly focused on the ideal of *l'homme moyen*:

> One of the principal facts of civilization is, that it more and more contracts the limits within which the different elements relating to man oscillate. The more knowledge is diffused, so much the more do the deviations from the average disappear: and the more consequently, do we tend to approach that which is beautiful, that which is good. (Quetelet [1835] 1842, 108)

In addition to using the relative time framework of the human life cycle,

---

[28]   This faith in the similarity of certain developmental and evolutionary processes is in one way inconsistent with Quetelet's vision of the progress of human civilization. He alleged that the civilizing course was one in which the variations decreased with time, as humans gravitated toward the ideal *l'homme moyen*. However, as he, Charles Darwin, and many others have observed, variation across a species is least at the embryonic stage and increases with the age of the cohort group.

Quetelet also explored the "laws of periodicity" in diurnal and seasonal variation. In using observations taken over time, Quetelet took pains to distinguish
variation over the day, variation over a month, and variation over a year. In
several cases these were treated as separate populations with distinct frequency
distributions. Quetelet compared ranges in different relative time periods and
concluded that often the periodic influences on variables were more significant
than constant or accidental causes. In such cases, the diurnal variation often
exceeded the seasonal. Quetelet's conclusions on the frequency of births by
time of occurrence illustrate his articulation of the laws of periodicity:

> The regular and periodic causes, which depend either on the annual or
> diurnal period, produce effects on society which are more sensible, and which
> vary within wider limits than the combined, non-periodic effects annually
> produced by the concurrence of all the other causes operating on society; in
> other terms the social system, in its present state, appears to be more dissimilar
> to itself in the course of one year, or even in the space of one day than during
> two consecutive years; if we have reference to the increase in population.
> The diurnal period seems to exercise a somewhat stronger influence than
> the annual period, at least so far as births are concerned. (Quetelet [1835]
> 1842, 108)

Quetelet was sensitive to the choice of intervals in selecting the observations
for analysis. His methods of social science had a major impact on the work
of the biometricians, but there was little choice involved in selecting biometric
analytical intervals. Francis Galton, Karl Pearson, and Raphael Weldon were
concerned with the phylogenous issues of evolution and inheritance. The most
important interval in such studies is that between generations.

Galton's Connection of Means in Logical Time

Francis Galton's first regression exercise is one of several variations on the
theme of connecting means in relative time. In February 1877, he presented
a study on the "Typical Laws of Heredity" to the London Royal Institution.
Pearson and other historians of statistics have treated Galton's 1877 paper
as the first major step in the development of correlation and regression analysis.
Galton's application of the law of deviation (the normal curve) to heredity,
his notion of reversion to the ancestral mean, and the articulation of "r" as
a mathematical coefficient of co-relation are all present in the 1877 study.
Galton's concluding remarks give a flavor for his metaphorical comprehension
of the typical laws of heredity:

> We see by them that the ordinary genealogical course of a race consists in
> a constant outgrowth from its centre, a constant dying away at its margins,
> and a tendency of the scanty remnants of all exceptional stock to revert to
> that mediocrity, whence the majority of their ancestors originally sprang.
> (Galton 1877, 298)

Unable to collect adequate data on humans, Galton first quantified the laws

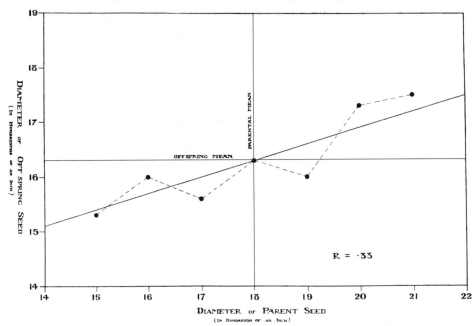

Diameter of Parent Seed	Diameters of Filial Seeds.								Total.	Mean Diameter of Filial Seeds.	
	Under 15.	15-	16-	17-	18-	19-	20-	Above 21-		Observed	Smoothed
21	22	8	10	18	21	13	6	2	100	17·5	17·3
20	23	10	12	17	20	13	3	2	100	17·3	17·0
19	35	16	12	13	11	10	2	1	100	16·0	16·6
18	34	12	13	17	16	6	2	0	100	16·3	16·3
17	37	16	13	16	13	4	1	0	100	15·6	16·0
16	34	15	18	16	13	3	1	0	100	16·0	15·7
15	46	14	9	11	14	4	2	0	100	15·3	15·4

Figure 5.12   The regression polygon and data table based on Galton's 1877 lecture to the Royal Institution. *Source:* Top graph – Pearson 1920, 35; Bottom table – Galton 1886, 260.

of heredity with the use of sweet pea seeds. Believing that sweet peas were self-fertilized, Galton compared the weight and diameters of the singular parent pea seeds against the weight and size of their offspring. Starting with a large number of parent seeds, Galton grouped them by size and until he had scores of seeds for each of seven sizes. The packets of homogeneously sized parent seeds were distributed among friends and planted. At the end of the growing season, Galton measured the sizes of the offspring seeds harvested from each bed, in which a few months before parent seeds of identical size had been sown. In essence, Galton broke the filial seeds into separate groups of observations determined by parental size. For each sample, he quantified the weight and diameter of the offspring and constructed a frequency distribution and a mean.

A data table for the exercise, which Galton reproduced in 1886, and the diagram based on the Galton's data, which Karl Pearson's assistant, Miss A. Davin, produced in 1920, illustrate Galton's method (see Figure 5.12). Galton's estimate of r, the correlation coefficient, for parent and offspring pod diameters was one-third. Galton arrived at that by smoothing the connected means of the seven samples into a straight line.[29] The means were connected not in cycle time but in the logical time framework of the parent seed dimensions ordered from smallest to largest.

This first exploration into regression was quite different from the frequency surface approach to correlation that Galton and Karl Pearson developed in later studies (see Chapter 7). Galton's x variable had a discrete, uniform distribution. Each of the seven parent groups, however, generated normal distributions in size of offspring. Although the y variable had a random component, the x variable did not. Also Galton was constrained by time's arrow. Starting the experiment with a uniform distribution of the size of sweet pea seeds, Galton could only go in one direction. He could not first observe the size of the offspring seed and from there pursue the size of the parents.

In his 1877 lecture, Galton made many visual and verbal references to the two-dimensional "law of deviation in its exponential form," but the image of the three-dimensional surface of deviation in an exponential form was not to come for several years. The regression approach of connecting means in the logical progression of the size of the x variable was more akin to the practical manipulations of financiers and almanac makers than the mathematical reasoning of Gauss and Bravais. What is notable about Galton's adaptation of Lubbock's, Quetelet's, Bowditch's, and Jevons's method of connecting means in cycle time was his leap from cycle time to logical time.[30]

Conclusion

The relative time framework is one of the most useful tools in statistics and time series analysis. The connecting of means of observations marshaled in cross sections of relative time can tell stories such as typical growth over a

---

[29] It is interesting to note that Galton labeled the last column of his data table "smoothed" rather than "estimated" or even "calculated."

[30] Galton had corresponded with all four. Quetelet had provided Galton with meteorological observations in his construction of European weather maps. Letters from Jevons and Lubbock can be found in the Galton Papers in the archives of the University College. Of particular interest to me was Jevons's answers in 1879 to Galton's "Questions on the Faculty of Visualizing." Galton had surveyed many distinguished scientists to "elicit the degree and manner in which different persons possess the power of seeing images in their mind's eye." Jevons, who made such stunning strides in the use of diagrams in both inductive and deductive economics, was obviously not up to par in the visualizing powers that Galton tested – across Jevons's return, Galton scribbled "lower quartile" (Galton Papers, 152/2B, University College, London).

 Another relative time influence on Galton was through correspondence with Henry Pickering Bowditch. In working on his growth charts for 24,000 Boston schoolchildren in the mid-1870s, Bowditch tried to quantify the relationship between weight and height for different ages. Helen Walker (1929, 100–101) has documented Bowditch's approach to Galton on this and Galton's reply on the construction of a curve to capture the relationship.

life cycle, the timing of high tide over a lunar cycle, the price of wheat over the course of a typical year, or the tug of war in inheritance between the parent and the ancestral mean of the species. The stories might be ends in themselves, as Quetelet's study of growth of the average man was, or they may be one stage of decomposition. As an example of the latter, Jevons wanted to map out typical seasonal variation in order to eliminate it and focus on irregular fluctuations.

Plots in cycle time continue to be used as statistical tools. With every recession, U.S. Federal Reserve Banks pull out the cycle time graphs and plot the average values of macroeconomic indicators against months or quarters after the peak of a typical cycle. The tradition of plotting average values in different stages of the business cycle originated with Wesley Mitchell and the National Bureau for Economic Research. The NBER method rearranged quarterly values into nine stages of the cycle: stage one is the quarter of the initial trough; stage five the quarter of the peak; stage nine the quarter of the final trough; and stages two, three, four, six, seven, and eight can have the average of one or several quarters of data depending on the length of the cycle. With this method, the absolute date loses importance, and place in the sequence of a typical cycle marks the time of these graphs. One of the remarkable features of Mitchell's innovative use of a relative time framework was his suggestion of unequal intervals between stages of the business cycle (time deformation as it is sometimes called nowadays); the distance between each relevant observation could vary between one or several quarters.[31]

Relative time played an important part in Francis Galton's first regressions investigating the laws of inheritance and evolution. In Galton's experimental work, control of the observation process replaces mere storytelling. With regression, Galton connected the offspring mean of the low values of the parent generation to the offspring mean of the next higher value of the parent generation. Galton's regression line pivoted on the hereditary center of gravity – the central point that coordinated the average from a cross-section of one generation with the average of the cross section of another generation. The use of a relative time framework in the statistical studies of change through cycle time or of logical time fed into the development of the notion of an autoregressive process. Udny Yule (1926) argued that perceiving variables as functions of place in a sequence was often more fruitful than modeling them as functions of absolute, calendar time.

There are links between the relative time framework of statistical models and the relative time framework of historical narratives. In *The Measure of Times Past: Pre-Newtonian Chronologies and the Rhetoric of Relative Time*, Donald Wilcox juxtaposes the linear, absolute time framework of most modern historians with the episodic, relative time framework of classical historians such as Herodotus and Thucydides. In absolute time studies, the first priority is the

---

[31]   The original suggestion for the method can be found Mitchell 1927 and 1929, with more development in Burns and Mitchell 1946. Howard Sherman's *The Business Cycle: Growth and Crisis under Capitalism* (1991) makes extensive use of the NBER method of connecting means in a cycle time framework. Also plots connecting typical monthly values ordered by months after the peak can be found in recession issues of the Federal Reserve Bank of Cleveland's *Economic Trends*.

dating of all events on the B.C./A.D. time line championed by Isaac Newton. Truth is approached through precision and accuracy; Wilcox echoes Thucydides in using the Greek work *akribeia* to describe this quality of truth. In relative time narratives, on the other hand, place in local sequences is important, divorced from notions of universal dating. Accuracy and quantitative precision give way to verisimilitude, *aletheia*. This approach to truth is related to notions of cycles in history; one driving force for Thucydides' use of a relative time structure was his belief that the events he described would probably happen again in a similar way. Wilcox argues that the honest approximations to the general truth in relative time histories are often more appropriate than the date-it-first, ask-questions-later approach of modern history. In this latter approach, rhetoric is used only as expression at the end of the historian's task in an effort to make the facts readable. With relative time narratives, rhetoric was used to investigate and discover the truths of historical processes.[32]

In relative time statistical studies, the story told by a line connecting the averages from the matrix of cross sections is a myth; the process under study never emerged by such a route. Myths can play important roles in the construction and expression of a culture, and Lubbock, Quetelet, Jevons, and Galton all saw their connections of means in relative time as laws revealed through science. Notions of science, mathematical laws, and statistics, however, all connote precision and accuracy. There might well be a trade-off between *akribeia* and *aletheia* that is not acknowledged by statisticians. Although there may be verisimilitude in the lines connecting means in relative time, we may be pushing our luck by also making claims of precision. Also, if the organic connections of processes in time are stronger within the cycle than between cycles, the mythical law of seasonal process may, like Quetelet's *l'homme moyen* of average arm length, average leg length, and average torso, be improbable, nonviable, or even impossible. Nevertheless, the relative time framework remains one of the most effective tools for the quantitative analysis of temporal processes, and its full potential, particularly when coupled with unequal intervals, has not been fully realized.

The rearranging of time series data into cross sections in cycle time had obviously proved profitable to bankers, speculators, and navigators. The lines added by the law-making scientists bridged time and decomposed and reconstructed processes of change. There was, however, some philosophical questioning of the use of law lines – for example, Alfred Russel Wallace's complaint to Francis Galton that Galton's persistent use of the law of errors curve hid the evidence of natural selection inherent in the empirical data points that deviated not just from the mean but the law curve itself (see Figure 7.4).

The greatest danger in placing too much confidence in the statistical structure in relative time lies with the interpretation of lines in a model time

---

[32] Wilcox laments the fact that few modern historians have used a relative time approach and argues for the use of that approach, particularly in histories of cultural, social, and political identities. I consider chapter 7 of Mary Morgan's *History of Econometric Ideas* (1990) a good example of the relative time history Wilcox is calling for. A sequence of imaginary letters by econometricians from 1900 to 1950 (appropriately signed with Greek names) gives clarity to the story of the development of econometric modeling.

framework. This is best illustrated with Galton's regression line. With the two-dimensional regression diagram, the viewer usually marks time in the logical progression of the x variable from the smallest to the largest value. With Galton's data on sweet pea seeds we would not make the mistake of saying that as the parent grows the offspring grows, or worse, as the parent shrinks, the offspring shrinks. We know from the nature of the experiment and the presence of the regression polygon, from which the smoothed line was constructed, that the correct interpretation is that large values of y are associated with large values of x. In many other cases of regression, however, we can easily slip into the process-of-change-over-time mode and allege that our line tells the story of how y changes with changes in x. Our comprehension is not simultaneous; it too is a process in time. As our eyes follow the regression line, the law unfolds from left to right as x gets larger. In cases of lines connecting the mean y values conditional upon the x values, logical time is easily confused for process or historical time.

Part II

Subject Context and
Statistical Theory

Statistics, state, static. Whether by word association or etymology, one is led to believe that statistics is a study of mass phenomena at rest. Yet statistics is and has been used in comprehending processes of change in economies, species, and weather. In Part II of this book we look at how mathematically inclined investigators reconciled static comparison and dynamic fluctuation. There is more concentration in this part on scientific arithmetic, in contrast with the emphasis on monetary and political arithmetic in Part I. I am particularly interested in how the *subjects* of the investigations engendered different routes in getting from fluctuation to deviation. What distinguished statistical reasoning in the investigative contexts of observation processes, biological processes, meteorological processes, and economic processes?

We will see that when natural philosophers used a statistical way of thinking to marshal observations from dice throwing or surveying there was little, if any, contradiction between the framework of static comparison and the temporal nature of the observation process. The contradictions were most pronounced with measurements on the economy and, to a lesser extent, the weather. It was with these subjects that statisticians drafted the algorithms of the traders and financiers for service in the decomposition of time series.

Part I of this book was a history of the practical roots of data manipulation methods used to reconcile the static nature of statistical method with data from temporal phenomena. We connected standard tools of mathematical decomposition, such as serial differences or moving averages, to a rich past of trading, speculating, persuading, and veiling. Part II is a history of theoretical searches for models of processes that could reside in "rest space" (the functional space in which one can effectively use equations and probabilistic algorithms associated with cross-section observations taken at one moment in time). It is about the who, how, and when of getting time series in forms amenable to the science of means and laws of deviation. This exploration also raises questions about the opportunity costs of conforming time series to rest space. Do we risk shedding the structure and texture that constitutes history when we decompose our time series until we reach the stationary residues? How is that opportunity cost tied in with our appropriation of the algorithms from men who traded in money and accumulated capital?

6

Laws of Chance and Error in the Observation Process

Whence, finally, this one thing seems to follow: that if observations of all events were to be continued throughout all eternity (and hence the ultimate probability would tend toward perfect certainty), everything in the world would be perceived to happen in fixed ratios and according to a constant law of alternation, so that even in the most accidental and fortuitous occurrences we would be bound to recognize, as it were, a certain necessity and, so to speak, a certain fate.

Jakob Bernoulli [1713] 1966, 65–66

Fixed ratios and certain fates are not terms we, at first glance, associate with playing cards or reconciling discrepant measurements of the same object. Had we eternity to observe, however, we would, according to Jakob Bernoulli, see the constancy and certainty veiled in shorter glimpses of chance. In itself that idea is not very novel, even for the eighteenth century. What was novel, however, was Bernoulli's demonstration that we didn't have to wait for eternity; a semblance of constancy and certainty would come to us in a relatively quick, nonlinear fashion as we increased the number of trials. What is more, we could determine how many trials would be needed for a specific level of certainty. After a while, summing observations from each trial and redistributing that sum over all the trials would yield an expected value consistent with experience and deductive reasoning. The sole role of time was to make things clearer.

Observing coin tosses over many trials and then summarizing the observations with an expected value are a far cry from capturing empirical laws of interest rates or barometric pressures over time. Yet, probability theory, built on a foundation of examples from games of chance, is an essential component of the statistical analysis of processes that do not proceed only by chance. This chapter lays the groundwork for judging the role of early probability theory in the development of time series analysis. We will see that the algorithm for determining the average value by summing and redistributing that sum over the inputs has a legacy in economic traditions and commercial practice.

The main story in this chapter, however, is not about roots of commercial practice but about the development of a theory built on logical comparison. It was philosophers and mathematicians, not merchants, who equated the average with the notion of mathematical expectation and took the further step of assessing the likelihood of deviation from that expected value. This chapter examines the statistical theory of the observation process developed in the studies of games of chance and measurement error from the seventeenth to the early nineteenth century. It begins with the late seventeenth-century and early eighteenth-century work of Christiaan Huygens and Jakob Bernoulli that seemingly had little to do with analyzing temporal phenomena. The chapter ends with the acknowledgments by Russian mathematicians, such as Pafnuty Lvovich Chebyshev, Andrei Andreevich Markov, and Aleksandr Mikhailovich Lyapunov, in the late nineteenth and early twentieth centuries that observing a game of chance was itself a process that evolved within time.

Similar to traversing the English countryside, one cannot help exploring the early history of statistical theory without being constantly aware that others have walked every acre before you. There is little wilderness left for historians of science in examining probability theory. The contributions of analysis of games of chance and observational errors to a statistical way of thinking have been thoroughly examined in other histories. What I have focused on here is how the investigators reconciled the timeless laws of comparison with the temporal nature of both their methods of observation and their subjects of exploration.

Games of Chance

Most histories of probability begin with a history of gambling and games of chance that includes studies such as those outlined in Table 6.1. Leisure speculation on the stability of frequencies in dice throws, or on equitable ways to distribute stakes should a game be halted before its intended finish, generated a mode for quantitative and mathematical reasoning that historians allege is the bedrock for the development of statistical theory. Archaeological evidence indicates that as early as 5000 B.C. the four-sided astragali bone was used as a die and there are many games of chance in a variety of cultures spanning thousands of years. Several historians (Kendall 1960, David 1962, Maistrov 1974) have asked the question, Why, given the long history of dice throwing and card playing, were a theory and a calculus of probability so long in emerging? Among the reasons considered are:

- imperfections in early dice
- persistence of primitive mathematics
- traditions of superstition
- absence of notions of randomness and chance
- evidence that gambling acquired mass popularity only in the seventeenth century

- absence of conditions, until the rise of capitalism, necessary for applications (e.g., quantification of political and social phenomena, a need for rational decision making in civil cases of uncertainty)

An analysis of games of chance gave seventeenth-, eighteenth-, and nineteenth-century natural philosophers a structure for creating order out of the chaos of mass phenomena with an economy of information. Its essential contributions to modern statistical theory were:

1. The notion of mathematical expectation
2. The law of large numbers and other guidelines that enabled investigators to balance increasing precision of prediction with the need to economize on observations
3. The equating of time with trials, such that frequencies of occurrence could be used to explain mass phenomena that seemed to follow no obvious law or pattern on an individual scale

Averages, Mathematical Expectation, and European Law

In the "normal" statistical case, the expected value is the arithmetic mean, the average value. Tracing the origins of the use of the word "average" gives us an indication of the links between the development of probability theory and commercial practice. One of the earliest uses of "average" was as a label for the expenses that were to be equitably distributed among merchants when part of a cargo was lost at sea.[1] An example given by Serjeant Marshall in McCulloch's *Dictionary, Practical, Theoretical and Historical, of Commerce and Commercial Navigation* (1856) illustrates the legal doctrine of average contributions:

> Thus where the goods of a particular merchant are thrown overboard in a storm to save the ship from sinking: or where the masts, cables anchors, or other furniture of the ship, are cut away or destroyed for the preservation of the whole; or money or goods are given as a composition to pirates to save the rest; or an expense is incurred in reclaiming the ship, or defending a suit in a foreign court of admiralty, and obtaining her discharge from an unjust capture or detention; in these and the like cases, where any sacrifice is deliberately and voluntarily made, or any expense fairly and *bonâ fide* incurred, to prevent a total loss, such sacrifice or expense is the proper subject of a general contribution, and ought to be rateably borne by the owners of the ship, freight, and cargo, so that the loss may fall equally on all, according to the equitable maxim of the civil law – no one ought to be enriched by another's loss: *Nemo debet locupletari aliena jactura*. (Marshall, quoted in McCulloch 1856, 50–51)

---

[1] William Stanley Jevons reasoned that average as a notion of redistribution of a whole into equal parts stemmed from the feudal term *averagium*, which referred to the entitlement of the feudal lord to the labor of serfs' farm horses (Jevons [1877] 1958, 363).

Table 6.1 *Analysis of games of chance*

When/where	Specific concept	Author and publication	Discussed in
16th century/ Italy	Relative frequency of outcomes from throw of 2 dice	Cardano, Girolama (1501–1576) 1526 *Liber De Ludo Aleae*	David 1962 Maistrov 1974 Hald 1990
	Arithmetic triangle to compute number of variations in throwing any number of dice	Tartaglia, Niccoló (ca. 1499–1557) 1556 *Trattato general treatist di numeri et misure*	David 1962 Maistrov 1974
	A & B intend to play until one wins 6 rounds. Game must stop with A having won 5 & B, 3. How should stakes be divided?	Pacioli, Luca (1445–1514) ca. 1494, *Summa de Arithmetica Geometria Proportioni et Proportionalita*	Kendall 1956
17th century/ Italy	Relative frequencies of 216 ways of throwing 3 dice	Galilei, Galileo (1564–1642) Before 1642 *Sopra le scoperta dei Dadi*	David 1962 Maistrov 1974 Hald 1990
17th century/ France	Fair distribution of stakes through equality of rational expectations	Port Royal (Antionne Arnauld & Pierre Nicole) 1662 *La logique, ou l'art de penser*	Hacking 1975
	Solution to Chevalier de Mere's problem of how stakes should be divided if game of chance ends before its time.	Pascal, Blaise (1623–1695) Fermat, Pierre de (1601–1665) 1654 *Correspondence*	David 1962 Maistrov 1974 Daston 1988 Hald 1990
17th century/ Netherlands	Mathematical expectation, first published text on calculus of probability	Huygens, Christiaan (1629–1695) 1657 Tractatus de *Rationciniis in Aleae Ludo*	David 1962 Maistrov 1974 Hacking 1975 Hald 1990

Table 6.1 (cont.)

When/where	Specific concept	Author and publication	Discussed in
18th century/ Switzerland	Law of large numbers, limit theorem	Bernoulli, Jakob (1654–1705) 1713 *Ars Conjectandi*	David 1962 Maistrov 1974 Hacking 1975 Daston 1988 Hald 1990
18th century/ England	Bell curve as limit to a binomial distribution, accuracy proportional to square root of number of observations, measurements of dispersion, mathematics of life insurance and annuities	De Moivre, Abraham (1667–1754) 1718, 1756 *The Doctrine of Chances*	Pearson 1923 David 1962 Pearson 1978 Stigler 1986 Hald 1990
	Derivation of binomial distribution "curve" and its properties, rule for obtaining the probability that the required probability lies within given limits	Bayes, Thomas (1702–1761) 1763 "An Essay towards Solving a Problem in the Doctrine of Chances"	Maistrov 1974 Pearson 1978 Stigler 1986

McCulloch points out that this fair principle of average contributions was embodied in Rhodian and Roman law. It is apparent in the *Oxford English Dictionary* that this legal, maritime use of "average" dates from at least as far back as 1500, and it was commonly used, with variations in spelling, in French, Spanish, Portuguese, Dutch, and Italian trade. Given the variety of circumstances under which a ship's cargo might be partially lost or destroyed and the need to ascertain the exact cause of the loss, the determination of the average was often a messy legal battle. McCulloch quotes Lord Tenerden on this aspect: "the determinations of the English courts of justice furnish less of authority on this subject (average) than on any other branch of maritime law" (McCulloch, 1856, 52).

The notion of an average was thus originally tied to the notion of equitable treatment under European commercial law. The notion of mathematical expectation had similar ties in the form of reasoning on aleatory contracts. Lorraine Daston (1988) explores these ties in her pursuit of the question of why some notions of probability were quantified more readily than others. She argues that seventeenth- and eighteenth-century analyses of games of chance focused on quantifiable, civil applications, particularly notions of equitable distribution, expected outcomes, and reliable evidence. In this context, the mathematical analysis of gambling provided rules for rational decision making in cases of uncertainty.

Aleatory contracts were particularly suited as cases that engendered a quantitative reasoning of expectation. Such contracts often involved possible payment of an interest rate and dealt with messy cases of uncertainty and chance. Settlements of these contracts were in terms of money, which lubricated commerce because it quantified value. Aleatory contracts also danced on a fine line between outlawed usury and just reward for risk. This called forth a precise and reasoned rhetoric that was to characterize mathematical writings on games of chance.

Christiaan Huygens was the first of the logicians of the games of chance to articulate formally the concept of mathematical expectation, calling it the "value of the chance" to win a fair game. Jakob Bernoulli in commenting on Huygen's work elaborated:

> The word "expectation" is not meant here in its usual sense in which "to expect" or "to hope" refers to the most favorable outcome; although the least favorable may occur; we would understand this word here as the hope of getting the best diminished by the fear of getting the worst. Thus the value of our expectation always signifies something in the middle between the best we can hope for and the worst we fear. (Bernoulli, quoted in Maistrov 1974, 57)

The emotions of fear and hope were canceled out in a reasoned middle. With the analogy of games of chance, philosophers, such as Bernoulli and Huygens and Abraham De Moivre, numerically determined that middle and proved it was fair, rational, and useful. They also showed that this reasoned middle could straddle one dice throw to the next or one month to another. In some cases, it made sense to declare a middle within the flow of time.

Relative Frequencies and the Stochastic Art

The strong connection between gambling and statistics is acknowledgment of the uncertainty of any individual outcome and the certainty of the outcome of many repeated trials. Gamblers who forsook superstition, which relied on a sense of individual luck or notions of winning and losing streaks, could become extremely sensitive to the relative frequencies of combinations of dice cast. Galileo Galilei was asked by such a gambler to confirm logically his subjective impression that the probability of a ten being thrown with three dice was greater than that for a nine, although both could be made from the same diversity of numbers. Galileo calculated that the probability of a ten being thrown was .125 and that of a nine was .116, a difference of only .009 (Galilei [1642] 1962, 195).

The approach of these gamblers and logicians such as Galileo was to divorce all expectations of the value of one observation from what was thrown immediately before and immediately after.[2] The event was not seen as part of the flow of individual experience. It was one observation picked out of an infinite population of all dice throws. The before and after of one throw can be ignored if one has the patience, as men of leisure and professional gamblers did, to observe many trials. One requires time to ignore time. Over many trials, and thus usually over time, the stability of statistical ratios or frequencies becomes apparent. This tendency toward stability, toward a formal law over time, was the basis for not only mathematical expectation, but also laws, theorems, and eventually geometric structures that could bridge experience and prediction.

In many games of chance we know a priori the probability of a particular outcome, because we are aware of the original design. With most phenomena, however, the probability cannot be determined a priori. The earlier probability theorists had confined themselves to calculating probable outcomes when the only requirement was that the number of cases be equally likely, as in faces of a die or a coin. In *Ars Conjectandi*, Jakob Bernoulli introduced the art of conjecturing, "measuring its probability" – "the stochastic art" – using "the way which is based on trials" (Bernoulli [1713] 1966, 13). Bernoulli was interested in determining a posteriori the probable outcome in order to apply "the art of estimation to civil, moral and economic affairs." A key to this achievement was a clear hypothesis on the relationship between accuracy of estimation and number of trials. An early articulation of a law of large numbers is found in a letter from Jakob Bernoulli to Gottfried Leibnitz written in 1703. Recognizing that common sense dictated that the larger the number of observations available the smaller the risk of falling into error, Bernoulli asked,

---

[2] Interestingly, among the early probability theorists there was at least one who put more stock in luck than in random chance. Cardano's logic of combinations coexisted with his belief in personal luck – for example, winning and losing streaks (see Daston 1988, 36).

whether the probability of an accurate ratio increases steadily as the number of observations grows, so that finally the probability that I have found the true ratio rather than a false ratio exceeds any given probability; or whether each problem, so to speak, has an asymptote – that is, whether I shall finally reach some level of probability beyond which I cannot be more certain that I have detected the true ratio. For if the latter is true, we will be done with our attempt at finding out the number of possible outcomes through experiments. If the former is true we will investigate the ratio between the numbers of possible outcomes *a posteriori* with as much certainty as if it were known to us *a priori*. And I have found the former condition is indeed the case; whence I can now determine how many trials must be set up so that it will be a hundred, a thousand, ten thousand, etc. times more probable (and finally, so that it will be morally certain) that the ratio between the numbers of possible outcomes which I obtain in this way is legitimate and genuine. (Bernoulli [1713] 1966, 70–71)

Abraham De Moivre elaborated on this and proposed that accuracy increased with the square root of the number of observations. De Moivre also deduced the function for the "normal" bell curve from the limit to the binomial distribution. These proofs and tools allowed the calculus of probability to be extended beyond the realms of games of chance where expected outcomes were known a priori. Inductive reasoning could be used to determine parameters a posteriori without having to exhaust the population being studied:

As upon the Supposition of a certain determinate Law according to which any Event is to happen, we demonstrate that the Ratio of Happenings will continually approach to that Law, as the experiments or observations are multiplied: so conversely, if from numberless observations we find the Ratio of the Events to converge to a determinate quantity, as to the Ratio of P to Q; then we conclude that this Ratio expresses the determinate law according to which the event is to happen. (De Moivre [1718] 1756, 251)

The widespread applicability of this analysis was not lost on philosophers of the seventeenth and eighteenth centuries. John Arbuthnot in his 1692 preface to his translation of Huygen's *Tractatus de Rationciniis in Aleae Ludo* noted:

The Reader may here observe the Force of Numbers, which can be successfully applied, even to those things, which one would imagine are subject to no Rules. . . . I believe the calculation of the Quantity of Probability might be improved to a very useful and pleasant Speculation, and applied to a great many Events which are accidental, besides those of Games. . . . all the Politicks of the World are nothing else but a kind of Analysis of the Quantity of Probability in causal Events, and a good Politician signifies no more, but one who is dexterous at such Calculations; only the Principles which are made use of in the Solution of such Problems, can't be studied in a closet, but acquired by the Observation of Mankind. (Arbuthnot, quoted in Pearson 1978, 140)

Similarly, Jakob Bernoulli argued that the art of conjecturing, quantifying probabilities of events, embodied "all the wisdom of the philosopher and all the discretion of the statesman" (Bernoulli [1713] 1966, 13). In a letter to Leibnitz, Bernoulli gave a prescription for the practice of the way which was based on trials: "The following suffices for practice in civil life: to formulate our conjectures in any situation that may occur no less scientifically than in games of chance; I think that all the wisdom of a politician lies in this alone" (Bernoulli [1713] 1966, 70–71).

Despite the advocacy of Bernoulli and others for the wisdom in relying on probability analysis, its diffusion to commercial and legal practice was slow. This is remarkably apparent in the cases of annuities and life insurance. Abraham De Moivre, who did considerable mathematical analysis of annuities and insurance argued that "Although chance produces irregularities, still the odds will be infinitely great, that in process of Time, those Irregularities will bear no proportion to the recurrence of the Order which naturally results from Original Design" (De Moivre [1718] 1756, 251). Annuities and life insurance policies were contracts in the process of time, but until the late eighteenth century, institutions dealing in such contracts ignored the order of mass phenomena and acted on individual assessment.

On one side of a life insurance contract was an insuring institution, which usually expected to stay in business for a long time. On the other was a person who was willing to pay some money now in order for his or her dependents to benefit in the case of that person's death. The timing of death was uncertain, and the insurer could guess by having a good look at the person or by having a good look at the mortality data, if it existed, for a lot of people and reckoning the chance of death at that age. The former was the most common practice until the late eighteenth century. Somewhere between the seventeenth-century insurer, who typically depended on individual evaluation to judge the timing of death, and the late nineteenth-century work of Karl Pearson, who decomposed a curve of British mortality into five chance distributions, lies eighteenth-century probabilists such as Abraham De Moivre and Thomas Simpson and actuaries such as James Dodson and William Morgan.[3] These eighteenth-century logicians argued that evaluating contracts based on a person's age located on a relative frequency distribution tabulated from a cross section of deaths at one time would clinch financial solvency for the insuring institution. Statistics in the form of frozen history were offered as the essential tools for negotiating profitable contracts in time.[4]

---

[3] Karl Pearson's decomposed law of mortality was reproduced (Figure 2.7) and discussed in Chapter 2. William Morgan, who was one of the first to apply mathematical probability theory as a professional actuary in life insurance, was the same Morgan who in 1797 used a mathematical key to decipher the scaled series of bullion holdings of the Bank of England (see Chapter 4).

[4] In their histories of probability theory, Lorraine Daston (1988) and Anders Hald (1990) thoroughly explore the links between probability theory and annuities and life insurance. Daston deals with more cultural and philosophical issues such as the sixteenth-century equating of gambling and life insurance versus the eighteenth-century perception of them as opposites; reasons why the practice of individual assessment persisted despite numerous demonstrations of the stability of ratios with mathematical theory and mortality data; and how the applications of annuities and life insurance influenced the words and

Time = Trials

The remarkable pattern of order observed in games of chance provided a foundation of mathematical reasoning for a science of observation. A set of dice or a deck of cards served as the elements of an experiment that could be repeated many times. The outcomes were discrete and easily measured by frequency ratios. Although each face of the die had an equal chance of being thrown, the numerical combinations and permutations possible with simultaneous throws of two or more dice had different relative frequencies that were revealed by many plays and confirmed by mathematical reasoning. Experience, experiment, and deductive reasoning were in consensus in the analogy of the games of chance.

The striking correspondence between experience and mathematical reasoning is illustrated in Karl Pearson's frequency curves drawn for four examples of games of chance (Figure 6.1). In each case, the dashed line plotting data on frequency of observation is almost identical in form and location to the dotted line plotting predictions from mathematical theory.[5] The experience of recording throws of dice, draws of cards, and tosses of coins was usually in time, but time could be ignored, and inductive and deductive reasoning led to the same vision. Similarly, the plotted pattern of results from one person throwing a die many times would be the same as that for many people each throwing a die at once. Even if not known a priori, the original design and the proof of stability would be revealed in repeated trials – in time without change. Within this context of equating time with trials, a calculus of probability became the basis for statistical theory.

The Treatment of Observational Errors

For mathematicians developing a calculus of probability, games of chance were an illustrative vehicle and life insurance, annuities, and other aleatory contracts their main focus of application. Astronomy and geodesy were the favored applications for mathematicians developing a system for accommodating observational errors. Some key developments in the history of the statistical treatment of errors of observation are highlighted in Tables 6.2 and 6.3. In her history of theories of observational errors, Laura Tilling (1973) states that the first algorithms for systematic treatment of errors in measurement were developed ad hoc for specific practical purposes. The most sophisticated work came out of the attempts to measure the ellipticity of the earth to determine

---

definitions used in the calculus of probability. Daston echoes some of these issues in *The Empire of Chance: How Probability Changed Science and Everyday Life* (1989), a work she co-authored with Gerd Gigerenzer, Zeno Swijtink, Theodore Porter, John Beatty, and Lorenz Krüger. In his mathematical, problem-solving approach, Hald links the earlier work of John Graunt and Edmund Halley with late eighteenth-century work on mortality; compares De Moivre's advocacy of a mathematical law of mortality with Simpson's construction of a life table; and works out formulas for single-life, joint-life, and reversionary annuities.

[5]   The experimental and theoretical curves differ most in the lower right plot of dice throwing. Pearson pointed out that this was due the inevitable bias and imperfection of dice (Pearson 1897, 12).

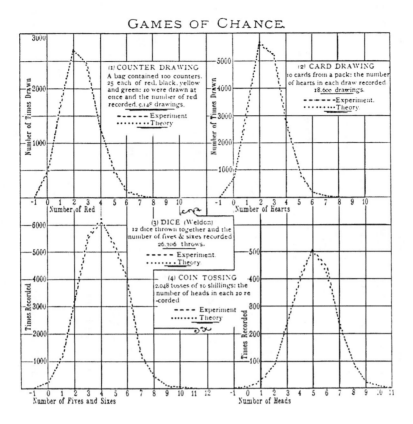

Figure 6.1   Pearson's frequency distributions showing the close correspondence between mathematical theory and the results of many experimental trials in four games of chance. Pearson used this in "The Chances of Death" to illustrate the "notion of law and regularity in chance distributions." *Source:* Pearson 1897, 13.

whether it was oblate, according to Newton's hypothesis, or oblong. Tilling argues that in this area alone there was enough discrepancy between theory and data to warrant a thorough treatment of the effect of errors of observation. Similarly, Stephen Stigler (1986) sees the generation of a method of least squares in eighteenth-century endeavors to determine mathematically the motions of the moon and of Saturn and Jupiter, as well as the shape of the earth. As Stigler points out, the significant contributions to statistical theory from these applications included not only methods of estimating parameters but also methods of quantifying accuracy of estimation and mathematical theories developed to prove that these methods were the best.

A major problem confronting scientists of the seventeenth and eighteenth centuries was, if the correctness of ideas was to be decided not on authority, or even just logic, but on observation, how did one systematically deal with errors of observation? Galileo Galilei was very critical of the blind reliance on authority and championed the virtues of observation. In his *Dialogue Concerning the Two Chief World Systems*, Galileo discussed methods of determining the position of a celestial body, the new star of 1572. Thirteen observations were

Table 6.2 *Analysis of errors in measurement: Nature of errors and frequency distributions*

When/where	Specific concept or method	Author, date of publication, publication	Discussed in
17th century/ Italy	Errors in measurement inevitable, symmetric distribution, small errors more probable than large ones.	Galilei, Galileo (1564–1642) 1630 *Dialogue concerning the two Chief World Systems – Ptolemaic and Copernican*	Maistrov 1974
18th century/ England	Mean of a great number of observations is preferable to any single observation, first consideration of continuous distribution of errors, each observation treated as one face of a many-sided die	Simpson, Thomas (1710–1761) 1755 "A Letter … on the Advantage of Taking the Mean of a Number of Observations in Practical Astronomy" 1757 *Miscellaneous Tracts on Some Curious and Very Interesting Subjects in Mechanics, Physical Astronomy and Speculative Mathematics*	Tilling 1973 Maistrov 1974 Stigler 1986
18th century/ Switzerland	Principle of maximum likelihood	Bernoulli, Daniel (1700–1782) 1778 "Dijudicatio maxime probabilis plurium observationium discreptantium atque verismilliam inductio inde formanda"	Kendall 1961
18th century/ Germany	Numerical rules for estimating precision of observations, principles of maximum likelihood and of minimization of maximum residual	Lambert, Johann H. (1728–1777) 1760 *Photometria, Sive di Mensura et Gradibus Luminis Colorum et Umbrae*	Sheynin 1971 Tilling 1973 Tilling 1975
19th century/ Germany	Probability distribution of errors	Gauss, Carl Friedrich (1777–1855) 1809 *Theoria Motus Corporum Coelestium*	Pearson 1923 Maistrov 1974 Stigler 1986
19th century/ France	Central limit theorem, hypothesis of elementary errors, use of Gaussian, (normal) distribution for inverse probability	Laplace, Pierre Simon (1749–1827) 1810 "Mémoire sur les approximations des formules qui sont fonctoins de trés grands nombers et sur leur application aux probabilités"	Stigler 1986

made, all of which gave conflicting positions. The problem was deciding which position was the correct one:

> Simplico: I should judge that all were fallacious either through some fault of the computer or some defect on the part of the observations. At best I might say that a single one, and no more, might be correct, but I should not know which one to choose. (Galilei [1632] 1967, 281)

Galileo's characters in the *Dialogue* eventually concluded:

- Errors were inevitable.
- There is no bias to overestimation or underestimation.
- Small errors were more probable than large ones.
- The size of the errors depended upon the precision of the instrument.

The only essential properties of the statistical theory of errors absent in Galileo's dialogue were those that can be derived from the notion of a measurement *process*: that increasing the number of observations reduced the likelihood of error of estimation, that this accuracy increased in proportion to the square root of the number of observations, and that an algebraic equation or geometric form could summarize the properties of errors in measurement.[6]

Simplico's belief that truth, if it were to be found, lay only in a single actual observation, was a common one in the fifteenth century. Even as late as the nineteenth century, philosophers such as William Whewell had to take pains to explain that a constructed value, such as the mean or a slope on a fitted line, was more true than individual, observed facts. The immensity of this conceptual leap was acknowledged by Thomas Simpson writing in 1755:

> The method practised by astronomers, in order to diminish the errors arising from the imperfections of the instruments and of the organs of sense, by taking the mean of several observations, has not been so generally received, but that some persons of considerable note have been of the opinion and even publicly maintained, that one single observation, taken with due care, was as much to be relied on as the Mean of a great number. (Simpson 1755, 83)

Simpson proved that "the taking of the mean of a number of observations, greatly diminished the chances for all the smaller errors and cuts off almost all possibility of any great ones." He did so by treating an error as if it were the face of a many-sided die, "each die having as many faces as the result of one single observation can come out different ways" (Simpson 1755, 86). A prerequisite for the application of the mathematical analysis of games of chance

---

[6] In an interesting illustration of the novelty of the first of these characteristics of the measurement process, Stephen Stigler (1986, 16–31) points to the differences between the approaches of the mathematician Leonhard Euler and the practical astronomer Tobias Mayer to a similar problem of combinations of observations in astronomy in the mid-eighteenth century. Euler was afraid that aggregation of observed equations would increase errors of estimation, but Mayer recognized that errors would cancel each other out and that the likely error of an estimate would decrease with a greater number of observations.

Table 6.3 *Analysis of errors in measurement: Combinations of observations subject to error*

When/where	Specific concept or method	Author, date of publication, publication	Discussed in
18th century/ England	Determine most probable place of true value in plane of several observations by taking weighted mean	Cotes, Roger (1682–1716) 1722 "Aestimatio errorum in Mixta mathesi, per variationes partium trianguli plani et spherici"	Kendall 1961 Eisenhart 1961 Eisenhart 1964 Tilling 1973 Stigler 1986
18th century/ France	Measuring irregularities in observed orbit of planets by extending zero-sum of residuals to multiparameter problem	Euler, Leonhard (1707–1783) 1749 *Piece qui a remporte le prix de L'Academie royale des sciences, sur les inegalities du mouvement de Saturne et de Jupiter*	Kendall 1961 Eisenhart 1964 Tilling 1973 Stigler 1986
18th century/ Germany	Method of averages applied to lunar libration and combination of observational equations when number of equations exceeds number of unkonwns, estimate of accuracy of determination	Mayer, Johann (1723–1762) 1750 *Abhandlung uber die Umwalzung des Mondes um seine Axe*	Kendall 1961 Eisenhart 1964 Tilling 1973 Stigler 1986
18th century/ France	Criteria for line of best fit for pair of observations measuring ellipticity of the earth: Σ of + and − residuals in y direction to be equal Σ of absolute values of all residuals as small as possible.	Boscovich, Roger (1711–1787) 1757 *De Litteraria Expeditione per Pontificiam ditionem ad dimetiendas duas Meridiani grandus*	Eisenhart 1961 Eisenhart 1964 Tilling 1973 Stigler 1986

Table 6.3 (cont.)

When/where	Specific concept or method	Author, date of publication, publication	Discussed in
18th century/ France	In $y = a + bx$, a & b be chosen so as to minimize the absolute value of largest deviation	Laplace, Pierre Simon (1749–1827) 1783 *Memoire sur la figure de la terre*	Whittaker 1944 Eisenhart 1964
	Determination of all unknowns through combination of equations of condition	1787 *Théorie de Jupiter et de Saturne*	Tilling 1973 Stigler 1986
	Algebraic formulation of Boscovich's algorithm for minimizing residuals	1789 *Sur les degres mesures des meridiens, et sur les longueurs observees sur pendule*	
	Method for minimizing absolute value of maximum error by weighting observations	1799 1805 *Traite de mecanique celeste*	
19th century/ France	Least sum of squared residuals of which the arithmetic mean is a special case	Legendre, Adrien Marie (1752–1833) 1805 *Nouvelles methodes pour la determination des orbites des cometes*	Whittaker 1944 Eisenhart 1964 Seal 1967 Tilling 1973 Stigler 1986
19th century/ Germany	Maximum probability of zero error of estimation, first connection of least squares with theory of probability	Gauss, Carl Friedrich (1777–1855) 1809 *Theoria Motus Corporum Colestium*	Pearson 1920 Whittaker 1944 Eisenhart 1964
	Least mean squared error of estimation	1821–1826 *Theoria combinationis observationum erroribus minimis obnoxiae*	Seal 1967 Maistrov 1974 Tilling 1973 Stigler 1986

to the science of observation was divorcing measurement error from cause and effect, from the individual observer, from measurements that had been taken sequentially before or would be taken sequentially after, and from time.

Laura Tilling has suggested that the establishment of a probabilistic theory of errors came more from the mathematician's search for applications of analysis of games than from the practitioner's search for mathematical analysis to eliminate the irregularities caused by observational error. States and learned societies encouraged the connection of mathematical theory and navigational and geodesic practice with the incentive of prizes, such as that offered for the best method of determining longitude at sea. By the early 1800s practical algorithm and probabilistic theory were philosophically joined. Pierre Simon de Laplace, Carl Friedrich Gauss, and Auguste Bravais formulated equations for a curve and a surface describing a law of distribution of errors and the least squares method for determining the best combinations of several observations to minimize error. Their treatment was almost totally mathematical, and when mention was made of applications it was to geometric relations between instrument readings and desired measurement arising in astronomy and geodesy. The key assumption for these developments was that the errors of observation being considered displayed random sequential variation and predictable logical variation:

> Certain causes of error depend for each observation, on circumstances which are variable and independent of the result which one obtains: the error that arises from such sources are called irregular or random, and like the circumstances which produced them, their value is not susceptible to calculation . . . and it is certainly necessary to tolerate them in observations. One can however by a suitable combination of results reduce their influences as much as possible. (Gauss [1821] 1957, 2)

Combinations of Observations and Least Squares

The importance of the philosophical and algorithmic work on observational errors is not only in its further generalization of probability distributions. The work on combinations of observations also gave a conceptual and mathematical basis to multiparameter estimation. There was no notion, however, of statistical dependence or stochastic relationships in the earliest uses of a least squares method to estimate parameters. Algorithms such as least squares were first used to reveal the true and singular relationship between two or more variables, which, because of errors in observation, were considered independent of each other. In several empirical problems of geodesy the true values of the variables were deterministically related through mathematical law. The observed pairs or groups of observations of these quantities, however, were subject to measurement errors. Gauss, for example, spelled out the rules governing the use of the method of least squares in a problem in practical geometry:

> To determine the position of a point from the horizontal angles observed from this point between other points whose position is known exactly . . . let us

suppose that for the angular measurements taken at the point whose position is unknown, a theodolite has been used without repetition, with the lens turned successively towards the various known points without the position of the instrument itself being changed. (Gauss [1823] 1957, 168–169)

The goal was to determine the precise location of a point. If the number of unknowns equaled the number of equations, then the solution was simple. Gauss and others of the same mind-set, however, thought accuracy increased with observations. So algorithms, such as the least squares method, were developed to reconcile discrepancies when the number of observations exceeded the number of unknowns. Gauss searched for the best algorithm in the theory of probability:

> Among the combinations, the most advantageous should be chosen, that is to say, those which furnish values whose standard errors to be expected is as small as possible. This problem is certainly the most important which the application of mathematics to natural philosophy presents.[7] (Gauss [1821] 1957, 32)

The development of a mathematical treatment of the combination of errors in observation was paralleled by the developments in graphical analysis of experimental data. For example, in his studies of temperature, magnetism, evaporation, and other physical variations, Johann Heinrich Lambert interposed smooth curves among the observations to discover periodic variation and bivariate correspondence (e.g., Lambert 1779). Lambert assumed symmetry of error and sought to construct the curves as near as possible to their true position by drawing through the middle of the empirical coordinates. His systematic graphical and theoretical treatment of errors of observation was rare for the 1700s.[8] It was not until the 1840s that graphical presentation became a popular technique. By that time, scientists such as James Forbes were graphically interpolating smooth curves through erroneous observations with the use of least squares, which had become the popular tool for sifting truth from facts.

Nowadays, least squares is usually associated with regression analysis. It is acknowledged as a convenient and, in some cases, the best way of fitting a line to estimate multivariate, stochastic relationships. It is important to remember, however, that regression was developed independently of least squares, and that the marriage of the two orchestrated by Udny Yule in 1897

---

[7] In his essay on "The Meaning of 'Least' in Least Squares," Churchill Eisenhart (1964, 24) argues that there were three distinct interpretations of this algorithm: (1) *Least Sum of Squared Residuals* (Legendre 1805); (2) *Maximum Probability of Zero Error of Estimation* (Gauss 1809); and (3) *Least Mean Squared Error of Estimation* (Gauss [1821] 1957).

The first interpretation, by Legendre, was not linked with probability or with a law of error. The most common interpretation used in modern statistics courses is the second, although Eisenhart argues that Gauss preferred the third. With English translations of letters written by and to Gauss and Legendre, R. L. Plackett (1972) documents the feud between the two over priority of discovery. In addition to Eisenhart's and Plackett's essays, readers will find a detailed history of least squares in Stigler 1986.

[8] Oscar Sheynin (1966, 1971) has argued that Lambert, not Gauss, should be seen as the originator of the theory of errors. Laura Tilling (1973, 1975) also treats the pioneering work of Lambert with high regard in her history of the theory of observation errors.

did not come naturally and was not without controversy. In contrast to the work of the biometricians, Yule reduced inexact relationships to single-valued functions and replaced the three-dimensional correlation surface with the two-dimensional regression line. In contrast to the astronomers and geometers, Yule shifted the criteria of normalcy from the observed variable to the residual of a relationship of statistical dependency. Yule essentially initiated the replacement of error in measurement with variation in a relationship. Through the work of Quetelet, Galton, and Pearson, the law of error in observations was transformed into the law of deviation of measurements of the same organ across a species. With Yule's marriage of regression and least squares, law and order in large numbers took the form of a law of the variation of an organic social relationship.

The appeal of Yule's orchestration was that a co-relationship could be statistically estimated without regard to the frequency distribution of the variables. Mathematicians liked it because they could now regress to their hearts' content on economic and meteorological data that rarely formed normal distributions. Indeed, they could achieve greater heights in their discipline by searching for geometric form in the residuals. Social scientists liked it because the benefit of quantitative and geometric *ceteris paribus* was achieved without the need for a real-time case of it in the form of the laboratory experiment. Economists came to appreciate least squares regression because they could, for the first time, draw fact curves in logical time.[9]

Adrien Marie Legendre and Carl Friedrich Gauss had used the criteria of least squares only in cases of variables that would have had an exact mathematical relationship when quantities were free of errors of observation. Some mathematicians, such as Karl Pearson, questioned the appropriateness of Yule using the algorithm to estimate a singular linear relationship between variables that were only organically and loosely related. To Pearson, the least squares method could not be divorced from the law of errors of observation.[10] Legendre, Gauss,

---

[9]   Fact curves refer to lines fitted to actual data. A logical time framework facilitates a comparison of static points, for example, comparing values of y as x is high or low. Many nineteenth-century bivariate plots of experimental data in physical science were fact curves in logical time. Although economists considerably developed fact curves in historical time, there were no economic fact curves in logical time until the advent of least squares regression (see Klein 1995b).

[10] Pearson's objections can be found in a letter to Yule on January 26, 1896, and two letters in September 1896 (all three are in Box 931 of the Pearson Papers, University College, London). For example, in the September 17 letter Pearson wrote that Yule had said that

> physics and biology have no essential difference. I say, yes, they have. In physics you know by experience that the finer your methods of observation and your powers of observation, the more nearly you get your two variables related by a single valued equation and you are justified in trying to find the value of its constants . . . . You speak of the method of Least Squares as being independent of normal variation or theory of errors. But I have never seen anything that I should call a satisfactory treatment of the subject, which is not based in the normal theory of errors and I think Laplace and all the big mathematicians thought so also.

Pearson persisted in another letter a few days later:

> In physics we assume that we reach the single-valued relation, which exists if they were fixed and the method of least squares leads us to its probable form. In biology we do not attempt to find the single-valued relation, and I cannot see any evidence whatever in favour of your average equation being the single-valued relation which would result if any of the unknown variables were fixed. Now will you turn to any proof of the method of least squares and see if it does not start from $y = f(x)$ as the actually true relation between y and x and then assume that single observations differ from this by a known Law of frequency, which in most cases will be found ultimately or in *a disguised form* to be the normal law?

and Laplace used the least squares criteria to deal systematically with error in measurement; they assumed that the presence of errors rendered the directly observed variables independent and unrelated. Gauss's attempt to prove that the least squares estimate was the best fit led to the first mathematical articulation of the exponential law of error. The equation for the normal curve, the Gaussian law of error, was a spin-off – a tangent – to the development of least squares.

The law itself was a good fit for the philosophical reflections on errors in measurement. It met all of Galileo's observations, including those of symmetry of mistakes and the greater likelihood of small errors as opposed to large errors. Gauss and Laplace used square roots, calculus, and exponential and inverse relationships, all closely associated Isaac Newton's successful analysis. Abraham De Moivre's equation for one of the laws of chance revealed after many trials became, for Gauss, a probability distribution of errors in measurement after many observations. Gauss's equation for the error distribution, combined with the work of Thomas Bayes and Pierre Simon Laplace on inverse probability and Laplace's articulation of a central limit theorem, enabled investigators to measure probability of error and the accuracy of estimation and to test significance.[11]

The Russian Probability School

As we will see in the next chapter, the work of Gauss, Bayes, and Laplace influenced many European natural philosophers and statisticians. The thread of pure mathematical reasoning on probability theory, however, was taken up most completely by Russian mathematicians. Although the time frame of this Russian development goes beyond that of the kernel of this chapter, a brief description of the contributions of Russian probabilists will clarify how the classical probability theory was eventually wedded to time series analysis. The key to this clarity is the Russian understanding of observing as a *process* and the treatment of the values of dice throws or measurements of the same object as a *sequence* of random events. For the Russians, an analysis of dice throws was time series analysis. Starting with the work of Pafnuty Lvovich Chebyshev, in the latter half of the nineteenth century, the Russian mathematicians took the approach of deducing the law of large numbers and limit theorems of Bernoulli, de Moivre, Laplace, and Poisson as "very special cases of limit theorems concerning *sums of independent random variables*" (Gnedenko

---

In a letter to George Darwin on December 27, 1896, however, Pearson gave his approval to Yule's presentation of an amended version of the least squares paper to the Royal Society. In that letter, which is in the archives of the Royal Society, Pearson went so far as to say, "This discovery seems to me of very great value . . . this sort of thing is wanted in the first place for the biologist & the economist & the anthropologist."

[11] Stephen Stigler (1986) gives a thorough exposition of the developments associated with Gauss's and Laplace's specifications of the Gaussian law of error or normal distribution in 1809 and 1810. There had been other formulations of laws of error before those of Gauss and Laplace, although they were not means of inference. In the "Law of Error" entry in the *Encyclopedia of Statistical Science* (1993), Churchill Eisenhart presents a useful table of the analytical and graphical expressions of these laws from Simpson's work in 1756 to Cauchy's distribution in 1853.

and Kolmogorov [1949], 3). The Russian approach was to search for an asymptotic estimate of probability by showing that the sum of the random variables observed eventually converged to a definite value.

Within the context of mathematical expectation following on from the summation of sequential values, Chebyshev (1867) proved what conditions ensured the law of large numbers. His pupils at St. Petersburg University, Andrei Andreevich Markov (1899) and Aleksandr Mikhailovich Lyapunov (1900, 1901), used the method of moments and the method of characteristic functions, respectively, to demonstrate what conditions ensured a central limit theorem that would allow observers to assume a normal distribution. With the exception of Markov, the early Russian probabilists took a single random variable – a one-dimensional random vector in which each observation was uncorrelated with the others – as the basic element.[12] Markov expanded this to look at the case in which the observations were only pairwise independent (see section on Markov chains in Chapter 10), and Kolmogorov and others took the next step in considering *each* observation as one dimension or as one random variable in a sequence of one realization of a stochastic process. The Russian school's emphasis on processes, mathematical expectation, summation of sequential values, operations on random variables, and limit theorems provided the basis for Andrei Nikolaevich Kolmogorov's ([1933] 1950) axiomatic approach to probability theory, which established it as a branch of additive set functions, Eugen Slutsky's ([1927] 1937) demonstration that cyclical processes could be the result of summation of random causes, and Aleksandr Yakovlevich Khinchin's (1932, 1934) classification of stationary stochastic processes (these studies are discussed in Chapter 10).

The Russian mathematicians saw themselves carrying on the mantle of mathematical probability theory that, with the possible exceptions of Wilhelm Lexis and Ladislaus von Bortkiewicz in Germany, had been neglected in the rest of Europe after Laplace. As Khinchin and Boris Vladimirovich Gnedenko wrote in their *Introduction to the Theory of Probability*:

> At the time in the last century when probability theory went into eclipse in the West, in Russia the brilliant mathematician P. L. Chebyshev found a new means for its development – the over-all investigation of a sequence of independent random variables. Chebyshev himself, and his students A. A. Markov and A. M. Lyapunov, obtained fundamental results by this means (e.g., the law of large numbers and Lyapunov's theorem). . . .
>
> The reason for the great importance of this theorem is that a significant number of phenomena whose origin depends on chance proceed, in their fundamental behavior, according to the following scheme: the phenomenon under study is subjected to the action of an enormous number of independently acting stochastic causes each of which exerts only a negligibly small

---

[12]   Although Gauss in the early nineteenth century talked of *random errors* of observation, it was not until the work of Russian mathematicians in the late nineteenth century that the notion of *random observations* became part of the language of mathematical statisticians. According to Oscar Sheynin (1989, 350; 1994, 337), the Russian expression "random quantities" was used before the English expression of "random variables." Given that "random quantities" suddenly appeared simultaneously in several Russian treatises, Sheynin speculates that Chebyshev first coined the term in his lectures on probability.

influence on the course of the phenomenon as a whole. The action of each of these causes is expressed by random variable $\xi_1, \xi_2, ..., \xi_n$, and their combined influence on the phenomenon equals the sum $s_n = \xi_1 + \xi_2 + ... + \xi_n. ...$

The central limit theorem, established by the works, principally, of Academicians P. L. Chebyshev (1821–1894), A. A. Markov (1856–1922) and A. M. Lyapunov (1857–1918), asserts that if the acting causes $\xi_1, \xi_2, ..., \xi_n$ are mutually independent, if their number n is very large, and if the action of each of these causes in comparison with their total action is not large, then the law of distribution of the sum of s_n can differ only insignificantly from a normal distribution law. (Gnedenko & Khinchin 1962, 119)

For Khinchin and the other mathematicians connected to Moscow University in the late nineteenth and early twentieth centuries the most fruitful approach to understanding chance was to perceive dice throwing or measurement taking as a process. The mathematics used to describe the observation process could be generalized in some cases to other, more active processes. Gnedenko and Khinchin followed their historical summary quoted here, with an example of a phenomenon that proceeded according to their description of a chance process: firing a cannon at a target. Target practice was the active counterpart to the more passive summation of random observations. As with trials in games of chance and with observations in the measurement process, the more shots, the more certainty and coherence. In all three cases, isolated instances could be connected as components of a random process.

The end result of these processes was a predictable, bell-shaped geometric form that enabled investigators to infer and reason a posteriori. Adolphe Quetelet spoke of the order and science generated in the observation process:

> When we stand in the Presence of Nature, and seek to interrogate her, we are at once struck with infinite variety which we observe of the least phenomena. Whatever may be the limits within which we concentrate our attention we find a diversity as astonishing as it is embarrassing.
>
> The most simple appreciations leave a vagueness incompatible with precision which science requires. One single object, measured or weighed several times in succession, notwithstanding every precaution that may be taken, nearly always presents dissimilar results. Our ideas, however, seem to fix themselves, and to settle on a precise number – on some mean which will show the results of the observations made, as free as possible from accidental error. . . . The theory of Means serves as a basis to all sciences of observation. It is so simple and so natural that we cannot perhaps appreciate the immense step it has assisted the human mind to take. (Quetelet [1846] 1849, 38–39)

In the measurement process, the observer aims her theodolite at a landmark and takes a reading. In target practice the gunner aims his cannon at a target and shoots. An end result of both processes could be a curve similar to a normal distribution. The notions of a reasoned middle and of a law of deviation from that middle were applicable to both the passive interrogation of nature and to the action of aiming and firing. The question that biometricians and later econometricians broached was what other forms of active processes could be analyzed with the algorithms that were so useful in the rest space of games of leisure.

Conclusion

We could perhaps force the theme we used in Part I, that of the commercial-political-scientific development of mental tools for the analysis of temporal phenomena, onto this history of probability theory. The algorithm of the average, as summing and redistributing that sum over all the parts, was first popularized in the commercial practice of maritime law. Jakob Bernoulli was a political arithmetician arguing that wise statesmen who conjecture on civil issues should adapt a similar algorithm for expected outcome. Carl Friedrich Gauss and Pierre Simon de Laplace then took this algorithm to the realm of scientific arithmetic. In early commercial uses, however, the average was not a tool for comparison over time. Also, there was no commercial counterpart to the notion of regulated deviations from the average. It was in the philosopher's context of time equals trials that logical variation was reconciled with temporal variation. More time meant more trials, meant more observations, meant more certainty.

In tossing coins or throwing dice, variation from one trial to the next is generated only by chance. Similarly, the errors of observations on several measurements of a position of a star could be treated as random, chance errors. In the early nineteenth century, Gauss and Laplace marshaled these chance errors into an exponential law of error. From this law, the probability of an outcome or a deviation from the expected value could be determined. In the late nineteenth century, the Russian mathematicians, including Pafnuty Lvovich Chebyshev, Andrei Andreevich Markov, and Aleksandr Mikhailovich Lyapunov, substituted "random quantities" for random errors. Within this context, the act of measuring objects or observing games could be seen as a *process* in which the values derived from algorithms based on summing and redistributing that sum approached a Gaussian law of error. The law of error is a structure of logical variation. In the pure observation process there is no thread of history linking the trials; ideally, the outcome of one toss does not depend on the outcome of previous tosses. The formidable task of translating this structure of logical variation to processes in which there was a thread of history is explored in the remaining chapters of this book. We will see, in Chapters 9 and 10, that it was in meeting this challenge of reconciling logical and historical variation that statisticians adapted monetary and political algorithms for decomposing time series. In the next chapter we explore how Francis Galton, Karl Pearson, and other biometricians and mathematicians in the late nineteenth century used the geometry of logical variation to explain changes in a world in which chance was not the result of limited human perception but was an integral part of natural order.

7

Laws of Deviation and the Capacity for Shifting Means in Early Statistical Models of Processes

> Thus the further we go back, the more we may find the *laws of motion* mechanism to be due to the structure of matter.
>
> Karl Pearson in a letter to Udny Yule, April 20, 1891
> (Pearson Papers, Box 931)

In this and the remaining chapters of this history of time series analysis we will be examining attempts by statisticians to link movement, witnessed in biology, meteorology, or political economy, to the geometric structure of static deviation from an expected value. By the late nineteenth century, some natural philosophers and mathematicians saw active processes of change as chance processes. They used the laws of chance, which had been specified by Jakob Bernoulli, Abraham De Moivre, Carl Friedrich Gauss, and Pierre Simon Laplace, to quantify and model the progress of civilizations, the dynamic properties of gases, and the evolution of species. The application of the laws of chance to social and natural processes was initiated by Adolphe Quetelet, James Clerk Maxwell, Francis Galton, Raphael Weldon, and Karl Pearson, who transformed the laws of error and chance into what Galton called "laws of deviation." These investigators then used laws of deviation to explain and predict laws of motion.[1]

In an essay penned in 1909, the French mathematician Henri Poincaré asserted that "chance is something other than the name we give our ignorance." Poincaré was writing of a new way of seeing chance that was tied to temporal processes of cause and effect. Until the mid-nineteenth century, chance had been a name for human ignorance. As we saw in the previous chapter, this was true even for those who immersed themselves in the calculus of probabilities. Those reasoning on the arts of conjecturing and measuring tried to surmount or freeze time in the hopes of seeing the certainty and the determinacy that God in eternity knew. For them, chance was a product of

---

[1] The nineteenth-century rotation of perspective from chance as a human illusion to chance as a real quality of natural processes is more fully explored in Ian Hacking's *The Taming of Chance* (1990). Ted Porter (1986) and Victor Hilts (1973) have documented the importance of nineteenth-century social and biological applications to the transformation of the law of error into a general and powerful statistical way of thinking.

passive observation or measurement. Time was only a factor as duration of play; it was equated to trials – the more trials, the more certainty and the clearer the law.

For the mathematicians and the probabilists, the term "law," as in "law of error," meant equation; from Quetelet onward, it implied a generic geometric form, which mapped out frequency of values that could be compared to each other or to a mean value. The use of the geometry of static comparison to explain motion, "mechanism by geometry" as Karl Pearson called it, reached its fullest vision in the statistical program initiated in the late nineteenth century to test and quantify Alfred Wallace's and Charles Darwin's theory of evolution by natural selection. For the biometricians, a geometric study of logical variation across a species could be used to understand evolution and inheritance; variation within cross sections carried the capacity for the temporal shifting of the mean value of measurements on populations.

This chapter begins with a discussion of Adolphe Quetelet's law of accidental causes as a bridge between the laws of error of early nineteenth-century astronomers and the laws of deviation of late nineteenth-century biometricians. Quetelet's work leads into an exploration of the links between statistical theory and the kinetic theory of gases. I then use Quetelet's ideas on social physics and Stanley Jevons's speculations on microscopic Brownian motion to examine the vision of cross sections carrying the capacity for temporal change. We conclude this chapter with a look at three contributions of the late nineteenth-century biometricians to a statistical theory of mechanism by geometry – the double-humped frequency distribution of a species as evidence of natural selection; and the regression "polygon" and bivariate frequency surface as means of quantifying laws of inheritance. Our study in this chapter of the use of a cross section as a starting point to comprehending change over time will help us to understand the issues raised in subsequent chapters regarding the use of time series data in the statistical analysis of changing phenomena.

The Law of Accidental Causes

Writing in the second quarter of the nineteenth century, the Belgian astronomer Adolphe Quetelet straddled the older view that chance was only a human illusion and the more modern idea of randomness as a part of the natural order:

> The powers of man are limited. Nature is unbounded. The Supreme Being can alone see events proceed in accordance with his laws. To him time is nothing, and all imaginable combinations may be realized in succession. These apparent differences are only found within the sphere of man and spread a remarkable variety over all the events in which he is concerned. This variety, which is in part his work, has however narrow limits, and cannot alter the general order of things. (Quetelet [1846] 1849, 64)

Quetelet also bridged the astronomer's law of error and the biometricians' law of deviation with his notion of a "law of accidental causes." Table 7.1

Table 7.1 *Statistical distinctions in the context of subject*

	Physical science (before 1800 – astronomy, geodesic surveys)	*Biology & social science* (after 1870 – inheritance, anthrometry, social policy)
Mean		
Jevons 1877	Precise or probable mean result	Fictitious mean or average result
Edgeworth 1887	Objective mean, true value	Subjective mean, representative value
Data		
Edgeworth 1887	Observations: "different copies of one original"	Statistics: "originals affording one generic portrait"
Probability distribution		
Galton 1869, 1877	Law of error	Law of deviation
Bivariate relationships & least squares method		
Pearson 1896, 1920	Exact, geometric, deterministic relationship between unobserved variables; directly observed variables are independent due to error in measurement; purpose is accuracy with least error	Inexact, organic relationship of statistical dependency between observed variables; purpose is best average equation
Philosophical approach		
Mayr 1982	Essentialist	Populationist

highlights the differences, perceived mainly by late nineteenth-century mathematicians, between the physical science and social science interpretations of statistical parameters, distributions, and multivariate relationships. Quetelet's work falls between the two columns. Although Quetelet took the astronomers' tools of frequency distributions and summary parameters into the realm of social statistics, his notion of dispersion was still intimately tied to the notion of error. For Quetelet, the mean was the ideal, limits to variation were desirable, and the progress of human civilization was manifested in a narrowing of the range in the measurements of a myriad of human and social characteristics.[2]

---

[2]   Ernest Mayr argued that Quetelet's philosophy was closer to the essentialist approach of Gauss and Laplace on error in measurement than the populationist approach of Darwin, Wallace, and the biometricians on natural selection: "The statistics of the essentialist are quite different from those of the populationist. When we measure a physical constant – for instance the speed of light – we know that under equivalent circumstances it is constant and that any variation in observational results is due to inaccuracy of measurement, the statistics simply indicating the degree of reliability of our results. The early statistics from Petty and Graunt to Quetelet was essentialistic statistics, attempting to arrive at true values in order to overcome the confusing effects of variation. Quetelet, a follower of Laplace, was interested in

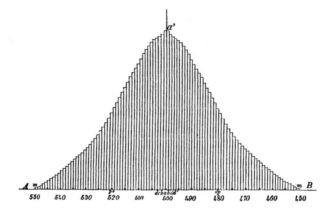

Figure 7.1a   Quetelet's geometric representation of the chances of drawing a number of white balls from a random drawing of 999 balls from a urn containing an equal number of white and black balls. The most probable draw, the draw with probably the greatest frequency, would be 499 white balls and 500 black balls or 500 white balls and 499 black balls. *Source:* Quetelet [1846] 1849, 68.

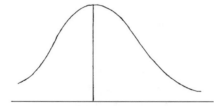

Figure 7.1b   Quetelet's "curve of possibility" when chances of accidental causes are unequal. Quetelet was giving vision to his observation that "Nature is like man in this, – when it differs from its type, it is more generally in exaggeration than in diminution." Frequency distributions skewed to the right are common, given that many measured quantities face a lower limit of zero but a far less distinct upper boundary. *Source:* Quetelet [1846] 1849, 114.

Unlike his fellow astronomers, Quetelet did not limit the use of frequency distributions to observations on the same star. Although Quetelet likened variation to error, he took a bold step in searching for a law of error in statistics on similar, but not identical people. Quetelet found bell-shaped distributions in social statistics and named the vision the "law of accidental causes." Indeed, Quetelet, is credited with the first published visual images of normal and skewed probability distributions (see Figures 7.1a and 7.1b).

Quetelet's law of accidental causes was similar to the old laws of error and chance, but this new law was constructed from statistics that embedded change over time. The elements were not measurements of the exact same object nor were they trials of throwing the same dice; the statistics Quetelet worked with were often time series, – for example, rates of crime, death, or birth for a

deterministic laws. He hoped by his method to be able to calculate the characteristic of the "average man" that is to discover the "essence" of man. Variation was nothing but "errors" around the mean values" (Mayr 1982, 47).

society year to year, or even in some cases hour to hour. Quetelet argued that these measurements of social phenomena were influenced by constant causes, variable causes (which were often periodic or seasonal), and accidental causes.

To Quetelet, the notion of accidental causes served as an explanation not only for mass social phenomena, but for errors and games of chance as well. For example, one might suspect that biases in coins would lead to different results in the case of many coins being tossed compared with trials in which the same coin is repeatedly tossed, but the law of accidental causes showed otherwise. Quetelet credited Siméon-Denis Poisson in demonstrating that the results were the same:

> The small variations which we find in passing from one coin to another may be ranged among the effects of accidental causes, which are obliterated when the experiments are sufficiently multiplied. So that the results are presented as if the trials had really been made with but one coin. In the case before us the experiments should generally be very numerous: it is for this reason that M. Poisson has designated the extension of Bernoulli's principle as *the law of great numbers*. We have already had occasion to consider analogous examples, particularly in reference to the measurements taken on a large number of men of the same age. We then saw that all the heights collected together gave a mean, from which they individually differed according to a well-defined law, and absolutely as if an individual type had been measured a number of times by means more or less defective.[3] (Quetelet [1846] 1849, 145)

So for Quetelet, it was useful to see the irregular variation as coming not just from the imperfection of human observational powers but also from the initial causes. The significance of Quetelet's shifting of the "accident" to cause itself is indicated in Karl Pearson's definition of statistics in his 1907 lectures on the subject at University College in London: "Statistics is the science that deals with the distribution of effects which follow a cause, not in itself uniquely deterministic" (Pearson Papers, Box 69, The Library, University College, London). Henri Poincaré qualified this cause–effect relationship even further. Effects had either simple, significant causes or they were the result of slight differences (or complex causes) that produced great effects. The latter he labeled chance:

> The greatest bit of chance is the birth of a great man. It is only by chance that meeting of two germinal cells, of different sex, containing precisely, each on its side, the mysterious elements whose mutual reaction must produce the genius. One will agree that these elements must be rare and that their meeting is still more rare. How slight a thing it would have required to deflect from its route the carrying spermatozoan. It would have sufficed to deflect it a tenth of a millimeter and Napoleon would not have been born and the destinies of a continent would have been changed. No example can better

---

[3] Quetelet was referring to Poisson's articulation of the law of large numbers published in 1837. Poisson's contribution to a statistical way of thinking is examined in Hacking's *The Taming of Chance*.

make us understand the veritable characteristic of chance. (Poincaré [1909] 1913, 410–411)

Having defined chance as slight variations in cause having great difference in effect, Poincaré explained why we could assume that a law of chance could be represented by a continuous function:

> Thus we see why phenomena obey the laws of chance when slight differences in the causes suffice to bring on great differences in the effects. The probabilities of these slight differences may be regarded as proportional to these differences themselves, just because these differences are minute, and the infinitesimal increments of a continuous function are proportional to a variable.[4] (Poincaré [1909] 1913, 404)

Even when the laws of chance are used in cases of our ignorance of exact cause and effect, Poincaré saw advantage. One could try to study how the force of a throw, the surface of a table, the resistance of the atmosphere, and so forth determines which side of the die will land face up, but the assumption of equal probability of all sides would yield useful results with an economy of information. The intricate knowledge of cause and effect of all life-styles and of each individual's habits and genetic and chemical makeup is usually of less use to insurers for profitable prediction of mortality rate compared with the usefulness of assumptions arising out of a frequency distribution of age of death. If we knew the velocity, paths, and laws of motion of each molecule of gas in a container, the snarled calculations would not allow us to explain or predict change; yet assumptions of random movement and mass phenomena do. In these cases often the best approach is to ignore the individual histories, the before and after, the cause and effect of individual outcomes and compare possibilities of all outcomes.

The Kinetic Theory of Gases and Brownian Motion

The kinetic theory of gases was held up by Poincaré and many others as an example of the fruitfulness of the law of accidental causes and a statistical way of thinking:

---

[4]   The *direction* of causality was important to Poincaré's argument. If one traveled faster than the speed of light and therefore experienced time in reverse, then one would perceive chance as great differences in causes having slight effects; laws (even the law of chance) would be inoperable and prediction would be impossible. Also in addressing the questions as to whether "chance" has objectivity, Poincaré argued that "very slight" was relative not from one person to another but from one age of the earth to another. The world was becoming more uniform, and the probability curves becoming smoother: "since the beginning of the ages, there have always been complex causes ceaselessly acting in the same way and making the world tend toward uniformity without ever being able to turn back. There are the causes which little by little have flattened the salients and filled up the reentrants, and this is why our probability curves now show only gentle undulations. In milliards of milliards of ages another step will have been made toward uniformity, and these undulations will be ten times as gentle; the radius of mean curvature of our curve will have become ten times as great" (Poincaré [1909] 1913, 409). This modern notion of the tendency toward uniformity sounds remarkably similar to Quetelet's idea that society would become more homogeneous with the progress of civilization.

the kinetic theory of gases, a well-known hypothesis, wherein each gaseous molecule is supposed to describe an extremely complicated trajectory, but in which through the effect of great numbers, the mean phenomena, alone observable, obey the simple laws of Mariotte and Gay-Lussac. (Poincaré [1908] 1913, 157)

Rudolph Clausius, James Clerk Maxwell, Peter Guthrie Tait, and Ludwig Boltzmann in the latter half of the nineteenth century and Albert Einstein and Marian von Smoluchowski in the early twentieth century were among those who used statistical reasoning to explain and predict motion in gases. These scientists used the motion of molecules in gases to explain the observed relationships between pressure, density, and temperature; and to investigate the diffusion of matter, momentum, and energy in order to comprehend the irreversible dissipation of energy.[5]

The investigations of the kinetic theorists led to estimates of molecular values such as relative and absolute masses, velocities, the length of their mean paths of motion, and the number of collisions per second. The use of studies of motion in gases to measure the unchanging qualities of molecules is illustrated in Maxwell's summary of the work of Josef Loschmidt:

> Now Loschmidt has deduced from the dynamical theory the following remarkable proportion:–As the volume of a gas is to the combined volume of all the molecules contained in it, so is the mean path of a molecule to one-eighth of the diameter of a molecule (Maxwell [1873] 1965, 372).

There were at least five threads of statistical thinking in the theoretical developments on motion in gases:

- The regularity of averages is at the level of perceptible changes.
- The velocity of particles follows a Gaussian distribution.
- The second law of thermodynamics is valid in a macro-statistical sense, even though it may be violated at the particle level.
- Statistical behavior is not exclusively a product of mass phenomena and even singular particles could display it.
- The random movement of particles in Brownian motion is caused by irregularities of structure.

Emphasizing the regularity of means, Maxwell argued for a forsaking of the historical method in favor of the statistical method of comprehending dynamics in gases. Dynamic phenomena could be explained if one ignored the actual paths of individual molecules, and thus cause and effect at the micro level, and focused only on the measurable behavior of averages at the macro level (Maxwell [1873] 1965). The basic elements, the individual

---

[5]   In the late eighteenth century and early nineteenth century, Daniel Bernoulli and John Herapath speculated on molecular motion in gases as the source of heat and other observable phenomena, but it was not until the latter half of the nineteenth century that statistical reasoning was brought to bear on this subject (see Brush 1976).

molecules, displayed neither logical variation (a hydrogen molecule in a laboratory was exactly the same as that in a distant star) nor historical variation
(molecules, as Maxwell conceptualized them, did not grow, decay, change, or
cease to exist). Variation was only a quality of the mass phenomena of gases and
the assumption of chance was necessary in order to model and quantify change:

> Thus molecular science teaches us that our experiments can never give us
> anything more than statistical information, and that no law deduced from
> them can pretend to absolute precision. But when we pass from the contempla-
> tion of our experiments to that of the molecules themselves, we leave the
> world of chance and change, and enter a region where everything is certain
> and immutable. (Maxwell [1873] 1965, 374)

Charles Gillispie (1963), Stephen Brush (1976), and Theodore Porter (1986)
have made a strong case for the influence of Quetelet's work on the theoretical
physics of Maxwell and Boltzmann. Echoing an essay of "Quetelet on Probabilities" by John Herschel, Maxwell went beyond just advocating the regularity
and stability of the average to specify the law of error as the most probable
distribution of the velocities of particles consistent with known properties of
gases: "It appears from this proposition that the velocities are distributed
among the particles according to the same law as the errors are distributed
among the observations in the theory of the 'method of least squares' " (Maxwell [1859] 1965, 382).[6] Boltzmann went on to demonstrate that the tendency
for a system to approach the distribution specified by Maxwell was equivalent
to the tendency to reach maximum entropy, and the equilibrium of a system
at the macro level became defined as the most probable state.

In many ways the work of Maxwell, Tait, and Boltzmann is similar to the
seventeenth- and eighteenth-century notions of chance: human ignorance and
the inadequacy of our senses force us to perceive what is really deterministic as
stochastic. At the particle level, dimensions were invariable and motion was
deterministic. At the macro level, however, behavior was consistent with
probability analysis. According to Maxwell, we had to acknowledge that "disturbance is a mere figment of the mind, not a fact of nature, and that in
natural action there is no disturbance" (Maxwell [1870] 1965, 229).[7]

Studies of Brownian motion and radioactive decay, however, called into
question the assumption that statistical behavior was exclusive to the realm
of mass phenomena. Lorenz Krüger (1990) argues that the real nail in the
coffin for physical determinism was the discovery that single atoms in the
process of radioactive decay, unaffected by any collision or outside forces,

---

[6] Maxwell's appropriation of the law of error was in keeping with the importance he attached to "scientific
    metaphor" and the transference of formal, mathematical relations from one branch of science to another
    in the generation of new discoveries (Maxwell [1870] 1965). Note Maxwell's linking of the law of error
    with the method of least squares.

[7] Maxwell saw the concept of entropy or the dissipation of energy in a similar light. The concept would
    be meaningless to a higher being who knew and could act upon the motion of every molecule: "Now,
    confusion, like the correlative term order, is not a property of material things in themselves, but only
    in relation to the mind which perceives them. . . . It is only to a being in the intermediate state, who
    can lay hold of some forms of energy while others elude his grasp, that energy appears to be passing
    inevitably from the available to the dissipated state" (Maxwell [1878] 1965, 646).

displayed stochastic behavior. For example, in their study of radioactive change in 1903, Ernest Rutherford and Frederick Soddy argued that chance was a property of the decay rates of individual atoms and of the time intervals between successive stages of disintegration. In the twentieth century, the connection of chance to real processes, rather than to human perception, has been a mainstay of quantum mechanics.

Even Robert Brown had noted as early as 1828 that a single particle isolated in a drop of water on the microscope slide had the same spontaneous irregular motion as seen with many particles. Although Brownian movement is frequently seen as the best illustration of random molecular motion, Stephen Brush (1968; 1976) points out that the kinetic theorists never wrote on the irregular movement in particles that had been observed at the microscopic level by Robert Brown. According to Brush, it was not until Einstein pursued his studies of statistical mechanics in 1905 and Smoluchowski in 1906 adapted the mean-free-path description of gas molecules to particle motion in fluids that the random motion of microscopic particles in fluids was linked to the theory of heat and motion in gases.

Brownian motion and the statistical mechanics of gases are often seen as examples of the erosion of determinism in the nineteenth century.[8] Nineteenth-century studies on microscopic Brownian motion, however, indicate a persistence of determinism even in the face of what we, with hindsight, might see as evidence to the contrary. For example, Stanley Jevons, a keen observer of the spontaneous motion of microscopic particles, adhered to the idea that it was only our deficient faculties that led to chance:

> Chance then exists not in nature, and cannot coexist with knowledge; it is merely an expression, as Laplace remarked, for our ignorance of the causes in action, and our consequent inability to predict the result, or to bring it about infallibly. In nature the happening of an event has been pre-determined from the first fashioning of the universe. *Probability belongs wholly to the mind.* (Jevons [1877] 1958, 198)

Jevons was one of the few scientists to take an interest in microscopic Brownian motion between the 1830s and 1900. Like Brown, Jevons witnessed this movement in isolated, single, inorganic particles and he did not think it was caused by heat (to the contrary, Jevons argued that increases in temperature decreased the motion). He called this self-animated movement *pedesis* from the Greek word meaning leaping or bounding (Jevons 1878a, 7). Although Jevons made reference to "spontaneous motion," he never used the words "random" or "chance" in describing the action he saw under the microscope, and his study of pedetic motion obviously did nothing to shake his belief in a deterministic world.[9] Jevons's study of Brownian motion does point, however,

---

[8] In his book, *The Taming of Chance* (1990), Ian Hacking documents, with a myriad of other examples from the nineteenth century, the death of determinism and the birth of the idea that fundamental processes followed statistical laws.

[9] Although I have found no discussion of the contradictions of Jevons's faith in determinism and his interest in the random motion of microscopic particles, John Aldrich (1987), Margaret Schabas (1990),

to another link with a statistical way of thinking. Jevons related pedetic motion to nonuniform structure. The more irregular the shape of the particles, the more intense and rapid the motion. Some key models of processes are based on a similar notion that cross-sectional variation (disparity, deviation) carries the capacity for temporal variation (historical fluctuation).[10]

Cross Sections in Temporal Processes

Statistical technique is grounded on the concept of variation as simultaneous comparison, usually comparison by subtraction (i.e., deviation from the mean). For investigations into human development, biological evolution, climatic change, and economic fluctuations, however, variation also meant a process of change. The confusion of the two meanings is quite blatant at times, as illustrated by the debate in 1901 between Karl Pearson and William Bateson over mathematical theories of evolution (discussed later in this chapter).

Part of the confusion arises because the two concepts of variation – deviation and change – are often linked in a cause–effect relationship. In thermodynamics and meteorology, scientists maintain that the simultaneous existence of different temperatures or different pressures in a closed system will inevitably lead to change. When all matter is in a homogeneous state, change will cease. Another nineteenth-century illustration of static disparity being the cause of movement is the meteorological reasoning of Christopher Hendrik Diederik Buys Ballot. Buys Ballot (1857) empirically determined that the greater the difference in the barometric pressure between two places, the greater the resulting force of the wind. Similarly, Buys Ballot's Law states that if you place yourself in the direction of wind, the place of least atmospheric pressure will be to your left.

In the social sciences there are also notions of change being the result of static disparity or deviation. Examples include the dialectical process (the confrontation and unity of the opposites – the thesis and antithesis – bring about the synthesis); and the notion voiced by the political opposites Karl Marx and Ronald Reagan that in the development of capitalism, the greater the disparity of income distribution in a society the greater the potential for economic growth of the productive forces of capitalism.[11]

The supply-side reasoning of Ronald Reagan's economic advisers echoed the philosophy of Charles Darwin in his argument that disparity or deviations from average income carried the capacity for economic growth. In his *Voyage*

---

and Sandra Peart (1993) have commented on the coexistence of his use of probabilistic inference with his commitment to the deterministic view of the way in which the world works.

[10] In using the phrase "carries the capacity," I am adopting Nancy Cartwright's (1989) suggestion that observing and measuring capacity is a fruitful way of comprehending causality.

[11] There are notions that change can cause deviation. The different rock strata in a cross section of a hill are the snapshot legacy of change. A three-dimensional form or a warped surface results when different parts of a flat two-dimensional surface grow at different rates. In morphology it is assumed that the form of an organism is determined by its rate of growth in various directions; organic form itself is seen as a function of time, as eloquently documented by D'Arcy Thompson (1942).

of the Beagle journal entry for February 6, 1833, Darwin evaluated the native society of Tierra del Fuego:

> The perfect equality among the individuals composing the Fuegian tribes, must for a long time retard their civilization. As we see those animals, whose instinct compels them to live in society and obey a chief, are most capable of improvement, so is it with the races of mankind. . . . In Tierra del Fuego, until some chief shall arise with power sufficient to secure any acquired advantage, such as the domesticated animals, it seems scarcely possible that the political state of the country can be improved. At present, even a piece of cloth given to one is torn into shreds and distributed; and no one individual becomes richer than another. On the other hand, it is difficult to understand how a chief can arise till there is property of some sort by which he might manifest his superiority and increase his powers.
>
> I believe, in this extreme part of South America, man exists in a lower state of improvement than in any other part of the world. (Darwin [1845] 1960, 219)

Darwin's faith in disparity or deviation leading to change was to become a cornerstone of his theory of biological evolution that he made public in 1858. In that year, Darwin and Alfred Wallace sowed the seeds for key developments in statistical theory and method with the publication of their idea that the transformation of a species depends on natural selection confronting differences across each generation of a species.[12] In subsequent biometric research on inheritance and evolution, the theoretical and empirical confronting of variation (as deviation across a species) with change in species over generations led to the development of new concepts such as correlation and regression. Intragenerational comparisons of cross sections were used to quantify intergenerational change. The notion that static deviation carried the capacity for shifting means over time was modeled as a stochastic process.

There are elements of these notions in Quetelet's idea, voiced in the 1830s, of the progress of human civilization. Like Wallace's and Darwin's natural selection, Quetelet's social physics was envisioned as a connecting of cross sections of populations over time. This is evident in Quetelet's hypothetical plot of the strength of man at different ages of the world (top right of Figure 5.8). The development of human nature was the curve enveloping the means of the cross sections of generations. It is a curve connecting the mean of one age of the world to the mean of the next age. In typical visions of gradual evolution by natural selection, however, a point of *deviation* from the mean of one cross section is connected to the mean of the next generation (Figure

---

[12] Wallace did not share Darwin's view of the necessity for disparity in order to improve human civilization. As Wallace explained, "I am a Socialist because I believe that the highest law for mankind is justice. I therefore take for my motto, 'Fiat Justia, Ruat Clum'; and my definition of Socialism is, 'The use, by everyone, of his faculties for the common good, and the voluntary organisation of labour for the equal benefit of all.' That is absolute social justice; that is ideal socialism. It is, therefore, the guiding star for all true social reform" (Wallace 1916, 390).

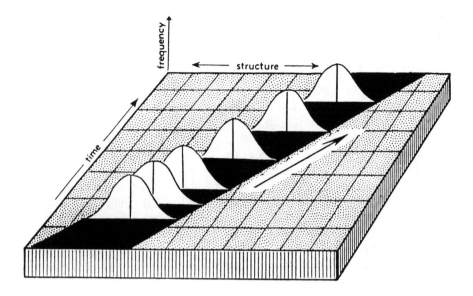

Figure 7.2   Evolution of species by natural selection acting on cross sections of generations. The fittest of one generation may well be different from the average. By passing on this fit deviation over time, the mean of the cross section of one generation shifts until eventually the species is very different in structure from the original. This model is critiqued in an essay on punctuated equilibria written by Stephen Jay Gould and Niles Eldredge reprinted in Eldredge 1985. *Source:* Moore, Lalicker, & Fischer 1952, 3.

7.2). In a similar vein, Quetelet's assumption of the goodness of moderation and the badness of extremes contrasts with Wallace's and Darwin's notion of the creative potential of deviation.[13]

Quetelet's vision is one of shifting means. There is, however, no organic connection between Quetelet's cross sections as there was in the inheritance models of Francis Galton and Karl Pearson. In Quetelet's model, with each generation (cross section), it is as if the target changes and the marksman (God) shoots again. The most significant difference between Quetelet's vision of the progress of civilizations and the biometricians' vision of inheritance and evolution is that Quetelet's cross sections did not carry the capacity for shifting the mean.

Biological Evolution by Natural Selection

The theory of the evolution of species by natural selection, publicly voiced by Charles Darwin and Alfred Russel Wallace in 1858, is one of the earliest speculations on processes dependent on chance variation. According to Darwin and Wallace, species evolved through a combination of changes in the environment, variation among individuals, inheritance, and what Darwin called "ancestral reversion." Notions of a gradually changing inorganic and organic

[13]   Quetelet's perception of deviation as error is explored in Hilts (1973) and Porter (1985).

world had been expressed for many decades before the 1858 Darwin and Wallace essays on species transformation. The *Scala Naturae* doctrine accepted by the church of static hierarchy from the simple to complex, or from plant to mammal, had been transformed to a dynamic ladder by several writers speculating on common descent and progression of life forms through the ages. The evolutionary theory of Darwin and Wallace was still, however, quite revolutionary. To Darwin and Wallace, evolution was not without direction, given the role of natural selection, but it did not have the goal orientation suggested by earlier theories of progression toward sophisticated perfection.

Wallace and Darwin argued that organic populations – species – experienced continual, gradual, nonteleological change. At any point in time there was variation, diversity among the individuals of the species. Unchecked a species would reproduce at a considerable rate, but nature ensured checks. Competition for resources existed between species, but also competition for food, space, and sexual mates existed among individuals of a species. Those who were able to survive and to reproduce the next generation were those whose slightly different traits allowed them to adapt most readily to their environment and to attract mates. Variable traits could be inherited so eventually members of a species would look and act quite different from their predecessors millions of years ago.

At a 1908 commemoration of Darwin's and Wallace's original presentations to the Linnean Society, Wallace listed the "curious series of correspondences, both in mind and in environment, which led Darwin and myself, alone among our contemporaries, to reach the identically the same theory" (Wallace 1916, 93). Both Darwin and Wallace were avid collectors of beetles, which offered more variety in form than any other organisms. Both had an intense interest in variety and through their extensive travels were able to observe local and geographical distributions and the effects of isolation in the biologically richest parts of the earth. Finally, after accumulating many observations, both naturalists were struck by the arguments of the political economist and the Reverend Thomas Malthus on the system of positive checks controlling the otherwise exponential growth of population.[14]

The characteristics of Darwin's and Wallace's theories that made them historically unique also rendered them ideally suited for the application of

---

[14]   At this commemoration on the fiftieth anniversary of the Darwin–Wallace communication, Wallace emphasized that while they had independently arrived at the theory of natural selection or survival of the fittest, Darwin deserved more credit:

> But, what is often forgotten by the Press and the public is, that the idea occurred to Darwin in 1838, nearly twenty years earlier than to myself (in February 1858); and that during the whole of that twenty years he had been laboriously collecting evidence from the vast mass of biology, of horticulture, and of agriculture; as well as himself carrying out ingenious experiments and original observations. . . .
>
> I was then (as often since) the "young man in a hurry"; *he*, the painstaking and patient student seeking ever the full demonstration of the truth that he had discovered, rather than to achieve immediate personal fame.
>
> Such being the actual facts of the case, I should have had no cause for complaint if the respective shares of Darwin and myself in regard to the elucidation of nature's method of organic development had been henceforth estimated as being, roughly, proportional to the time we had each bestowed upon it when it was thus first given to the world – that is to say, as twenty years is to one week. (Wallace 1916, 92–93)

statistical analysis. Raphael Weldon and Karl Pearson wrote of this remarkable statistical foundation in the editorial for the first issue of *Biometrika*, the journal established to investigate mathematical laws of evolution:

> Whether we hold variation to be continuous or discontinuous in magnitude, to be slow or sudden in time, we recognize that the problem of evolution is a problem in statistics, in the vital statistics of populations. . . . every idea of Darwin – variation, natural selection, sexual selection, inheritance, prepotency, reversion – seems at once to fit itself to mathematical definition and to demand statistical analysis. (Editorial, *Biometrika*, 1901a, 3–4)

Darwin did not apply statistical analysis – that was to come several years later with the work of Pearson, Galton, Weldon, and other biometricians. He was not comfortable with mathematical or statistical analysis and admitted being "muzzy" on the subjects of proportion and chance.[15] Darwin was, however, aware of the importance of measurement, and in particular the Rule of Three (see Chapter 2), in verifying his ideas, and he frequently quoted quantitative results. Wallace, although not inclined to use equations, did use concepts of mean and variation and visual images of distributions in explaining his ideas. It was primarily with the work of Francis Galton, Raphael Weldon, and Karl Pearson from 1877 onward that Darwin's and Wallace's ideas were modeled and empirically investigated with statistical methods.

The elements of the statistical foundation laid in the theory of natural selection and evolution by Darwin and Wallace included:

- use of population as the primary unit of analysis
- emphasis on logical variation rather than central tendency
- linking of variation across a population with the process of change

The term "evolution" was originally applied to growth of the individual; in fact, Charles Darwin never used the word in characterizing his ideas. Naturalists before Darwin had closely investigated the development of organisms. Darwin did not dwell on this ontogeny, however; his focus was phylogeny. Following Thomas Malthus's cue, Darwin's subject was a population, not an individual organism. The current use of the term "evolution" is to describe the history of a population or a system undergoing irrevocable change.[16] For Darwin, a species was a population of similar but not identical individuals.[17] Darwin recognized that diversity within the population created the potential

---

[15] In a letter to Karl Pearson on July 8, 1901 (in Box 245 18/E of the Galton Papers, The Library, University College, London) Francis Galton wrote: "I have just spoke to Frank & Leonard Darwin, first separately then together. Their views about their father's attitude toward statistics are the same as mine except that Frank's were more strongly expressed. I fear you must take it as a fact that Darwin had no liking for statistics. They even thought he had a 'non-statistical' mind rather than a statistical one."

[16] As Georgescu-Roegen (1971, 206) has pointed out, "The tenet in biology is that only an aggregate of similar but not identical individuals, i.e. a species can evolve; an individual never evolves, it only comes into existence, lives and dies."

[17] Although Darwin was instrumental in linking the concept of a species with the concept of population, his definition of species in *The Origin of Species* was not the one in present use. Ernest Mayr (1982, 265–269) argues that Darwin's definition in his *Voyage of the Beagle* journal was actually closer to the modern definition; it was based on zoological evidence and assumed reproductive isolation. By

for change in the entire population over time. At first Darwin argued that favorable variation was rare but in a letter to Darwin on July 2, 1866, Wallace encouraged him to consider variation ubiquitous:

> Now, such expressions have given your opponents the advantage of assuming that *favourable variations* are *rare accidents*, or may even for long periods never occur at all and thus Janet's argument would appear to many to have great force. I think it would be better to do away with all such qualifying expressions, and constantly maintain (what I certainly believe to be the fact) that *variations of every kind* are *always occurring* in *every part* of *every species* and therefore that favorable variations are *always ready* when wanted. You have, I am sure, abundant materials to prove this, and it is, I believe, the grand fact that renders modification and adaptation to conditions almost always possible. I would put the burden of proof on my opponents to show that any one organ, structure or faculty does *not vary*, even during one generation, among all the individuals of a species. (Wallace 1916, 143)

Darwin and Wallace reached their theories on population change over time by noticing inexplicable, simultaneous differences in races of a species living close to each other. Climatic change could possibly explain why different species and varieties inhabited a region at different times. Likewise, different physical environments could explain differences in flora and fauna in different geographical areas. Darwin and Wallace, however, in their world travels were confronted with considerable variation in organs at the same time and in the same physical environment with small bodies of water being the only isolating barriers. In the Galapagos Islands, or even on opposite banks of the same river, they were forced to explain the existence of remarkably different races of the same species under isolation but thriving in nearby and physically identical environments. The only explanation was variation in isolated subpopulations of the same species.[18]

The variation across the population was the result of accidental causes.[19] The change in species that resulted from this variation was not, however, random. Natural selection ensured a probable success to a favorable few. In the words of Darwin:

> But let the external conditions of a country alter. . . . Now, can it be doubted from the struggle each individual has to obtain subsistence, that any minute variation in structure, habits or instincts, adapting that individual better to

1859, Darwin, under the influence of botanists, ignored reproductive isolation and distinguished species merely by degree of difference. According to Mayr, the modern biological definition of species – "*a reproductive community of populations (reproductively isolated from others) that occupies a specific niche in nature*" – was not clearly articulated until the turn of the century (Mayr 1982, 272–273). In addition to looking at the history of taxonomy, Mayr thoroughly explores the history of evolution, variation, and inheritance in biological thought.

[18] For example, the remarkable variation in isolated subpopulations was apparent to Wallace in the Malay Archipelago. A narrow sea, sometimes referred to as "Wallace's line" separates the western group of islands whose fauna were Asiatic, from the eastern group with animals similar to those in Australia (see Wallace 1916, 35; Camerini 1993).

[19] Explanations for the variation consistent with present-day biological thinking would include genetic mutation or recombination in the linking of maternally and paternally derived chromosomes.

the new conditions would tell upon its vigour and health?[20] (Darwin [1858] 1958, 261)

For Darwin, although natural selection was creative as well as destructive, evolution was not progressive. There was no potential being realized, nor a development from simple to complex, imperfect to perfect. Final causes, special creation, and teleological determination had no place in Darwin's scheme. The idea of variation across a population confronting natural selection yielded a complex process. As Sewall Wright (1967, 117) described it, "The Darwinian process of continued interplay of a random and a selective process is not intermediate between pure chance and pure determination, but in its consequences qualitatively utterly different from either."

The Law of Deviation

Considerable advances in statistical inferences were made in the late 1800s in the investigation of the mechanics of inheritance and evolution through natural selection. Biometricians such as Francis Galton, Raphael Weldon, and Karl Pearson applied the "law of error" to organic populations. In attempting to substantiate Darwin's theory, they formulated new frequency distributions, more refined statistical parameters of dispersion, and both geometric visions and coefficients of correlation and regression. Their goal was to quantify change over time and their use of tools of logical variation to do so was unique.[21]

Galton called the law of error or accidental causes by a new name in two works that inspired the biometricians' research program. In his 1869 book on *Hereditary Genius* and in his 1877 talk on "Typical Laws of Heredity," Galton referred to it as the "law of deviation." With the biometricians' quantitative

[20] Although some advocates of Darwin's theory of natural selection saw it as the "survival of the fittest," Karl Pearson lamented that his observations on humans and poppies pointed instead to "survival of the most fertile." In a letter to Udny Yule on Dec. 30, 1895 (Pearson Papers, Box 931, The Library, University College, London) Pearson wrote, "there is another nail in the coffin of natural selection as applied to civilised man. The battle is to the most fertile, not the most fit & he would be a bold statist who identified the two." This lament is in keeping with Pearson's eugenic agenda, which is discussed later in this chapter and thoroughly documented by Donald MacKenzie (1981). In a letter to Francis Galton on January 2, 1896 (Pearson Papers, Box 293B), Pearson voiced his eugenic frustration: "I still find that natural selection in man seems utterly ineffective as compared with reproductive selection. It looks as if the survival of the most fertile completely replaced the survival of the fittest in civilized man."

[21] Other historians of science have examined the biometricians' contributions to statistical theory and method: Helen Walker (1929) takes a technical look at the history of correlation and the origin of terms used in statistics; Egon Pearson (1938; 1965) uses correspondence and lecture notes to supplement the published work of Weldon, Karl Pearson, and Edgeworth on biological variation; Victor Hilts (1973) contrasts Galton's approach with that of Quetelet; Donald MacKenzie (1981) stresses the eugenic mission and the debates between Pearson, who professed eugenics, and Yule, who did not; Theodore Porter (1986) chronologically details the development of Galton's statistical way of thinking and his theory of heredity; Stephen Stigler (1986) shows the conceptual steps Galton took in reconciling the theory of error with inheritance, Edgeworth's role in bridging the work of Galton and Pearson, and the mathematical contributions of biometry to tests of significance, variance component models, and correlation; and Ian Hacking (1990) looks at Galton's and Pearson's achievement in using statistics for explanation and in replacing causation with correlation. With the exception of Egon Pearson, these histories have stressed inheritance rather than evolution through natural selection as the driving force in biometric work. The history of this period is also enriched by Karl Pearson's own documentation of developments (see Pearson 1906b; 1914–1930; 1920).

investigations of Darwin's and Wallace's theory, measuring variation was no longer relegated to second status behind measuring central tendency:

> The starting point of Darwin's theory of evolution is precisely the existence of those differences between individual members of a race or species which morphologists for the most part rightly neglect. The first condition necessary, in order that any process of Natural Selection may begin among a race, or species, is the existence of difference among its members and the first step in an enquiry into the possible effect of a selective process upon any character of a race must be an estimate of the frequency with which individuals, exhibiting any degree of abnormality with respect to that character, occur. (Editorial, *Biometrika*, 1901a, 1)

With the biometricians' investigation of the process of natural selection, deviation from the mean became as philosophically and analytically significant as the mean itself and it was celebrated and quantified in new ways. It was with the biometric work of Karl Pearson that our most common measurement of dispersion – standard deviation – was first articulated.

Simultaneously, the arithmetic mean was divorced from God, truth, or perfection and took on the mere garb of the typical. Although dispersion was now emphasized, the mean still served a useful purpose as a summary parameter. There was a major conceptual distinction between the mean of different observations of one physical entity and the mean calculated from statistics on similar, but not identical organisms. Francis Ysidro Edgeworth (1887) called the former an objective mean and the latter a subjective mean (see Table 7.1). The subjective mean of the biometricians' data was not the true value of the astronomer's stellar position or even the bull's-eye around which errant shots were distributed. It was a summary parameter of a whole population. The raw materials of the biometricians' studies were not observations, but statistics, and deviation from the subjective mean had become an essential component to what Edgeworth called the "Science of Means."

The Double-Humped Signature of Natural Selection

Among the biologists, it was Raphael Weldon who most clearly pursued the problem of evolution through searching for laws of deviation. In a memorial tribute to Weldon, Pearson described him as one who "realised to the full that the great scheme of Darwin was only a working hypothesis, and that it was left to his disciples to complete the proofs, of which the master had only sketched the outline" (Pearson 1906b, 282). Weldon first searched for proofs with morphological and embryological studies. These methods, however, emphasized homogeneity and Weldon soon turned toward the study of variation and distributions that Galton used in his work on inheritance. Weldon went beyond using a frequency distribution for describing a population to asking how natural selection affected a distribution. In his work on shrimp and crabs, Weldon (1890, 1892, 1893) discovered:

- The "probable error" of the measurements of the same organ is different in different races of the same species.
- The degree of correlation between a given pair of organs is approximately the same in local races of the same species.
- Variations in size of the organs usually occur with the frequency indicated by the Gaussian law or error.
- In one species of shore crabs the frequency distribution for measurements of one organ was asymmetrical.

Weldon's observation of a double-humped distribution in the breadth of the foreheads of Naples crabs (Figure 7.3) gave him and Pearson hope that they were gaining a glimpse of the bifurcation of a species by natural selection. If this pattern became more exaggerated over many generations, eventually there would be two separate species. Alfred Russel Wallace had predicted that evidence of natural selection would be found in empirical plots that deviated from a bell curve. In two letters to Francis Galton on March 7, 1886, and December 1, 1893 (Galton Papers, Box 336, The Library, University College, London), Wallace spoke of his difficulties in accepting the normal law curve at the expense of data points. Wallace acknowledged Galton's flair for "averages exhibited diagrammatically." In studying Galton's work, Wallace had not been able to "follow the formulas & tables in their mathematical form," but he had clearly comprehended the diagrams and curves. Wallace observed, however, that "mathematical treatment of the subject does not bring out some of the most interesting points as regards evolution by natural selection." He went on to suggest that Galton use empirical dots to represent every observation on his diagrams, rather than smoothed lines. Wallace thought that the mathematical curves, such as the superimposed exponential law of error, obscured the empirical discovery of the "modification by natural selection." Wallace suspected that mapping out the actual observations would highlight "irregular deviations" such as in his hypothetical sketch reproduced in Figure 7.4. For Wallace, the interesting evolutionary story was the deviation of the mass of dots, not from the mean value, but from the law curve of deviation.

Galton had already been thinking along those lines, as is evident in a letter Weldon wrote to him on November 27, 1892, describing his finding of a double-humped distribution: "Therefore, either Naples is the meeting point of two distinct races of crabs, or a 'sport' is in process of establishment. You have so often spoken of this kind of curve as certain to occur, that I am glad to send you the first case which I have found."[22]

---

[22] Egon Pearson quotes this passage in his essay on the early history of biometry, and he describes the stimulus of Weldon's finding of a double-humped distribution on Karl Pearson's work. By 1895, the biologist Weldon was complaining to Galton that Pearson's mathematical mind was finding skewness where it was not warranted. Weldon argued that Pearson's approach to curve fitting, this time in the case of Plymouth crabs, emphasized the goodness of fit for the edges of the distribution at the expense of fitting the majority of observations (see Egon Pearson 1965, 337; Stigler 1986, 336–337). One wonders how the species of Naples shore crabs has evolved since Raphael Weldon's investigations in the 1890s. Has any tendency toward a bifurcation of the species, which Weldon and Pearson claimed evidence of, persisted? Or have human selection and economic progress wiped out the variety altogether?

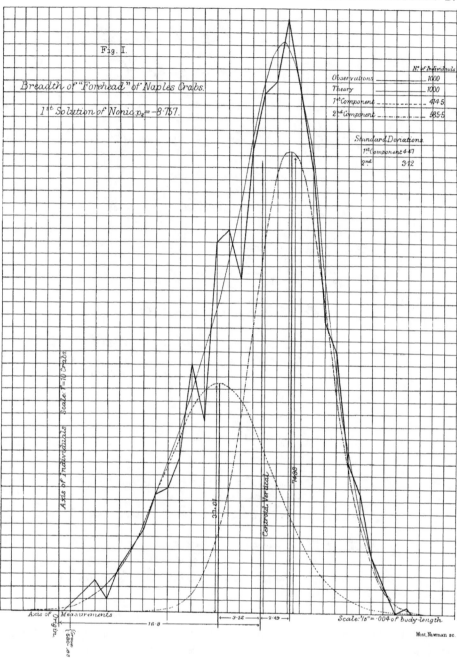

Figure 7.3   The bimodal frequency distribution of the breadth of foreheads of 1,000 Naples crabs based on Raphael Weldon's measurements. The horizontal axis measures the breadth as a ratio of the forehead to body length and the vertical axis measures the frequency – that is, the number of crabs with that ratio. The actual distribution was smoothed to an analytical curve and the latter was decomposed into two normal distributions – two separate populations with different means and standard deviations. Weldon and Karl Pearson used this case as evidence that natural selection was at work and could, in the future, generate two separate species. *Source:* Pearson Papers, Box 107, The Library, University College, London.

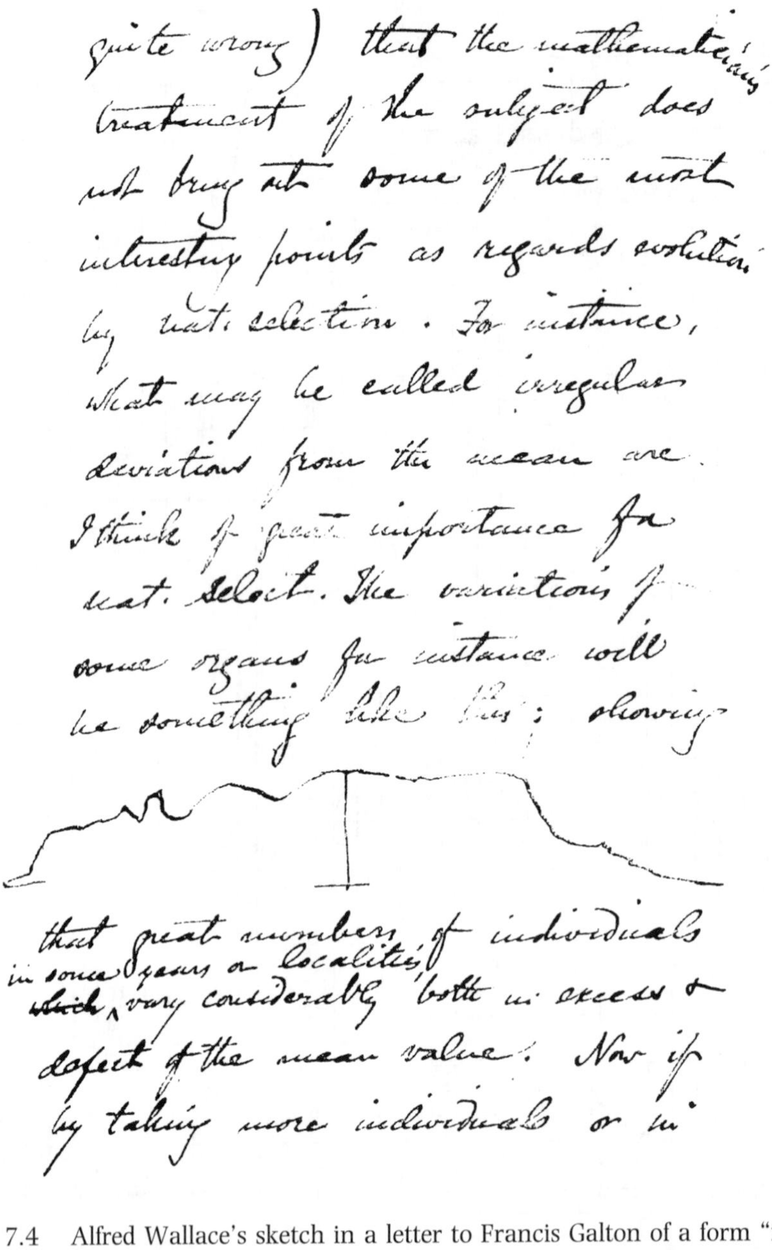

quite wrong) that the mathematical
treatment of the subject does
not bring out some of the most
interesting points as regards evolution
by nat. selection. For instance,
what may be called irregular
deviations from the mean are.
I think of great importance for
nat. select. The variations of
some organs for instance will
be something like this; showing

that great numbers of individuals
in some years or localities
which vary considerably both in excess &
defect of the mean value. Now if
by taking more individuals or in

Figure 7.4   Alfred Wallace's sketch in a letter to Francis Galton of a form "irregular deviations" might take if natural selection were at work. Wallace urged Galton to plot dots for each individual observation on frequency distributions rather than relying on mean values or smooth mathematical curves, which could obscure modification by natural selection. *Source:* Letter from Wallace to Galton, December 1, 1893 (Galton Papers, Box 336, The Library, University College, London).

In his February 1, 1894, lecture on "Problems in Evolution," which was part of his Gresham College series on "The Geometry of Chance," Karl Pearson explained the significance of the double-humped distribution as evidence of natural selection:

> Suppose for example a fishmonger receives a consignment of sales from Grimsby. They are a chance selection from the oceanic population, and with a high degree of probability from a normal frequency distribution. He gets them at 8 a.m. and at 9 the good housewife begins her purchases; the large fish are too expensive and the small only suited for the club dinner of the bachelor. We get an asymmetric distribution by the evening which may or may not be double humped according to whether it's the price of the big soles, or the keenness for the moderate sized fish which most influences the house-wife. Such abnormal frequency curves are common owing to human selection in the shops. I have found them in purchasing screws, tennis bats, vegetables, marrows, etc. etc. – legs of mutton. Now just as man makes by selection a normal frequency group into an abnormal one, so nature by the struggle for existence may achieve exactly the same result. Like the house-wife she may be selecting the mediocre or the giants or the dwarfs as unsuited to survive. . . . [23]
>
> Selection could produce such double-humped and asymmetrical frequency curves. Is it doing so and to what extent? The answers that may be given to these questions are the verdict of modern science on the great problem of evolution. They are essential to the problems of development and of heredity. For the first time in the history of biology, there is chance of the science of life becoming an exact, a mathematical science. Men are approaching the questions of heredity and evolution from a new standpoint. Hitherto evolution has been a name, and natural selection a most brilliant suggestion, a very honorable hypothesis. . . . We want to know whether the distribution is a normal one, – a pure chance distribution or whether we have an abnormal curve and something which suggests a tendency to deviate more in excess or defect of the mean is really present. We want shortly to know whether evolution is at work *now* and to *what extent*. It is largely to Professor Weldon that we owe this attempt to give an exact aspect to the problem of evolution, his interesting laborious & careful measurements on the organs of shrimp and crabs, are the first steps in the right direction, but what he is doing ought to be done by dozens of trained researchers. (Pearson 1894b, 9–12)

Wallace, Pearson, Weldon, and Galton all expected skewed or double-humped distributions to be evidence of the presence of natural selection.[24] Weldon's findings and Ysidro Edgeworth's problems with skewed price curves inspired Pearson to examine mathematically nonnormal frequency

[23]   Wallace would not have been pleased with Pearson's analogy of the housewife selecting the best fish. In a letter to Darwin in 1866 (Wallace 1916, 140–143), Wallace said that too many readers had interpreted "natural selection" to mean that an "intelligent chooser" selected the favorable variations. Whereas the process he and Darwin were describing was one in which those with unfavorable variations died off before reproducing. Wallace suggested that Darwin replace the metaphor of "natural selection" with Herbert Spencer's term, "survival of the fittest."

[24]   Most present-day visual models of evolutionary change by natural selection, such as Figure 7.2, use the normal distribution to represent the cross section of a generation. The reasoning of the biometricians suggests a more complex form.

distributions, which led to the analysis of skewed, chi-square, and F distributions. In response to a request from Weldon on breaking up a frequency distribution into two normal components, Pearson published in 1894 the first of a series of papers entitled "Mathematical Contributions to the Theory of Evolution." In this series, Pearson developed:

- the method of moments as a means to fitting a theoretical curve to observational data
- a comprehensive system of frequency curves linked together by their derivation from a single differential equation
- the chi-square test for goodness of fit
- a method for correlating attributes
- solutions to problems in multiple correlation
- statistical tables that are still in use today for determining values corresponding to probabilities from various frequency distributions

The stimulus to these developments of statistical analysis was the study of evolution. Pearson paid tribute to Weldon's 1893 study of crabs as the starting point for this statistical research program, calling it "a paper which biometricians will always regard as a classic of their subject. It first formulated that the method of the Registrar-General is the method by which the fundamental problems of natural selection must be attacked, and that is the essential feature of biometry" (Pearson 1906b, 185). [25]

In that biometric classic, Weldon urged biologists to measure organs across populations to quantify deviation. The geometry of that logical variation would indicate the rate of change and the possible evolutionary future of species:

> It cannot be too strongly urged that the problem of animal evolution is essentially a statistical problem: that before we can properly estimate the changes at present going on in a race or species we must know accurately (a) the percentage of animals which exhibit a given amount of abnormality with regard to a particular character; (b) the degree of abnormality of other organs which accompanies a given abnormality of one; (c) the difference between the death rate percent in animals of different degrees of abnormality with respect to any organ; (d) the abnormality of offspring in terms of the abnormality of parents and vice versa. These are all questions of arithmetic; and when we know the numerical answers to these questions for a number of species we shall know the deviation and the rate of change in the species at the present day – a knowledge which is the only legitimate basis for speculations as to their past history, and future fate. (Weldon 1893, 329)

[25]   As Darwin appropriated the notion of population thinking from the political economist Thomas Malthus, Raphael Weldon and Karl Pearson borrowed the political arithmetic of the registrar general to empirically investigate Darwin's theory of natural selection. As we saw in Chapter 2, the shop arithmetic and population thinking of the seventeenth-century merchant John Graunt had greatly influenced the goals and methods of the British registrar general. So once again, we see this theme of monetary to political to scientific arithmetic played out.

Replacing Forces of Inheritance with Laws of Inheritance

Darwin's theory and the many supporting examples he presented in *The Origin of Species* focused on diversity within a population. Temporal continuity of some of the diversity ensured the transformation of species. This temporal continuity came from inheritance. Darwin argued for a theory of "soft" inheritance – characteristics acquired within an organism's lifetime could influence the germ cells and be passed on. Darwin did not accept a true theory of blended inheritance; for Darwin fertilization led to a mixture and not a true fusion of two distinct individuals. His theory of pangenes, however, lacked the arithmetic simplicity and determinacy of modern genetics:

> To sum up on the origin of our domestic races of animals and plants. Changed conditions of life are of the highest importance in causing variability, both by acting directly on the organisation, and indirectly by affecting the reproductive system. It is not probable that variability is an inherent and necessary contingent, under all circumstances. The greater or less force of inheritance and reversion, determine whether variations shall endure. Variability is governed by many unknown laws, of which correlated growth is probably the most important. Something, but how much we do not know, may be attributed to the definite action of the conditions of life. Some, perhaps a great, effect may be attributed to the increased use or disuse of parts. The final result is thus rendered infinitely complex. (Darwin [1859] 1928, 48)

Darwin's notion of the forces of inheritance left much to be desired in explaining the persistence of variable traits. As Karl Pearson noted in his *Grammar of Science,*

> The reader can hardly fail to have been impressed in his past reading and experience with the great burden of explanation which is thrown on that unfortunate metaphysical conception force. . . . He may perhaps have concluded, with the present writer, that the word is not infrequently a fetish which symbolises more or less mental obscurity. But the reason for the repeated occurrence of the word is really not far to seek. Whenever motion, change or growth were postulated, there in the old metaphysics, force as the cause of change in motion was to be found. (Pearson [1892] 1969, 132)

An obvious weakness in Darwin's argument was his scheme of inheritance. For example, he left himself open to criticism that minute variations were not sustainable from one generation to the next since they could be easily canceled out in sexual reproduction with individuals not possessing the same variation of characteristics. It is one of the ironies of the history of science that the hereditary flaw in Darwin's argument led to considerable development in statistical methods that would not have taken place in the time and the form it did had Gregor Mendel's genetic theory of particulate inheritance been widely known and accepted.[26] It was in pursuit of replacing the ambiguous "force of inheritance" with mathematically precise "laws of inheritance" that the concepts of correlation and regression analysis were conceived and applied. The measurement approach of the biometricians bore little fruit in the biological understanding of inheritance, but the techniques developed to test their hypothesis of blending inheritance remain today as essential components of statistical analysis.

Eugenics

Proving Darwin's theory on the origin of species was not the only reason the biometricians sought to quantify the law of inheritance. Francis Galton, Karl Pearson, Charles Spearman and Ronald A. Fisher were eugenists. They believed that inheritance was more important than environment in determining a person's character and behavior, and they argued that the way to improving society was by social control of human reproduction – state provision of incentives and regulations that would ensure that more children would be born to those who were "fit" than to those who were "unfit."

In the years immediately after the 1907 founding of the Eugenics Education Society, members adopted Galton's notion of judging fitness by "civic worth." Civic worth, according to Galton, was formed by qualities such as intelligence, character, and energy, which were in turn mainly determined through heredity. Galton argued that the distribution across society of the talents which fed into civic worth followed the normal law of frequency. He recommended the augmentation of favorable stock through awarding diplomas in civic worth to deserving young adults, offering dowries to newlyweds of the higher classes, persuading females in the classes "where the brains of our nation lie" to marry early, and subsidizing housing for exceptionally promising young couples (Galton 1909, 25–29).[27] Galton went so far as to argue that eugenics had strong claims to becoming a new national religion and hoped that further statistical inquiry would enable eugenists to "proclaim a 'Jehad', or Holy War against customs and prejudices that impair the physical and moral qualities of our race."

---

[26]   Gregor Mendel wrote up his study of genetic inheritance in peas in 1866, but it was not until 1900 that his ideas were widely distributed and tested. William Bateson, a biologist who was instrumental in publicizing Mendel's work at the turn of the century, was very critical of the biometricians' approach to the study of heredity: "That such work may ultimately contribute to the development of statistical theory cannot be denied, but as applied to the problems of heredity the effort has resulted only in the concealment of that order, which it was ostensibly undertaken to reveal. A preliminary acquaintance with the natural history of heredity and variation was sufficient to throw doubt on the foundations of these elaborate researches. To those who hereafter may study this episode in the history of biological science it will appear inexplicable that work so unsound in construction should have been respectfully received by the scientific world" (Bateson [1913] 1930, 6).

[27]   With regards to the need to reduce the age of marriage for "fit" women of "better stock," Galton wrote: "There is unquestionably a tendency among cultured women to delay or even to abstain from marriage; they dislike the sacrifice of freedom and leisure, of opportunities for study and of cultured companionship. This has to be reckoned with. I heard of the reply of a lady official of a College for Women to a visitor who inquired as to the after life of the students. She answered that one-third profited by it, another third gained little good, and a third were failures. 'But what become of the failures?' 'Oh, they marry' " (Galton 1909, 26).

Karl Pearson's commitment to the eugenic religion is evident in his Huxley lecture in 1903 on "The Laws of Inheritance." Pearson concluded that social control of reproduction could do far more to raise national intelligence than education:

> We are ceasing as a nation to breed intelligence as we did fifty to a hundred years ago. The mentally better stock in the nation is not reproducing itself at the same rate as it did of old; the less able and the less energetic are more fertile than the better stocks. No scheme of wider or more thorough education will bring up, in the scale of intelligence, hereditary weakness to the level of hereditary strength. The only remedy, if one be possible at all, is to alter the relative fertility of the good and the bad stocks in the community. (Pearson 1904, 159)

Pearson, considered an advocate of women's rights and socialism, stressed the importance of incentives rather than force in carrying out eugenic policy. Reminiscing on the achievements of the biometric school at a dinner given in his honor in April 1934, however, Pearson expressed hope in Adolph Hitler's rise to power:

> The climax culminated in Galton's preaching of Eugenics, and his foundation of the Eugenics Professorship. Did I say "culmination"? No, that lies rather in the future, perhaps with Reichskanzler Hitler and his proposals to regenerate the German people. In Germany a vast experiment is in hand, and some of you may live to see its results. If it fails it will not be for want of enthusiasm, but rather because the Germans are only just starting the study of mathematical statistics in the modern sense![28] (*Speeches Delivered at a Dinner Held in University College, London in Honour of Professor Karl Pearson, 23 April 1934,* 23)

As Donald MacKenzie (1981) documents, eugenics motivated the statistical work of the biometricians and affected the nature of the theory and tools developed and the resources available for statistical research. The first university department of applied statistics was a combination of the Biometric and Eugenic Laboratories at University College in London, and the first professorial chair for this department was the Galton Professor of Eugenics endowed by Galton and held by Pearson. Galton and Pearson developed and used correlation and simple and multiple regression in order to quantify the contribution of parents and previous generations to human characteristics. Similarly, as Stephen Jay Gould (1981) has shown, the eugenist Charles Spearman designed factor analysis to justify his theory of the physical structure of inherited intellect.

---

[28] Pearson did not live to see the horror of this culmination of eugenic philosophy – he died in April 1936. Hitler's "experiment" led to the genocide of millions of people and to the bombing of London, where Pearson's children and grandchildren lived.

Correlation Surfaces and Laws of Inheritance

Much of Pearson's work in the 1890s was directed toward obtaining "coefficients of heredity" on pairs of parents and offspring for all measurable characteristics. The foundation for this procedure was given by Galton's work, first on sweet pea seeds and eventually on humans. Galton's 1877 study of sweet peas (discussed in Chapters 5 and 9) yielded a zigzag regression path that Pearson called a regression "polygon." It is unlikely, however, that Galton would have pursued this method had he not discovered a bivariate normal surface in the joint frequency distributions in his human inheritance studies.

After resorting to offers of prizes for family records, Galton was finally able to collect enough data on humans to examine correlation of heights from one generation to the next. The data on 205 parents and 930 adult children yielded "the numerical value of the regression towards mediocrity in the case of human stature, as from 1 to 2/3 with coherence and precision" (Galton 1886, 247). With these data, Galton worked out joint (bivariate) frequency distributions. Galton "smoothed" the entries by summing at each intersection of a horizontal and vertical class the entries in the four adjacent squares. Galton in essence constructed a bivariate normal surface from the elliptical contour lines of the bivariate frequency table:

> I then noticed that lines drawn through entries of the same value formed a series of concentric and similar ellipses. . . . The points where each ellipse in succession was touched by a horizontal tangent, lay in a straight line inclined to the vertical in the ratio of 2/3; those where they were touched by a vertical tangent lay in a straight line inclined to the horizontal in the ratio of 1/3. Those ratios confirm the values of average regression already obtained by a different method, of 2/3 from the mid-parent to the offspring, and of 1/3 from offspring to mid-parent. (Galton 1886, 255)

Once again the law of error or deviation appeared, though this time in three-dimensional form. Frequency surfaces were subsequently used in almost all work on correlation until Yule's introduction of least squares regression in 1897. Pearson, Galton, and Yule used the surfaces to quantify the laws of inheritance. A typical example of this is given in Figure 7.5, where the height of the surface is the frequency of pairs of heights for fathers and sons. The correlation surface was picked up by other statisticians in the correlation of social data. Luigi Perozzo's skewed surface of the joint distribution of the age of marriage of Italian husbands and wives (Figure 7.6) was on view at the Royal Statistical Society for several years during the 1890s. Yule's generic vision of the contour lines of the bivariate frequency table that form the normal correlation surface are shown in Figure 7.7, and his drawing of the ideal normal surface is in Figure 7.8. The geometric construction of correlation surfaces was complemented by Karl Pearson's algebraic formula for a single coefficient of correlation (see Appendix 1) explained in papers published in 1896 and 1898. Although the correlation surface soon lost favor to the

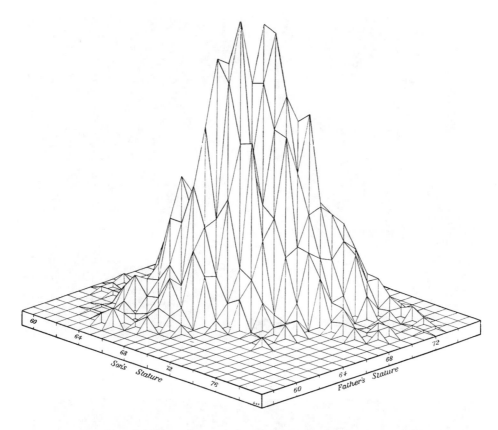

Figure 7.5   Yule's sketch of the bivariate frequency surface of the heights of fathers and the heights of sons. The data on 1,078 pairs of father and sons were compiled by Karl Pearson and Alice Lee. *Source:* Yule 1911, 166.

regression line, the Pearson product–moment correlation coefficient remains one of the most widely used tools in multivariate analysis.

The normal correlation surface between a measurement of the parent and a measurement of the offspring lent visual rationale to the eugenic mission but, ironically, little support to the theory of natural selection. Galton concluded that "the characteristics of any population that is in harmony with its environment, may remain statistically identical during successive generations" and that the applications of the law of error "were found eminently suitable for expressing the processes of heredity" (Galton 1889, 192). Galton's work in particular illustrates the remarkable stability of species. Galton was less likely than Alfred Wallace, Raphael Weldon, or Karl Pearson to countenance a law of deviation or frequency distribution that was not the Gaussian law of error. Nor could he easily mathematically embrace a nonnormal frequency surface. He left it to other biometricians to explore the nonnormal substantiation of evolution by natural selection: "The limits of deviation beyond which there is no regression but a new condition of equilibrium is entered into, and a new type comes into existence, have still to be explained" (Galton 1889, 258).

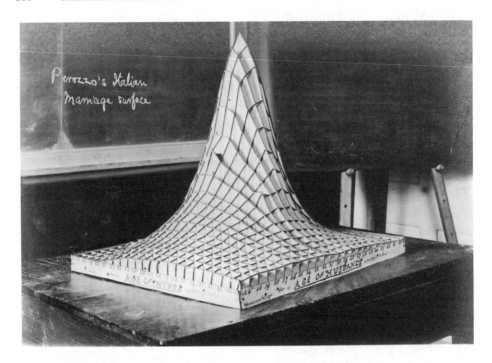

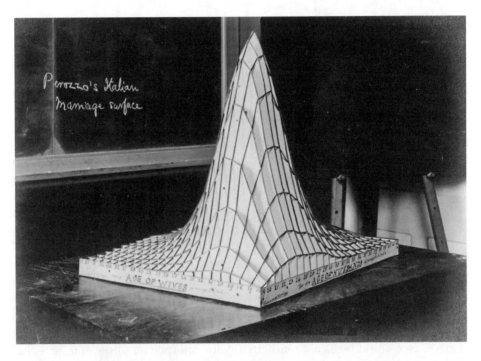

Figure 7.6   Pearson's photographs of the bivariate frequency surface constructed by Lugio Perozzo. The height of the skewed surface shows the number of marriages for a given age of husband and a given age of wife. *Source:* Pearson Papers, Box 230, The Library, University College, London.

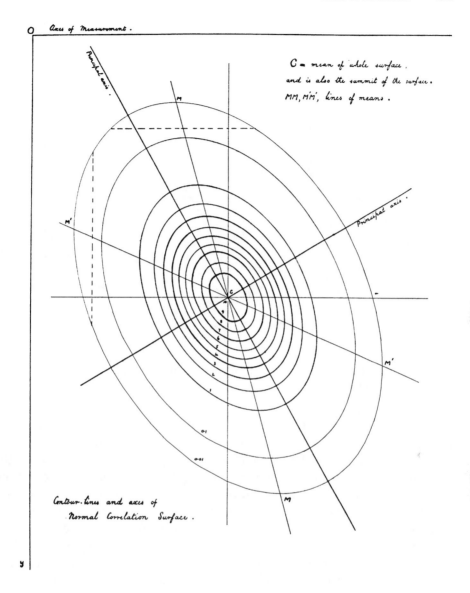

Contour lines of Normal Frequency Surface, drawn by G.U.Y.

Journal Royal Statistical Soc. Dec 1897. p.843 fig 6.

Figure 7.7   Yule's 1897 sketch of the contour lines of a bivariate frequency table that form the normal correlation surface. *Source:* Pearson Papers, Box 230, The Library, University College, London.

With the use of frequency distributions of cross sections of species and the bigenerational correlation surface, the stochastic processes of natural selection and inheritance became "mechanism by geometry." The geometry of the cross sections of the biometric samples was premised on population as species and

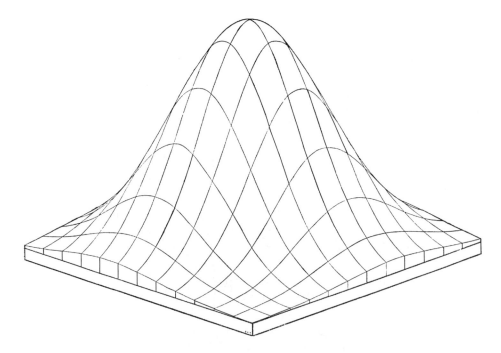

Figure 7.8   Yule's sketch of the ideal normal frequency surface with the extremes truncated. *Source:* Yule 1911, 166.

variation as deviation. The statistics that the biometricians formed into frequency distributions were often measurements of the same organ (e.g., height or frontal breadth) in different individuals from the same generation of the same species. The statistical techniques of frequency distributions, correlation, and regression are now often applied to time series, not just cross sections. With most time series cases, the clear generational boundary is nonexistent and it is doubtful whether we are working with a statistical population analogous to one generation of a species. In the next two chapters, I pursue this lack of the formative conditions of generations and species in meteorological and economic statistical investigations. I want to conclude this chapter with a brief exploration of another dilemma raised in the statistical analogy of natural selection and inheritance – the great burden we place on the word "variation."

Different Interpretations of "Variation"

We use the word "variation" to mean both static deviation and change over time. The debate between Karl Pearson, with his multiple correlation view of ancestral heredity, and William Bateson, with his particulate, Mendelian view of genetic heredity, is indicative of the ambiguity that arises in discourses on variation. According to the biometricians, two variables were correlated (either in the same organism or in parent and offspring) because their variation was partly due to common causes. The focus of the biometricians' investigation was a process of change – inheritance and/or evolution. Examining samples of populations at one moment in time revealed the disparities or deviations that were preconditions for change.

Variation, in the vocabulary of Galton, Weldon, and Pearson, was logical variation and it took on systematic form only in the context of a population at one moment in time. The idea that deviation leads to change was taken to the extreme in Pearson's "On the Principles of Homotyposis and Its Relation to Heredity" (Pearson 1901b). In this essay Pearson suggested that resemblance between two offspring of the same parent could be seen as a special case of resemblance between undifferentiated like organs in the parent. The correlation between two siblings is possibly an expression of the same phenomena as the correlation between two leaves on the same tree or any two measurements of similar characteristics of one organism:

> Now the reader will perceive at once that if we can throw back the resemblance of offspring of the same parents upon the resemblance between the undifferentiated like organs of the individual, we have largely simplified the whole problem of inheritance. . . .
>
> If this view be correct, variability is not a peculiarity of sexual reproduction, it is something peculiar to the production of undifferentiated like organs in the individual and the problem must largely turn on how the resemblance between such organs is modified, if modified at all, by the conditions of nurture, growth and environment generally. (Pearson 1901b, 287–288)

In an article typical of the acrimony between the biometricians and the Mendelians, William Bateson (1901) was very critical of Pearson's suggestions. In that article and in Pearson's reply (Pearson 1901c) it is clear that the different meaning each attached to the word "variation" was one of the chief sources of conflict between the two men. Bateson argued:

> By the word *variation* we are attempting to express a great diversity of phenomena in their essence distinct though merging insensibly with each other. The attempt to treat or study them as similar is leading to utter confusion in the study of evolution. (Bateson 1901, 204)

Pearson quoted Bateson's definition of variation from an earlier work and juxtaposed his own understanding of the word:

> Mr. Bateson's definition of variation: "For though on the whole the offspring is like the parent or parents, its form is perhaps never identical with theirs, but generally differs from it perceptibly and sometimes materially. To this phenomenon, namely the occurrence of differences between the structure, the instincts or other elements which compose the mechanism of the offspring, and those which were proper to the parent, the name *Variation* has been given . . ."
>
> Mr. Bateson's conception of variation is not that of a measure of the deviations of a population from its mean. To the biometrician variation is a quantity determined by the class or group without reference to its ancestry. To Mr. Bateson it is a measure of the deviation of the offspring from the parent. (Pearson 1901c, 325)

The subject of the biometricians' study was that of a temporal process. There is discontinuity in the process from one generation to the next. Correlation, a measurement of degree of likeness or association was developed to study this discontinuous process. The data, however, were not in time series form. Cross-section observations were used for each generation. Although the ultimate goal of the biometric investigation was to quantify laws of motion, the statistical populations existed at one moment in time; variation measured deviation or static difference, not change.

> The Primary object of Biometry is to afford material that shall be exact enough for the discovery of incipient changes in evolution which are too small to be otherwise apparent. The distribution of any given attribute, within any given species, at any given time, has to be determined, together with its relations of external influences. . . . The organic world as a whole is a perpetual flux of changing types. It is the business of Biometry to catch partial and momentary glimpses of it, whether in a living or in a fossil condition, and to record what it sees in an enduring manner. (Galton 1901, 10)

For Bateson, variation was the perpetual flux; for the biometricians variation was dispersion in the momentary glimpse. The biometricians used momentary glimpses to explain perpetual flux. These glimpses, the cross sections of a generation of a species, carried the capacity for change, and it was in that way that the laws of deviation were used to connect chance with the processes of evolution and inheritance.

Conclusion

Gauss's 1809 law of error became Quetelet's 1849 law of accidental causes, which in turn became Galton's 1869 law of deviation. In all three, the associated visual image is usually the exponential distribution curve of bell-shaped symmetry, but the metaphysical trappings that accompany all three are quite different. With games of chance, errors in measurement, and Quetelet's social physics, the search had been for the essence. Galton and the biometricians, however, focused on the creative potential of deviation. With the biometricians and the kinetic theorists of the late nineteenth century, the mean changed from the manifestation of truth, divine order, and perfection to a description of the typical constituent of a momentary population. Although Quetelet pursued the essence, his liberation of the error law from multiple observations of a single object was an inspiration to social scientists and other physical scientists. In their studies of dynamic interactions in gases, Maxwell, Boltzmann, Einstein, and others used the law of accidental causes to hypothesize stochastic processes. The velocities of particles of gas were marshaled into frequency distributions, and the laws of chance were used to model the laws of motion in the mass phenomena of the interaction of molecules in gases.

In the last quarter of the nineteenth century, the biometricians used laws of chance as a tool for studying evolution by natural selection according to the ideas voiced by Charles Darwin and Alfred Wallace in 1858. At any moment in time there were small differences in the members of one species. Those members possessing the characteristics most suited to adapting to their environment thrived, reproduced, and in some cases passed on their deviant characteristics. Variation in characteristics across the species at any point in time confronted with environmental exigencies led to change within the species and eventually to origins of new species. Deviation within the cross section was a condition for evolutionary change.

The concept of statistical population reached its full maturity with late nineteenth-century investigations of evolution. The biometricians Raphael Weldon, Francis Galton, and Karl Pearson started with measurements of one organ of one generation of one species. Their raw materials were statistics on similar but not identical members of a species, and the image ordering the measurements on the population often looked remarkably close to the exponential curve of errors in multiple observations of a single object. That encouraged Galton to trust his geometric reasoning as an appropriate and fruitful way of exploring evolution and inheritance. The curve of errors was a good fit for the frequency distributions of many observations on organisms. Francis Galton renamed it the law of deviation and Galton and Karl Pearson referred to it as the "normal" distribution.

Even when the law of deviation for an organ of one species didn't look exactly like the Gaussian law of error, the biometricians were heartened. If the frequency distribution was skewed or really the combination of two chance distributions, then it was a sign that Darwin and Wallace were right. Raphael Weldon and Karl Pearson treated the double-humped curve, the bimodal distribution, as the signature of natural selection. With awe, they witnessed in a momentary glimpse of the frontal breadths of crabs from the Naples shore the potential for the distinction of new species and the extinction of an old one that would not come to pass until centuries after their deaths. It was like James Clerk Maxwell seeing God in the invariance of molecules and seeing the Creation at the edge of all our calculations backward through the entropy process.

Karl Pearson and other late nineteenth-century enthusiasts of projective geometry tried to explain mechanism, the laws of motion, by looking at spatial structure. The frequency distribution of a species as evidence of natural selection was one of three geometric pillars of biometric investigations. Another pillar was the zigzag regression line or "polygon" showing the tension between inheritance and ancestral reversion. This autoregressive stochastic process, first formulated by Galton in 1877, is discussed in Chapter 10. A third pillar was the normal correlation surface showing the stabilizing influence of inheritance. Francis Galton and Karl Pearson and other biometricians searched for geometric form to support their eugenic philosophy. The burden on statistics was to produce evidence and quantification of how characteristics were passed on from one generation to the next. The pointed symmetry of the frequency surface enveloping the heights of fathers and sons gave weight to nature over nurture. As with Weldon's and Pearson's search for the signature of natural selection in the two-dimensional frequency distribution, Galton and Pearson used the three-dimensional surface as a tool of logical variation to analyze temporal variation. The distinction between these two meanings of variation, however, was at times blurred. For example, whereas the biometricians used the term "variation" to refer to deviation from a mean value at one point in time, William Bateson, a Mendelian, used variation to refer to the change in a characteristic from one generation to the next.

The attempt by the biologists to apply statistical analysis to understanding a process of change over time was carried on in studies of meteorology and economics. The biometry practiced by Galton, Weldon, and Pearson soon gave way in biology to the individualistic, deterministic approach of the geneticists in the study of inheritance and to experimental methods such as the analysis of variance developed by Ronald Fisher.[29] It was the investigators of social policy and economic theory who carried on the development of the techniques of correlation and regression. In these studies there was no obvious grouping like a species and no obvious boundary in time like a gap between generations. Also missing was the concept that cross sections carried the capacity for shifting the mean over time. In the correlation of economic time series, time and the schizophrenia of variation presented far more serious problems. These problems are explored in the next three chapters.

[29]   Biologist Lundy Pentz pointed out to me that the measurement approach of the biometricians and the pheneticists plays very little role in modern studies of evolutionary genetics partly because there are few one-to-one relationships between genes and traits that can be readily measured in the field. Most of such traits in organisms are polygenic – the result of the combined action of different gene products – and many genes are pleiotropic – they effect a variety of observable traits. Ironically one of the few recently documented examples of significant change in measurable traits indicating natural selection was a study by Peter Boag and Peter Grant (1981) of Darwin's finches on an island in the Galapagos. During a drought in 1977, birds that were relatively heavy with larger beaks capable of cracking the large hard seeds that were the only food were more likely to survive. Boag and Grant concluded that their results were "consistent with the growing opinion among evolutionary ecologists that the trajectory of even well-buffered vertebrate species is largely determined by occasional 'bottlenecks' of intense selection during a small portion of their history" (Boag & Grant 1981, 84). Boag and Grant's work is discussed in Jonathan Weiner's *The Beak of the Finch* (1994).

8

A Funny Thing Happened on the Way to Equilibrium: Economic and Statistical Ways of Thinking around the Turn of the Century

> I suggest therefore that the proper attitude for those of us who are primarily theorists is to ask in what possible ways our view of the economic world and the theories we have built up to account for it are influenced by the methods and results of the quantitative workers. . . . Is the normal of the statistician the same as that of the theorist? Does the statistical work strengthen a view of the world running in terms of equilibrium?
>
> Eveline Burns, December 1927[1]

In this chapter we continue our investigation into the importance of subject in statisticians' attempts to use the geometric reasoning of logical variation to investigate temporal processes. The focus of this chapter is the interaction of economic theory and statistical theory. In the chapter following this, we will continue with the subject matter of economics but emphasize the impact of empirical economic research on the development of time series analysis. As we saw in Chapters 6 and 7, philosophical musings on games of chance, errors in measurement, social physics, and biological evolution provided fertile contexts for the development of probability and statistical theory. In this chapter we ask what influence did economic theory have on statistical theory, and vice versa?

At a superficial glance there seems to be a good correspondence between nineteenth-century economic theory and statistical theory. With European economic thought, there were not only schools that encouraged inductive, empirical investigation, but there was as well a tradition of thinking in terms of populations. Also, economists used words such as "variation," "long run" tendencies, "normal" prices, and "stationary" equilibrium. A few economists, however, such as Eveline Burns, questioned whether the vocabularies of the statistician and the economist were the same. Political economists, for example, usually used "variation" to describe fluctuations over time. Although disparity was a theme for some nineteenth-century political economists, they attached little significance to deviation from a mean. Similarly, there was little voicing

---

[1] A copy of Eveline Burn's remarks at the roundtable discussion on quantitative economics, sponsored by the American Economic Association in December 1927, can be found in Box 3, Oscar Morgenstern Papers, Special Collections Library, Duke University.

in neoclassical economic rhetoric of the notion of cross sections carrying the capacity to shift means. The point of tangency between economic theory and statistical theory was process, not deviation.

In the 1930s, Aleksandr Yakovlevich Khinchin and Herman Wold described and modeled the stationary process that was to dominate time series analysis for decades to come. A stationary process was one for which the probability structure and thus the mean and variance remained constant over time. The appeal of the stationary process was that if the data generating process could be classified as "stationary," then least squares regression and probabilistic reasoning were appropriate tools of analysis. Economic theory played a major role in the specification of stationary stochastic processes, but it was often through indirect routes of frustration and contradiction rather than direct routes of deductive reasoning.

The economic value theorists of the nineteenth century hypothesized a nonstationary process in which the market price of a commodity tended to damp to the normal equilibrium price – the process of *tâtonnement*, as Léon Walras named it. This nonstationary convergence process, however, was rarely expected to be observed because there were always disturbances that caused the oscillations to persist (see the top plots in Figure 8.1). On the other hand, the business cycle theorists in the late nineteenth and early twentieth centuries wanted to focus on what statisticians now call a "stationary process" of the nine- to eleven-year trade cycles, but trends ensured that their data series were evolutive, not stationary (see bottom plots in Figure 8.1). This double dilemma, of economists at the micro level hypothesizing *damped* oscillations but finding no empirical support for them and at the macro level wanting to ignore trends but finding them ubiquitous in the data, led to tools and metaphors that fed into the ARIMA (autoregressive integrated moving averages) modeling of stationary processes.

The tone of this chapter may sound rather negative in contrast with that of the previous chapter on the biometricians' input into statistical theory. One point of this history of time series analysis, however, is that contradiction, along with parsimony and deception, was a creative force in the development of statistical method. We begin this chapter by exploring Karl Pearson's perception of the links between the political arithmetic, political economy, and statistics. After a brief review of nineteenth-century methodological debates, we look at the attempts of Ysidro Edgeworth to connect utility and probability theories. The economic vocabulary of the late nineteenth-century value theorists, in particular that of Alfred Marshall and Léon Walras, is compared with the vocabulary of contemporary statisticians. We will see how Walras's *tâtonnement* and Marshall's and Walras's metaphors of disturbed tendencies fed into the statistical theory of Oscar Anderson, Udny Yule, Gilbert Walker, and Ragnar Frisch in the first few decades of the twentieth century. We will also see that there were some missed opportunities on the part of the value theorists. Neither Oscar Anderson's statistical test for the empirical demonstration of a process of *tâtonnement*, nor Walker's test for a model of disturbed damped oscillations, were taken up by neoclassical economists. We end the

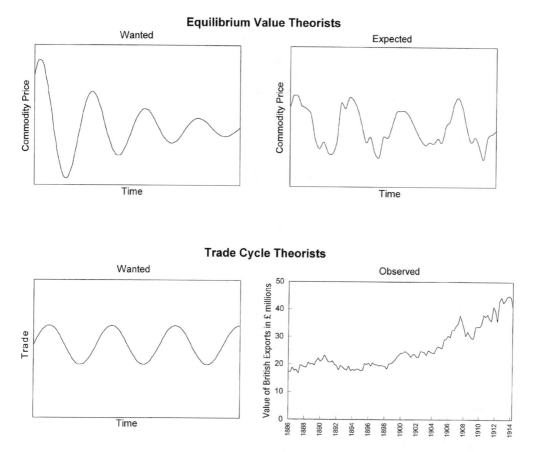

Figure 8.1   Time sequence plots illustrating processes relevant to late nineteenth-century and early twentieth-century political economy. The value theorists hypothesized a market price damping to an equilibrium point of rest (top left), but expected there to be disturbances stopping this tendency (top right). The trade cycle theorists wanted to work with the "barometers" of the seven- to eleven-year business cycle (bottom left), but their raw data were in the form of fluctuations (bottom right), which also displayed evolutive, seasonal, and irregular patterns.

chapter with an overview of the empirical approach to economics that coupled the focus on the nine- to eleven-year trade cycle in industrial economies with the propensity of statisticians to decompose economic time series. That leads into the next chapter, which contrasts the decomposition approach of most time series statisticians in the late nineteenth century with the function-of-time studies that flourished around 1914.

Political Economy, Political Arithmetic, and Statistics

In his observations on the bills of mortality in 1662, John Graunt constructed political arithmetic from the algorithms he had used in his shop to compute exchanges of cloth and money (see Chapter 2). From the seventeenth century to the late nineteenth century, political arithmetic, political economy, and

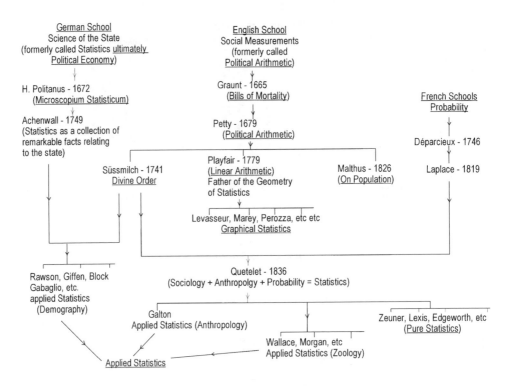

Figure 8.2   Karl Pearson's (1891) diagram of the history of the definition of statistics.

statistics, although not synonymous, were closely linked. Karl Pearson tried to disentangle the bonds in his introductory lecture to his course on the geometry of statistics in 1891. He presented Gresham College students with the chart reproduced in Figure 8.2 and argued that political economy and statistics had switched definitions in the nineteenth century:

> Thus traced from the historical and philological standpoint, statistics refers to *states-craft*, or perhaps we had better say *Political Economy*. The name itself seems to have first made its appearance about 1670 and was used pretty frequently for works dealing with the science of government for nearly a century. Thus Achenwall in 1749 defines Statistics as a "collection of remarkable facts relating to a state," while he terms his "outline of the Science of Government," a "guide to statistics." ... We may conclude therefore that the name statistics was rather used originally in the sense of *political economy*, than as a branch of the abstract science of number. We shall speak of this as the German conception of statistics. ... In the political arithmetic of our countrymen Graunt and Petty lies the root of modern statistics, while in the statistics of Achenwall lies the root of modern political economy. Thus we see that the words political and statistic have in the course of time just interchanged places. ... In the end the political arithmetic of Graunt has become statistics and the statistics of Achenwall political economy. (Pearson 1891, 2, 3 ,6)

Pearson tried to dispel the notion that statistics was related only to social phenomena. In their treatises on statistics, Georg Mayr (1877) in Germany, Maurice Block (1878) in France, and Antonio Gabaglio (1880) in Italy had argued that statistics was not only a method of observing aggregates that could be applied in any science, but it was also a science in itself. They perceived the science of statistics as a branch of sociology that could only be studied by means of the statistical method. Block used the words "la statistique" and "demography" interchangeably to describe the science of the political, economic, and social condition of a population. Block's term of "demography" stuck and other statistical theorists, such as Pearson, fashioned a different meaning to "statistics."

In Britain in the latter half of the nineteenth century, statistics had been strongly identified with the empirical studies of members of the Royal Statistical Society or Section F of the British Association. Members of these groups generally resisted the calls from the Continent for statistics to be recognized as a science. As Wynnard Hooper argued before a meeting of the Statistical Society in London in 1881:

> Indeed, it is remarkable that though in the practical business of conducting statistical investigation, and in the application of the results of those investiga-tions to the solution of the problems presented by political and other branches of practical social science, Englishmen are at least as advanced as foreigners, in almost all that concerns the theory of the subject, they are, comparatively speaking, "nowhere." I know of no work in English in any way similar to those of Dr. Georg Mayr, M. Maurice Block, or Dr. Antonio Gabaglio, to name the three best authorities on the subject. (Hooper 1881, 32)

The aim of Karl Pearson, Francis Galton, and Udny Yule was to take up the Continental idea of a theory and science of statistics, but to generalize it beyond demography, to marry it with probability theory, and to couch it in the abstract language of mathematics. Most of the studies in the 1870s–1890s presented to Section F or the Statistical Society had been for the "public man," as we saw with Robert Giffen's work in Chapter 3.[2] The presentations were usually numerical investigations into issues of public policy that relied on tables, the Rule of Three, arithmetic means, first differences, and percent change, but rarely on geometric laws of deviation, frequency, or probability. Pearson cautioned that, "We associate statistics too readily with Mr. Giffen's periodical demonstrations that we are really wealthier and happier than we feel ourselves to be" (Pearson 1891, 7). Using the analogy of geometry changing

---

[2] In his essay on "The Place of Economics in the Hierarchy of Sciences: Section F from Whewell to Edgeworth," James Henderson (1994) has documented the founding of Section F in 1833 and the attempts by Francis Galton in 1877 to abolish it because of its unscientific approach. Those instrumental in initially setting up a statistical section of the British Association included Thomas Malthus, Richard Jones, William Whewell, Charles Babbage, and Adolphe Quetelet. By the 1870s there were calls from Whewell, Nassau Senior, and Cliff Leslie to reform Section F, the Section of Economic Science and Statistics, into a more scientific endeavor. Robert Giffen, John Ingram, and Stanley Jevons were among those who challenged the calls for reform or abolition. By the 1890s, Section F was more closely linked with the Economic Society and neoclassical mathematical economics than with the Statistical Society and empirical political economy.

from a "measurement of land" to a branch of abstract science dealing with space in general, Pearson argued that statistics, originally a "measurement of state," should be treated as a branch of abstract science dealing with numerical aggregates (Pearson 1891, 14). By the turn of the century, both economics and statistics were becoming more abstract, theoretical, and mathematical. Although there had been the centuries-old intertwining of statistics and political arithmetic, there was not a late nineteenth-century convergence of mathematical economics with probabilistic statistics that had been approached in physics and biology.

The Methods of Political Economists

In the 1870s and 1880s considerable scholarship in political economy was devoted to questions of method. During these and previous decades many political economists perceived a distinct chasm between a deductive, abstract approach and an inductive, historical approach. At times this separation was embodied in separate people and even in separate national schools. The work of David Ricardo – for example, his *Principles of Political Economy* published in 1820 – was held up as the thesis, the standard to which English classical economists aspired and the foundation of a mathematical approach. The attempt by William Roscher and associates in Germany in the 1840s to grasp the laws of the evolution of economies through historical and statistical observation was the antithesis.

The thesis was the method of abstraction and isolation; deduction through *ceteris paribus*. Heinrich von Thunen eloquently defended this method in the preface to the second edition of *The Isolated State*.

> I hope that the reader who is willing to spend some time and attention on my work will not take exception to the imaginary assumptions I make at the beginning because they do not correspond to conditions in reality and that he will not reject these assumptions as arbitrary and pointless. They are a necessary part of my argument, allowing me to establish the operation of a certain factor, a factor whose operation we see but dimly in reality where it is in incessant conflict with others of its kind. This method of analysis has illuminated and solved so many problems in my life, and appears to me to be capable of such widespread application, that I regard it as the most important matter contained in all my work. (von Thunen [1842] 1966, 3–4)

Thomas Malthus, whose work inspired Charles Darwin and Alfred Wallace, was one of the early critics of Ricardo. The most cohesive opposition in Britain to the Ricardian method was, however, a group of writers on political economy led by William Whewell in Cambridge. In the 1830s and 1840s, Whewell and his followers criticized Ricardians for a priori generalizing on human behavior without observation. The Cambridge or Whewell group argued that methodical, inductive investigation was needed before the axioms of economics could be determined. They embraced the use of mathematics in this endeavor, but only mathematical models that could be verified with observations.[3]

The most striking antithesis to the Ricardian deductive method came in the mid-nineteenth century with the advocacy, primarily in Germany, of a historical method. Proponents of the historical method, including William Roscher and Gustav Schmoller, made the subject of the economic inquiry a population related through nationality. The object of study of the thesis had been the "economic man," an individual, separated from time, place, and others, acting under the singular influence of self-interest. The antithesis was aggregation – of individuals, of motives, of causes. The thesis had searched for universal laws of human nature. The focus was on essence, not population. The antithesis assumed differences relative to place and time. Advocates of the historical method emphasized induction, observation, and measurement to capture the variety of real life. Their audience, as with the political arithmeticians, was often the state. Political economists in the German historical school turned to biological analogies of human growth, development, and evolution to guide their investigation. Roscher called the historical method the "Anatomy and Physiology of Public Economy," and saw his task as capturing evolutionary themes of economic development. For Roscher, economics as well as economies evolved and the historical method was a natural maturing of the science of political economy:

> The abstraction according to which all men are by nature the same . . . , as Ricardo and von Thunen have shown, must pass as an indispensable stage in the preparatory labors of political economy. It would be especially well, when an economic fact is produced by the cooperation of many different factors, for the investigator to mentally isolate the factor of which for the time being, he considered as not operating and as unchangeable, and then the question asked, what would be the effect of a change in the factor to be examined, whether the change be occasioned by enlarging or diminishing it? But it never should be lost sight of, that such a one is only an abstraction after all, for which, not only in the transition to practice, but even in finished theory, we must turn to the infinite variety of real life. (Roscher [1877] 1878, 105)

Historians of economics see a synthesis of the abstract and historical methods by the 1890s in the works of John Neville Keynes and Alfred Marshall. The previous preoccupation of the classical economists with a one dimensional "economic man," or *Homo oeconomicus*, was to give way to a science of measurable motives. Like Roscher and Richard Wagner, Marshall was interested in

---

[3]   Norton Wise and Crosbie Smith (1989) discuss Whewell's criticism of Ricardo and his insistence on the importance of disturbing causes, dynamic reasoning, the elusiveness of equilibrium, and the influence of culture and morality on economic development. In his book, *Early Mathematical Economics: William Whewell and the British Case* (1996), and in an 1985 essay, James Henderson looks at the network of economists that worked on a mathematical, inductivist counter to Ricardo's a priori method. The "Whewell Group" included William Whewell, Richard Jones, Charles Babbage, Edward Rogers, Colonel T. Perronet Thompson, John Edward Tozer, Dionysius Lardner, and Sir John William Lubbock. I discussed the work of the last two in Chapter 5.

the stages through which the science of economics itself evolved. Marshall, quite unsuccessfully, urged economists to see their Mecca not in physics, but in biology:

> There is a fairly close analogy between the earlier stages of economic reasoning and the devices of physical statics. But is there an equally serviceable analogy between the later stages of economic reasoning and methods of physical dynamics? I think not. I think that in the later stages of economics better analogies are to be got from biology then from physics; and consequently, that economic reasoning should start on methods analogous to those of physical statics, and should gradually become more biological in time. . . . economic problems are not mechanical, but concerned with organic life and growth. (Marshall 1898, 39, 44)

Marshall argued that the assumptions of static equilibrium or of steady motion that enabled deduction through mere addition of forces or through mathematical formulas were characteristic of the earlier stages of economic reasoning. If the Mecca of economists was biology, however, Marshall and mainstream economists were never to complete the pilgrimage. Marshall is remembered for his systematic, mechanical analysis of markets, not for his biological analogies (see, e.g., J. M. Keynes [1925] 1966 and Gordon 1972). Marshall had argued that equilibria should be seen as the balance of the forces of growth and decay rather than static points where the sum of mechanical forces cancel each other out (Marshall 1898). The equilibrium analysis of *The Principles of Economics*, however, enabled Marshall to build up a "Copernican system" of balance. This system of points at rest or in uniform motion was strengthened with the logical, mechanistic concepts of "margin" and "substitution." It was not just that the reversible processes of balance and substitution at the margin were emphasized at the expense of processes of evolution, growth, and decay, but also that the abstractions of the economists often remained immeasurable, unobservable, and incommensurate with statistical and biological notions of population and variation.

Edgeworth's Connection of Probability and Utility

In the late nineteenth century the links between economic theory and statistical theory were few and far between. Economic theory did not provide a clear definition of a statistical population, and the variation hypothesized was unobservable. The concepts that were shared between the two – tendencies, normal, long run – had different contextual meanings. Ysidro Edgeworth stands out as a rarity in trying philosophically to match the theories of statistics and economics. He published extensively in both fields and explored the possible analogies between the two. For example, in an article explaining methods of calculating the modulus and comparing two means Edgeworth stated: "It is useful to have the ideal of proof before our eyes, even when we cannot realize it in practice. This function of the Calculus of Probabilities – to present an unattainable ideal – resembles that which the mathematical theory of Political Economy performs" (Edgeworth 1885, 194).

The strongest analogy Edgeworth drew was that between probability in statistical theory and utility in economic theory (see Bowley 1928).[4] Edgeworth perceived several elements common to both probability and utility: results were often in nonnumerical mathematical statements; parameters were determined by maximizing probability or utility; and both had subjective elements of personal belief or personal satisfaction. Edgeworth's approach to economics and statistics was a philosophical one. From that perspective he saw, as he wrote in 1908, a very close relationship between utility and probability:

> To return to the comparison between the mathematical theory of statistics and that of economics: there is common to both studies a certain speculative or dialectical character which recalls the ancient philosophies. "In wandering mazes lost," too often both pursue inquiries which seem to practical intellects interminable and uninteresting. These characteristics, it is to be feared, may seem to attach to inquiries, like those pursued in an earlier portion of this Paper, into the *a priori* probabilities of various measurements. In economics, too, other peoples' mathematics are apt to resemble the
>
> > "dark-lantern of the spirit,
> > Which none see by but those that bear it."
>
> This similarity of complexion is symptomatic of a deeper affinity between the two studies: the peculiarity that they are both in part metaphysical, unlike the recognised mathematical sciences in that they deal with subjective states of consciousness, belief and satisfaction. Jevons, in his powerful plea for the measurement of utility has dwelt on this analogy: "previous to the time of Pascal who would have thought of measuring doubt and belief?" The successors of Pascal had already before the time of Jevons thought of measuring utility. Bernoulli had initiated the mathematical treatment of advantage, under the head of "moral expectation." Bernoulli, in effect, formulated the law of diminishing utility which plays so large a part in the mathematical theory of Political Economy. . . .
>
> The cognate studies of probability and utility do well to keep together and support each other, for they have not yet won a recognised position among the arts and sciences. They occupy an insecure place between philosophical literature and mathematical physics, frowned on as pedantically precise by the one, and by the other as suspiciously inexact. (Edgeworth, 1908, 659–660)

This philosophical link was, however, not reproduced in a common conceptual structure that would have enabled statistical verification of economic hypotheses. Edgeworth eloquently described why the path of applied economics was so slippery:

---

[4] The mathematical theory that Edgeworth alluded to was the calculus of pleasure and pain used to analyze, among other things, how consumer satisfaction changed during a typical consumption cycle. For example, with the so-called marginal revolution in economics in the 1870s, economists began to talk of and plot out a law of "diminishing marginal utility" to illustrate how the extra satisfaction associated with consuming an additional quantity of a good diminished with each additional increment.

We have laws almost as simple and majestic as that of gravitation, in particular those relating to value and distribution; but these laws do not afford middle axioms, such as the proposition that planets move in ellipses deduced from the law of gravitation. So dense is the resisting medium which obstructs the free movement of the market; and not only in general dense, but also variable from case to case. (Edgeworth 1925, 8)

Foundering on a lack of middle axioms, Edgeworth's acknowledgment of a metaphysical connection of probability and utility did not lead to any major connection of the economic and statistical ways of thinking.[5] John Maynard Keynes took up the mantle of a philosophical approach to probability in his highly acclaimed *Treatise on Probability* published in 1921. Keynes explored the logical foundations of probability but there was little mention of, let alone connection to, economists' reasoning on value and distribution. Keynes was skeptical of the use of probability distributions and statistical inference in the study of economic phenomena. Although Keynes included seven chapters on statistical inference, he directed most of his attention to work of eighteenth- and early nineteenth-century probabilists such as Jakob Bernoulli and Pierre Simon Laplace rather than his contemporaries such as Karl Pearson or Udny Yule. Keynes began his work on the treatise in 1906, but he was not inclined to pursue the geometry of correlation surfaces, the notion of chance processes, or the possibilities for inductive investigations opened up with least squares regression.[6] Keynes's relative neglect of contemporary statistical techniques is illustrated in correspondence with Karl Pearson. In a letter to Pearson written on March 29, 1915, Keynes expressed concern that he had been appointed as sole external examiner for the University of London exams on economics and statistics:

In some parts of the papers in connection with the Faculty of Economics I shall be very dependent on Bowley. My main reason for writing, however, is that a few days ago I was much dismayed to receive particulars of a new schedule in connection with the Faculty of Science, of which I had received no previous information on in time. The knowledge of statistical theory, which is required for this, travels I find quite outside my knowledge. I could not possibly pass the examination myself and it would be farcical for me to examine in it as sole examiner responsible for the external students. (Letter from Keynes in Box 734/7 of Pearson Papers, The Library, University College, London)

---

[5] Edgeworth's work on probability, however, was not without influence. Stephen Stigler (1986) demonstrates Edgeworth's influence on Karl Pearson and biometrics, and Theodore Porter (1986) looks at Edgeworth's role in the development of mathematical statistics. In *Edgeworth on Chance, Economic Hazard, and Statistics* (1994), Philip Mirowski reproduces several key papers of Edgeworth on statistical theory and discusses the links between Edegworth's mathematical psychics and probability theory.

[6] When statistical geometry was applied to economic observations, money was usually there. John Maynard Keynes wrote treatises on both probability and money, but he was reluctant to join the two in a research program. Neither was he inclined toward statistical geometry. He drew neither law curves in logical time (as in frequency distributions or least square lines) nor fact curves in historical or relative time (as in Jevons's sketches of wheat prices, interest rates, and bankruptcies). In a sentiment that expressed both respect and caution, Keynes described Jevons as a pioneer of the "black arts of inductive economics" (Keynes 1936, 53).

Although William Stanley Jevons and Ysidro Edgeworth did ponder the philosophical links between utility theory and probability theory, few other nineteenth-century economic *theorists* contemplated connections between the economic and statistical ways of thinking.

Flow, Motion, and Rest in Economic Theory

The most essential process in the minds of many turn-of-the-century economic theorists was the unobservable, nonstationary, teleological process of prices and quantities demanded and supplied tending toward an equilibrium point of rest. This focus on the point of rest, or on the damped oscillatory movement toward that point, stands in contrast to an interest in earlier decades on the flow of economic systems. One of the themes of Karl Pearson's 1891 lectures on modern science at University College was, "Heraclitus: 'All things flow', contrasted with the modern view: 'All things are in motion.' " It was in the nineteenth century that political economy rotated perspective from flow to what Pearson described as the "modern view" of motion. Adam Smith, Thomas Malthus, William Playfair, David Ricardo, John Stuart Mill, and Karl Marx asked questions regarding population growth, economic progress, the interaction between capital accumulation and class relations, and the birth and death of economic systems. These studies from the late eighteenth to the mid-nineteenth century were generally speculations on flow. Assumptions of change-as-motion and mechanical analogies are not absent from classical reasoning. For example, Smith's invisible hand and François Quesnay's *Tableau Economique* seem more closely associated with motion than flow. Many questions of change in early nineteenth-century writing, however, concerned long time horizons and processes of growth, accumulation, and crises.

In contrast, Stanley Jevons, Carl Menger, Léon Walras, Alfred Marshall, and most economists after 1870 drastically reduced or eliminated the time frame of reference and broke up the whole into finer units of analysis.[7] With the rise of marginal analysis in the 1870s, economists' interest in population, as Joseph Schumpeter (1954, 890) described it, "tended to wilt." Charles Darwin and Alfred Wallace each remembered the day that Malthus's hypothesis on the unchecked geometric increase of populations sparked his insight into natural selection.[8] At the time that Galton, Weldon, and Pearson, spurred on by Darwin's theory of the evolution of populations, were statistically investigating variation and selection in species, economists rarely sustained an interest in population. Economists who empirically investigated temporal fluctuations focused on revocable nine- to eleven-year trade cycles manifested in prices and production of commodities; the trend or flow element was eliminated from the theory and the data. The short-time horizon and the analogies of mechanical motion were also a part of the "static" method of the marginal

---

[7] In *The Origins of American Social Science* (1991), Dorothy Ross carefully documents the North American economists' abandonment of history in the early twentieth century.

[8] For Darwin it was September 28, 1838, and for Wallace it was in February 1858 (see Wallace 1916, 92, and Mayr 1982, 478, 495).

utility theorists.[9] As Amiya Dasgupta (1985) explains, Léon Walras's "crying of prices" and Ysidro Edgeworth's "recontract" are illustrations of the reversible, particulate nature of a process of substitution in determining eventual equilibrium in commodity markets.[10]

Normal Value versus Normal Distribution

Although there were empirical investigations into the fluctuations of economies, which we will examine in detail in the next chapter, there was not a strong theoretical link between neoclassical economics and a statistical way of thinking.[11] We can see this even if we narrow our focus to three words frequently used by Alfred Marshall in his writings on value and distribution: "normal," "long run," and "stationary." Marshall's *Principles of Economics*, first published in 1890, set the scope and method of political economy at Cambridge University, in most of Britain, and in parts of continental Europe for a few decades. As Marshall explained in his preface to the first edition, the fundamental idea of economic theories of distribution and exchange was equilibrium of demand and supply, and laws of economics were "statements of tendencies expressed in the indicative mood" (Marshall [1920] 1961, vi). In this same preface, Marshall described normal values as "those which would be ultimately attained, if the economic conditions under view had time to work out undisturbed their full effect" (Marshall [1920] 1961, vii). In all the editions of Marshall's *Principles*, equilibrium was at the end of a hypothetical process, a point achieved in the "long run":

> The normal or "natural" value of a commodity is that which economic forces tend to bring about *in the long run*. It is the average value which economic forces would bring about if the general conditions of life were stationary for a run of time long enough to enable them to work out their full effect. (Marshall [1920] 1961, 347)

[9]   In *More Heat Than Light: Economics As Social Physics, Physics As Nature's Economics* (1988), Philip Mirowski argues that the physical metaphors appropriated by neoclassical economists, while long on the determinism and static mechanism of nineteenth-century energetics, were short on the principles of conservation and the dynamic implications that follow from those principles.

[10]   Following the lead of physicists, economists embodied motion in differential calculus and the balancing of marginal increments. Although differential equations have been labeled the "mathematics of time" (see, e.g., Ingrao & Israel [1987] 1990, 305), they proved more useful in the static rather than dynamic analysis of late nineteenth- and early twentieth-century economic theorists. A more appropriate label is Marshall's description: "the science of small increments" (Marshall [1920] 1961, xvii). The ambiguity of differential calculus as the mathematics of time is illustrated in Paul Samuelson's cautious qualification of differential equations as dynamic analysis: "By a liberal interpretation of the circumlocution 'variable at a different point of time,' we may bring differential equations under the definition [of dynamical system], remembering that differential coefficients characterize the behavior of a function in the neighborhood of a point" (Samuelson 1947, 314).

[11]   The lack of correspondence between economic and statistical ways of thinking is particularly acute after the "marginal revolution" in economics in the 1870s when economic theorists appropriated the calculus of variation to compare incremental changes in utility in the consumption cycle. Norton Wise and Crosbie Smith argue that before that time political economists talked in terms of the balancing act of statistical variations and natural philosophers saw the balancing act in variational calculus. Early nineteenth-century political economists – defined broadly by Wise and Smith to include, for example, Adolphe Quetelet – saw variation as empirically observed accidental fluctuations, while the natural philosophers deduced virtual variations and periodic oscillations (Wise & Smith 1989, 291).

Varations des Prix acheteurs-consommateurs dans chaque Epoque

Figure 8.3   Pierre Samuel Du Pont de Nemour's curve of a commodity price going to its natural terminal point after a tax has been eliminated. The graph should
be read from right to left as the price changes through nine stages. Du Pont assumed that the incidence of tax had been on the producer; thus the above curve
shows the price to consumers oscillating until it comes to rest at its original value.
Du Pont's original work on economic curves was presented in 1774, and he reported on this in letters, published in 1792, to Margrave Carl Friedrich of Baden.
The figure was redrawn from part of a set of economic curves, which included the
producer price changes, from a photograph of the original in Spiegel's 1955 translation of Du Pont's essay.

In his earlier work, as John Whitaker (1975, 70) points out, Marshall
qualified this tendency to the normal with the condition of competition: "Normal results are those which would be brought about by competition if it acted
freely, and always had time to cause those effects which it had a tendency to
cause" (Marshall & Marshall 1881, 148). Mary Paley and Alfred Marshall's
definition of normal price in *The Economics of Industry* is similar to that of
Adam Smith's and François Quesnay's concepts of natural value. For Smith it
was the value toward which market prices would go in a climate of competition
without the distortions of monopoly and government protection; for Quesnay
it was the value toward which prices would go if the government eliminated
the tax. These were essentialist notions of true, natural value prevalent in the
late eighteenth century.

The process of the market going toward its essence, the natural terminal
point, was sketched out by Pierre Du Pont de Nemours, a French physiocrat,
in 1792. Du Pont drew elaborate curves of the complicated path followed by
the producer price after a tax had been suppressed. Using the language of a
multiplier, Du Pont looked at the "wavelike movement" in price due to changes
in profit in successive periods or epochs. A part of one of his diagrams that
show the "*Variations des Prix*" for buying customers in each round is reproduced
in Figure 8.3. As Du Pont described the curve, viewing it from right to left,
"the waves progressively becoming less pronounced as the curves approach the
natural terminal point at which all must stop" (Du Pont [1792] 1955, 11–12).

This damped oscillatory motion is the image of the key process in nineteenth-
century economists' theories of value and distribution – the long-run tendency
to a point of balance and rest.[12] As with Du Pont, Marshall treated the normal
value as a terminal point of a singular process of change that had been isolated

[12]   In *Stabilizing Dynamics*, Roy Weintraub cautions us not to attach "linguistic fixity" to the term equilibrium: "'Equilibrium' has two meanings in a stable dynamic system – as a state of no motion, and as
an attractor of arbitrary motions of the underlying dynamic process" (Weintraub 1991, 18). While
Marshall's mechanical treatment of market equilibrium supported the state-of-rest notion, the work of
Léon Walras, Ysidro Edgeworth, and P. H. Wicksteed gave credence to the notion of equilibrium as
the coordinated outcome of individuals acting in their self-interest. Weintraub's book also illustrates
that we would be unwise to assume a linguistic fixity with the term "stationary." The stationary

from other processes. This is evident in his earlier writings and the editions of *Principles*. By 1890, however, when the *Principles* was published, Marshall's concept of normal no longer referred to the natural essence stressed by the British classical economists and the French physiocrats. In a letter to J. B. Clark on November 11, 1902, Marshall wrote:

> I then believed it was possible to have a coherent though abstract doctrine of economics in which competition was the only dominant force; and I then defined "normal" as that which the undisturbed play of competition would bring about: and now I regard that position as untenable from an abstract as well as from a practical point of view. (Letter from Marshall to Clark, in *Memorials* 1925, 414)

In another letter to Clark, Marshall wrote that in his doctrine, "'normal wages' = 'terminal' " (*Memorials* 1925, 412). Similarly in his *Principles*, Marshall divorced normal from competitive:

> Of course, Normal does not mean Competitive. Market prices and Normal prices are alike brought about by a multitude of influences, of which some rest on a moral basis and some on a physical; of which some are competitive and some are not. It is to the persistence of the influences considered, and the time allowed for them to work out their effects that we refer when contrasting Market and Normal price. (Marshall [1920] 1961, 347–348)

Marshall did not draw a geometric vision of this process of the market price tending to the normal price – there was no law curve in historical time, as with Du Pont, to show the path to a stable equilibrium. In his visions, the normal value was a point of intersection of two law curves in logical time (see Klein 1995b). Marshall also never drew a frequency distribution of possible market prices. Marshall's normal price was not representative of observed market values. In contrast, the biometricians appropriated the term "normal" to describe an entire distribution of observations, the mean of which was the typical value.

There are also differences in economists' and statisticians' use of the "long run." For eighteenth- and nineteenth-century geometricians and natural philosophers writing on probability, the "long run" was the number of trials it would take before empirical observations clarified into mathematically deduced order – it was the cutoff that yielded an acceptable level of stability in statistical ratios and thus accurate inferences. The long run of Marshall and other twentieth-century economists was the time period that would allow one to realize the ultimate effect of a steady force in isolation from all other causes and to draw conclusions about historical variation. In particular, the long run in Marshallian analysis of market value was the period in which there are no production constraints and the full potential of flexibility is realized.

equilibrium of the mathematical economics of Ragnar Frisch and Paul Samuelson, as discussed by Weintraub, might in cases be compatible only with nonstationary processes of trends or damped oscillations eschewed by mathematical statisticians.

Marshall's long run was a condition based on the rare simultaneity of time and *ceteris paribus*. The two usually converge only in the realm of abstraction or controlled experimentation. Marshall recognized that time was the chief difficulty of almost every economic problem:

> It is true however that the condition that time must be allowed for causes to produce their effects is a source of great difficulty in economics. For meanwhile, the material on which they work, and perhaps even the causes themselves, may have changed; and the tendencies which are being described will not have a sufficiently "long run" in which to work themselves out fully. (Marshall [1920] 1961, 36)

Both images of the ideal process of movement toward equilibrium realized in Marshall's long run and the messy reality of disturbed tendencies were taken up by those reasoning on stochastic processes.

Groping toward Equilibrium under Stationary Conditions

Although I have used only Marshall's vocabulary to illustrate the lack of a viable correspondence between economic and statistical terms, the same holds true for other late nineteenth-century neoclassical theories of value and distribution. Léon Walras and Vilfredo Pareto, of the Lausanne school, used mathematics more extensively in their study of marginal utility and the determination of prices in markets. Their mathematics, however, was not an edifice for inductive investigation into market processes.[13] In the tradition of Augustin Cournot, Walras's mathematics was deterministic functional analysis. It was a tool for rational deduction on a static system based on the analogy of classical mechanics. Although, some minor attention was paid to the possible dynamic reasoning on the process, Walras and Pareto focused on simultaneous mechanism, and an essential component of that mechanism, *rareté* or marginal utility, was deemed immeasurable.[14]

---

[13] Although Pareto did not pursue his study of preferences and competitive optimums with empirical fervor, he did help Swiss authorities in analyzing data on income distribution. Pareto's equation that generated a fat upper tail and the subsequent suggestion that such a distribution was best illustrated with a logarithmic scale for both x and y axes were both acknowledged in twentieth-century studies involving frequency distributions of incomes and prices (see Cirillo 1979; Arnold 1983). Paul Levy, Frederick Cecil Mills, H. F. Lydall, and Benoit Mandelbrot were among those who extended the analysis of characteristics of Pareto-like distributions. Philip Mirowski (1989) discusses how Mandelbrot began his explorations of chaos theory (e.g., Noah and Joseph effects and time-invariance in geometric structure) through his studies in the 1960s on hyperbolic price distributions. Although he does not link the irony with Pareto's work on general equilibrium, Mirowski argues, as did Mandelbrot himself, that Mandelbrot's findings on typical price distributions in capitalist economies are irreconcilable with neoclassical economic theory and econometric estimation techniques such as least squares regression, ARIMA, and spectral analysis.

[14] Bruna Ingrao and Giorgio Israel ([1987] 1990) have thoroughly documented the general equilibrium theories of Walras, writing from 1870 to 1900, and Pareto, writing from 1890 to 1920, in the context of the late Enlightenment and nineteenth-century mathematics and science. In their book, *The Invisible Hand: Economic Equilibrium in the History of Science*, Ingrao and Israel also examine the influence of the Lausanne school on John Hicks and Friedrich Hayek at the London School of Economics in the 1930s and 1940s and compare the aims and methods of Walras with the axiomatic treatment of Gérard DeBreu in the 1950s.

Although Walras assumed an arbitrary beginning in his illustrations of the process of the market price oscillating to the equilibrium value, the *tâtonnement* he specified was far from a random process. Walras's vision of a nonrandom process of prices slipping or groping toward an equilibrium value inspired the Russian mathematician Oscar Anderson in his classification of time series. In his study on the decomposition of time series, Oskar Anderson (1927) proposed a test of the Walrasian notion of equilibrium based on the presence or absence of random components in a price series. Anderson proposed classifying series by the "character of the behavior of the standard deviations of the series at its successive differences" (Anderson 1927, 562). Anderson classified series as either types Z, R, or G:

- Z stood for *zackig* or zigzag. Group Z series displayed an alternating pattern with negative correlation between successive observations.
- R stood for random. With Group R series the values of the standard deviations of the series for different order of differences would remain constant. A group R series could be the random component of a decomposed time series.
- G stood for *glatt*, meaning smooth or slippery. Group G series would vanish after a certain order of differencing. The G series could be the deterministic component of a decomposed series and could be modeled by determining what order of differencing was necessary to eliminate the G component and maintain only the R component.

Anderson asserted that his classification of series was analogous to that of German empirical economist Wilhelm Lexis. A theme throughout Lexis's work was the testing of the stability of social statistics over time. Lexis derived measurements of stability that made comparisons between series possible. These measurements led to the qualitative distinction of "super-normal," "normal," and "sub-normal" dispersion. Supernormal dispersion was an indication that random fluctuations were combined with "physical fluctuations of the underlying probability." Only in the case of normal (or "random-normal") dispersion was there demonstration of a "constant probability underlying the observed numerical relation showing the same uncertainty as would be expected in a proper game of chance" (Lexis [1879] 1942, 7). Subnormal dispersion indicated that the individual events of the mass phenomena were interrelated, subject to regulations or norms, and divorced from free will.[15]

Lexis perceived that the tight enforcement of a law could result in a series that was of subnormal dispersion or supernormal stability. He provided the example of the rate of school attendance among children as the enforcement

---

[15]   These three qualitative distinctions of stability of series depended upon the value of Q, Lexis's index of dispersion, which was the ratio of the actual dispersion to the dispersion predicted from combinatorial formulas. In the case of a supernormal series, Q was > 1; $Q = 1$ in the case of normal series; and $Q < 1$ in the case of subnormal series. Lexis found no evidence for subnormally dispersed series in his empirical work, but he found many instances of supernormal distributions in moral statistics. "Typical" series in the form of ratios had "normal" dispersion; one example of that was the ratio of male to female births. Although the "typical" series could be found in the physical sciences, most economic series were of the progressive, evolutionary type – there was a trend.

of compulsory education became stricter year to year. This series of attendance rates would map out an "evolutionary movement" that would test as a "subnormal series," which displayed less dispersion than one would expect even from a random series oscillating about a constant value:

> With sufficient legal compulsion the fluctuations of the ratio as it approaches unity become much less than those of an unrelated series with a constant underlying probability. Some compensating relations may occur between successive individual values when there is a pronounced tendency to enforce the law. The fact that the ratio is somewhat smaller in one year will induce a stricter enforcement in the following year. (Lexis [1879] 1942, 5)

In the cultural context of late nineteenth-century Germany, Lexis was very sensitive to the effect of government law enforcement on social and moral statistics. His example, however, indicates that a series of price ratios that tended to a unique value and had a index of dispersion $Q < 1$, might support the hypothesized economic law of *tâtonnement* to an equilibrium price.

That was at least Oskar Anderson's take on his analogy to Lexis's classification. Anderson's Group G series corresponded to Lexis's case of a subnormally dispersed series. Anderson argued that if the standard deviation of a manipulated series remained constant after several steps of differencing, then the series had a random component (a Group R series). If a stage of constant standard deviations with successive levels of differencing was never achieved, however, then there was likely no random component:

> If the behaviour of the series u is *incompatible* in its final differentiation with the hypothesis of a random component, this will itself be of considerable scientific interest, throwing light from a new point upon the inner construction of the series. Let me note the importance such discovery might have in connection with the reconsideration of the old ideas of Quételet, with the new theories of price-value, with the theory of the "equilibre économique" of the Lausanne school, etc. Unfortunately, I have not yet met such results, except in the still somewhat doubtful "dynamic law of Valenti" for the Italian crops of wheat. (Anderson 1927, 565–566)

Anderson had thus constructed an empirical test for the presence of *tâtonnement*. No economist to my knowledge followed up on Anderson's suggestion, but Anderson's method of differencing a series until the standard deviations converged became the standard method of differencing a series until it was stationary, then modeling it as an autoregressive and/or moving average series (see Chapter 10). There was an analogous situation in economists' speculations on disturbed tendencies to equilibrium. The metaphor was a fruitful one for the specification of stationary stochastic processes, but economic theorists did not take up empirical tests suggested by Gilbert Walker for distinguishing between a process in which damped oscillations were disturbed and a process in which the stationary oscillations were generated by an external cyclical force.

Disturbances to the Groping Process

Anderson had speculated that if equilibrium theory of the Lausanne school was correct, only the "smooth" component and not a random component would be evident in a price series. This would be similar to the case of Lexis's subnormal dispersion or supernormal stability. Even among advocates of equilibrium theory, however, it was acknowledged that the process of a market groping toward the normal equilibrium value was unlikely to be observed. Observable *ceteris paribus* was more likely to be witnessed in throw after throw of the dice than in quote after quote of a price. In economics, the actual observations were not expected to reveal a lawful or an ordered process. Even Adam Smith acknowledged that the "natural" price was unlikely to be observed:

> But though the market price of every particular commodity is in this manner continually gravitating, if one may say so, towards the natural price, yet sometimes particular accidents, sometimes natural causes, and sometimes particular regulations of police, may, in many commodities, keep up the market price, for a long time together, a good deal above the natural price. (Smith [1776] 1910, 53)

As Marshall later put it, "the fitful and irregular incidents of the market cannot for the greater part be reduced to order" (*Memorials* 1925, 157). According to Marshall, "the fact that the general conditions of life are not stationary is the source of many of the difficulties that are met with in applying economic doctrines to practical problems" (Marshall [1920] 1961, 347). The word "stationary" is another whose meaning bore different nuances in economics and statistics. Marshall's use of "stationary" is close to the twentieth-century stochastic meaning of a constant mean and constant variance in sections from a time series. For Marshall, a stationary country was one "in which each year is just like the past, in which each generation is like that which went before" (Marshall 1898, 46). The stationary process for Marshall, however, was not the microeconomic process of a market tending toward equilibrium, but the macroeconomic background of "steady flows."[16] Neither the "stationary" background nor the long-run process of market prices going to an equilibrium point of rest was commonly observed; there were, as Marshall pointed out, always disturbances. Stationary conditions in the background would lead to a nonstationary data-generating process as a price went to its natural terminal point; nonstationary conditions in the background held out the promise of an observable stationary data generating process of market prices:

> The economic conditions of the country are constantly changing, and the point of adjustment of normal demand to normal supply is constantly shifting its position. There are, indeed, constant tendencies towards that point as surely as, to use an old simile, there is a constant tendency of the surface of

---

16   Although Léon Walras also referred occasionally to a stationary state, he also used the term "stationary" to describe the state of equilibrium, the terminal point, in the auction process (Walras [1900] 1969, 85).

the sea towards a position of rest; but the moon and the sun are always shifting their places, always therefore changing the conditions by which the equilibrium of the sea is governed; and meanwhile there are ceaseless currents of the raging winds; the surface is always tending towards a position of normal equilibrium, but never attains it. (Marshall, quoted in Edgeworth [1891] 1925, 8–9)

Léon Walras had used a similar image in accepting the reality of the dynamic state of the market. In contrast to Marshall, who wrote from a large island surrounded by sea, Walras, in a move appropriate to his setting on Lake Geneva, used the image of an "agitated lake":

> Such is the continuous market, which is perpetually tending towards equilibrium without ever actually attaining it, because the market has no other way of approaching equilibrium except by groping, and, before the goal is reached it has to renew its efforts and start over again, all the basic data of the problem, e.g. the initial quantities possessed, the utilities of goods and services, the technical coefficients, the excess of income over consumption, the working capital requirements, etc., having changed in the meantime. Viewed in this way, the market is like a lake agitated by the wind, where the water is incessantly seeking its level without ever reaching it. But whereas there are days when the surface of a lake is almost smooth, there never is a day when the effective demand for products and services equals their effective supply and the selling price of products equals the cost of the productive services used in making them. (Walras [1900] 1969, 380)

As we will see in Chapter 10, a few decades after Marshall and Walras wrote on the reality of markets, the notion of a system tending to a point of rest, but always disturbed, was to become a powerful metaphor in Udny Yule's, Gilbert Walker's, and Ragnar Frisch's models of stationary, autoregressive, stochastic processes. Their image was that of a pendulum, or a rocking horse, which if allowed to pursue its tendency to a point of rest would map out a process of damped harmonic oscillation. In Yule's imagery, boys using this pendulum for target practice would persistently but randomly disturb this tendency to rest. The subsequent disturbed to-and-fro movement would map out a stochastic autoregressive process. Although Frisch gave considerable credit to Knut Wicksell for the economic notion of random shocks, the idea of continual disturbances to a damped oscillatory process of groping toward equilibrium can be found in the earlier work of Alfred Marshall and Léon Walras. Wicksell's insight was to see that the time curve of the effect could be very different from the temporal pattern of the cause – irregular disturbances could generate periodic fluctuation.[17]

Another quantitative worker who extended Yule's model of a dampening process subject to random disturbances was Gilbert Walker. In 1931, Walker generalized the autoregressive model of a physical system of natural

---

[17] In her *History of Econometric Ideas* (1990), Mary Morgan has a detailed discussion on Ragnar Frisch's theories on cyclical behavior. She also examines the work of Udny Yule and Eugen Slutsky on random disturbances within the context of theories of business cycles.

oscillations, all subject to dampening but buffeted by random disturbances, to take into account dependence on more than two previous values. He also demonstrated that a diagram of the autocorrelation coefficients plotted against the intervals, what Wold was to later call a correlogram, could be used to distinguish the source of the cyclical fluctuations. Walker used the correlogram to determine whether the oscillations of a variable were due to the fact that the external disturbances were cyclical (e.g., solar influences) or the disturbed system itself had an inherent oscillatory nature, which must be damped (as in Walras's *tâtonnement*). As with Oskar Anderson's test, Walker's method of discerning the nature of the process from time series data did not feed back to the economic theorist.

In her remarks at the American Economic Association's 1927 Roundtable Discussion on Quantitative Economics, Eveline Burns lamented the fact that the discussion between quantitative workers and economic theorists was so acrimonious. The discussion at that conference was a harbinger of the 1940s debate over measurement without theory versus theory without measurement. Trying to patch up relationships, Burns argued that:

> In calmer moments we are all willing to concede that there is a danger that the quantitative worker may concentrate too exclusively upon those things which are capable of measurement, and may even shape his concepts to the limited nature of his available data, while the qualitative worker – the pure theorist – may become so pure as to be unhelpful in a world where measurable quantities play an important role. Moreover in the last resort neither school will insist that it can progress without entering the domain of the other. (Burns 1927)

Burns was speaking a year after Oskar Anderson suggested his test of the equilibrium process. Three years later, Gilbert Walker demonstrated a method of distinguishing between oscillations that were generated from an external cyclical influence and oscillations that were the product of a dampening process continually altered by random disturbances. In later years, quantitative workers, including Herman Wold, George Box, and Gwilym Jenkins, would build on the differencing work of Anderson and the autoregressive models of Yule and Walker, which had been partly inspired by the mismatch of economic theory and reality. In her conciliatory role at the session on quantitative economics, Burns had pleaded with the theorists to learn from the quantitative workers: "Does the statistical work strengthen a view of the world running in terms of equilibrium? Certainly there seems no doubt that quantitative work will reveal to us new entities and concepts whose significance in the economic process we had not hitherto suspected" (Burns 1927). Burn's plea to the economic theorists went unheeded.

Empirical Investigations and Trade Cycles

In the late nineteenth and early twentieth centuries the links between economics and statistics were more likely to come from empirical investigations into the aggregate movements of the markets rather than economic theories of value and distribution. In particular, the focus on the trade cycle and the idea that an investigator could decompose a time series to capture this cycle generated reconciliations with the law of deviation and the mess of fluctuations. By 1890, it seemed a good start had been made toward answering Stanley Jevons's plea: "The deductive science of economics must be verified and rendered useful by the purely empirical science of statistics. Theory must be invested with the reality and life of fact" (Jevons [1871] 1970, 90). The synthesis, however, was not a comfortable one. For the majority of theorists, such as Jevons and Walras, macroeconomic empirical work and microeconomic theoretical work often remained separate. Measurement of actual economic phenomena spanned a spectrum from anecdotal empiricism to statistical inference. Alfred Marshall, who was a professor of political economy at Cambridge from 1885 to 1905, was nearer to the former end of the spectrum. He was on the one hand very critical of the application of frequency distributions, least squares, and regression analysis to economics, but on the other very enthusiastic on the necessity of observation. Observation through what Marshall called "field work" took the form of numerous conversations with employers and unionists, diary entries of correlated events, and visits to factories and commercial ports. A good example of his method used to investigate Giffen's idea of inferior goods is illustrated in a letter to Edgeworth in 1909.

> Ever since I saw Giffen's hint on the subject I have set myself to compare the amounts of bread (and cake, wheaten biscuits, and puddings) eaten at first class dinners in private houses and expensive hotels, with the consumption in middle class houses and second-rate hotels; and again with the consumption in cheap inns, including a low grade London hotel: and I have watched the baker's supplies to cottagers. And I am convinced that the very rich eat less than half as much bread as the poorer classes; the middle class coming midway. This proves nothing: but it is a fair basis, I think, for a surmise as to a probability. (*Memorials* 1925, 438)

Marshall's often-stated quest was for "the One in the Many, the Many in the One." His selective observation and armchair "data manipulation" enabled him to achieve empirical *ceteris paribus*. What was lacking in this approach compared with that of statistical inference was numerical precision and measurement of the reliability of conclusions. Marshall's approach was a quaint marriage of deduction and induction, but it was not the stuff from which the dynasty of econometrics descended.

Over half of all key works in applied time series analysis before 1930 used economic data (see Appendix 2). Most of these were investigations into seasonal variation or cycles of several years' duration in agricultural prices, exports and imports, and industrial production. In the 1860s to 1890s, Stanley Jevons and Clément Juglar, among others, used tables, graphs, and simple data manipulation techniques to determine the existence and quantify the duration of trade and business cycles. In the early 1900s Reginald Hooker, Henry Moore, and Warren Persons used correlation and regression analysis to estimate cyclical relationships. In order to determine whether one series was related to another in cyclical movement, investigators had to decompose their economic time series. The trend or flow elements, which might have caught the interest of the earlier classical economists, were discarded. Statisticians gleaned the methods for eliminating the trend and embracing the cycle – percent changes, first differences, deviations from moving averages, relative time frameworks – from merchants' and financiers' quantitative tools of the trade. The focus on the cycle and the bold notion that one could decompose a time series to quantify laws of motion came from political economists concerned with the short-term stability of capitalist economies. Henry Moore described the essential role of the trade cycle in economic analysis:

> There is a considerable unanimity of opinion among experts that, from the purely economic point of view, the most general and characteristic phenomenon of a changing society is the ebb and flow of economic life, the alternation of energetic, buoyant activity with a spiritless, depressed and uncertain drifting. . . . What is the cause of this alternation of periods of activity and depression? What is its law? These are the fundamental problems of economic dynamics. (Moore 1914, 1).

To capture the law of cycles with statistical tools of correlation, regression, or harmonic analysis, Moore, like other economic statisticians of his day, had to first decompose the time series of prices and production and eliminate the seasonal and secular trend components.

Lexis on the Stability and Decomposition of Time Series

In almost every empirical work of late nineteenth-century political economy, measurements taken at different points in time were used. In most studies, with the exception of the relative time studies of Jevons and Norton, averages and measures of dispersion were calculated from samples formed by consecutive measurements. Wilhelm Lexis was one of the few political economists to recognize that statistical ratios from such time series were often estranged from probability foundations and potentially unstable. Lexis was also one of a few statisticians to approach probability theory from induction rather that deduction. His attempts to measure and test for stability were based on the question of singularity of population. Lexis, influenced by his fellow Germans writing on the historical method, argued that statistical method was an essential tool of political economy for the study of *Massenerscheinungen* (mass phenomena). Lexis's notion that empirical work was an economical means of determining laws was clearly spelled out in his review of Karl Marx's third volume of *Capital*:

> But the facts of social life cannot be reduced to such a simple scheme; while the immanent social laws which Marx assumes to find in them are no more than hypothetical abstractions.

I conceive that political economy is an empirical science. The economic dealings of the conscious individual are its fundamental facts. From these, economic phenomena as they appear in the mass are to be explained. There being a large number of individual actions, the effects of some may serve to offset the effects of others. But other effects, again, are intensified, and bring about general phenomena, which, for the very reason that they made up a large number of individual actions, are subject to no rapid changes, and so possess a good degree of stability. Thus they become in a way independent of the will of the individual: they may even appear as forces controlling the action of the individual. In the flow of time they show such constancy that we may speak of "economic laws." This expression, while in strictness only figurative, is not open to objection, provided that it be not forgotten that the observed uniformities do not rest, like the law of gravitation, on some external force controlling the individual phenomena, but are simply the results of a number of individual acts, which, while doubtless reacting one on the other, yet are each independent. . . . Thus we may reach, by the most trivial empirical means, and without any reference to immanent ideas or laws of evolution, the same conclusion as Marx's law of surplus value. (Lexis 1895, 32–33)

A theme throughout Lexis's empirical research on economic and moral statistics was the testing of the stability of social statistics over time. Those statistics directly related to natural conditions (e.g., population statistics) were very stable but moral statistics less so. Time series data could reveal a variety of principal forms of fluctuation:

- evolutionary – displaying historical development
- undulatory – of which periodic is one type
- oscillatory – of which a special class is the typical[18]

The "typical" series was a group with the unique characteristics that individual values were in essence approximators of a constant underlying value differing from it only by random deviation. In all series, average deviation could be calculated; however, if the series had an evolutionary or undulatory character, one could only empirically characterize its variability, and inference could not be drawn. Only in the case of "typical" series, where the distribution of observations approximated a law of chance, was the relationship between individual values and the mean of a probability character. The Q value of the "typical" series indicated "normal" dispersion and thus "normal" stability.

---

[18] Lexis's use of "oscillations" in a statistical sense highlights the assertion by Norton Wise and Crosbie Smith that nineteenth-century political economists and natural philosophers shifted the concept of a balancing system from regular variation to accidental disturbances: "Oscillations average out at the position of stability; that is how a balance balances. All of these writers, however, use this idea to slide rhetorically from the averaging effect of periodic oscillations, controlled by constant natural causes, to the averaging effect of aperiodic fluctuations and variations, produced by 'accidental,' 'temporary,' 'irregular,' or 'disturbing' forces. Accidental disturbances are simply assumed to produce variations equally above and below the natural state. The image of a stable condition maintained by regular oscillation is thereby transformed, without explicit justification, into that of averaging out irregular variations" (Wise & Smith 1989, Part I: 280).

Lexis applied the analogy of games of chance in his classification of statistics that were in the form of ratios. For example, the ratio of male to female births was like the ratio of white to black balls in an urn. The analogies of target practice and the law of error were appropriate for series of absolute values, but Lexis concentrated on ratios. He therefore used the analogy of the urn and the binomial distribution to reason on the stability of series. Supernormal dispersion (subnormal stability) within a series indicated that the probability structure had changed, that the balls were drawn from different urns, that the samples came from different populations.

With time series data, probability analysis and analogies could be applied only if values formed "typical" series and thus were neither interrelated, nor subject to an enforced law, or the result of "physical" dispersion due to changing probabilities. Lexis did speculate on formulating curves of changing underlying probabilities in the case of evolutionary or undulatory series, as other statisticians were to attempt in their decomposition of time series. Lexis refused, however, to accord it a status of law:

> The curve of the underlying probabilities can be formulated only hypothetically. If one finds then that the average deviation between the calculated and the observed values is not appreciably larger or smaller than would be expected according to the theory of probability, the hypothesis is justified. One may assume then that the hypothetical curve reproduces approximately the true variations of the underlying probability in the given period of time. Such a curve, however, cannot be extrapolated since it did not represent a law in the past. It is nothing else but geometrical representation of what has taken place. The exact determination of such curves is usually not worth the effort. (Lexis [1879] 1942, 12)

Lexis did not see all periodic undulatory series as interrelated series, but he did argue that each phase of the cycle would have to be treated as a separate population to apply statistical analysis:

> The periodicity of the death rate is still more blurred by the seasons of the year. Series of this kind do not belong to interrelated series at all since the periodicity here is not determined by a definite rule but depends upon the periodical variation of external factors, the effect of which is not strictly uniform, varying greatly with many other conditions. In any case the periodicity of such a series cannot be neglected and each phase of the fluctuations must be treated separately. (Lexis [1879] 1942, 6)

Although Lexis took an empirical approach to political economy and statistics, he searched for probability foundations in his work.[19] His aim was not to capture laws of motion so much as to determine the distortions of temporal

---

[19] In *The Rise of Statistical Thinking* (1986), Theodore Porter discusses the influences on Lexis's mathematical reasoning, his insistence on breaking data down into observations from elementary populations, his concern with the relationship between the stability of statistical ratios and determinism and free will, and Lexis's influence on Ladislaus von Bortkiewicz, Alexander Chuprov, Andrei A. Markov, and Francis Ysidro Edgeworth.

change on statistical series and classify the series amenable to probabilistic analysis. In that determination he made the assumption that more than one population could be the source of observations taken over time on one variable. The observations had to be from a single population, the balls all from one urn, to apply the analysis whose beauty lay in the stability of the parameters summarizing a chance process.

In their bridging of commercial practice and economic statistics, Stanley Jevons, Reginald Hooker, Henry Moore, and others were in essence trying to determine the boundaries of populations. Statistics, as Edgeworth described it, was "the science of 'Means' . . . the term 'Means' of course implies the correlative conception: members of a class, or terms of a 'series' " (Edgeworth 1885, 182). Statistical analysis of time series data continually begged the question as to whether values from a time series of one variable were members of a single class or a homogeneous population. Economic data, with the evolutionary or trend component so prevalent, precluded assumptions of stability or homogeneity that Lexis and other probabilists insisted upon. The task of investigators who would apply statistical techniques of frequency distributions, correlation, and regression to economic data became one of decomposing series and eliminating the problem components – trends and seasons – until all that remained were oscillations with characteristic stability. The acknowledgment of the necessity of decomposing until you hit oscillations coincided with economists' embracing of the trade cycle. Detrending the data went hand in hand with detrending the economic way of thinking. Along with the rest of the sciences, economists abandoned flow to celebrate motion.

Conclusion

Nineteenth-century economic inquiry seemed suited for statistical measurement and verification. The subject matter was often a society or a market of many players. Economic laws were treated as tendencies, not the rigid certainties of physical laws. Equilibrium in value determination was revealed in the long run. Thomas Malthus, who inspired Charles Darwin, Alfred Russel Wallace, and the biometricians with his theory of population growth and checks, was a political economist. Also, in reaction to the a priori, deductive method of Ricardo, there was an increasing interest in the mid-nineteenth century in inductive, empirical approaches and in the quantification of relationships. There was, however, no theoretical grouping of economic phenomena into statistical populations with means and deviations. *Homo oeconomicus* was no *l'homme moyen.*[20] The late nineteenth-century neoclassical theories of value and distribution that shared with statistics adjectives such as normal, long run, and stationary, were deterministic with rarely any hypothesizing on sums of independent, accidental causes or stochastic processes.

[20] Not only was "economic man," in the stories of Ricardo and neoclassical economists, never presented as the average or the typical, he was also a lone individual maximizing his pleasure, minimizing his pain, and making choices with no influence from family, society, and the needs and actions of those around him. The biases and limitations of a theory based on such an individual are explored in essays in *Beyond Economic Man* (1993), edited by Marianne A. Ferber and Julie A. Nelson.

Under the influence of the historical antithesis, Marshall recommended that economists set their sights on the Mecca of biology. Ironically it was the twentieth-century application of the tools of the biometricians, not the organic models of growth, form, and evolution that eventually set the course for economics and econometrics. Regression and correlation analysis, combined with refined commercial practices of decomposition, formed the kingpin of twentieth-century econometric and time analysis of economic data. The key problem in this econometric practice was the unidirectional, evolutionary character of secular change. Time posed minor, surmountable problems if change was of a random or short-term, oscillatory nature.

The neoclassical economist was hoping not to find what we would now call stationary stochastic processes. Late nineteenth-century value theorists hypothesized damped oscillations of market price tending to an equilibrium point of rest. This nonstationary convergence process, however, was not expected to be observed because the tendencies were always disturbed. On the other hand, for economists searching for empirical laws on the workings of national economies, the trend was the element to be avoided. The presence of a trend in the data was undesirable in terms of theory – the focus was now on the cyclical behavior of economies – and it made probabilistic inference impossible.

With regard to the micro problem, Oskar Anderson suggested a method of classifying time series that could test the Lausanne school's theory of convergence without randomness, and Udny Yule and Gilbert Walker used the analogy of disturbed tendencies to model autoregressive stationary processes (see Chapter 9). With regard to the macro problem, statisticians adopted algorithms of traders and financiers for decomposing time series. Also, mathematicians' attempts to mimic trends in experimental data led to new classifications of "dangerous" series and evolutive processes. These developments in the classification and the statistical modeling of processes are discussed in Chapter 10.

Within the context of a science of means, deviation from the mean has a special significance. If deviation is to be more than just an empirical calculation, if it is to be used for inference, then the observations from which it is calculated should be related within a singular statistical population or constant probability structure. As Wilhelm Lexis argued, there was often the possibility that observations in an economic time series came from more than one population. The particular problems for the analysis of economic time series were what Lexis called the "undulatory" and "evolutionary" components. Seasonal variation and directional long-term change begged the questions, What is an average? and What is a statistical population? It was in this context that decomposition and, in particular, detrending became standard tools in the analysis of economic data. Decomposition as a means of solving the time–statistical problem is the subject of the next chapter.

9

Decomposition and Functions of Time

We are now concerned with data in the study of which the essential problem is the analysis of chronological variations. Such series are of major importance in the field of economic statistics, for most of the data of economics and business are variables in time – as bank clearings, steel production, volume of sales, etc. This dominating importance of series in time is not found in any other field of statistical research, and the development of methods of analysis appropriate to time series has come, accordingly, only within recent years with the wider adoption of statistical methods in the field of economics.

Problems connected with time series arise both in the ordinary routine of internal administration and in the analysis of general economic conditions. Sales, purchases, profits on the one hand, stock prices, interest rates, business failures on the other, are variables which fluctuate with the passage of time. In the analysis of such series it is generally desired that the rate and character of growth be determined and that periodic and accidental fluctuations be isolated for study.

Frederick Cecil Mills 1924, 252

Time is the great independent variable of all change – that which itself flows on uninterruptedly, and brings the variety which we call motion and life.

William Stanley Jevons [1877] 1958, 307

Our task in Part II has been to examine how natural philosophers and mathematicians working in different disciplines applied a statistical reasoning based on logical variation to comprehend phenomena observed over time. In this chapter, the subject contexts are empirical economics and, to a lesser extent, meteorology. We will see that these subjects presented formidable challenges to the reconciliation of logical variation and temporal fluctuation. In the late nineteenth and early twentieth centuries, statisticians turned to the commercial tools of first differences, moving averages, and relative time frameworks to make their time series data compatible with the mathematical tools of correlation and regression, which had been constructed for cross-section data.

So it is in this chapter that we can pick up the thread of Part I and see the outcome of influences of commercial practice on the shaping of stationary time series analysis.

In Chapter 6, we saw that in the early nineteenth century Carl Friedrich Gauss and Pierre Simon Laplace constructed a law of errors that they expected to be plotted out from measurements of a single object. For example, when several people measure the height of the same person, the frequency distribution of the measurements is likely to be the bell-shaped curve of the Gaussian law of errors centered on the arithmetic mean of the measurements. In the 1830s, Adolphe Quetelet used a similar observation process and law to describe what happens when we measure the height of many people from a population. Can we justify a further step of using the same tools to measure the height of a person through different stages of youth or the average height of a population through different decades? In what circumstance do measurements from processes observed over time constitute a statistical sample from a homogeneous population? When, if at all, does it make sense to calculate an arithmetic mean or a standard deviation to summarize time-ordered data? How can time series data be made analogous to a cross-section sample from a single population at one point in time?

Late nineteenth-century and early twentieth–century statisticians were confronted with these questions in their attempts to reconcile the messiness of fluctuations with a static law of deviation. Innovations in statistical method and theory in the eighteenth and nineteenth centuries had come from the disciplines that either could equate time to trials, as in dice throwing, or could freeze time and observe a cross section of a population, as in measuring the foreheads of 1,000 crabs on the same beach. Although the biometricians had statistical visions of a temporal shifting of the mean, the geometric structure was based on deviations across a species at one moment in time. The empirical investigations of Raphael Weldon, Francis Galton, and Karl Pearson into the processes of natural selection and inheritance were able to thrive on cross-section data with no urgent need for time series analysis. When other statisticians applied correlation and regression to time series data, however, it was immediately obvious that there were problems. Statisticians often got results in the correlation of two and more time series that were at best difficult to interpret or at worst nonsensical. Udny Yule called it the "time-correlation problem" (Yule 1920).

In the remaining chapters, I explore solutions pursued by statisticians in the first three decades of the twentieth century to the time-correlation problem in particular and the time-statistical problem in general. Table 9.1 outlines the various approaches to the time statistical problem. In this chapter, we look at the history of the first three approaches of isolating and correlating the cyclical components, decomposition into sinusoids, and modeling series as functions of time plus a random component. That lays the foundation for the final chapter, which looks at stationary stochastic processes modeled as autoregressive series or as moving summations of random disturbances.

Table 9.1 *Approaches to the time-statistical problem*

SEPARATE THE DIFFERENT MOVEMENTS

Assumption	Series are composed of trend, cyclical, seasonal, and irregular components
Goal	Isolate cyclical component to correlate it with cyclical components of other series
Decomposition tools	Moving averages, trend lines, first differences, % change, link relatives
Final step	Correlation of cyclical components of variables
Early studies	Hooker 1901, 1905; Norton 1902; March 1905; Persons 1923

MODEL SERIES AS FUNCTIONS OF TIME

Assumption	Series are functions of time and superimposed random error
Goal	Decompose into sinusoids
Decomposition tools	Relative time frames, Fourier transformations, periodograms, harmonic analysis
Final step	Declaration of periodicity
Early studies	Schuster 1906; Moore 1914, 1923; Beveridge 1922

ELIMINATE THE FUNCTION OF TIME COMPONENT

Assumption	Series are composed of functions-of-time and irregular components
Goal	Model and eliminate the function-of-time component and correlate residual series
Decomposition tools	Difference series until function-of-time component is eliminated
Final step	Correlate residual series or classify series according to univariate model
Early studies	Student 1914; Anderson 1914, 1927; Cave & Pearson 1914

MODEL SERIES AS SELF-DETERMINED DYNAMICS

Assumption	Values are at least partly self-determined; they are functions of place in a sequence
Goal	Classify series by serial correlation and/or model oscillatory process
Decomposition tools	Correlogram
Final step	Model the series as an autoregressive process with random disturbances
Early studies	Yule 1926, 1927; Walker 1931; Wold 1938

MODEL CYCLIC PROCESSES AS CUMULATING RANDOM DISTURBANCES

Assumption	Variables are partly functions of the interaction of random disturbances
Goal	Univariate model of oscillatory process
Final step	Model stationary series as a moving average of random disturbances
Early studies	Slutsky 1927; Yule 1927; Kuznets 1929; Working 1934; Wold 1938

Correlation and Subject Context

In the hands of the biometricians, correlation and regression coefficients were applied to a variety of measurable characteristics of organisms. In his classic 1896 article on regression, Karl Pearson lists some of these earliest studies of correlation of sizes of organisms. There are several things the early biometric studies have in common that were not shared by later economic and meteorological investigations:

1. The co-relationship was between the same organ of different generations or different organs of the same organism. Thus the x and y variables were measured in comparable units and although they were samples drawn from different populations, they were organically related.

2. The observations for each variable were taken from a cross section of the population at one point in time. Although the goal was to study heredity and evolution, the observations comprised a sample from a static, single population.

3. The observations for each variable usually displayed a "normal," bell-curve frequency distribution similar to the law of error. Similarly, the correlation table of paired variables yielded a near-normal bell-shaped surface.

Within a few years of the biometricians' investigations on anthrometry and inheritance, Pearson Product Moment correlation coefficients proliferated in studies of meteorology, psychology, social policy, and political economy. Each new subject area to which correlation and regression were applied presented unique problems and subsequent new parameters or techniques. For example, the relationships studied in psychology were often measured by incomparable units. Charles Spearman posed the problem:

> Suppose that we wanted to measure the correlation between the skin's spatial sense and its sensitivity to pain; we should measure both senses at a great many different places all over the body. . . . But then arises the obvious question, how far are the variations of distance between the two points of the aethesiometer legitimately comparable with the variations of pressure of the algometer? (Spearman 1906, 91)

Spearman tackled the problem with the suggestion that measurements of the two different attributes be converted into ranked data then tested for correlation. Spearman's rank correlation coefficient became a standard tool of measurement in psychological experiments.

The problems of applying correlation and regression to economic and meteorological data were of a different nature. Two decades separate Galton's first regression of the diameter of sweet pea seeds and the first application of this technique to political economy and time series data. Political economy shared with meteorology temporal mass phenomena. These two fields of inquiry had the following in common:

1. The data were usually in the form of time series.
2. The series usually displayed some periodicity. The temporal variation hinted at repetitious patterns of seasonal variation and multiyear cycles.
3. The frequency distribution of each variable was usually skewed and the amount of variation was a considerable fraction of the mean. Bivariate frequency surfaces were also skewed.[1]
4. There was spatial as well as temporal variation (e.g., in prices or barometric heights at different locations).

The problem of skewed frequency distributions was tackled by both Ysidro Edgeworth and Udny Yule. Edgeworth (1885) demonstrated a central limit theorem: even though samples displayed skewed distributions, the distribution of the means of the samples from a population would be approximately normal.[2] Yule (1897) used the condition of least squares to estimate a line of regression and deduce the formula for correlation and its properties without reference to the form of frequency distribution of the variables. With Yule's suggested approach of regression with ordinary least squares, rather than correlation through the frequency surface approach, the limiting criteria of "normal correlation" for the raw data became seemingly insignificant. We saw in Chapter 8 that there was some uneasiness about transferring the least squares algorithm, used to eliminate errors in measurement in exact physical relationships, to the estimation of inexact social relationships. For example, Alfred Marshall in a letter to Alfred Bowley in February 1901 expressed his concern of the drift of statistics embodied in Bowley's new book, *Elements of Statistics*:

> Perhaps the best way to begin is to confess that I regard the method of Least Squares as involving an assumption with regard to symmetry that vitiates all its applications to economic problems with which I am acquainted. In every case that I have considered at all carefully, I think harm has been done by treating the results as "economic." I regard them as mathematical toys. (*Memorials* 1925, 419)

---

[1] Egon Pearson (1965) argues that it was economic data that provided the first stimulus to Karl Pearson's interest in skewed distributions. In 1893, Ysidro Edgeworth asked Karl Pearson for suggestions in dealing with skewed distributions of commodity prices.

[2] In an essay in 1905, Edgeworth extended this even more by stating: "*The law of great numbers* states that if numerous observations, each obeying (almost) any particular law of frequency, are taken at random, their sum (or more generally linear functions, or approximation thereto) will approximately obey the normal law of error" (Edgeworth 1905).

   Warren Persons recognized Edgeworth's statement as essential to the statistical analysis of economic data: "Professor Edgeworth acknowledges indebtedness to Laplace for this principle, but it is clear that to Professor Edgeworth himself is due the credit for stating, explaining, and extending it. . . . Although this theorem is not even mentioned in most current textbooks in economic statistics it provides the justification for applying the theory of probability to the problems of sampling and computation of means from economic data differing markedly from the normal type" (Persons 1925, 185).

The momentum of least squares regression, however, was unstoppable. Economists, in particular, latched onto least sum of squares estimation that enabled them to mimic the *ceteris paribus* properties of the laboratory experiment, draw law curves in logical time, and estimate inexact relationships between variables with skewed distributions. Although only 36 percent of all time series studies from 1847 to 1938 listed in the International Statistical Institute's *Bibliography on Time Series and Stochastic Processes* were economic applications, 90 percent of all studies involving regression were in economics (see Appendix 2). Within a quarter century, Yule's suggestion was to become the standard practice in the measurement of economic relationships. In his classic article on the history of correlation, Karl Pearson asked, "Are we not making a fetish of the method of least squares as others made a fetish of the normal distribution?" (Pearson 1920, 45). Even Yule admitted, however, that least squares did not solve all the problems of estimating relationships between economic time series.

Yule's Study of Pauperism

The obstacles confronting statistical investigations in meteorology and economics were demonstrated in the first attempt to apply correlation to economic data. In a series of articles Yule (1895; 1896 a, b; 1899) investigated Charles Booth's assertion that the proportion of relief given outdoors, as opposed to in the workhouse, had no general relation to the total percentage of pauperism in those districts that administered such an out-relief policy. Booth, a social reformer, was concerned about the loss of liberty and the breakup of the family inherent in policies that were limited to indoor relief (i.e., the workhouses). Booth asserted that outdoor relief would not reduce the incentive to work.

Yule used data on over 500 unions in England that had been gathered in a survey in 1871 and again in 1891. Yule was first struck by the skewed frequency distribution displayed by measurements of the ratio of outdoor to workhouse paupers and of the percentage of the population that was paupered. In his first article, Yule calculated for both surveys a positive correlation coefficient, but warned that "as no theory of skew correlation has yet been published (excepting Professor Edgeworth's recent work which deals with an approximation not covering any considerable degree of skewness) we cannot say what weight can be attached to the coefficient under these circumstances" (Yule 1895, 604). He concluded, however,

> Whether we deal with general pauperism at all ages, or with the case of males over sixty-five years of age, whether in the latter case we take an Urban or a Rural group of unions, whether we take the year's count or the day's count, we find the proportion of the population in receipt of relief to be positively correlated with the proportion of relief given out-of-doors, i.e. we find that a high pauperism corresponds on the average to a high proportion of out-relief. (Yule 1896a, 618)

In the first few decades of the application of regression analysis, the interpretation of regression was that it gave the average value of y corresponding to a value of the x variable. This was consistent with the technique of fitting a line of regression to a regression "polygon" (see discussion of Galton's regression polygon in Chapter 5). In no publication of that time was a coefficient of regression translated as $\Delta y / \Delta x$. Yule, however, did make a table ranking districts from smallest to largest ratios of out-paupers to one in-pauper. For each class he gave the corresponding mean percentage of population in receipt of relief. Yule used the language of fluctuations – "rise" and "increased" – to make static comparisons between high and low rankings in his table; he described this table as showing "that the rise in pauperism, as the out-relief ratio was increased was well marked and uniform" (Yule 1896a, 613). A step had been taken in substituting logical time for historical time.

In his most thorough treatment of poor-law statistics, Yule (1899) investigated causes of *changes* in pauperism. In his textbook on statistics, Yule explained why he concentrated on changes:

> On the whole, it would seem better to correlate *changes* in pauperism with *changes* in various possible factors. If we say that a high rate of pauperism in some districts is due to lax administration, we presumably mean that as administration became lax, pauperism rose, or that if administration were more strict, pauperism would decrease; if we say that the high pauperism is due to depressed condition of industry, we mean that when industry recovers, pauperism will fall. When we say, in fact, that any one variable is a factor of pauperism, we mean that *changes* in that variable are accompanied by *changes* in the percentage of the population in receipt of relief, either in the same or reverse direction. It will be better, therefore, to deal with changes in pauperism and possible factors. (Yule 1911, 192)

Yule captured the "changes" by correlating cross-section data of one year's value as a ratio to the value recorded ten years previously. The changes in pauperism and his explanatory variables were all measured as percentage ratios – for example, pauperism in 1881 multiplied by 100 and divided by pauperism in 1871. Yule did not use simple differences or percentage change over the decade because he did not want to work with negative signs.

Yule's study was also one of the first applications of multiple regression; in addition to the out-relief ratio, he used the proportion of elderly and population as independent variables. Yule noted that this method of splitting an effect into portions due to several causes yielded estimates of the algebraic parts of the whole change not fractional parts. In some cases the change ascribed to a change in out-relief was greater than the whole change that had taken place, but against that there would be something to offset it due to another cause. Yule concluded that his method of multiple correlation of changes from 1871 to 1881 and 1881 to 1891 revealed that changes in pauperism were due to changes in administrative policy, not external causes such as growth of population or economic changes.

Despite his own contribution to the study of nonnormal distributions, Edgeworth in his discussion of Yule's presentation to the Royal Statistical Society in 1899 worried about the lack of compliance with the laws of error:

> Perhaps he went a little further than Mr. Yule in the importance which he attached to normality, but to him it appeared that if one diverged much from that rule, one was on an ocean without rudder or compass. This law of error was more universal perhaps than the law of gravity. (Edgeworth's discussion in Yule 1899, 288)

Edgeworth encouraged Yule to devote his attention to moral and social phenomena which fulfilled the law. Edgeworth's plea was made a few years *after* his own demonstration of the asymptotic normal distribution of means from nonnormal samples and Yule's work on least squares regression.

Although Yule's data consisted of pairs of time-ordered data, his analysis was on the cross sections of these pairs. Additional problems appeared when Yule and other statisticians used correlation and regression on pure time series. The earliest examples of this are summarized in Table 9.2. Problems that were immediately obvious to the investigators, in addition to skewed correlation, were time lags, and the influence of trends on the results. Time presented to economists, as well as meteorologists, the question of intervals between cause and effect. Correlation with lagged values tackled this; the independent variable was dated at earlier times than the dependent variable. Trends were perceived to be a problem because economic statisticians were usually interested only in cyclical phenomena. To grasp the co-relationships within the trade cycle, statisticians had to first decompose their raw time series.

Correlation of Decomposed Time Series

Although empirical investigations in economics and meteorology shared similar problems in the application of correlation and regression to time series data, there were some differences:

1. In meteorological correlation studies, the measurements of the x and y variables were usually measurements of the same type of instrument, for example, the barometer. Although the two samples being related were time series from two different stations, the assumption was often that the weather at one station would, in a few hours, be the weather at the other. The correlation of barometric heights at different stations was thus very similar to serial correlation. In correlations of economic data, the x and y variables were usually measurements from *different* instruments or phenomena, for example, the price of wheat correlated with the marriage rate or exports of cotton.
2. Economic observations were often aggregates, averages, or relative numbers.
3. The meteorological observations used in the early studies rarely exhibited a perceptible secular change. There were random, cyclical, and

seasonal components, but there was rarely a trend, which was so prevalent in economic data.

Economists turned to statistics in search of "barometers" of trade cycles and of short-term oscillations. Unlike barometric pressure, however, measurements of economic and commercial phenomena showed secular changes through "general movement" as well as random and periodic changes. Ironically, capturing the laws of motion with economic data was difficult, if not impossible, because of the ubiquitous presence of flow.[3] For the economist, correlation analysis begged the question of which of the several components of the time series were to be correlated. Several of the earliest studies mention the different movements of a variable due to forces acting in different time frameworks. Among the movements described were:

- rapid, irregular movements from observation to observation
- seasonal movement within the year
- oscillations of about ten-years corresponding to the "wave in trade"
- slow, secular movement either nonperiodic or periodic with a very long period – the trend or evolutionary or progressive element

The earliest writers saw the time-correlation problem as isolating the different components and correlating only similar components of two or more variables. It was usually of greater interest to economists to investigate correlation of short-term oscillations, in particular the movement through the trade or business cycle. Economic statisticians recognized that the correlation coefficients of unmanipulated observations only indicated a relationship between the secular changes.[4] In a *Handbook of Mathematical Statistics* published in 1924, the Harvard statistician Warren Persons summarized the decomposition approach that had been the standard practice for two decades:

> If our problem is to ascertain the relationship between two series ordered in time it is of little avail (or actually misleading) to compute the coefficient of correlation from pairs of the actual items. In case the two series possess definite trends or seasonal variation the coefficient of correlation for the items will yield a value different from zero. Having found such a coefficient we would be unable to say what contributed most largely to the result – similar (or diverse) trends, seasonal variations, cyclical movements, or irregular fluctuations. Generally in the comparison of two time series it is the relation between their respective cyclical variations that is most interesting from the practical point of view. In order that this relation may be set forth either graphically or by use of the correlation coefficient, it is necessary to remove from the actual items that portion of their values ascribable to secular trend

---

[3]   The trend was a problem peculiar to economics. This is evident in the *Bibliography on Time Series and Stochastic Processes* (see Appendix 2). Although only 36 percent of all time series studies between 1847 and 1938 were in economics, 88 percent of studies involving trend analysis were in economics.

[4]   This is illustrated in Figure 1.4 in the introductory chapter. In the short-term movements from point to point, as x increases, y decreases. The slope coefficient estimated from least squares regression, however, is positive; because of the presence of a trend in both x and y, over the entire sample higher than average values of x are associated with higher than average values of y.

Table 9.2 *The earliest applications of regression analysis to time series data*

Date	Author	Title	Perceived problem	Solution	Comments
1897	K. Pearson A. Lee	"On the Distribution of Frequency (Variation and Correlation) of Barometric Heights at Divers Stations"	Skewed frequency distributions Possible irregularity due to periodicity	Yule (1897) had shown correlation still reliable Selected observations to cover entire period	x and y variables measured the same phenomena at the same time at different locations There was no trend present
1899	G. U. Yule	"An Investigation into the Causes of Changes in Pauperism in England"	Skewed frequency distributions Causation of change	Least squares regression used Cross-section data of ratios of one year over previous decade's value	x causes, y effect, Multiple regression
1901	R. H. Hooker	"Correlation of the Marriage Rate with Trade"	Compounding of several movements due to different causes, correlation only picks up trend not oscillations Marriage Rate does not respond immediately to general prosperity	Deviations calculated from instantaneous average of all observations in the period of which that moment is the central point Determine lag of relationship by highest R^2	Coined the term "trend" Population from which the mean is calculated is determined by annual observations from one complete cycle
1902	J. P. Norton	*Statistical Studies in the New York Money Market*	Correlation of periodic movements without trends	Deviations calculated from "growth axis," an interpolated logarithmic curve Relative time framework of weeks in a year	First correlation of weekly financial data Used first differences and regression polygons
1905	F. E. Cave-Brown-Cave	"On the Influence of the Time Factor on the Correlation between Barometric Heights at Stations More Than 1000 Miles Apart"	To forecast barometric pressure from earlier reading someplace else Summer and winter different	Lag measurements from one station Divide sample by equinoxes	First serial correlation Correlation of first differences

Table 9.2 (cont.)

Date	Author	Title	Perceived problem	Solution	Comments
1905	R. H. Hooker	"On the Correlation of Successive Observations; Illustrated by Corn Prices"	To eliminate trends	If cyclical, then calculate deviations from instantaneous average If not periodic, correlate first differences	Distinguished practice of correlating deviations from moving average and correlating first differences
1905	L. March	"Comparison numérique de courbes statistiques"	To distinguish "des changement annuels, de changement polyannuel, des changements séculaires" in financial data	Correlate deviations from instantaneous average determined by graphical interpolation Correlate annual changes	Coined the term "decomposition"

and seasonal variations. It would be desirable also to eliminate the irregular fluctuations, but this appears to be impossible in general because, by definition, such fluctuations are unsystematic. Our problem, then, resolves itself into two parts, first, the measurement and elimination of seasonal variation and secular trend from each series under investigation, and, second, the measurement of the correlation between the two series of items thus "corrected." (Persons 1924, 150–151)

Decomposition and Trade Cycles

As Persons pointed out, generally early twentieth–century investigators were only interested in correlating the components of time series that corresponded to four- to ten- year cycles in social and economic variables. The emphasis on the cycle and the problem of the trend can be seen in Arthur Bowley's (1901) and Reginald Hooker's (1901) studies of the relationship between the marriage rate and the price of wheat and trade. The relationship between the marriage rate and trade was one of the most investigated topics in late nineteenth- and early twentieth-century statistics. As early as 1798, Thomas Malthus had hypothesized a cyclical relationship between economic prosperity and the marriage rate. Malthus argued that if food became plentiful and real wages increased, the marriage rate, and thus the fertility rate, would increase. The subsequent increase in population would lead to lower real wages, less food for everyone, and eventually a lower marriage rate; then the cycle would begin again. Hooker and Bowley, both writing in 1901, were not alone in trying to determine the extent of this relationship originally hypothesized by Malthus: William Farr, the registrar general of Britain, used tables in several reports in the 1870s and 1880s to link fluctuations in trade and the marriage rate; William Ogle in 1890 and Reginald Hooker in 1898 used graphs of absolute values; and Udny Yule in 1906 and William Beveridge in 1912 used correlation coefficients and graphs to explore the relationship.[5] These British studies followed the periodization of forms of quantitative reasoning spelled out in Chapter 1 with Farr working through tables, Ogle and Bowley working through graphs of data, and Hooker working through graphs of results.

In his 1901 study, Bowley argued that in the early nineteenth century, when wheat was the major object of working-class expenditure, an increase in the price of wheat would lead to a decrease in the marriage rate. In the latter quarter of the nineteenth century a different relationship became important: "On the other hand, now that wheat is cheap and wages higher, a change in the price of the loaf is only of great importance to a minority; it is now the general prosperity of the country, well indicated by the condition of foreign trade, that raises the marriage rate" (Bowley 1901, 176).

---

[5]   Several of the early statistical investigations of trade and marriage were summarized by Dorothy Swaine Thomas in *Social Aspects of the Business Cycle*. The book, published in 1925, also includes Thomas's own investigation, which used the statistical methods pioneered by Bowley, Wesley Mitchell, and Warren Persons.

Bowley's hypothesis of connecting links was not, however, immediately obvious from a simple diagram of the three variables. The problem can be seen in Bowley's plot of the marriage rate, total exports and imports per head, and the price of wheat from 1860 to 1896 (Figure 9.1a). He used this and subsequent plots to illustrate the diagrammatic method in his *Elements of Statistics*. Although Bowley did not speak in terms of trends, it is evident from the diagram that there is very little long-term relationship between the marriage rate and the other two variables; there is a very slight tendency for the marriage rate to decrease over the period; there is a considerable downward trend in the price of wheat; and there is an upward trend in total trade per capita. To highlight the correspondence of their cyclical fluctuations, Bowley plotted the marriage rate and total trade per capita with each variable scaled on a separate y axis such that their average value for the thirty-six years was at the same height (Figure 9.1b). Bowley also plotted these two variables such that their fluctuations were proportional to one another. He calculated the average differences between local maximums and minimums and then took the proportion between these two averages; he thus hypothesized that a change of £1 in the total trade per head synchronized with a change of .5 in the marriage rate per thousand. Despite these manipulations, there were still problems:

> Our conclusion is, that since 1870 the causes which affect foreign trade have also affected the marriage rate at the same dates and in the same sense, and that the more marked the effects on the one, the more marked are the effects on the other also, but that there is no law of simple proportion between them. (Bowley 1901, 177)

Hooker, however, went after that "law of simple proportion" with more sophisticated tools. Bowley's "corrected" series were the deviations from the arithmetic mean of the entire sample of annual observations from 1860 to 1894; he used the Rule of Three and a graphical method of testing for the simultaneous relationship. Hooker's "corrected" series were the deviations from a moving average; he used a correlation coefficient to estimate and test for relationships; and he used the graphical method to determine the optimal lag. Bowley talked only of the curves rising or falling together, and did not dance around the idea of a "trend." Bowley saw the difficulty of assuming a fixed simple proportion between his two "corrected" series as a trade-off between the graphic closeness of curves in the latter part of the series and graphic closeness in the earlier part.

Hooker named the problem a "trend," isolated it with a moving average spanning the trade cycle, then eliminated it by subtracting the moving average from the actual value. Hooker calculated correlation coefficients for pairs of "corrected" series: the marriage rate and various variables measuring trade including exports per head, imports per head, total trade per head, and the price of wheat. In the first step in this process, Hooker used the smoothing

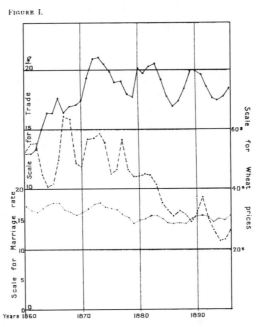

Figure 9.1a   Arthur Bowley's plot of annual observations on the marriage rate, total trade per head, and the price of wheat from 1860 to 1896. *Source:* Bowley 1901, 175.

algorithm that had been first used by the Bank of England in its veiled public reporting of cash and bullion from 1832 to 1844 (see Chapter 4). In appropriating the moving average, Hooker alluded to the humble nature of his method of detrending:

> What I wish to suggest here, however, is an elementary method of eliminating the general movement in the particular case – which is of frequent occurrence – of phenomena exhibiting similar regular periodic movements, so as to enable us to correlate the oscillations.
>
> To correlate the oscillations of two curves, I propose that all deviations should be reckoned, not from the average of the whole period, but from the instantaneous average at the moment. The curve or line representing the successive instantaneous averages I propose to call the *trend*. Any point on the trend will be represented by the average of all the observations the period of which that moment is the central point; e.g. if a curve shows a period of *p* years, the instantaneous average in any year is the average of the *p* years of which that particular year is the middle. By working out this instantaneous average for consecutive observations, we obtain the trend of the curve; i.e., the directions in which the variable is really moving when the oscillations are discarded. (Hooker 1901, 486)

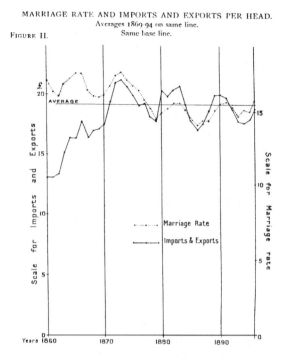

MARRIAGE RATE AND IMPORTS AND EXPORTS PER HEAD.
Averages 1869-94 on same line.
FIGURE II.   Same base line.

Figure 9.1b   Arthur Bowley's plot of annual observations on total trade per head and the marriage rate, with the former measured on the left y axis and the latter on the right y axis. Bowley highlighted the correspondence of their cyclical fluctuations by making the average of the two series the same height. *Source:* Bowley 1901, 175.

Reginald Hooker's method of decomposition was therefore to construct a new "corrected" series by calculating deviations from a moving average of the original series. Hooker reckoned that there were about nine years between maximums in trade; the nine years became his span for calculating a moving average. Each raw observation successively served as a central point in the moving-average calculation, with each value being the average of the actual value for that year and the four years before and the four years after. It was the method suggested by John Poynting (see Chapter 4), but Hooker went beyond visual confirmation to quantify correlation. Of more significance, he recognized that the statistical foundation of this method of averaging was the periodic movement of a series.

Hooker had calculated a correlation coefficient of only $r = .18$ for the correlation of the raw values of annual exports per capita and the marriage rate for Britain from 1861 to 1895. With his detrended series, constructed from the deviations from the respective nine-year moving averages, Hooker calculated $r = .80$. He bettered that even more to $r = .86$, by correlating the detrended marriage rate in any one year with detrended exports per head a half year earlier (he formed the series of trade figures that lagged half a year by taking the mean of one year and the previous).[6] Although Hooker had in

---

[6]   See Appendix 1 for an explanation of correlation coefficients.

his 1898 study relied on diagrams of the absolute values of trade and marriage rates plotted over time, the only diagrams Hooker presented to the Royal Statistical Society in 1901 were the correlation coefficients plotted against time lags of trade series (see Figure 9.2). Not only was Hooker stepping from the elementary, commercial, and political realms to the scientific, empirical realm of data manipulation, he was also stepping from the realm of plotting out variables over time to calculating correlation coefficients and plotting out the statistical results against time lags in the models. His plots and those of F. E. Cave-Browne-Cave (see Figure 10.1) were precursors to Yule's visual investigation of autoregressive series and Wold's correlograms.

The method of correlating deviations from an instantaneous or moving average was recognized as only being applicable if there was a periodic movement in a variable. Reginald Hooker (1905) and Lucien March (1905) independently suggested that correlation of first differences could be used to capture the correlation of short-term changes in cases of nonperiodic variables. Just as Hooker coined the term "trend," March was apparently the first statistician to use the term "decomposition" with reference to manipulating time series.[7] In his study, which included analysis of bullion and deposits of the Bank of France as well as the marriage and birth rates, March explained the danger in capturing the long-term relationship between variables at the expense of neglecting the relationship from one year to the next. He illustrated this with a hypothetical diagram (Figure 9.3), in which two series both show a parallel general upward movement, but from one sequence to the next their movements are inversely related and nonparallel.

John Norton, who at the same time that Hooker was studying British trade was investigating the workings of the New York money market, suggested a similar method for decomposing and eliminating the trend. Norton did not, however, use a moving average; he graphically interpolated a line that he labeled a "growth axis," from which he calculated deviations. A corner of Norton's large graph of weekly fluctuations in money flows in New York from 1879 to 1900 is reproduced in Figure 9.4. As Norton saw it, when weekly observations of time series were connected on a graph the result was a "complex polygon." Norton argued that the statistician's task was to "resolve the motion of the polygons into elements . . . to isolate these elements and further to go beyond the time elements to the causes." An element was an "ideal influence which is at work in the curve in a certain motion correlate with time" (Norton 1902, 23).[8] The elements that Norton isolated were:

- growth element due to a continuous passage of time
- periodic elements due to recurrent periods of time

---

[7] Although March was the first statistician to name the "decomposition" process of empirically breaking a time series down into various components, the recognition and naming of the components were not new. For example, Augustin Cournot argued that when looking at the price of a commodity over a long period, "as in astronomy, it is necessary to recognize *secular* variations, which are independent of *periodic* variations" (Cournot [1838] 1927, 25).

[8] As discussed in Chapter 5, a major part of Norton's analysis of the New York money market was done in the relative time framework of the fifty-two weeks of the typical year.

Correlation of the Marriage-Rate with Trade.

1.—*Marriage-Rate and Exports per Head.*

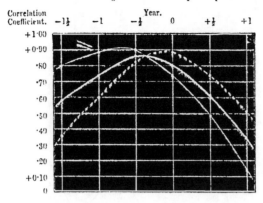

4.—*Marriage-Rate and Total Trade per Head.*

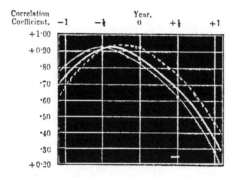

Correlation of Marriage-Rate with Trade, Wheat Prices, &c.

——————— 35 years, 1861-95.

————— 20   „   '76-95.

· · · · · · · 15   „   '61-75.

Figure 9.2   Reginald Hooker's "coefficient curves." The values of the correlation coefficients between the marriage rate and exports per head (top plot) or between marriage rate and total trade per head (bottom plot) are measured on the vertical axis against the lag between each pair on the horizontal axis. Each of the lines measures the relationship for a different time period. From these diagrams, Hooker concluded that the marriage rate did not respond to trade prosperity as quickly in the latter quarter of the nineteenth century as it had in the third quarter and that the highest correlation for the whole period, 1861–1895, was between the marriage rate and total trade per head a half year earlier ($r = .91$). *Source:* Hooker 1901, 491–492.

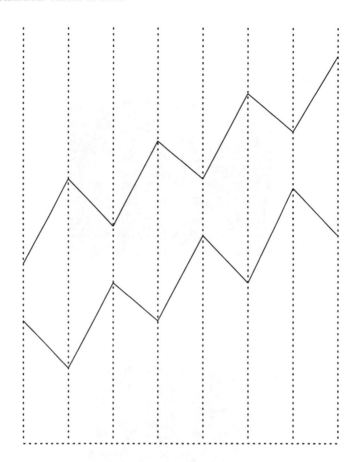

Figure 9.3   Lucien March's law curves in historical time illustrating that while the relationship between two variables over the long term, for example, seven years, may be positive, the annual changes could be negatively related – *antiparallèles*. March used this illustration to argue for the decomposition of time series before analyzing the co-relationships. *Source:* March 1905, 270.

- dynamic elements including business cycles, catastrophes, and minor irregular components

To capture the growth element, Norton graphically interpolated growth axes in each series (the ascending straight lines in Figure 9.4). His primary interest, however, was in the percentage of deviations of reserves, loans, and deposits from the respective growth axes and the correlation of these deviations:

> In this Chart are represented the really important movements in these financial statistics. The motion of the growth element is slow and gradual. Its effect is scarcely felt. But in the deviations are the movements which are forever puzzling financiers, and upon whose often apparently eccentric movements great fortunes are made or wrecked, panics are bred and crises precipitated. (Norton 1902, 36)

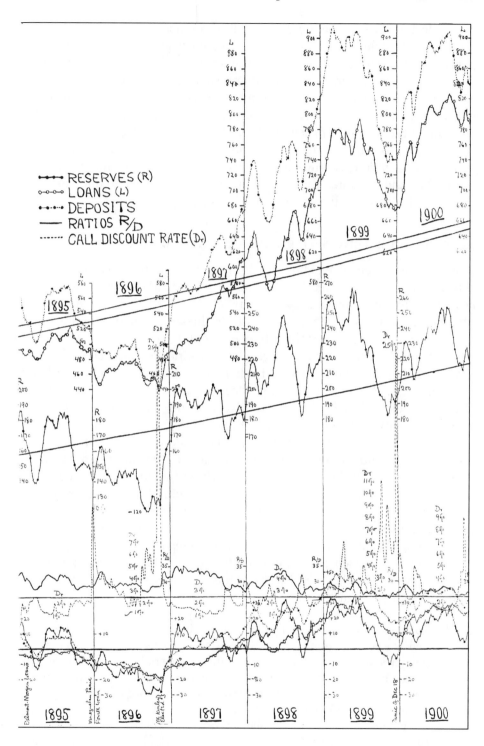

Figure 9.4   A portion of John Norton's plot of the weekly averages of total re-serves, loans, and deposits of the New York Associated Banks, 1879–1900. The solid, upward-sloping lines are "growth axes" from which Norton calculated deviations in each series. *Source:* Norton 1902, backpiece.

The deviations from the trend, the cyclical components, attracted the attention not only of financiers, but also of economists and econometricians. The pursuit of the cyclical component, by Wesley Mitchell, Arthur Burns, Warren Persons, Jan Tinbergen, and institutions such as the National Bureau for Economic Research, the Harvard Committee on Economic Research, the *Review of Economic Statistics*, the Berlin Institute, and the Konjuncture Institute of Moscow, is carefully chronicled by Mary Morgan in *The History of Econometric Ideas*. The aim of most statisticians who decomposed time series in the first half of the twentieth century was to get to the cyclical component, but in identifying and isolating the other components, new techniques and new elements of statistical theory were developed.

Transforming Time Series with Percent Change

One common means of avoiding trends in economic data is to use the percent change rather than the absolute levels of a variable. This approach was fully articulated in Irving Fisher's 1925 study of "Our Unstable Dollar and the So-called Business Cycle." Fisher gave a strong theoretical justification for using rates of change of prices rather than eliminating a secular trend through other means. He argued that the price level "cannot properly be said to have any secular trend" and he accused other investigators of ignoring inflation by confusing high prices with rising prices (Fisher 1925, 181). According to Fisher, the "oscillating barometer" that corresponded with the alternation in business activity was the *rate of change* of the price level, not the level itself.

In addition to advocating the use of percent changes, Fisher introduced the notion of a distributed lag to estimate the effect of the rate of growth of the purchasing power of the dollar in one month on the volume of trade several months later. Fisher got a correlation coefficient of .727 between an index of the volume of trade and the percent change in the price level seven months earlier. Fisher improved upon these results based on a *fixed* lag of seven months, by spreading the effect over several months – a distributed lag on the rate of growth of prices yielded a correlation coefficient of .941.[9] Fisher's explanation and justification for the use of a distributed lag was totally in terms of the analogy of targets and shooting:

> To visualize this distribution of influence – beginning in May, then increasing and afterwards diminishing – we may think in terms of the analogy of a gunner shooting at a target. According to this analogy we conceive of the horizontal line drawn to the right of April as representing not only time, but a physical road. Our imaginary gunner shoots forward on the time road, so to speak, a number of bullets proportional to the April P'. . . . Thus we assume the gunner aims at a target about 9½ miles (months) ahead on the time road, but like all gunners, sometimes overshoots and sometimes undershoots the mark. . . . We may think of each height (ordinate) of the P' curve as a

[9] In their introduction to *Foundations of Econometric Analysis*, David Hendry and Mary Morgan discuss the significance of Fisher's work and the problems they encountered in replicating it. They also reproduce most of Fisher's original article.

vertical pile of bullets to be shot forward on our time road. . . . The rule finally adopted as best for this study is somewhat analogous to the laws of probability according to which a gunner would distribute a bullet pile (P') by shooting each bullet of that pile at a target on the road ahead. (Fisher 1925, 184, 187, 188, 200)

Although Fisher made no reference to Karl Pearson's essay on "The Chances of Death" (see Chapter 2 and Figure 2.8), the similarity is striking. For example, Fisher argued that "target distance" and "gunner's accuracy" for each month's marksmen yielded variants on the "general law of the lag." Fisher talked of the "dance of the dollar" as Pearson talked of the "dance of death."[10] Although Fisher did not decompose a curve into chance distributions from different marksmen, he did decompose the distribution of one month's price increase into bullet piles fired by the marksman of inflation on April 1917 (see Figure 9.5). Based on his correlations between indices of business activity and a distributed lag of the rate of change of purchasing power, Fisher concluded that the business cycle from 1915 to 1923 was "largely mythical" (Fisher 1925, 201). Other statisticians joined Fisher in questioning not only the assumption of the cyclical component, but also the assumption of the trend component.

Trends and Long Waves

Trends were usually only isolated so that they could be eliminated; it was not until the late 1920s and 1930s that the trend received much attention in its own right.[11] The isolation of the trend was achieved by modeling it as a moving average spanning the cycle period, or fitting an arithmetically linear line, or log-linear line with least squares, or assuming a function such as a parabola or simple logistic or Gompertz equation. In his classic text on *The Analysis of Economic Time Series*, Harold Davis has documented the history of some of these methods and the state of the art of trend analysis in 1941. Another good source of examples is *Statistical Methods* published by the National Bureau of Economic Research economist Frederick Mills in 1924 and revised in 1938. A taste of the variety of methods of fitting trends can be gleaned from Edwin Frickey's table of twenty-three different statistical studies on pig iron production (Table 9.3). Most of these methods in essence assumed that the trend component was a function of time.

In the words of Frickey, the trend was usually defined as "the gradual and persistent movement of the series over a period of time which, contrasted with the short run fluctuations of the series, is long" (Frickey 1934, 199). In his

[10] It is likely that Fisher carefully studied Pearson's work, and in particular the "Chances of Death." Like Pearson and Galton, Fisher was a eugenist and a card-carrying member of a society that called for government control of the reproduction of the human species for the improvement of society.
[11] Wesley Mitchell (1927) saw a high opportunity cost in economic statisticians isolating trends for the sole purpose of eliminating them: trends were not studied in their own right and thus little was known about trends, their causes, their causal relationship with cycles, and their co-relationships with other trends.

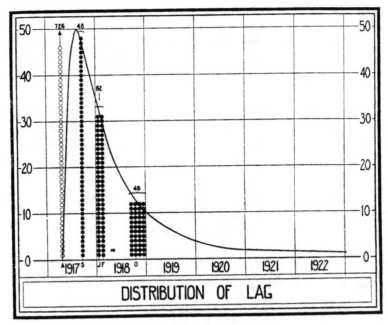

CHART 2

Showing how the pile of 726 bullets representing *P'* at April 1917 is distributed over the months following. The letters A, S, J, F, O stand for April, September, January, February and October.

Figure 9.5   Irving Fisher's "law of the lag" for the percent change in prices. In April 1917, prices in the United States increased at an annual rate of 72.6 percent. Fisher translated that into a pile of 726 bullets that were fired down the time road at a target 9½ months ahead. The hollow circles at April 1917 signify the 726 bullets that had been there before and the dark circles represent the bullets as they were distributed around the target after being shot. If the "time road" is measured on a logarithmic scale, the law of the distributed lag is near normal, symmetrically distributed around the mode of 9½ months. *Source:* Fisher 1925, 185.

survey of statistical techniques dealing with trends, German economist Paul Lorenz gave this definition:

> Technically speaking, the trend is the representation of the evolutionary changes in an economic phenomena brought about by the gradual transformation of economic institutions. Expressed methodologically, it is a line which obeys a simple mathematical law that gives only the general tendency of the economic series but not its details. . . . the trend fitting an economic curve must give the main tendency of the curve as perfectly as possible, but must not introduce any strange elements of movement into its course.
>
> The requirement concerning the matter consists in being able to recognize in the trend the geometric symbol of certain economically significant concepts. (Lorenz 1935, 460–461)

With respect to the latter point of linking the statistical estimation to the theoretical hypotheses, Lorenz cited the work of Simon Kuznets. Based on his

Table 9.3 *Edwin Frickey's summary of twenty-three attempts to fit trends to pig iron production. The "cycle" Frickey refers to was not based on a priori reasoning or the raw data, but was a mere mechanical "recurrence of different phases of plus and minus departures" from the trend line. The first column on the left gives an indication of the variety of techniques for isolating the trend component used in the 1920s.*

THE REVIEW OF ECONOMIC STATISTICS

TABLE I. — MEASUREMENTS OF AVERAGE LENGTH OF "CYCLE" FOR PIG IRON PRODUCTION, WITH REFERENCE TO MATHEMATICALLY-FITTED TRENDS

Type of curve, and trend interval	COMPUTATIONS EMPLOYING TREND INTERVAL AS BASIC PERIOD		COMPUTATIONS EMPLOYING 1877–1914 AS BASIC PERIOD	
	Interval from first to last "trough"*	Average length of "cycle" (*years*)	Interval from first to last "trough"*	Average length of "cycle" (*years*)
(1)	(2)	(3)	(4)	(5)
(1) Straight line, 1875–1920 (apparent length of "cycle" read from unsmoothed data).........	1875–80 to 1920	45–40	1875–80 to 1920	45–40
(2) Straight line, 1871–1910.....................	1872–1913	41	1872–1913	41
(3) Straight line, 1860–1915†...................	1872–1907§	35	1872–1907§	35
(4) Straight line, 1879–1913....................	1880–1913	33	1880–1913	33
(5) Logistic curve, 1854–1924 (actual items smoothed before making count of "cycles")............	1863–1932‡	23	1877–1932‡	27.5
(6) Logistic curve, 1854–1924 (count of "cycles" made from actual figures)......................	1861–1921	15.0 or 12.0	1876–1921	15.0 or 11.2
(7) Straight line fitted to logarithms, 1854–1926......	1861–1921	12.0 or 10.0	1876–1914	12.7 or 9.5
(8) Parabola, 1860–1915†.......................	1865–1908	10.8	1876–1908	10.7
(9) Compound-interest curve, 1879–1913...........	1876–1908	10.7 or 8.0	1876–1908	10.7 or 8.0
(10) Modified Gompertz curve fitted to logarithms, 1854–1926................................	1861–1921	10.0	1876–1914	9.5
(11) Third-degree parabola fitted to logarithms, 1854–1926................................	1861–1921	10.0	1876–1914	9.5
(12) Compound-interest curve, 1860–1915†..........	1865–1914	9.8	1878–1914	9.0
(13) Logistic curve, 1884–1926 (actual items smoothed before making count of "cycles")............	1885–1921	9.0	1876–1914	9.5
(14) Parabola fitted to logarithms, 1870–1922........	1876–1921	9.0 or 7.5	1876–1914	9.5 or 7.6
(15) Two straight lines fitted to logarithms, 1879–95 and 1902–15.............................	1876–94 and 1904–14	7.0 or 5.6	....	......
(16) Fourth-degree parabola, 1881–1913............	1876–1914	6.3 or 5.4	1876–1914	6.3 or 5.4
(17) Two straight lines, 1879–96 and 1897–1913.......	1879–1914	5.8 or 5.0	1879–1914	5.8 or 5.0
(18) Four straight lines, 1877–84, 1885–97, 1898–1902, and 1903–16...........................	1878–1914	4.5 or 3.6	1878–1914	4.5 or 3.6
(19) Straight line, 1903–16......................	1904–19	3.8	....	......
(20) Straight line, 1899–1913¶...................	1900–14	3.5	....	......
(21) Compound-interest curve, 1901–13............	1904–14	3.3	....	......
(22) Straight line, 1902–23......................	1904–24	3.3	....	......
(23) Straight line, 1904–14......................	1904–14	3.3	....	......

* For the first four entries, interval extends from first to last *peak*.   § 1872 selected as high point, since fit of line prior to 1870 is very poor.
† Fitted to per-capita data.   ¶ Fitted to pig iron consumption.
‡ Precise location of terminal date for smoothed series is uncertain.

Source: Frickey 1934, 204.

observation of many production curves, Kuznets formalized the requirements for a typical trend for industrial production: the curve had to rise or fall continually; there was a border value, which when the curve approached it the rate of growth had to decrease; and the absolute increase depended on the present level as well the border value. The simple logistic or learning curve was an obvious example meeting Kuznet's criteria. In 1927, Harold Hotelling suggested a novel means for fitting a logistic curve to data on population growth in the Unites States. Hotelling did not assume that the differential equation held for all times, but rather, "that the most probable value of the derivative at any instant is that assigned by the differential equation" (Hotelling 1927, 286). Hotelling's differential method enabled him to find the most probable value of population at any time by interpolation or extrapolation and to determine the probable errors of that interpolation or extrapolation.

Some statisticians saw a trade-off in generalizing the trend, to reduce or eliminate bendings and twistings, and in getting a good fit to the component. Several writers tried to push beyond mere statistical description and link decomposition with either different causes influencing time series, with economic theory, or with historical description. For example, Frickey quotes Abbot Payson Usher's review of a J. H. Clapham's text on economic history:

> The secular trend supplies the realist with the focus of attention essential to any vigorous portrayal of the movement of economic phenomena. It imparts to a historical narrative the requisite unity without resort to any artificial device. . . . The primary task of the general economic historian is to establish the general characteristics of these basic secular trends. (Usher, quoted in Frickey 1934, 201)

The links between economic theory and statistical description, however, were usually ambiguous. Some economic statisticians came to question whether the trend was anything more than a statistical construct. Charles Roos was critical of the practice of Henry Moore and others in equating trends, and thus dynamics, to a simple linear function of time:

> Professor Moore passed from the static equilibrium theory to a dynamic equilibrium theory by means of the trend ratio; that is, he proposed to fit an empirical trend curve to the data and substitute for actual prices and actual quantities the ratios of actual prices and actual quantities to their respective trends. As a first approximation to a dynamic theory of economics, this theory cannot be criticized, but it must not be thought that Moore's theory is the general dynamic theory of economics that will reconcile much of the apparent contradiction in economic theory.
>
> Although the method of trend analysis developed by Professor Moore and his students occupies an important historical position, statisticians are more and more beginning to question the significance of results obtained by those methods and are asking for increasingly realistic treatments. . . .
>
> In a workable dynamic theory, speculation, debts, interest, depreciation, obsolescence and other familiar economic functions of time, must assuredly be assigned important roles. Thus, it is not enough to lump all these quantities together in a trend curve and develop a so-called dynamic theory as H. L. Moore has done.[12] (Roos 1934, 4, 8)

Roos went on to argue that the common technique of eliminating the trend and correlating the residuals could, in some cases, eliminate the only significant component and lead to nonsensical results. He cited Karl Jordan (1929), who constructed examples in which the correlation of deviations from a trend were

---

[12] In his essay on "Differential Equations Subject to Error," Harold Hotelling (1927, 289), argued that Moore was constructing theories and models of "forced oscillations," whereas monetary phenomena were more likely to be "free oscillations" resulting from internal rhythms and disturbances. Similarly, Paul Samuelson (1947, 315) classified Moore's trend line of moving equilibrium to be a "statical type" rather than dynamic because it did not incorporate economically significant variables at different points of time.

meaningless, with the correlation coefficient being a mere function of the parameters of the trend functions. Roos argued that economists should treat all correlation of residuals from trends with suspicion and should recognize that the use of a trend was "a confession of ignorance" of the fundamental factors involved (Roos 1934, 250).

Although the financiers and most statisticians were entranced with only the trade cycles or the deviations from trends, a few statisticians and theoreticians celebrated the trend. In reviewing Wesley Mitchell's book on business cycles, Joseph Schumpeter said, "trend analysis will be the central problem of our science in the immediate future and the center of our difficulties as well" (Schumpeter 1930, 150). Carl Snyder, statistical economist for the Federal Reserve Bank of New York, saw the trend as analogous to the rate of fall of bodies to the earth in physical studies. It was "a kind of momentum or inertia that sweeps on in spite of all obstacles" (Snyder 1933, 77). Snyder used annual observations from 1879 to 1929 on a variety of U.S. time series data: cotton, coal, and pig iron production, population, employment, imports, and composite indices of manufacturing trade and production. He generally fitted log linear lines and concluded a fairly constant average rate of growth of 2.8 percent from 1800 to 1929, which he alleged was close to the rate of growth of 3 percent from colonial times to 1860. Snyder concluded that:

> What we find in almost every kind of economic measurement we have undertaken, and this has covered in the last ten years a wide variety, is the evidence for the same persistent tendencies or long-time trends of growth and change. Nowhere, almost, the revolutionary or the abrupt, but as a rule, quite the reverse, definite and often undeviating rates of change. All of which is almost precisely analogous to what we find in mechanics, in physics, in chemistry, and the physical sciences generally. (Snyder 1933, 82)

Little did Snyder realize that the U.S. economy had already gone over the precipice of a depression that would be so deep and span so many years that his celebration of a constant trend would look naive and irrelevant a few years hence (see Appendix 2 for the demise of trend analysis in the 1930s). The great depression of the 1930s, however, was not inconsistent with speculations on the existence of long waves in economic activity. Studies of long-term oscillations proved another rare exception to the focus on the four- to ten-year cycles. In a 1928 study, Nikolai Kondratieff applied a variety of decomposition techniques to test his theory of "long cycles" in the development of capitalism. He used least squares to fit trend lines to per capita data of several time series. He then smoothed deviations from the trend using a nine-year moving average. His purpose was to eliminate all movements other than long waves of approximately fifty-year periods. Without exploring direct causes, Kondratieff treated these long cycles as empirical manifestations of capitalist development.[13]

[13] Decomposition was a political act in the Soviet Union in the 1920s, and Kondratieff paid dearly for his hypothesis of fifty-year cycles in capitalist development. His 1922 study on the subject generated criticism from Leon Trotsky and other Marxists who argued that while the shorter trade cycle was consistent with Karl Marx's theory, a broken trend line showing an inevitable demise of capitalism,

Seasonal Variation

Like the trend components, the seasonal components were usually isolated only to be eliminated in favor of a focus on the cyclical components. Unlike trends, however, seasonal variation was often strictly periodic and the models and techniques for estimating and isolating the component were more obvious. As can be seen in Appendix 2, a high percentage of time series studies in the early twentieth century were devoted to seasonal variation and the search for periodicity. The techniques used were generally either types of harmonic analysis or the construction of indices of seasonal variation. For the latter, statisticians used either monthly arithmetic means, ratios to twelve-month moving averages, ratios to linear trend lines, or link relatives. Applications of harmonic analysis are described in more detail in the section on functions of time. Suffice to say, the periodicity of the seasonal component allowed economic statisticians to adopt and develop harmonic analysis that was otherwise closed off to them due to the irregularity of fluctuations in other cyclical components of most economic time series.

A typical way of eliminating the seasonal component was to divide the actual monthly or quarterly observations by an index that isolated the seasonal variation. The index could be constructed by simply using the arithmetic mean for each month over many years and dividing each of the twelve averages by the mean of those averages. Some statisticians modified this by correcting the arithmetic averages for secular trend. In his construction of indices of business conditions, Warren Persons (1923) developed the method of link relatives, which became one of the most popular tools for measuring seasonal variation. The first step in constructing a link relative was to calculate each month's value as a percentage of the previous month's; the second step was to calculate the median link relative over all the percentages for a particular month; the third step was to calculate a chain relative by making the January median link relative to the base; the fourth step was to adjust for a secular trend assuming a fixed rate of growth from one month to the next. Finally, one divided the actual raw monthly values by the corrected chain relative index value and ended up with a seasonally adjusted series.

In a 1924 issue of the *Journal of the American Statistical Association*, Helen Falkner and Lincoln Hall suggested the construction of seasonal indices by averaging, for each month, the actual monthly values expressed as a percentage of a trend value. The trend was usually a linear function of time or a polynomial of greater order, and the method of averaging the monthly ratios was determined by a frequency distribution of the individual ratios. A similar method was used by Frederick Macaulay and the NBER; the difference being the trend used in calculating the monthly ratios was a twelve-month moving average. Macaulay (1931) suggested a variety of methods of averaging the

and not a long cycle, was the other essential component of economic time series (see Klein 1995b; Day 1977). Within months of Kondratieff's 1928 publication of *The Long Wave Cycle* the authorities publicly denounced Kondratieff and closed down his Moscow Conjuncture Institute for the study of business cycles. Kondratieff was deported to a Siberian prison camp in 1931 and executed there in 1938.

monthly ratios. The notion of a seasonal index formed by ratios of monthly values to a twelve-month moving average was eventually used by U.S. government agencies in the Census I, Census II, X-1 and X-11 methods of decomposition.[14] As with trends, Mills (1924) and Davis (1941) are excellent sources for examples of methods used in the 1920s and 1930s to isolate and eliminate seasonal components.

Random Components

Very little attention was paid in the early decomposition studies to the irregular or random components. Statisticians saw them as unsystematic, and they were either unable and/or uninterested in isolating them for further study. Also, it was reckoned that several of the detrending and smoothing techniques eliminated a great part of the irregular component. The Russian statistician Oskar Anderson was one of the first to take a methodical interest in the random components. In 1914, he and Student (William Gosset) proposed the variate difference method of differencing time series until the correlation coefficient for a pair of variables was the same for that difference as it was for the previous stage of differencing. Udny Yule saw this as decomposing until all that was left were the irregular or random components, and he questioned whether correlation of random components was useful (see Chapter 3). Anderson (1927, 1929), however, incorporated Yule's insights, began to focus on the differencing properties of single series, and used the variate difference method to classify series, to test for the presence of random components, and to determine functions that were appropriate univariate models for the nonrandom components. For example, Anderson distinguished series by the behavior of the variance of the series at its successive differences (see his classification scheme of Z, R, and G series in Chapter 8). If at some stage of differencing, a constant variance was reached, the raw series contained a random component and the differencing had eliminated the systematic component.

With univariate models, Anderson came to see the foundation of the variate difference method as the assumption that any time series was composed of two parts: a systematic component, which was some function of time with a mathematical expectation different from zero, and a random component.[15] His method of decomposition was to eliminate the random component and model only the systematic component. Thus Anderson did not eliminate trends or seasonal variation, but incorporated them, along with any cycles, into one systematic component. Examining the behavior of the variance of a series with each stage of differencing would reveal the functional nature of the

[14] Sypros Makridakis (1974, 50–57) outlines the steps in the Census II method, first used in 1954, and discusses criticisms of and the links between Census I and Census II methods and Frederick Macaulay's work.

[15] Anderson's notion of decomposition preceded Herman Wold's theorem that all stationary time series could be decomposed into a deterministic function of time and a linear combination of random elements (see Chapter 10). Anderson's work was cited in the list of references of the first edition of Wold's 1938 treatise on time series analysis but not in the second edition.

systematic component. For example, if the variance was identical for the series of first differences and the series of second differences, then the systematic component was a linear function of time; if the variances were only constant between the second and third differences, then a parabola was indicated. Anderson used the variate difference method as a means of eliminating the random elements by fitting a moving polynomial to the data – the degree of the polynomial having been determined by the differencing. Anderson adopted W. F. Sheppard's smoothing formula as his means of graduating the series.

Anderson was critical of the traditional method of eliminating trends and seasonal components and illustrated how Warren Persons's technique of link relatives transformed a series without an original seasonal component into one with a spurious seasonal pattern.[16] Similarly, Anderson, starting with a series constructed without a cyclical component, demonstrated that Persons's method of decomposition resulted in an incorrect "corrected" series with a prominent, artificial cyclical component.[17]

Anderson, who was a professor at a school of *commercial sciences* in Bulgaria, acknowledged that the techniques of decomposition were unsophisticated tools of trade. Anderson saw statistical science as a substitute for experiment in the understanding of social life. The social investigator, Anderson wrote, had to "replace the physical experiment by other *much more crude methods*, and it is here that different methods of decomposition of the statistical series into components appear upon the scene" (Anderson 1927, 551; italics are Anderson's). These crude methods were the monetary algorithms that we explored in Part I. Anderson and other mathematical statisticians, however, transformed these commercial tools into "methods of scientific arrangement and separation of statistical series" (Anderson 1927, 549).

---

[16]   The dispute between Persons and Anderson, over whether statisticians should decompose a series by eliminating the trend component or whether they should difference the series until it was statistically manageable, has been echoed in the 1980s and 1990s. Some econometricians now refer to series as being either "trend stationary," in which case the trend is a removable, deterministic component, or "difference stationary," in which case the trend or secular component is stochastic and differencing is the appropriate tool for getting a series in the stationary form for linear regression (see, e.g., Nelson & Plosser 1982; Perman 1991). If, as Charles Nelson and Charles Plosser maintain, most macroeconomic series are not trend stationary, then the typical procedure for detrending (working with the residuals from a regression of a variable on a time trend) is inappropriate.

The parallels between Persons versus Anderson and trend stationary versus difference stationary are not exact. The concept of a "stationary" process had not been fully articulated in the 1920s. Anderson suggested differencing until the variance of the series that had been taken to the nth difference was the same as the variance of the series at the nth $-$ 1 difference. It is also important to keep in mind that Udny Yule criticized both Persons and Anderson for assuming that variables were mere functions of time. Although Anderson eschewed the simple linear trend, he assumed that the systematic component could be modeled as a higher order function of time that would be revealed by the order of differencing necessary to attain convergence of the variances.

[17]   The thirty-six-term time series that Anderson used to illustrate the spurious cycle generated by Persons's method of decomposition was constructed from:
   - a trend – generated by the series of natural numbers, one to thirty-six
   - a seasonal component – generated from a sinusoidal function
   - irregular fluctuations – generated by taking the number of letters from each of the first thirty-six lines of Persons's 1923 article on decomposition

Anderson graphically compared the values of the constructed series with the estimated normal values from Persons's method and Anderson's method of smoothing after elimination of the random component. He argued that Persons's method yielded a poorer fit because it created a cycle that was really nonexistent (Anderson 1927, 559–561). In Chapter 10, I further explore the analysis of stochastic processes by

Although Anderson changed the purpose to which he applied the variate difference method from his first application in 1914 to his studies in the late 1920s, all his work was based on the assumption that differencing would eventually eliminate the components that were functions of time. For example, as we saw in Chapter 3 on first differences, Anderson assumed that the source of the time-correlation problem was that there was a spurious correlation between variables because both were functions of time. Anderson's solution was to eliminate this functional relationship by differencing. Anderson and Student's work and that of Henry Ludwell Moore was to mark 1914 as a stellar year for statistical studies based on the assumption of variables as functions of time.

Variables as Functions of Time

Henry Moore is considered by many to be the "father of econometrics." His statistical analysis, while professor of economics at Columbia University, set a standard and agenda for empirical investigations into markets and economic cycles.[18] In the early part of his career, Moore was strongly influenced by both Léon Walras and Karl Pearson. Moore was writing during what I call the "Iron Age" of Europe and the United States; in the nineteenth century, the most frequently graphed variable in fact curves in historical time had been the price of wheat. In the second and third decades of the twentieth century, the most frequently plotted variable was the volume of pig iron production. Moore's goal was to explain economic cycles in industrial activity and he took the production of pig iron as the best "barometer" of this:

> It is a common observation of writers on economic crises that the production of pig-iron is an unusually good barometer of trade. The amount of pig-iron that is annually produced swells with the activity and volume of industry and trade, and it is among the first commodities to indicate the general shrinking in the ultimate demand which checks the activity of trade and causes its temporary decline. (Moore 1914, 147)

In addition to annual observations of pig iron production, Moore used yield per acre of several crops and rainfall at critical growing periods from 1870 to 1910. Using the motto of the U.S. Department of Agriculture as an epithet, "Agriculture is the Foundation of Manufacture and Commerce," Moore concluded that:

> The fundamental, persistent cause of the cycles in the yield of the crops is the cyclical movement in the weather conditions represented by the rhythmically changing amount of rainfall; the cyclical movement in the yield of the crops is the fundamental persistent cause of Economic Cycles. (Moore 1914, 149)

the modeling of random components initiated by Anderson, Udny Yule, and Eugen Slutsky and compare Anderson's classification of time series to that of Yule's and Herman Wold's.

[18] Moore's contributions to econometrics are examined in Stigler 1962, Mirowski 1990, and Morgan 1990.

The statistical methods Moore used in his 1914 work on economic cycles included:

- a periodogram to determine the periodicities of rainfall[19]
- a correlation of raw series with time to infer the existence or nonexistence of secular change
- a regression of the raw series on time to get the slope coefficient that was used in the elimination of the trend
- fitting a harmonic equation to crop yields if the correlation between these yields and rainfall was high
- correlating deviations from a three-year moving average of pig iron production with the lagged deviations from a three-year moving average of an index of yield per acre of four crops
- correlating deviations of the three-year moving average from linear trend lines of pig iron production and crop yields with various lags
- correlating the percentage changes in the product and price of pig iron
- correlating the cyclical components and the irregular components of the indices of crop yields and general prices

Moore used similar techniques in his 1917 study on *Forecasting the Yield and the Price of Cotton.* In a letter to his former instructor Karl Pearson, written on August 26, 1918, Moore outlined his hopes for this new approach to forecasting:

> My chapter on the "Law of Demand for Cotton" shows that the *a priori* theory of Professor Marshall and Professor Edgeworth does not touch the concrete either in its premises or its conclusion. But by the use of your methods I have shown how their problem can be solved inductively and practically.
>
> One of the reasons that led me to take up the investigation of forecasting was the probability that, if a practical question of the first importance could be solved, the claim of the newer methods for consideration would be greatly strengthened. Such a question is solved, I hope, in my essay. It is a large claim to make that, notwithstanding the many tens of thousands of dollars spent upon the cotton-crop reports, it is possible, by means of the methods I describe, for a single competent scientist who does not leave his study to reach more reliable forecasts than those supplied by the extensive and costly

[19]   In constructing periodograms, statisticians use a least-squares algorithm to estimate the values of the square of the amplitude for a variety of sinusoids composing the time series. A relatively high value for an amplitude suggests a significant cycle of the corresponding period. Moore danced around the application of periodograms to economic series in his 1914 work. His goal had been to explain economic cycles, but in 1914 he did not directly use the periodogram on any economic series. He started with a periodogram of rainfall, then correlated rainfall to crop yield, which was then correlated to pig iron production. The economic series was so divorced from true periodicity that Moore had to use several steps of error-augmenting methods to get a feel for it. In his review of Moore's 1914 book, Udny Yule (1915, 304) pointed out that no one had yet applied harmonic analysis to economic data and evaluated the different periods. Yule wondered why Moore, who argued that economic cycles were more than just irregular waves, had used a periodogram on rainfall but not on the data for crop yields, prices, or pig iron production. Moore had mentioned the labor involved in such an endeavor, but also he may have suspected the inadequacies of the periodogram in handling "errors in periodicity." In any case, Moore did include some periodograms of economic series in his 1923 study, *Generating Economic Cycles.*

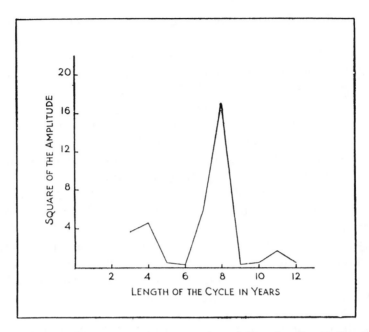

Figure 9.6   Henry L. Moore's periodogram of rainfall in the Ohio Valley. The vertical axis on the periodogram measures the values of the squares of the amplitudes
of the sinusoids as estimated with a least squares algorithm for cycles of varying
lengths. Moore interpreted the significant peak at eight years as the period of the
most important cycle in annual rainfall. He found a similar eight-year cycle in rainfall in the United States as a whole. *Source:* Moore 1923, 6.

> bureaus of the Department of Agriculture. (Letter from Moore to Pearson,
> Pearson Papers, Box 764, The Library, University College, London)

In his 1923 book on *Generating Economic Cycles*, Moore explained that his
primary object was no longer to forecast, but to "establish the existence of real
cycles and to trace the causes of the specifically cyclical elements in the total of
economic changes" (Moore 1923, 5). With a periodogram measuring the square
of the amplitude against the length of cycles (Figure 9.6), Moore concluded that
the eight-year cycle in rainfall in the United States accounted for 42 percent of
the total variability of annual rainfall. He went further back in the line of causation in the 1923 study and related the rainfall cycle, and thus economic cycles,
to the transit of Venus. The underlying theme in Moore's perception of dynamics and his analysis of time series data was that variables or their components
were functions of time. His pioneering use of the periodogram and Fourier
transformations, his fitting of linear trends, and his attempts to connect economic cycles to the transit of Venus were all based on this assumption.

The linking of the trend component with time, through least squares regression on time or the fitting of some polynomial based on time, was a common
procedure in the 1920s and 1930s. As we saw in the previous section, even
the method of link relatives, used to eliminate the seasonal component,
assumed that the trend component was a function of time. This assumption

was also the basis of all harmonic analysis on time series data. Harmonic analysis included Fourier transformations on the series and analysis in what is now called the frequency domain. One constructs graphs and models in the frequency domain to search for the existence of and to measure the intensities of periodicities. Visual tools in the frequency domain include periodograms and spectral density functions.

As we can see from Table 9.4, Moore was not the first to use harmonic analysis for time series data. Maurice Kendall (1945) argued that the Dutch meteorologist Christopher Buys Ballot was the first to make effective use of the tabular approach to exploring periodicity and that this was the basis for the modern periodogram.[20] Buys Ballot (1847) used the table now named after him to determine the period of the sun's rotation from daily observations of temperature in the Netherlands from 1729 to 1846. He built on the work of Professor Nervander, who in 1845 had, according to Buys Ballot, articulated three theorems regarding periods revealed in a relative time framework of a table in which a long time series is arranged in rows such that each column becomes a cross section of each stage of the cycle:

1. If the rows are the lengths of the true period, and thus the fourteenth observation of a periodic series of thirteen terms is under the first observation and so forth, the sums of the columns will form a periodic series.
2. If the table is arranged in such a way that the rows are not the lengths of the true period, the sums of the columns will show little periodicity.
3. If you add series of different periods and arrange the sums in a table, the sums of the columns from this new table will form periodic series that correspond to one of the original series as long the length of the rows are equal to the terms in one of the series.

Buys Ballot found Nervander's three theorems sufficient only if one knew the true period. Buys Ballot was working with time series of mean daily temperatures, which he argued were affected by at least four periods: two due to the movement of the moon, another due to the 365.25 days of the earth's revolution around the sun, and a fourth due to the rotation of the sun approximately every 27.25 days. Buys Ballot was particularly interested in finding evidence for the latter and determining its exact period from the temperature data.[21] To determine the unknown duration of a period, Buys Ballot added two more theorems, which were essentially built on Nervander's second theorem:

[20]   In his essay "On the History of the Statistical Method in Meteorology" (1984–1985), Oscar B. Sheynin discusses other contributions of Buys Ballot, including his emphasis on deviations from means.

[21]   Buys Ballot (1847) and Arthur Schuster (1898) were both interested in the twenty-six to twenty-eight day cycle that was thought to be the period of the sun's rotation. The evidence for that period had come from observations of the rotation of sunspots, but as Buys Ballot (1847, 38) pointed out, astronomers had come to doubt the fixity of those spots. A more complicated picture of differential rotation of the nonrigid body of the sun is acknowledged nowadays: the interior rotates with a different period than the exterior and the lower latitudes rotate with a different period than the higher latitudes. According to the *Cambridge Encyclopedia of Astronomy* (1977, 138–139), Doppler shifts of photospheric lines indicate that the polar regions of the sun take forty-one days to rotate with respect to the earth, whereas the sun's equator rotates in twenty-seven days.

Table 9.4 *Early applications of harmonic analysis to time series data*

Date	Author	Title	Perceived problem	Solution	Discussed in
1847	Buys Ballot	"Les changements périodiques de température, dépendants de la nature du soleil et de la lune"	How to determine period of sun's rotation from series of daily temperature	If series is arranged in a table with row lengths ≠ true period, examining column sums with additional rows will indicate true periodicity	Kendall 1945 Makridakis 1974
1879	Stokes	"Note on the Above Paper" [by Stewart and Dodgson on Sunspots]	Search for periodic inequalities of unknown period	Suggested use of harmonic analyser of Sir William Thompson to plot intensity of each harmonic	Cargill 1974 Makridakis 1974
1906	Schuster	"On the Periodicities of Sun Spots"	Search for hidden periodicities in sunspot variability; separate natural variability of Fourier coefficients from true periodic causes; determine the average intensity and the phase of periodic variation	Periodogram of Wolfer's monthly sunspot numbers 1749–1905	Davis 1941 Kendall 1945 Makridakis 1974
1913	Turner	"On the Expression of Sun-Spot Periodicity as a Fourier Sequence, and on the General Use of a Fourier Sequence in Similar Problems"	How to detect harmonics of the values of an arithmetic sequence	Checked for changing signs with Fourier Transformations	Cargill 1974 Davis 1941
1914	Moore	*Economic Cycles*	Determine cycles in rainfall that could explain economic cycles	Periodogram of rainfall in Ohio Valley	Cargill 1974 Morgan 1990
1922	Beveridge	"Wheat Prices and Rainfall in Western Europe"	Test for periods between 2.5 and 84 years in index of wheat prices from 1545 to 1844, relate to rainfall from 1850 to 1921, justification of composite index of wheat prices from five countries	Periodogram with tests for intensity, changing signs, continuity, and agreement with other records	Davis 1941 Cargill 1974 Kendall 1945 Makridakis 1974 Morgan 1990

1. If one makes a mistake in guessing the true period and makes the rows too long or too short, the false appearance of periodicity in the column sums will rapidly fade with each additional row of new observations added to the table. This theorem allowed Buys Ballot to determine how much one deviated from the truth by calculating how each additional row affected the difference between the maximum and minimum column sum.[22]

2. In the case of a mistaken guess on periodicity, the movement of the maximum column sum (or the minimum column sum) with each additional row of new observations indicates by how much one has overestimated or underestimated the true period.

Buys Ballot demonstrated with an example of a series of thirteen terms that he arranged in rows of only twelve terms each. By looking both at the diminishing difference between maximum and minimum with each new row added and the shifting of the position of the maximum column, he was able finally to determine the true period.

Buys Ballot took an empirical, algorithmic, tabular approach to determining periodicity. He did not directly use Fourier transformations or probability theory, and the Rule of Three was his most sophisticated mathematical tool in the determination of the existence and duration of periods. In contrast, Arthur Schuster's use of periodograms involved the direct use of the mathematical harmonic analysis of Jean Baptiste Fourier as well as graphs and probability theory. Schuster pointed out that he was not the first to use Fourier's theorems to discover hidden periodicities, but he was the first to formalize a method for deciding whether a maximum in the amplitude of a harmonic term corresponded to a true period or was generated from chance:

> What distinguishes the method which I am endeavouring to introduce from that of others, is the discussion of the natural variability of the Fourier coefficients according to the theory of probability, independently of any periodic cause which may have influenced the phenomenon. I have shown that where the phenomena are detached and the probability of the occurrence of any one event does not depend on the occurrence of a previous one, there is a definite probability for the value of the amplitudes of the harmonic terms

---

[22] Buys Ballot was not the first to notice this property of periodic series rearranged into cross-sectional tables. In his 1829 study of the cycles of solar and lunar winds and wheat prices in Britain, George MacKenzie noted that only a fifty-four-year grid, rearranging a series of wheat prices from 1200 to 1827, distinguished maxima and minima in average wheat prices: "It is proper to remark in this place, that an arrangement of the prices into fifty-three or fifty-five years, or any other term of years than the fifty-four, give no preponderance in the rates, either of cheap or dear, in any of the divisions of such periods, – thus proving, that the fifty-four year period is the natural term" (MacKenzie 1829, 42). In 1847, Hyde Clarke further elaborated on and updated an empirical verification of MacKenzie's hypothesis of a fifty-four-year cycle of famine and panics. Clarke's work caught the attention of William Stanley Jevons, who from 1875 onward also used grids and a relative time framework to investigate a periodic relationship between sunspot activity and economic cycles (see Chapter 5 for more details on early work in relative time frameworks and Morgan 1990, 18–39, for a discussion of Jevons's, Moore's, and William Beveridge's work on periodicity).

into which the recurrence of the phenomenon can be resolved. (Schuster 1906, 72)

With a periodogram of Wolf's and Wolfer's numbers measuring sunspot activity from 1750 to 1900, Schuster found a well-defined peak at 11.25. Most of the earliest uses of periodograms and harmonic analysis of time series data, including Schuster's, were investigations into the periods of or those generated by solar activity: the rotation of the sun, sunspot activity, or terrestrial magnetism, which many considered a function of solar activity. It was not until the 1920s that periodograms were applied to economic time series.

The most famous economic application of harmonic analysis at that time was Sir William Beveridge's periodogram of a detrended index of annual wheat prices in Britain, the Low Countries, France, North Germany, South Germany, and Austria from 1545 to 1869. Beveridge found evidence of nineteen cycles varying in length from 2.735 to 68 years. Harold Davis described Beveridge's work as "One of the most heroic computations in the history of periodogram analysis" (Davis 1941, 312). Davis saw harmonic analysis as one of the most fruitful avenues of time series investigations and he developed a comparable structure for analyzing the periodograms of Beveridge, other statisticians, and several of his own, including ones based on his invention of a "moving periodogram." Maurice Kendall, writing only four years later, was not so impressed with periodograms. Using correlogram analysis, Kendall detected only two oscillatory movements, at five and fifteen years, in Beveridge's index. He concluded that seventeen of the nineteen periods indicated by Beveridge's periodogram were due to sampling error and that the tests of significance usually applied to periodograms were invalid. Kendall saw the function-of-time, harmonic route of Beveridge and Schuster as a dead end for economic statisticians:

> In considering the work of these writers, we have to remember that the ideas of all investigators of the theory of cyclical movements in the nineteenth century, and of most of those in the twentieth, were conditioned by the mathematics of Fourier analysis. Their object was to exhibit the series as a sum of sine or cosine terms, and, if the fit between observation and theory was not exact, the differences were regarded as random errors of observation. Their methods have met with success in the domain of the very small, such as the oscillations which we believe to compose light-waves, and also in the domain of the very large, such as tidal effects generated by planetary motion. But I am sorry to say that in most of the intervening domain Nature does not seem to have studied the mathematical theory of harmonic analysis nearly so thoroughly as she ought. If there is one thing more clear than another in economic series, it is that they do *not* behave as if they were composed of harmonics with a superposed random element, for they shift continually in amplitude, distance between peaks and phase. By taking enough harmonics, of course, one can represent almost anything by a series of sine and cosine terms, but I do not think anyone who has tried to obtain

a close fit to an economic series of any length would feel that he was really probing into the essential causes of the generating process. (Kendall 1945, 96)

Kendall saw the real hope in analysis of time series in the "new approach to the problem" by Udny Yule, Eugen Slutsky, and Ragnar Frisch. These three eschewed the notion of representing time series by errors of observations superimposed on a function-of-time scheme. Yule, for example, replaced the search for "hidden periodicity" with the search for "flexible periodicity"; his autoregressive equations modeled phase shifts and variable, rather than fixed, amplitudes and periods. Slutsky, Yule, Frisch, and later Wold looked to stochastic schemes of random disturbances or erratic shocks that were integrated into oscillating systems. Their models of autoregression on variables and moving averages of disturbance terms were to prove more fruitful in economic time series analysis than the function-of-time-with-errors approach. Their work on stochastic processes is the subject of the next chapter.

Conclusion

By the turn of the century, statisticians were using correlation and regression analysis to explore law and order in economic and meteorological data. Although their ultimate aim had been to prove and quantify laws of inheritance and evolution, the biometricians who originally devised these techniques had worked with cross-section data. The basis of correlation and regression was a comparison of deviations from an average. The basis of that comparison was a statistical sample from a single population: a grouping of measurements of the same object or a grouping of measurements of the same organ of members of the same species. The raw materials for statisticians working with meteorological and economic data were usually time series. Time series begged the question of "What is an average?" Even in the earliest applications of correlation and regression to time series, empirical investigators realized there were problems. Skewed frequency distributions, nonrandom and successively dependent observations, time lags between cause and effect, and periodic and secular movement threatened the applicability of techniques grounded in logical variation and probability. Ysidro Edgeworth's articulation of a central limit theorem and Udny Yule's use of the least squares algorithm for regression analysis took the onus off variables for meeting the criteria of normality and apparently solved the problem of skewed distributions. Reginald Hooker, F. E. Cave-Browne-Cave, and others dealt with the problem of nonsimultaneous correlation by lagging one of the variables in a correlated pair. They made use not only of graphs of the variables plotted against time, but also of correlation coefficients plotted against time lags.

Even with least squares regression and time lags, economic statisticians were continually faced with a "time-correlation problem." The problem was not only that many correlations of time series data led to nonsensical estimates of coefficients, but also that in the 1890s and first two decades of the twentieth century, economists were usually only interested in short-period changes.

Reginald Hooker named part of the problem the "trend," and suggested eliminating the problem by correlating deviations from a moving average or correlating first differences. Lucien March argued for "decomposition" of time series to separate the year-to-year changes from the decennial changes or secular movement. Detrending catered to both the economist focusing on the cyclical component and the statistician trying to reconcile fluctuations with deviations. In addition to having to deal with the trend, investigators working with monthly or quarterly data had to isolate and eliminate seasonal components. In the 1920s and 1930s they "corrected" their series with harmonic analysis or seasonal indices constructed with link relatives or ratios to moving averages.

The earliest users of regression and correlation on time series data saw the solution to the time-correlation problem as isolating and then correlating only the corresponding components in each series – in practice this meant just the cyclical components. In addition to the trend and the seasonal component there was the irregular component. Oskar Anderson was one of the first to name this the "random component." In 1914, he suggested going beyond first differences, if necessary, and differencing until all correlation between the variables and time was eliminated, then correlating the differenced variables. In 1927, Anderson suggested that instead of seeing series as composed of trend, seasonal, cyclical, and irregular components one should see them as composed of a function-of-time component and a random component. Differencing would reveal the law with time, whether it be, for example, linear or parabolic. One would then use the appropriate smoothing function to model the series.

Anderson was not the only advocate of the function-of-time approach to estimating relationships. The harmonic analysis of Arthur Schuster, Henry Moore, and William Beveridge was also based on the assumption that the variables under investigation were functions of time and that any series could be ultimately represented by sums of sines and cosines. Stanley Jevons called time the "great independent variable of all change." This was taken to heart by Moore, as is evident in his regressions on time to model linear trends, his use of periodograms to determine the periodicity of rainfall, and his hypothesized links of earthly activity with the transit of Venus. Moore, like almost all statisticians writing in the first three decades of the twentieth century – the pig iron age – was unable to contemplate a more organic, self-determining notion of dynamics that was based not on a functional relationship with time, but on a functional relationship with previous states of a process.

Although periodograms and harmonic analysis in general got little attention from economic statisticians in the first quarter of the twentieth century, the variate difference method and regressing variables on time became popular solutions to the time-correlation problem. Time as the causal factor in this problem did not sit well with Udny Yule. Yule came to the conclusion that periodicity was not only "hidden" but "flexible" and that movement in a series was often partly self-determined. In such cases, it was more useful to see values as functions of previous values rather than as functions of time. In his presidential address to the Royal Statistical Society in November 1925, Yule suggested classifying series by the properties of their serial correlations (Yule 1926). The classification of time series into "dangerous series" or "stationary processes," and the introduction of models of random disturbances and autoregressive relationships, are the substance of the final chapter of this history.

10

Autoregression, Random Disturbances, Dangerous Series, and Stationary Stochastic Processes

Statistics then supposes a state to be for an instant stationary, so that the elements attached to its existence may be enumerated; whilst political history follows it in its march, and verifies all the phenomena it presents. The one science is to the other what, in a different order of things, statics are to dynamics, what rest is to motion. Generally, statistics relate to the present, leaving the past to history, and the future to politics.

Adolphe Quetelet [1846] 1849, 176

Sagredo: And what kind of natural events are motion and rest?
Simplicio: So great and basic that nature itself is defined by them.
Sagredo: So that moving eternally and being completely immovable are two very important conditions in nature, show the very greatest dissimilarity, and are the main attributes of the chief bodies in the universe. Consequently from them only the most different results can follow.
Simplicio: This is surely so.

Galileo Galilei [1632] 1967, 130

Many decades after Adolphe Quetelet wrote, statisticians were not content to leave the past to history and the future to politics. At first they looked into the past to see if, how, and why the economy seemed to ebb then grow then peak then ebb. Then they looked into the future to see if they could forecast a price thirty days from now, the weather twenty-four hours ahead, the variance of foreign exchange rates ninety days from now, or volume of output next month. Forays into the past and future with the tools of probability analysis required some preservation of the "stationary" conditions to which Quetelet alluded. Quetelet had used statistical analysis on cross-section data for the study of a state at rest. As we saw in Chapter 5, he often connected the means of these states in, for example, plots in cycle time, but the building blocks of his social physics were frequency distributions and means and deviations from cross sections of measurements taken at one point in time. When statisticians began to explore the past and future through time series data they abandoned frozen states of rest for conditions of motion. Yet, as Sagredo in Galileo Galilei's dialogue remarked, rest and motion are greatly dissimilar. Galileo and, fifty years later, Isaac Newton did, however, find a case in which motion and rest could be treated as equivalents. Both scientific philosophers demonstrated that from an internal frame of reference within a physical system, straight-line, *uniform* motion was indistinguishable from a state of rest.[1] Similarly, early time series studies attempted to isolate fluctuations that could be the analytical equivalent of a state of rest. These attempts culminated in the 1930s with the classification of time series as either stationary or evolutive and with prescriptions for manipulating evolutive series until they displayed stationary motion.

Aleksandr Yakovlevich Khinchin's and Herman Wold's naming and defining of stationary stochastic processes was preceded by Udny Yule's work on autoregressive processes, Yule and Eugen Slutsky's studies of linear transformations of random disturbances, Yule and Oskar Anderson's classification of time series, and Andrei Nikolaevich Kolmogorov's axiomization of probability theory and random processes. These major steps in the development of time series analysis form the structure of this last chapter in the history of time series analysis up to 1938. I begin by linking Yule's applications of autoregression with earlier regressions in biology and meteorology. Yule's notion of autoregression was that values in a time series were at least partly determined by previous values. This idea was also embodied in Karl Pearson's specification of random walks and Andrei Markov's specification of what are now called Markov chains or Markov processes, and I briefly look at their work in the context of a general functions-of-previous-states approach.

In his attempt to demonstrate the limitations of the function-of-time approach of Oscar Anderson and Student, Yule noted the generation of spurious cycles in linear operations on random variables. Eugen Slutsky took this a step further in his argument that moving averages of random disturbances could serve as useful models of economic cycles. Building on the theoretical work of Khinchin and Kolmogorov, Wold brought together the diverse strands of harmonic analysis, autoregression, moving averages, and classification of time series by their statistical properties. In his seminal work in 1938, Wold demonstrated that any stationary time series could be decomposed into a generalized process of hidden periodicities, and autoregressive and moving-average processes. Wold also demonstrated that if the data-generating process could be classified as "stationary," then least squares regression and probabilistic reasoning were appropriate tools of analysis. The stationary time series was to the cross section as uniform motion was to a state of rest.

A word of caution – although a superficial outline of this chapter paints a picture of progression from crude, diverse beginnings into an integrated, stunning whole, I wonder if the end product was more like a hole than a whole. Wold's integration of all these strands is historically important because least

---

[1]   Uniform motion is motion without either acceleration, deceleration, or change of direction. Roger Penrose (1989, 162–167) has a concise summary of this principle of Galilean relativity.

squares regression on stationary time series was to dominate time series analysis for decades to come. This approach, however, has several limitations:

- Many processes in the real world, particularly in the realm of economics, are not stationary.
- The data manipulation techniques borrowed from speculators and financiers to make series stationary were first used either as tools of persuasion and deception or as means of narrowing the focus to the very short term.
- Each step in the data-massaging process is fraught with dangers of generating spurious components and of destroying the essential, interesting features.
- The "uniform motion" of stationary processes that renders the statistics of states of rest applicable is often inadequate for understanding the past and future paths of processes of change.

Autoregression: The General Model

$$y_t = f(y_{t-1}, y_{t-2}, ..., y_{t-n})$$

This simple formulation of previous values of a variable predicting future values, with some random error, has a complex history. Udny Yule is usually given credit for the first specification of the autoregressive process in 1927. The roots of the specification for what he labeled a "statistical series," however, lie with the nineteenth-century work of Francis Galton and Karl Pearson on inheritance and Pearson, Alice Lee, and F. E. Cave-Browne-Cave on meteorological phenomena. An exploration of the similarities and differences between the ideas of Galton, Pearson, Cave-Browne-Cave, and Yule raises questions of the role of life cycles in comprehending change, the choice of an external or internal clock in dynamic models, the contrast between seeing change as a function of time or as a function of previous values, the definition of $(t, t-1)$, and the role of autoregression in time series analysis.

Autoregression: Biometry and Inheritance

$$y_t = f(y_{t-1}, y_{t-2}, ..., y_{t-n})$$
$$t = \text{one generation at adult stage}$$
$$t - 1 = \text{the previous generation at adult stage}$$

As we saw in Chapter 7, Francis Galton and Karl Pearson created correlation surfaces and regression polygons to quantify their eugenic hypothesis of determination by inheritance. Although the correlation surfaces were eventually generalized to examine the correlation between the measurement of one organ with that of another for the same person (e.g., correlation of the circumference of the head with foot size), the focus of the biometricians' work was correlation of identical organs through inheritance. Galton's first use of regression was his 1877 study of the relationship between the sizes of parent and offspring sweet pea seeds (more details of Galton's sweet pea experiment can be found in Chapter 5). Within a few years of the sweet pea experiment, Galton had obtained enough data on human families to perform regressions on measured characteristics of parents and offspring. The biometricians' mathematical formulation of inheritance was essentially $y_t = f(y_{t-1}) + e$. For example, the stature of the child was a function of the stature of the midparent (the weighted mean measurement of both parents was often used as the independent variable) and of some random variation across the species.

A distinctive feature of the biometricians' estimation of the laws of inheritance was the capacity of their subject for determining qualitative frontiers in the statistical process (i.e., generation gaps). There is little room for question as to the appropriate intervals between the elements of the sequence in the biometric models. The life cycle path of human development, the normal distribution of measured characteristics across the population, the normal surface of the reproductive relationship all yielded a structure and geometry that gave order to processes of heredity. Intervals between the subscripted times in the equation were determined by generation gaps. Galton, for example, took measurements of the parent at the adult stage of the life cycle and measurements of the offspring also at the adult stage of the life cycle. The acts of observing t and $t - 1$ were usually simultaneous – the height of the parent was measured and recorded at the same time as that of the child. The age difference within each pair varied from one pair to another, but the important thing was to be consistent in stage of life cycle and, of course, to separate the life cycles by generation. The clock or calendar in this process was internally generated by the development of the subjects of the analysis.

Serial Correlation: Meteorology and Isobars in Time and Space

$$y_t = f(y_{t-1}) + e$$
t = a place, a time
$t - 1$ = another place 1,090 miles southwest and another
time twenty-six hours before

The first meteorological study using correlation was that of Karl Pearson and Alice Lee in 1897. They correlated barometric readings at various pairs of stations in the British Isles. Their time series comprised daily observations spanning up to thirteen years. The correlation coefficients were computed for simultaneous readings. This was also the case in the 1902 study by F. E. Cave-Browne-Cave and Karl Pearson that included observations from north of Norway down the west coasts of Europe and Africa. Their study concluded that the correlation of simultaneous barometric heights between two stations, approximately on the same meridian, diminished to a negative minimum and then began to increase as the distance between selected stations increased.

The correlation coefficients calculated for various pairs of stations in the British Isles were high, between .75 and .98, but simultaneous correlation was not the most useful approach for forecasting. Two years later Cave-Browne-Cave (1905) lagged measurements at one station in each pair and used the criteria of greatest value of correlation coefficient to choose the most appropriate time interval between stations (see Chapter 3 and Table 9.2). Cave-Browne-Cave noted that the best interval was remarkably shorter in summer than in winter; therefore, she split the data into equinox-to-equinox sets. She also correlated the daily rise and fall (first differences) in barometric pressure at pairs of stations with different time intervals between the readings. In her article, she solicited physical explanations of the time intervals that she had determined to be the best, but she warned meteorologists that it would not necessarily be due to the average interval between the arrival of the same isobar at two stations since "correlation depends not upon the equality of pressure, but upon the proportionality of deviations from local means" (Cave-Browne-Cave 1905, 407).

Cave-Browne-Cave concentrated on the correlation for two pairs of stations: Wilmington, North Carolina, and Halifax, Nova Scotia, in the Northern Hemisphere and St. Helena and Cape Town in the Southern Hemisphere. With regard to the former, her correlations indicated that the change of pressure passed from southwest to northeast. Cave concluded that the best interval for prediction, using the given daily recordings, was the reading in Wilmington twenty-six hours before the reading in Halifax. She went further in interpolating a curve of correlation coefficients (Figure 10.1) that would give meteorologists some idea of the best forecasting interval if readings could be taken and compared at any time of the day. For Wilmington and Halifax this estimate was 14.07 hours in the summer and 23.22 hours in the winter.

As a shortcut to estimating the correlation of the daily differences in reading (e.g., correlating the daily rise or fall in Wilmington and Halifax), Cave-Browne-Cave serially correlated the barometric heights on consecutive days for each station separately. This first published example of serial autocorrelation yielded relatively high correlation coefficients (e.g., .62 for Wilmington in the summer). Cave-Browne-Cave suggested that future studies could improve upon hers by "making the prediction for one station depend upon observations at two or more other stations, so situated as to give suitable intervals for maximum correlation; and it may also be desirable to take into account the height observed on the previous day at the station for which the prediction is required" (Cave-Browne-Cave 1905, 412).[2]

Even without considering the explicit autocorrelation of barometric heights in Cave-Browne-Cave's study, the statistical meteorological studies helped to lay a foundation for the concept of an autoregressive stochastic process. A previous time corresponded with a place further southwest. This combination of spatial and temporal relationships was a key to Yule's formulation of a statistical series.

[2]   In this chapter, the term "autocorrelation" refers to the correlation of values of y with previous values of y, and not to the autocorrelation of residuals in regression. Helm Clayton (1917) also used serial autocorrelation in his meteorological studies. Clayton plotted the correlation coefficients of solar radiation for different intervals and the correlation coefficients of temperature to compare their periodicities.

Table I.—Correlation of Barometric Heights at Halifax and
Wilmington.

Interval between readings.*	Summer, 1879—1888.	Winter, 1879—1888.	Interval between readings.	Summer, 1889—1898.	Winter, 1889—1898.
hrs.			hrs.		
−118	+ 0 ·0585	—	−119	−0 ·0134	—
− 94	+ 0 ·0605	—	− 95	−0 ·0247	—
− 70	+ 0 ·0668	+ 0 ·0496	− 71	−0 ·0141	+ 0 ·0512
− 46	+ 0 ·1391	+ 0 ·0379	− 47	+ 0 ·0418	+ 0 ·0598
− 22	+ 0 ·2385	+ 0 ·0416	− 23	+ 0 ·1742	+ 0 ·0420
+ 2	+ 0 ·3432	+ 0 ·2878	+ 1	+ 0 ·3038	+ 0 ·2456
+ 26	+ 0 ·3714	+ 0 ·5206	+ 25	+ 0 ·3143	+ 0 ·4701
+ 50	+ 0 ·2176	+ 0 ·2344	+ 49	+ 0 ·1538	+ 0 ·2263
+ 74	+ 0 ·1138	+ 0 ·0842	+ 73	+ 0 ·0581	+ 0 ·0839
+ 98	+ 0 ·0816	+ 0 ·0342	+ 97	+ 0 ·0150	+ 0 ·0736
+122	+ 0 ·0881	+ 0 ·0217	+121	−0 ·0050	+ 0 ·0881

* Positive when the reading is taken later at Halifax.

Table III.—Correlation of Barometric Heights on Consecutive Days.

Station.	Summer, 1879—1888.	Winter, 1879—1888.	Summer, 1889—1898.	Winter, 1889—1898.
Halifax	0 ·5924	0 ·3998	0 ·5155	0 ·4270
Wilmington	0 ·6151	0 ·4827	0 ·6510	0 ·4916

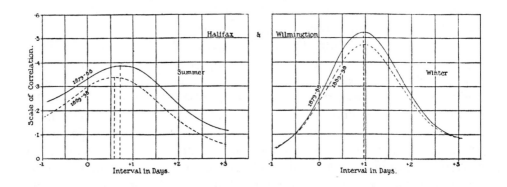

Figure 10.1   Cave-Browne-Cave's tables and plots of correlation coefficients of
barometric pressure at Wilmington, North Carolina, and Halifax, Nova Scotia, by
intervals between readings. *Source:* Cave-Browne-Cave 1905, 405, 408.

Autoregression: Yule's Specification

$$y_t = f(y_{t-1}, y_{t-2}) + e$$
t = a place in a sequence
$t - 1$ = the previous place in a sequence

Udny Yule's specification of an autoregressive stochastic process was a by-
product of his attempts to explain why statisticians, and in particular those
who worked with economic and social data, often got strange correlations

from time series data. Yule stands out as one of the few that philosophically struggled with the blending of the law of error and laws of motion. The titles of two of his papers illustrate this: "On the Time-Correlation Problem . . ." (1921) and "Why Do We Sometimes Get Nonsense-Correlations between Time-Series? – A Study in Sampling and the Nature of Time-Series" (1926).[3]

In his 1921 article, Yule reviewed several of the major studies that had applied correlation and regression to time series data. He argued that turn-of-the-century quantitative workers perceived the essence of the time-correlation problem as "the difficulty of isolating for study different components in the total movement of each variable: the slow secular movement, probably non-periodic in character . . . the oscillations of some ten years' duration, more or less, corresponding to the wave in trade: the rapid movements from year to year . . . the seasonal movement with the year, and so on" (Yule 1921, 501).

Around 1914, some statisticians switched the focus of time series analysis from the decomposition of series to techniques that assumed variables were functions of time. In the 1914 volume of *Biometrika*, Oskar Anderson and "Student" (William Gosset) suggested that the variables to be correlated be differenced until the correlation of the nth difference of x and y was the same as the correlation of the $(n + 1)$th difference (see Chapter 3). The advocates of the variate-difference method saw the time-correlation problem as "spurious correlation" due to variables being functions of time. Their solution was to eliminate all components which were functions of time and to correlate the serially independent residuals.

Yule speculated that appropriate models of many economic time series would include harmonic terms, and he questioned Anderson's assumption that differencing would tend to eliminate these periodic terms. Yule constructed a series from a simple harmonic function and examined the effects of repeated differencing on the amplitude for different intervals. He concluded that far from eliminating all the periodic terms, repeated differencing of a series generated from a harmonic function selectively emphasized the term with a period of two intervals (Yule 1921, 509). Yule hypothesized that the two-year oscillations would dominate the results of repeated differencing whether the series was based on a harmonic function or not. He tested this hypothesis by repeated differencing of a random series and concluded that

> differencing tends more and more to emphasize the alternation as against the random fluctuations. The variate-difference correlation method *tends*, we must conclude – slowly and subject to more or less dilution by longer periodicities and by the effects of random fluctuations – to give correlations due to two-year oscillations.[4] (Yule 1921, 519–520)

---

[3] Yule's 1926 essay and his 1927 investigation into sunspot activity are reproduced by David Hendry and Mary Morgan in *Foundations of Econometric Analysis*. In their introduction, Hendry and Morgan discuss their replication of Yule's experiments from the 1926 investigation. Holbrook Working's essay on random-difference series discussed later is also in that collection.

[4] Yule's 1921 and 1926 demonstrations that repeated differencing of a random series generated cyclical patterns were one-half of the claim to name in the "Yule–Slutsky effect." While Yule was explicit about the spuriousness of the cycles generated by the linear operations on random series, the other half of the duo, Eugen Slutsky, had no intention of demonstrating spurious cycles. Slutsky, as we will see in a later section of this chapter, was seeking a model of true cycles in capitalist systems.

The time-correlation problem continued to puzzle Yule, and he was not satisfied with the assumption, implicit in the variate difference method and harmonic analysis, that variables were functions of time: "While there is a sense – a special and definite sense – in which this may perhaps be said to cover the explanation, as will appear in the sequel, to my own mind the phrase has never been intellectually satisfying. I cannot regard time per se as a causal factor" (Yule 1926, 4).

Yule's formal education was that of a mathematical physicist. He served as Karl Pearson's lab assistant and he and Alice Lee were the only students in Karl Pearson's first formal lectures on applied statistics that were directed toward those with engineering backgrounds. In keeping with his physics background, Yule tackled the problem of nonsense correlation of time series with experimentation. In his 1925 presidential address to the Royal Statistical Society, Yule first demonstrated that nonsensical correlations (e.g., a perfect positive or inverse correlation in cases where there was actually zero correlation) could arise from a sampling period too short to capture the full harmonic motion of two experimental series (Yule 1926).

With these experiments, Yule realized that the nonsensical results were related to the fact that his series were "either rising or falling, not more or less level" (Yule 1926, 14). This prompted Yule to classify time series by the nature of their serial correlations. Random series with zero serial correlation posed no problem for bivariate correlation (see top plot in Figure 10.2). Series that were positively serially correlated, but whose first differences were not serially correlated, yielded high standard errors but did not tend definitely to mislead (middle plot in Figure 10.2).

Yule had used a sine wave in his experimental generation of time series. Such a series has the property that the serial correlation for the first differences are precisely the same as those for the values of the variables. This was an example of a third type of series – one whose values were positively serially correlated and whose differences were positively serially correlated (bottom plot in Figure 10.2). This type was the "dangerous" series that was particularly likely to lead to fallacious conclusions in bivariate analysis. Correlations between such series (Yule called them "conjunct" series with "conjunct" differences) tended to yield high positive or high negative correlations between the samples, without any regard to the true value of the correlation. Yule had solved the puzzle that had been perplexing him for years. He was able to identify and mathematically describe what he called the "dangerous class of series." The time plot of these series with serially correlated differences displayed

---

Figure 10.2 *(facing page)*   Yule's experimental generation of three pairs of series classified by their serial correlations. In the top plot, the values and the first differences of each random series are uncorrelated. In the middle plot, the values are serially correlated, but the differences are not; Yule referred to this as conjunct series with random differences. In the bottom plot of conjunct series with conjunct differences, both the absolute values and the differences are positively serially correlated. These are the "dangerous" series that yield nonsense correlations between series. *Source:* Yule 1926, 27–29.

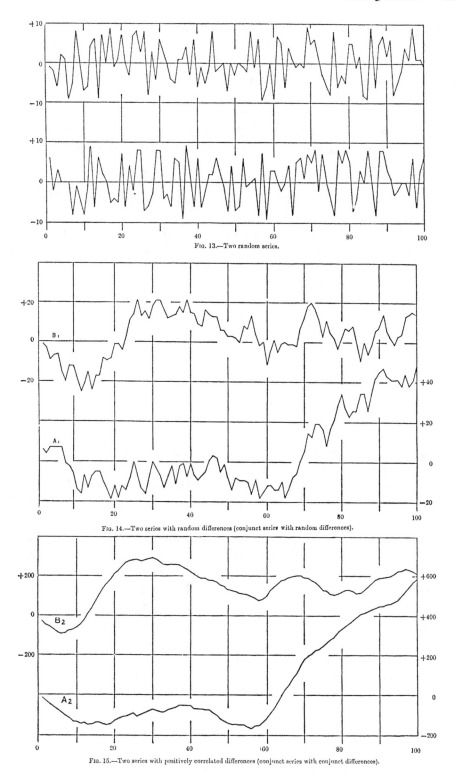

Fᴵɢ. 13.—Two random series.

Fɪɢ. 14.—Two series with random differences (conjunct series with random differences).

Fɪɢ. 15.—Two series with positively correlated differences (conjunct series with conjunct differences).

a tendency to rise or fall consistently over prolonged periods. While this gave the series some "continuity with time," time was not a causal factor and the series were not correlated with time. The movement manifested by many time series, particularly those used in economic analysis, was partly self-determined. Variables were not simply functions of other causal variables, as implied in a regression of x on y; nor were they simply functions of time, as implied in a periodogram of y. They had a clock and a life of their own. Yule chose to interpret this self-determining process as positions in a sequence or places in a series:

> In a mathematical series any term u_s is some definite mathematical function of s, and has precise and definite mathematical relations to the terms that precede and the terms that follow. In a statistical series u_s is no longer a definite mathematical function of s, and no longer has precise and definite relations to the terms that precede and follow it. I have suggested replacing, as we usually have to do in statistics, the conception of mathematical functionality by the conception of correlation, and thus specifying the characteristics of the series by its serial correlations. Apart from its application to the theory of sampling in time-series, such a specification is of interest in itself as a method of analysis. (Yule 1926, 41)

Yule demonstrated the use of serial correlation as a method of analysis in its application to William Beveridge's index numbers of wheat prices in Western Europe from 1545 to 1844 and recordings of rainfall at Greenwich from 1815 to 1924. His method, for each of the two examples, was to calculate the serial correlation coefficients for intervals up to $(t - 20)$ and for a range of serially correlated differences. He tabulated and plotted these correlation coefficients searching for patterns that would aid in the decomposition of each series and that would enable him to draw conclusions on whether the series was periodic or just oscillatory with no periodic movement (Figure 10.3).

Cave-Browne-Cave had used correlation to determine which station could best predict barometric height a few hours later at another station and which interval was best for prediction for a pair of stations. Yule used correlation to determine which previous value was most highly correlated with another value. His questions were similar to, What intervals, which stations yielded the highest correlations? Within two years of his presidential address, Yule applied the techniques of serial correlation and autoregression to investigate periodicities in the time series of Wolfer's sunspot numbers. His two formulations of sunspot activity were:

$$u_x = (2 \cos\theta)u_{x-1} - u_{x-2} + e$$
$$u_x = b_1 u_{x-1} - b_2 u_{x-2}$$

This work became the foundation for modern time series analysis. It was the first complete formulation of what was later to be called a stationary stochastic process of the autoregressive type. It was also the first instance in

TABLE XIII.—Serial correlations for Sir William Beveridge's index-numbers for wheat prices in Western Europe, 1545–1844. All correlations are positive.

k.		r_k.	k.		r_k.
1	....	0·92240	21	....	0·63432
2	....	0·83353	22	....	0·62901
3	....	0·79639	23	....	0·61136
4	....	0·79560	24	....	0·59658
5	....	0·79146	25	....	0·59193
6	....	0·76013	26	....	0·60030
7	....	0·72850	27	....	0·61241
8	....	0·71063	28	....	0·60680
9	....	0·72170	29	....	0·60770
10	....	0·75356	30	....	0·60789
11	....	0·78013	31	....	0·60877
12	....	0·77661	32	....	0·59589
13	....	0·74508	33	....	0·58851
14	....	0·73330	34	....	0·58553
15	....	0·73625	35	....	0·57505
16	....	0·73609	36	....	0·56441
17	....	0·70015	37	....	0·55683
18	....	0·65054	38	....	0·55342
19	....	0·62692	39	....	0·54495
20	....	0·62319	40	....	0·53479

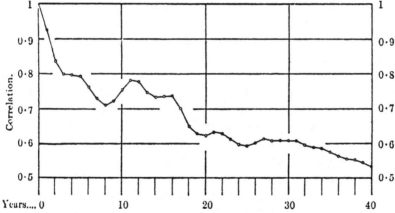

Figure 10.3 Yule's table and graph of serial correlation coefficients plotted against intervals of Beveridge's trend-free index of wheat prices in Western Europe. Wold would later label such a plot a correlogram. *Source:* Yule 1926, 43.

which an error term (e) was used to signify random disturbance in a relationship, not just errors in measurement.

Yule's variables were not functions of time, they were functions of previous terms in a sequence. It was as if Yule had taken scores of generations of one family of sweet peas. He was correlating measurements from parent and offspring, but the observations were not across a population at one moment in time. The offspring of the one regressed triad was the parent in the successive group and the grandparent in the next. In Yule's approach, the subscripts t, $t - 1$, analogous to his subscript s in U_s, were more closely linked with place in a sequence than with time. In fact in his work on serial correlation and autoregression, Yule never subscripted time.

Four years after Yule's study was published, Gilbert Walker (1931) generalized the autoregressive model of a physical system of natural oscillations, all subject to dampening but buffeted by random disturbances, to take into account dependence on more than two previous values. Through mathematical deduction, Walker showed that if the number of observations was great, the equation relating the autocorrelation coefficients for different pairs of terms in a series would be similar to the autoregression equation relating the actual terms of a series. He concluded that the graph of the autocorrelation coefficients plotted against the intervals linking the values correlated would be smoother than plots of the actual terms and could be used to determine the natural periods of the series. From the serial correlation plots of quarterly data on barometric pressure at Port Darwin from 1882 to 1926, Walker concluded that there were periods in the data of $34\frac{1}{2}$ months and $11\frac{1}{2}$ years.

Walker had argued that his method could be used to determine whether the oscillations were due to the fact that the external disturbances were cyclical (e.g., solar influences) or the randomly disturbed system itself had an inherent oscillatory nature, which must be damped. Walker concluded that the $11\frac{1}{2}$-year cycle was imposed from without, presumably from solar influences, but there were not enough observations to determine if the $34\frac{1}{2}$-month cycle was an internally generated damped cycle subject to random disturbance or one generated by an external factor that was in itself cyclical.

The notion of oscillations was central to the analyses of Yule and Walker. Also, both used autoregression and serial correlation, not to forecast the next value in a sequence or at some future time, but to explore serial relationships – either to determine the presence or absence of periodicity or to estimate the intervals between cycles. It was another tool to be used in the decomposition of time series in order to separate different causes and different resulting patterns of change. Yule's specification of the autoregressive process, however, was to become one of the most common tools of forecasting with univariate time series models. Autoregressive is the AR in ARMA and ARIMA (autoregressive integrated moving average) models, so widely used in the Box-Jenkins approach to time series modeling, and in VAR (vector autoregression) models. In addition to Yule's general specification of autoregressive processes, there were two other early twentieth-century univariate time series models based on a statistical dependency on previous values that became popular models of stochastic processes: Karl Pearson's specification of a random walk and Andrei Andreevich Markov's notion of dependent states of a chain.

Random Walk

$$y_t = y_{t-1} + e$$

A variation of the autoregressive process commonly found in structural time series models is the case where y depends on just the previous value and the coefficient on that previous value is equal to one. Karl Pearson was the first to name this the "random walk." As with the general autoregressive model, a spatial analogy preceded the pure time specification of Pearson's model of the random walk. In his statistical explorations of natural selection and evolution, Pearson asked,

> What is the rate of infiltration of a species into a possible habitat? . . . Now taking a centre, reduced in the idealised system to a point, what would be the distribution after n random flights of N individuals departing from this centre? . . . How far with a broad average of environment in relation to food supply, breeding places, shelter, foes, etc. is the spread of a species random? Are any of the geographical limits to plant or insect or animal life non-environmental and in course of change? (Pearson 1906a, 3, 4, 53)

In his search for a mathematical model of random migration of a species, Pearson publicly called for a solution to the problem of the random walk in a 1905 issue of *Nature*:

> A man starts from a point O and walks l yards in a straight line; he then turns through any angle whatever and walks another l yards in a second straight line. He repeats this process n times. I require the probability that after these n stretches he is at a distance between r and $r + \delta r$ from his starting point, O. (Pearson 1905, 294)

Pearson received replies and queries from scientists working in fields as diverse as the theory of sound waves and pest control of mosquito populations.[5] Lord Rayleigh suggested that if n was very large, an analogous solution existed in the problem of the addition of sound amplitudes in notes of the same period. Pearson summarized Lord Rayleigh's approach in an image that, with variation, is used today to describe the random walk: "The lesson of Lord Rayleigh's solution is that in open country the most probable place to find a drunken man who is at all capable of keeping on his feet is somewhere near his starting point!" (Pearson 1905, 342).

There is a difference in Pearson's metaphor and the description of the rambles of a drunken man used in present-day classes on time series analysis: for Pearson the spatial displacement, the yards walked, in each stage was equal but the angle was variable; in the modern autoregressive story the time intervals are equal and the distance stumbled in one direction is variable. In the autoregressive story, the random walk is an example of a nonstationary process; although the mean is relatively stable over time, the variance is not. In very general forms, the problem of the random walk is found in models of limiting diffusion processes, sequential analysis in experimentation, investiga-

---

[5] Letters to Pearson suggesting solutions to the random-walk problem are in the Pearson Papers at University College in files 122 to 127. The authors of these letters include John Blakeman, Geoffrey Bennett, Sir Ronald Ross, J. C. Kluyver, and John Strutt (Lord Rayleigh).

tions into the size of queues with finite waiting rooms, and first-passage-time problems dealing with recurrence to either a point or a given set.[6]

In recent decades, financial analysts have used the random walk to model stock market prices. This is not a new application; although he did not use the expression "random walk" in his 1900 doctoral thesis for the École Normale, Louis Bachelier used a similar diffusion model for speculation in securities.[7] At the start of his thesis, Bachelier qualified his use of probability theory to understand speculation in stocks, bonds, and options:

> The calculus of probabilities, doubtless, could never be applied to fluctuations in security quotations, and the dynamics of the Exchanges will never be an exact science.
>
> But it is possible to study mathematically the static state of the market at a given instant, i.e., to establish the law of probability of price changes consistent with the market at that instant. If the market, in effect, does not predict its fluctuations, it does assess them as being more or less likely, and this likelihood can be evaluated mathematically.
>
> Research for a formula which expresses the likelihood of a market fluctuation does not appear to have been published to date. Such is the object of this study. (Bachelier [1900] 1964, 17)

In determining the mathematical expectation of the change in security prices from a given state, Bachelier explored the notion of independent increments. In essence, he saw the random walk as a stochastic difference equation:

$$y_t - y_{t-1} = e$$

The price changes, the first differences, were the random elements and the expected value of the change in price from $t - 1$ to t was zero:

> It seems that the market, the aggregate of speculators, at a given instant can believe in neither a market rise nor a market fall since, for each quoted price, there are as many buyers as sellers. . . .

[6]   George Weiss (1986) summarizes these variations on the random walk in his technical and historical review in the *Encyclopedia of Statistical Sciences.*

[7]   Paul Cootner, who included James Boness's English translation of Bachelier's thesis in his book on *The Random Character of Stock Market Prices,* pointed out the extraordinary ways in which Bachelier was before his time in his analysis of stochastic processes:

> So outstanding is his work that we can say that the study of speculative prices has its moment of glory at its moment of conception. Bachelier's doctoral dissertation is both a remarkable theoretical study of speculative prices and an imaginative empirical investigation, and in both fields it is far ahead of its time. It also marked the beginning of the theory of stochastic processes, a beginning which went unrecognized for decades.
>
> In this paper we find the Chapman-Kolmogorov-Smoluchowski equation for continuous stochastic processes, the derivation of the Einstein-Wiener Brownian motion process and the recognition that this process is a solution of the partial differential equations for heat diffusion. . . . In addition, Bachelier solves the first passage problem for the Wiener process, the probability law for diffusion in the presence of an absorbing barrier and other problems of interest, all of these solutions occurring many years before they were solved independently by the men who laid the basis for the modern theory of stochastic processes. Most of this theory was later to be developed by the mathematicians who were transforming probability theory into a rigorous discipline, Levy, Kolmogorov, Borel, Khinchine, and Feller. . . . If Bachelier was before his time in the development of probability he was even farther ahead in the analysis of stock market prices. It was not until 1934 that H. Working revived the idea of a random walk in commodity prices. (Cootner 1964, 3, 5)

> *The mathematical expectation of the speculator is zero.* It is necessary to evaluate the generality of this principle carefully: It means that the market, at a given instant, considers not only currently negotiable transactions, but even those which will be based on a subsequent fluctuation in prices as having a zero expectation. (Bachelier [1900] 1964, 26, 28)

In 1934, Holbrook Working suggested, as Bachelier had done, that price series on financial assets, particularly stock prices, had characteristics resembling a "random-difference series." Working used that label to emphasize the fact that although the series was not random, the first differences were. Working constructed a standard random-difference series table and graph so that other researchers could test the extent to which their commodity or stock price series resembled his standard.

Not all economists and statisticians have been comfortable with the random walk. This discomfort was eloquently expressed in the work of Maurice Kendall, who much to his surprise found a random walk in his analysis of first differences of weekly wheat prices from 1883 to 1934. Although Kendall's study is several years beyond the time scope of this history, his reaction to the results, which indicated a random walk, serve as good descriptions of the properties of this model. Kendall was apparently not familiar with either the work of Bachelier or the term "random walk" (although he used the term "economic Brownian motion"), but he captured the spirit of the random walk through the market:

> At first sight the implications of these results are disturbing. If the series is homogeneous, it seems that the change in price from one week to the next is practically independent of the change from that week to the week after. This alone is enough to show that it is impossible to predict the price from week to week from the series itself. And if the series really is wandering, any systematic movements such as trends or cycles which may be "observed" in such series are illusory. The series looks like a "wandering" one, almost as if once a week the Demon of Chance drew a random number from a symmetrical population of fixed dispersion and added it to the current price to determine the next week's price. And this, we may recall, is not the behaviour in some small backwater market. The data derive from the Chicago wheat market over a period of fifty years during which at least two attempts were made to corner wheat, and one might have expected the wildest irregularities in the figures. To the statistician there is some pleasure in the thought that the symmetrical distribution reared its graceful head undisturbed amid the uproar of the Chicago wheat-pit. The economist, I suspect, or at any rate the trade cyclist, will look for statistical snags before he is convinced of the absence of systematic movements. . . .
>
> A comparison of the variances of the two parts of the series suggests that there has been an increase in variability since World War I. This is what one might perhaps have expected, but it is rather a nuisance from the point of view of analysis because it suggests that the series is not stationary. We have here an interesting and rather unusual case of a time-series for which the mean remains constant but the variance appears to be increasing. (Kendall 1953, 13, 15)

For those studying the short-term behavior of prices, perhaps the greatest frustration that arises from specifying a random walk model is the admission that in a volatile market characterized by continual change, the best prediction one can make with sophisticated mathematics is that there will be no change.[8]

Markov Processes

$$P\ [(character_t = vowel)\ |\ character_1,....,character_{t-1}] =$$
$$P\ [(character_t = vowel)\ |\ character_{t-1}]$$

Similar to the random walk, the Markov process is a model of the dependency of a value in a series on only its immediately preceding value. The preceding equation is a description of a Markov stochastic process in which the *probability* of a character in a string of characters being a vowel, conditional upon all previous states in the character string, is identical to the probability of that state conditional upon only the previous character; whether or not the next letter is a vowel essentially depends only on whether the previous letter was a vowel or consonant.

Andreevich Markov, a professor of mathematics at St. Petersburg University from 1880 to 1905, was a practitioner of Chebyshev's mathematical problem-solving approach to probability theory. Markov's work on probability was characterized by proofs and demonstrations of limit theorems with the tools of continued fractions and the method of moments. In the tradition of Lexis, the urn was the starting point for Markov's logic.[9] He took an interest in the more esoteric sides of probability including hypothetical cases illustrating the "law of small numbers" and Lexis's subnormal dispersion ratios ($Q < 1$, or supernormal stability). The reasoning that led to his specification in 1906 of what are now called Markov chains can be seen in his correspondence with Alexander Alexandrovich Chuprov. Markov's unique focus on cases of "dependent variables" in sequences and his reliance on Russian reasoning tools of mathematical expectation, binomial distributions, and Lexis's classification of series are evident in his letter to Chuprov on November 15, 1910:

[8]   An analogous paradox can be found in the economist's use of the first derivative in curves drawn to illustrate the cyclical behavior of, for example, unemployment. At the peak, when the economy is going through a great qualitative change from expansion to recession, we interpret the mathematics as telling us that there is no change (dy/dt is equal to zero).

[9]   The Russian probability theorists' interest in urns and mathematical expectation comes through in a variety of communications. In a letter to Chuprov on November 28, 1912, Markov compared the geometric approach of Karl Pearson with his own: "But I must say that the derivation given by Pearson himself and his school runs quite differently. There is no discussion of urns" (*Correspondence between A. A. Markov and A. A. Chuprov* 1981, 9). With regards to mathematical expectation, Major Greenwood made the following statement in reviewing Chuprov's book on the theory of correlation: "Professor Tschuprow's pupil, Dr. Anderson, and Professor Tschuprow himself, have reproached English statisticians, particularly those of the Biometric School, with a neglect of the method of 'Mathematical Expectation' in their treatment of statistical problems" (Greenwood 1926, 322). A year later, Oskar Anderson commented on Greenwood's statement: "To what he has said I would like to add that an important advantage of this method consists in the rehabilitation in its rights of the idea of the *discontinuity* of the examined masses, and it is well known that this idea is now also gaining more and more ground in the realm of theoretical physics" (Anderson 1927, 564).

In order to consider the mathematical expectation of a squared sum, pairwise independence of the variables is sufficient. Corresponding to this, the dispersion in the sense of Lexis, which does not go beyond the mean squared deviation, can be shown to be normal for dependent trials if they are pairwise independent. Believing that this can be of interest to you I shall give an example. Let all the odd trials $1, 3, 5, \ldots 2i - 1, 2i + 1, \ldots$ be independent of each other and let the probability of event E for each of them be $\frac{1}{2}$.

For the even trials we shall assume that event E must occur on the $2i$th trial if the results of the $(2i - 1)$st and $(2i + 1)$st trials are the same, but it does not occur on the $2i$th trial if the results of the $(2i - 1)$st and $(2i + 1)$st trials are different. Our trials are pairwise independent. And therefore the dispersion in the sense of Lexis must be normal although the complete independence of the trials is out of the question. (*Correspondence between A. A. Markov and A. A. Chuprov* 1981, 9)

Markov then went on to demonstrate that the mathematical expectation for the first two moments was the same for his example (of the even trials being dependent on the adjacent odd trials) and that of Lexis's normal dispersion of totally independent trials. Chuprov replied the same day with a variation:

Your example is extraordinarily interesting for statistics. It is instructive in two respects. First of all, of course, because you constructed it: it brings out boldly that independence is not a necessary condition even for normal dispersion (in the sense of Lexis), not to speak of the law of large numbers in general, and that consequently normality of dispersion is not firm evidence of independence. . . . it is very easy to see from your example how normal dispersion is attained here, despite the lack of independence, because of the mutual compensation of the moments increasing dispersion against the norms, and those decreasing it. (*Correspondence between A. A. Markov and A. A. Chuprov* 1981, 10)

Chuprov went on to give two variants on Markov's example that yielded supernormal and subnormal dispersion. In a letter to Chuprov a few weeks later, Markov stated that the aim of his work was to show that "independence is not a necessary condition, but that another condition is necessary in order to show the real facts – the *constancy* of the probability" (*Correspondence between A. A. Markov and A. A. Chuprov.* 1981, 52). Markov's chief contributions to time series analysis include this shift in emphasis away from independence of trials toward constancy of probability structure and his mathematical examination of the statistical properties of dependent trials and sequences.

Markov generally avoided not only axiomatic approaches to probability theory but also empirical work on the subject. The only application he developed to illustrate his hypotheses was an investigation into sequences of characters in writing. He worked out the conditional probability that a letter would be a vowel given that the preceding letter was a vowel and the conditional probability that a letter would be a vowel given that the preceding letter was a consonant, then looked at the properties of various groupings of letters. It was Markov's demonstration of the appropriateness of the statistics of Bernoulli and Lexis in some cases of dependent trials and his interesting variant on serial dependency – the probability of a state depends on the nature of the previous state and looking *past* the previous state yields no more information on the present than would have been the case had we looked only at the previous state – that served as the basis of the theory of ergodic processes that are now called Markov chains. In the 1930s, Aleksandr Yakovlevich Khinchin and Andrei Nikolaevich Kolmogorov extended Markov's analysis of discrete-time random processes to continuous time. Cross tabulations on entries in the International Statistical Institute's *Bibliography on Time Series and Stochastic Processes* (see Appendix 2) sheds some light on the earliest studies of Markov processes up to 1938. Although 13 percent of all of the 979 entries on time series analysis were in French and 14 percent were in German, 30 percent of all investigations of Markov processes were in French and 24 percent were in German. Of the 140 entries coded as general Markov processes, 51 percent had no field of application, 18 percent were in physics, 16 percent were in genetics and only two studies were on economic applications.

Slutsky's Summation of Random Causes

$$\xi(t) = b_0 \cdot \eta(t) + b_1 \cdot \eta(t-1) + \cdots + b_h \cdot \eta(t-h)$$

As Holbrook Working pointed out in his 1934 essay, a random-difference series could be created by cumulating random numbers. Working and others credited Eugen Slutsky with being the first to systematically explore the properties of a model of cumulative effects of random disturbances. As with other Russian probability theorists, Slutsky was interested in the properties of the random components of time series. His work, along with that of Udny Yule and Ragnar Frisch, rotated the perspective of statisticians from one of seeing the random components as errors of observation to seeing them as disturbances that were an important part of the data-generating process. In a study published in Russian in 1927 and translated into English ten years later, Slutsky asked, "is it possible that a definite structure of a connection between random fluctuations could form them into a system of more or less regular waves?" (Slutsky [1927] 1937, 106). For Slutsky the answer was "yes," and he proceeded to demonstrate this with a variety of models and manipulated random series.

Slutsky argued that "an especially prominent role is played in nature by the process of *moving summation*" (Slutsky [1927] 1937). This moving average of random causes generated autocorrelation in the series of consequences, because through the summation, the consequences now possessed causes in common.[10] Slutsky visually compared his Model I series, generated from a

10 Slutsky called the original random series a "random function" and described it as an "incoherent series." The moving summation of the random series was a "chance function," and because of its serial correlation, a "coherent series." Slutsky described his model as a "moving summation" or just "summation" rather than a "moving average." Herman Wold labeled Slutsky's model a "moving average process," and in the second edition of *A Study in the Analysis of Stationary Time Series* also called it a "Slutsky process."

Черт. 3. ——————— Индекс английской кон'юнктуры за 1855 — 1877 г.
(масштаб слева)
·············· Модель I, точки 20—145. (Масштаб справа).

Figure 10.4   Slutsky's plot of a ten-term moving summation of the last digits of numbers drawn in a government lottery (dotted line) juxtaposed with Dorothy Swaine Thomas's quarterly index of business cycles from 1855 to 1877 (solid line). Slutsky used this to demonstrate the cyclical effects of the accumulation of unconnected random events. To get a good graphic match, Slutsky had to search for and isolate segments from Thomas's plot of quarterly observations from 1855 to 1914 and his series of 1,009 terms. From the latter, Slutsky chose terms 20 to 145 of his Model I to overlay on the early years of Thomas's data. *Source:* Slutsky 1927, 38.

ten-item moving average of the last digits in numbers drawn for a Soviet lottery, with Dorothy Swaine Thomas's quarterly index of English business cycles from 1855 to 1877 (Figure 10.4). He concluded that his model of a moving average of a random variable was a suitable one for simulating economic cycles. Slutsky constructed more elaborate models of moving averages of random series and examined their properties. He demonstrated that moving averages of random series could not only generate undulatory movement, but also regular, periodic waves with a strong tendency to sinusoidal forms. This ability of the summation of random causes to simulate regular harmonic oscillations was, however, tempered with abrupt changes in "regimes":

> *The summation of random causes generates a cyclical series which tends to imitate for a number of cycles a harmonic series of a relatively small number of sine curves. After a more or less considerable number of periods every regime becomes disarranged, the transition to another regime occurring sometimes rather gradually, sometimes more or less abruptly, around certain critical points.* (Slutsky [1927] 1937, 123)

In his investigation of what circumstances would lead to a suspension of regime changes and thus a tendency toward a pure, constant sinusoidal form, Slutsky articulated the "Law of the Sinusoidal Limit": repeating indefinitely moving summations followed by repeated differencing of a random series produces a sinusoidal process (Slutsky [1927] 1937, 131).[11] For Slutsky, the sinusoidal limit was an extreme case – practical models of moving summations of random disturbances would include the regime changes that were also typical of the real world. It was Slutsky's sinusoidal limit theorem, however, that led to the coupling of his name with Yule in the notion that linear operations on random series produce oscillations that tend toward a regular pattern.

Although the Yule–Slutsky effect is now associated with the generation of spurious cycles, Slutsky saw true, not spurious, cycles resulting from moving average operations on random variables. This is indicated in the title of Slutsky's work: "The Summation of Random Causes As the Source of Cyclic Processes." Slutsky argued that not only could moving averages of random disturbances generate periodicity, but that other statisticians such as Wesley Mitchell had been wrong in denying the periodicity of business cycles because of the crudeness of their models and their descriptive orientation. Slutsky also perceived harmonic analysis with the summation of sinusoids as crude and ineffective, but praised those who intuitively sensed cycles in the economy: "Those investigators of economic life are right who believe in their acumen and instinct and subscribe to at least an approximate correctness in the concept of the periodicity of business cycles" (Slutsky [1927] 1937, 119).[12] Slutsky even extended his confidence in the summation of random disturbances as the explanation of economic cycles to that most periodic of all movements – the heavenly bodies: "The paths of the planets, if regarded during billions of years, should be considered therefore, as chance functions" (Slutsky [1927] 1937, 132).

Although Slutsky did not specify a mechanism, such as expectations, by which a moving summation of random disturbances was achieved in an economy, it was obvious that he was searching for true causes of cycles in

---

[11] In *The Analysis of Economic Time Series*, Harold Davis (1941, 57–58) relates Slutsky's "sinusoidal limit theorem" and his general theory of random series to the work by Herbert Jones and others on the theory of runs and Harold Cramer's work on the probability distributions of functions of random variables.

[12] In the late 1920s in Moscow, it would have been in Slutsky's interest to have emphasized the mathematical properties of the generation of spurious cycles rather than a stationary cyclical model of the way capitalism proceeds. In the 1927 essay, written while he was employed at Nikolai Kondratieff's Conjuncture Institute, Slutsky made no mention of crises, historical materialism, class struggle, or even dialectical processes in his analysis of British trade cycles. Slutsky assumed the stochastic process of the moving summation of random disturbances was a *natural* one, and the "regime changes" predicted by his model were relatively crisis-free transitions from one sinusoidal form to another. He argued that his models of the "sinusoidal wave which rises and falls on the surface of the social ocean with the regularity of day and night" could be applied to both the business cycle of five to eleven years and the long cycle revealed in Kondratieff's empirical work (Slutsky [1927] 1937, 107). In 1928, within months of Kondratieff's publication of *The Long Wave Cycle*, the authorities closed down the Conjuncture Institute. As is evident in Figure A2.4 in Appendix 2, Russian studies in time series analysis decreased dramatically in the economic and political climate of the early 1930s. Unlike his colleague Kondratieff, Slutsky could rely on the political credentials of his revolutionary student days and he could take refuge in his mathematics, which as a discipline suffered far less from Stalin's purges than economics (see Demidov 1991). After 1927, Slutsky published only in the areas of meteorology and pure math, making contributions to probability theory particularly in the area of stochastic processes. The same year that Kondratieff was sent to prison in Siberia, Slutsky took on a new position studying solar activity at the Central Institute of Experimental Hydrology and Meteorology. There, one could more easily model cyclical processes *sans* discontinuous trend lines without provoking political wrath.

his models.[13] Slutsky did not mention the possibility of "spurious" cycles being generated by data manipulation. His subsequent reputation for discovering spurious qualities of random functions is probably due to his subsequent need to distance himself from formal, crisis-free models of capitalism, the association of his work with that of Yule, who did use linear transformations on random variables to demonstrate spurious cycles, and Ragnar Frisch's spin on Slutsky's work:

> One aspect of the problem to which I attach great importance is what might be called the *Slutsky effect*. This is the fact that linear operations applied to a random variable may produce fluctuations of a more or less cyclical character. I study the laws of such spurious cycle corrections and show in particular that it is possible to construct operations Ω which, when applied to a random variable, will produce nearly rigorous sine curves, the period and amplitude (but not the phase) of which can be predicted almost exactly when the operation Ω is known. I call this the Slutsky effect because I believe the Russian statistician, Eugen Slutsky, was the first to take up this effect in a systematic study. My results go somewhat further than Slutsky's. In particular, I derive coefficients by which the amplitude of observed cycles are compared with the amplitude of spurious cycles generated through the Slutsky effect. The knowledge of the laws of spurious cycle creation thus obtained may be combined with the key equation approach in a manner which goes a long way toward eliminating the spurious cycles. The procedure simply consists in, so to speak, setting aside one root of the key equation to take up the spurious effect. (Frisch 1931, 78)

Due to Frisch's naming of the *Slutsky effect*, Slutsky is now more closely associated with the generation of spurious cycles than with his advocacy of the summation of random disturbances as the source of true cycles. In some ways, however, Slutsky's legacy, without his name, has been revived through the MA part of ARMA and ARIMA models. Slutsky's study remains one of the few eloquent justifications for the use of moving averages of random causes as a model of how the world works.[14]

---

[13] Slutsky's interpretations of the cyclical effects generated by linear combinations of random disturbances is analogous to how a rational expectations theorist might interpret Andrew Harvey's and Albert Jaeger's 1993 study indicating that the Hodrick–Prescott filter initiates spurious cycles through the Yule–Slutsky effect. Some expectations theorists have attempted to model the way in which agents form their expectations with the same equations that econometricians use to model the economy. These theorists might well take up Harvey and Jaeger's critique of the Hodrick–Prescott filter as a theory of how economic cycles are generated. The mental machinations of forming expectations could act like a Hodrick–Prescott filter on the initial input of a random reality. The output of this form of rational expectations would be a cyclical process, constructed by human behavior. Where Yule, or Harvey and Jaeger, see spurious cycles generated by the manipulations of fellow econometricians, Slutsky, or some enterprising expectations theorist, sees true cycles generated from a filtering process by actors within the economic system.

[14] There were some economists who saw possibilities in Slutsky's work for a theory of business cycles. In an addenda to his 1927 treatise on business cycles, Wesley Mitchell briefly summarized Slutsky's study. Noting that Slutsky had worked only with uniform, rectangular distributions, Simon Kuznets (1929) used simulations and graphs to explore which shapes of distributions of random causes, which periods of moving averages, and which weighting systems yielded the most cyclical effects. Kuznets also clearly distinguished between the demonstration that the summation of random causes yielded

The Active Random Elements in the Models of Yule and Frisch

The demonstration that someone else's data manipulation practices led to the generation of spurious components is part of the one-up-manship among academic statisticians. We saw, for example, in the previous chapter how Oskar Anderson (1927) generated spurious cycles from Warren Person's decomposition techniques on a series that was partly formed by Warren Persons's own writing. In a similar vein, Udny Yule (1921) demonstrated that Anderson's variate-difference method applied either to a harmonic function or a random series set up an alternating pattern in the residual series and thus generated two-term cycles. If we take, as Wold did, the term "moving average" to describe a general linear transformation on successive values of a series, Yule's differencing showed that moving averages of outcomes of dice throws could generate spurious cycles.

Four years later while trying to simulate the time-correlation problem Yule (1926) used a moving average summation on a random series to generate a "dangerous" series in which the observations were serially correlated and the first differences were serially correlated. Yule took this a step further in this 1927 study of sunspot activity by giving the random term an active role as a disturbance term. As we saw in the previous chapter, Arthur Schuster and others had used harmonic analysis and, in particular, periodograms to determined the periodicity of annual measurements of sunspot activity. In using the periodogram, Schuster assumed that the true periods were hidden partly by random errors of observation, or "superposed fluctuations," as Yule called them. The larger the magnitude of such errors, the more irregular the curve, but amplitude and phase would hardly be affected and the periodogram would still be able to determine the true periods. Yule argued that in a more realistic model of oscillatory behavior, amplitude and phase should also change as a result of random action. Using the analogy of the pendulum, Yule wondered what would happen if,

> unfortunately boys get into the room and start pelting the pendulum with peas, sometimes from one side and sometimes from the other. The motion is now affected, not by *superposed fluctuations* but by true *disturbances*, and the effect on the graph will be of an entirely different kind. The graph will remain surprisingly smooth, but amplitude and phase will vary continually.[15] (Yule 1927, 268)

cycles and its inversion: "But can one invert the proposition and say that, therefore, cyclical oscillations may be conceived primarily as results of summation of random causes? . . . If cycles arise from random events, assuming the summation of the latter, then we obviously do not need the hypothesis of an independent regularly recurring cause which is deemed necessary by some theorists of business cycles" (Kuznets 1929, 273–274).

[15]   Harold Hotelling, in his essay on "Differential Equations Subject to Error" published a few months after Yule's, suggested a similar analogy of youthful male disturbance to a tendency to free oscillation: "Like a weight suspended from a spring, an index of the business cycle moves up and down, but as when the spring is in the hands of a small boy, one can never be quite sure what is going to happen next" (Hotelling 1927, 290).

Yet again, there was the metaphor of target practice, but the target was a moving one. Even more significant, the usefulness of the analogy was not that the random error of the inaccurate marksmen mapped out a static picture of a bell curve, but that the hit and miss of several boys served as random disturbances to a movement that would have been one of damped oscillation. This disturbed motion mapped out a dynamic stationary stochastic process. Yule was suggesting a very different role for the random component as one of active disturbance rather than passive error of observation. As Herman Wold described it, Yule was replacing "the approach of strict periodicity by a hypothesis containing an acting random element" (Wold [1938] 1954, 143). Yule's understanding of disturbance was linked with patterns of serial correlation and autoregression:

> Disturbance will always arise if the value of the variable is affected by external circumstance and the oscillatory variation with time is wholly or partly self-determined, owing to the value of the variable at any one time being a function of the immediately preceding values. (Yule 1927, 417)

In his models of dynamic economics, Ragnar Frisch elaborated on this notion of active random disturbance shocking a damped oscillatory system and thus serving as the source of energy in maintaining oscillations:

> One way which I believe is particularly fruitful and promising is to study what would become of the solution of a determinate dynamic system if it were exposed to a stream of erratic shocks that constantly upsets the continuous evolution, and by so doing introduces into the system the energy necessary to maintain the swings. If fully worked out, I believe that this idea will give interesting synthesis between the stochastical point of view and the point of view of a rigidly determined dynamical system. (Frisch 1933, 197–198)

Frisch suggested that economic fluctuations could be modeled by the components of a trend, damped oscillations, and a moving average of random disturbances.[16]

An important point to note is that Frisch, Yule, Walker, and Slutsky all took oscillations as their starting point. Although they criticized the harmonic analysis of the periodogram, the oscillatory behavior of economic time series was acknowledged and at some stage of their analysis all four statisticians

---

[16]   In Chapter 8, I look at Alfred Marshall's and Léon Walras's notions of disturbances to a process of market price tending to an equilibrium value. In her *History of Econometric Ideas* (1990), Mary Morgan has a detailed discussion on Ragnar Frisch's theories on cyclical behavior. She also examines the work of Udny Yule and Eugen Slutsky on random disturbances within the context of theories of business cycles. Roy Weintraub (1991) examines the details and significance of Frisch's ideas in relation to that of Paul Samuelson's work on dynamics. There are interesting parallels between changes in notions of what was dynamic in mathematical statistics and mathematical economics. As statisticians rotated their perspective from functions of time to autoregressive models, Samuelson encouraged the use of differential equations and argued that a model could not be classified as "dynamic" unless it included economically significant variables at different points of time. The mere inclusion of a time trend was not sufficient (see, e.g., Paul Samuelson 1947, 315).

used harmonic functions.[17] As Schuster, Moore, and Beveridge had pursued "hidden periodicity," Yule, Walker, and Wold pursued "flexible periodicity."

Bringing It All Together in Wold's Stationary Process

As we saw in the introduction to this history (see, e.g., Figure 1.6) oscillations were the intermediary between fluctuations and deviations. Theoretical investigations into stochastic oscillatory behavior, by Yule, Walker, Frisch, and Slutsky, were essential ingredients of the Herman Wold's study of stationary random processes. Early twentieth-century Russian probability theorists, such as Markov, were concerned with limit theorems in cases where the underlying probability structure was constant.[18] The Russian mathematicians essentially asked:

- What were the necessary, sufficient, and broadest conditions for the applicability of limit theorems?
- Under what conditions could one assume limit theorems with an empirical time series in which the observations were not independent?
- When could deviations be a simile for oscillations?

In work published in 1932 and 1934, Aleksandr Yakovlevich Khinchin answered these questions by defining the stationary stochastic process. A time series was stationary if its probability structure, including estimates of the mean and variance, did not change with samples from different time periods.

In his 1933 study on probability, Kolmogorov had examined the properties of general random processes. He demonstrated that a set of distribution functions could be seen as the equivalent to a single probability function in an infinite number of dimensions. Each observation of a time series generated from a random process could be treated as a random variable or the entire series could be treated as a sample value of a distribution with dimensions equal to the number of observations. Khinchin narrowed the scope of probability analysis of random processes to stationary processes. He demonstrated that random processes that were stationary were ruled by the law of large numbers. Wold provided a variety of translations of Khinchin's definition of stationary processes:

> Letting $(t) = (t_1, t_2, \ldots, t_n)$ represent an arbitrary set of time points and fixing arbitrarily a translation in time of this set, say $(t^*) = (t_1 + t, t_2 + t, \ldots, t_n + t)$, a random process as defined by a set $\{F\}$ of distribution functions is called

---

[17] Yule was careful in pointing out that his use of the word "oscillations" did not imply a strict periodicity: "They are wave-like movements . . . movements in which the length of time from crest to crest of successive waves is not constant, and in which, it may be added, the amplitude is not constant either, but would probably, if we could continue our observations over a sufficient number of waves, exhibit a frequency distribution with a fairly definite mode; to avoid the suggestions of strict periodicity and the use of the term *period* I propose to speak of them as *oscillations* of a given *duration*, the word *duration* to imply, not a fixed and constant duration, but an average only" (Yule 1921, 501).

[18] As can be seen in Table A2.10 in Appendix 2, 34 percent of time series studies before 1938 involving classical limit theorems were in Russian compared with only 6 percent in English. This illustrates the context for Andrei Markov's, Oskar Anderson's, and Alexander Alexandrovich Chuprov's verbal disdain for the English mathematicians' neglect of urns and mathematical expectation.

stationary if the two functions F belonging to the two sets (t) and (t^*) are identical. Thus, the probability laws assumed to rule the observational time series depend on time in such a way that if we replace time as measured from a fixed time point by a time variable measured from another time point, the probability laws will remain the same. In other words, if the development in a time series is known up to a certain time point say t, the probability laws ruling the continued development will depend only on the behaviour of the time series up to the time point t, not on the actual value of t.[19] (Wold [1938] 1954, 4)

Wold narrowed the scope of the analysis further by looking only at what he called "discrete" stationary processes. The discreteness lay in the fact that the series was restricted to observations taken at equidistant time intervals. This restriction insured that the number of dimensions of the distribution capturing the entire series was finite.

The classification of stationary series adopted by Khinchin and Wold was a mathematical one in contrast with the earlier empirically derived classifications of Wilhelm Lexis, Oskar Anderson, and Udny Yule. Lexis ([1879] 1942) had suggested that one calculate the dispersion of a series and compare it with the dispersion one would expect from a chance distribution. Anderson (1927) had argued that series should be classified according to the behavior of the variance in successive stages of differencing. Yule (1926) had classified series by the serial correlations of levels and differences. These classification systems all involved empirical manipulation. Although statisticians would eventually construct empirical tests or indications of stationarity (e.g., unit root tests), the starting point for the definition and classification of time series as stationary was hypothetical, mathematical deduction not empirical induction. A related difference between Khinchin's and Wold's classification scheme and those of Lexis, Anderson, and Yule was that the alternatives to the stationary process were neither clearly defined nor fully explored. Wold labeled all observational series that were not stationary processes as "evolutive," and he rarely mentioned them.[20]

In his thorough 1938 study of stationary processes, Wold integrated the probability theory of Kolmogorov and Khinchin with the experimental and empirical investigations of Schuster, Beveridge, Yule, and Slutsky. Wold demonstrated that the models of hidden periodicities, autoregression, and moving averages of random disturbances were special cases of discrete stationary processes. Wold grouped Yule's and Slutsky's schemes of moving averages with Yule's scheme of autoregression into a comprehensive scheme that he called models of "linear regression" (Wold [1938] 1954, 3). These models of

[19] The definition of identical distributions given by Wold is now described as "strong" or "strict" stationarity. The condition of "weak" or "second-order" stationarity is that the mean and variance are constant and the autocovariances depend only on the time lag. Strict and weak stationarity are equivalent if the distribution is normal.

[20] One of the few references to nonstationary processes was the stochastic difference equation that is now called the random walk. Wold described this as a case of a "discrete homogeneous process." He labeled it as "evolutive" because the oscillations tended to increase in amplitude over time (Wold [1938] 1954, 96).

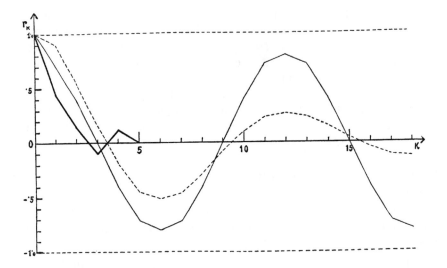

Figure 10.5   Wold's hypothetical correlograms used to illustrate the structural properties of three schemes of discrete stationary processes: hidden periodicities (thin line), linear autoregression (broken line), and moving averages (thick line). *Source:* Wold [1938] 1954, 147.

linear regression in which the random element plays an active role stand in contrast to the scheme of hidden periodicities in which the random element is merely analogous to passive errors of observations. Although he reiterated Slutsky's sinusoidal limit theorem as a demonstration that schemes of hidden periodicity were limit cases of processes of linear autoregression, Wold did not dismiss the harmonic approach of Schuster and Beveridge. In a structure parallel to that of Oscar Anderson, Wold argued that all stationary processes could be decomposed into a deterministic function of time and a linear combination of random elements. More specifically, Wold stated that the general discrete stationary process was composed of the process of hidden periodicities and of linear regression, the latter of which could be composed of a moving average and autoregression processes. Any stationary series, from which the deterministic component had been eliminated could be reduced to some linear combination of random disturbances.

Wold saw the stationary process as an oscillatory system and searched for a substitute to the classical periodogram as a means of determining which hypothetical model was an appropriate description of empirical stationary phenomena. Although periodograms had been the essential tool in determining hidden periodicities, they had not proved useful in modeling schemes of moving averages of disturbance terms and linear autoregression. Wold turned instead to the graphical practice of Yule and Walker, which was based on serial correlation coefficients plotted against intervals. Wold called these graphs of serial or autocorrelation coefficients "correlograms," and he used them as the chief means of modeling stationary processes. He demonstrated how correlograms could be used not only to distinguish schemes of autoregression and hidden periodicities, but also to indicate the presence of a moving average process. Wold generated hypothetical correlograms for the three key models (see Figure 10.5) and then compared these with the correlograms from empirical series, such as Beveridge's wheat index, to determine the appropriate model for that time series.[21]

With Wold's approach, correlograms and ordinary least squares regression became common and efficient tools for the analysis of stationary time series. The theoretical rationalization for the use of these tools was provided by a sweeping consolidation of past work on time series analysis: Wold clarified the definition of stationary processes rooted in Russian probability theory and decomposed the general stationary process into models of hidden periodicity, autoregression, and moving averages of random disturbances. If oscillations could be tamed, then a law of deviation could be assumed. If you were a time series person who liked your distributions normal and your regressions ordinary, the stationary process was for you. Cementing the relationship between this tamed motion and the law of error/deviation, Wold called the discrete stationary process the "normal process."

Wold not only defined "normal" motion, he also showed those working with empirical data what specific forms tamed series could take (see Figure 10.5). The only loose end left untouched by Wold was how to tame the series. Statisticians had been in training for that one for a long time, and they met the challenge with their algorithms for decomposing, detrending, and deseasonalizing. The precursors of most of those algorithms – differencing, percent change, index numbers, and moving averages – were the crude tools used by merchants and financiers to make a short-term profit, to persuade, or even to deceive. As we saw in Part I, the Bank of England's publicity of its bullion accounts from 1832 to 1844 with a three-month moving average demonstrated the advantages of an algorithm that veiled the extremes and traced out the secular movement. By the early twentieth century, statisticians were mapping out deviations from a moving average to get to the stationary oscillations. The nineteenth-century speculator, out to make a quick profit, focused on the net changes – the first differences. Economic statisticians, uninterested in the evolutive qualities of the economy, eager to examine relationships in a trade cycle, and desiring to use the cross-section tools of regression and correlation, differenced their series until they were tame and oscillatory. To both money movers and number crunchers, these algorithms proved to be fine tools for freezing history.

Conclusion

Until the late nineteenth century the statistical analysis of social data was seen as "frozen history." The law of deviation and the techniques of correlation and regression were designed for use with cross-section data. When statisti-

---

[21]   In an interview with David Hendry and Mary Morgan (1994), Wold explained that he searched for structure in the time series data while Frisch and econometricians in the Cowles Commission looked for structure in the behavioral equations of their models. Wold also told Hendry and Morgan that the most important development that he had added to the work of Yule and Slutsky was his decomposition theorem. In that interview, Wold discussed the influences of Kolmogorov, Frisch, and Cramér on his work.

cians, however, applied these techniques to time series data they often got nonsensical results. One solution to this problem was to search for a type of process, generating time series data, that was essentially equivalent to a state of rest. The discrete stationary process, the "normal process," was fully articulated by Herman Wold in 1938. Wold mathematically defined the stationary process, explained how it was compatible with ordinary least squares regression analysis, and demonstrated that autocorrelation coefficients plotted against serial intervals could indicate the appropriate model to describe an empirical stationary process. The three models that Wold argued composed the general stationary process were those of hidden periodicity, autoregression, and moving averages of random disturbance terms.

Wold adopted the autoregression model that Udny Yule had used in his 1927 study of sunspot activity and that Gilbert Walker had generalized in 1931. The seeds for autoregression, however, go back to Francis Galton's first regression on inheritance in sweet peas and F. E. Cave-Browne-Cave's interval correlation of barometric pressure at two stations. An understanding of this history of autoregression and serial correlation should make us more respectful of the myriad of interpretations of t, $t - 1$, and time itself, and more cautious in the applications of these techniques to comprehending processes of change. There are considerable problems in combining time series data with statistical methods that are based on rigorous sampling assumptions. Time series observations of a variable do not necessarily comprise a sample from a unique population. They are successive terms in a sequence, and each term may itself be the sole observation from a population. Yule's formulation of an autoregressive stochastic process and his suggestion of a disturbance term that took on the statistical properties that before were accorded to variables opened doors for statisticians who had been plagued by problems with economic time series. Yule, however, intended for serial correlation and autoregression to be methods for giving sampling structure, for determining where one generation ended and another began. They were aids to the decomposition of time series and to revealing oscillatory patterns rather than predicting future outcomes.

In his pursuit of the cause of nonsense correlations, Yule noted in both his 1921 and 1926 studies that linear transformations of random disturbances could generate cyclical patterns. Eugen Slutsky explored this in more detail and went as far as to argue that moving summations of random disturbances could be the source of cyclical patterns in economic variables. Building on Slutsky's work, Wold used moving averages of random disturbances as one of this three generic models of discrete stationary processes.

The Russian school of probability theorists, which included Slutsky, Andrei Andreevich Markov, Andrei Nikolaevich Kolmogorov, and Aleksandr Yakovlevich Khinchin, based their analysis of probability theory on notions of mathematical expectation, random processes, and the conditions under which limit theorems were applicable. Drawing on the work of Wilhelm Lexis, Markov demonstrated that the law of large numbers and normal dispersion were appropriate even in some cases of dependent sequences. The key assumption, Markov argued, was not the independence of successive observations in a time series, but the constancy of the underlying probability structure.

This constancy of probability structure became Khinchin's anchor in defining the stationary process. With time series generated from a stationary stochastic process, the probability distribution, including the mathematical expectation of the first and second moments, remained constant with samples taken from different time sets of the same series. In his 1938 treatise, Wold narrowed this analysis of stationary random processes to cases where measurements were recorded at equidistant time intervals. Wold argued that series were either evolutive or stationary, and if the latter then they could be modeled as either schemes of hidden periodicity or of linear regression. The correlogram and ordinary least squares regression could be effective tools of analysis if series were not evolutive. The "if" was a major obstacle, however, particularly for economic time series. Despite Wold's claim to the contrary, many time series are not stationary in their raw form. Often, neither our frequency distributions nor our bivariate correlation surfaces nor our data generating processes are "normal." In manipulating the data until we arrive at the stationary – "normal" – process we usually come close to measurement without history. That should be questioned as seriously as measurement without theory or theory without measurement.

Epilogue

Measurement does not necessarily mean progress. Failing the possibility of measuring that which you desire the lust for measurement may, for example, merely result in your measuring something else – and perhaps forgetting the difference – or in your ignoring some things because they cannot be measured. ... To my mind Freudian psychology made more progress in a few years than measurement-psychology had made for decades. Mendelism again meant more progress than Biometry.

Udny Yule in a letter to Maurice Kendall (Kendall 1952, 160)

I think the economic, as distinguished from the mathematical, student is hurt by being invited to spend his time on them [mathematical toys, such as least squares], before he has made a sufficiently realistic study of those statistics to know roughly, without calculation, on which side of the target the centre of the shots lies. He assumes there is no wind. I believe that a Boer marksman, who takes account of the wind, will by instinct get nearer the truth than he by mathematics. To study the wind and guess how it will deflect the bullets is, in my opinion, *the* work of the statistician. Do not you encourage men to neglect the wind?

Alfred Marshall in a 1901 letter to Alfred Bowley (*Memorials* 1925, 419)

There will be practitioners of time series analysis who think this history ends where it should begin. Herman Wold's 1938 treatise on stationary stochastic processes is a significant starting point for several reasons: Wold spelled out the autoregressive, moving-average, modeling approach that would be used in the coming decades to investigate stochastic processes, his work spurred further development in spectral analysis, he gave justification for the use of sums of squares in the analysis of stationary time series, and he put correlograms front and center as the key means to model specification. I would argue, however, that an interesting and revealing history lies with the groping toward the concept of stationary stochastic processes. I want to use this final space to review two of the overarching themes that have come out of this historical exploration: the importance of practice to the development of mathematical statistics; and contradictions that can arise when we use tools of logical comparison to analyze processes of change.

Importance of Practice

Until recently, most historians of mathematics and science have not dwelled on the key role of practice in forming methods and ideas. We readily accept that in our economic system time is money; it stands to reason that commercial arithmetic could be a source of algorithms for time series analysis. Merchants, financiers, and speculators were among the earliest manipulators of time series data, and it is from their practice that many of the tools associated with the analysis of stationary time series derive. Although the tools have been appropriated to different contexts, an understanding of their earlier uses sheds light on their present capacities. Differencing time series is a key technique for getting from fluctuations to deviations by freezing history. It is no coincidence that a financier with a short-term profit perspective should find first differences as useful as the statistician anxious to make her or his data "stationary." Similarly, studying the veiling/persuading history of truth-seeking tools such as index numbers and moving averages enables us to understand their potential and shortcomings for revelation.

The intimate relationship between mathematical statistics and practical finance continues today, and the transfer of insight is still two-way. At a workshop on new time series techniques, I was struck by an argument between two financial analysts over whether there was market trading in fourth moments. In our sophisticated financial markets, bets are placed not only on the mean and variance of price movements, but also on measurements related to skewness, kurtosis, and the volatility of the volatility. The financial press has been tracking corporate research on "analytics" used to identify and model unusual trades. Many of the new algorithms developed in this research on trading are corporate secrets, but it is likely some will trickle upward and be appropriated and generalized by academics in mathematics, statistics, and computer science.[1] In a similar fashion, academic statisticians eventually learned of William Gosset's (alias Student's) formulation of the t-distribution to handle sampling problems at the Guinness brewery.

The unusual analytical connection of time and dispersion that arises when a trader or institution attempts to stay one step ahead in financial capitalism is a likely starting point for statistical theory. For example, many players in stock and derivative markets use the high-low-close chart to track the daily range of and changes in prices. This is a visual image of the historical variation of a logical variation of prices. The length of the vertical line measures the range for each day and the shifting of the range and closing price maps out the fluctuations from day to day. I have wondered which came first, the high-low-close chart or the standard error chart used to show the dispersion of y

---

[1]   A 1991 article in the *Wall Street Journal* ("Mathematicians Race to Develop New Kinds of Trading Instruments," October 18, C1) gives a flavor for the recent synergy between mathematics and finance: the author, Craig Torres, suggested that the only source of monopoly power in Wall Street was the "proprietary mathematics of analytical systems"; one of the firms he reported on that developed mathematical systems for securities trading was called Algorithmics Inc.; and the director of International Business Machine's mathematical science department was quoted on his mathematical model developed with a Wall Street firm, in which time was measured by the daily worldwide volume of trading activity in a security.

values conditional upon an *x* value. I would not be surprised to see eventually the candlestick charts, favored by Japanese traders, adopted and adapted for statistical investigation.[2] Of course, commercial and financial practices are not the only possible source of algorithms and graphical tools for time series analysis. Perhaps some new empirical procedure will be sparked from female habits of day-to-day tracking of changes in temperature and mucus as part of the sympto-thermal method of birth control.[3] Whatever the mathematical future of the candlestick or basal temperature chart, we would do well to remember that the daily habits of quantitative reasoning in the affairs of business and home have been and will be a viable source of analytical tools for mathematicians and statisticians.

Measurement without History

In his letter to Maurice Kendall, quoted at the start of this chapter, Udny Yule, the "inventor" of ordinary least squares regression and models of autoregressive stochastic processes, cautioned against the lust for measurement. That humbling thought is appropriate to this history of time series analysis. There are limits to the net benefits of measurement, particularly measurement arising from a probabilistic strategy. Logical variation is a potent analytical tool, but we must be aware of its historical rationale, the analogies on which it is based, and thus its capacity, or lack thereof, for comprehending sequential variation. Throwing dice, drawing balls from an urn, and shooting at a target can all occur over time. The transfer of these analogies, however, to reasoning on changes in the weather or the economy is beset with problems. The fit of economic time series data into probability theory is rarely a very good one and we have to continually massage the data or even the results to make the fit. In our massaging, we neglect not only the wind, as Marshall feared, but history itself.

There are at least two reasons why the statistical analysis of stationary stochastic processes might be measurement without history:

- The manipulation of a time series necessary to render it stationary or "normal" can destroy the features that represent historical changes.

---

[2] The top of a candlestick measures the high price of the day, the bottom the low price and the heights of the horizontal tic marks across the stick indicate the opening and closing prices. On days when the closing price is lower than the opening price, the box between these two prices is filled in. In addition to this coding by shading, traders have given names to generic forms, such as the hanging man, the *doji* candlestick, and the hammer, that indicate market direction (see, for e.g., Holliston Hill Hurd's article on "Congestion Phase Analysis with Candlesticks" in the February 1993 issue of *Technical Analysis of Stocks & Commodities* or Steve Nison's (1991) book on *Japanese Candlestick Charting Techniques*.

[3] The uniqueness of the high-low-close or candlestick charts is the juxtaposition of logical dispersion over one day with the tracking in discrete time of the closing-to-closing or opening-to-closing fluctuations. With the daily plotting of basal temperature, the interesting features include the blend of qualitative and quantitative observations, rules-of-thumb connected with pre-shift and post-shift levels, and the addition of persistence to the analysis predicting the fertile period before and after the turning point of ovulation. The sympto-thermal method of birth control can serve as a useful analogy in macroeconomics classes to explain governments' use of leading, coincident, and lagging indicators to track the business cycle. With the reproductive cycle, consistency of mucus is a leading indicator, *mittelschmerz* is a coincident indicator, and elevation of temperature is a lagging indicator of ovulation. The analogy also

- Statisticians rarely use history as a tool in the choice of intervals between observations or the structuring of complementary samples.

Some of the natural philosophers mentioned in the this book, including Adolphe Quetelet, James Clerk Maxwell, and Henri Poincaré, have gone so far as to assert that the historical method and the statistical method are mutually exclusive enterprises. Historians are concerned with dating events and they are interested in the specific and the unique. Such concerns go against the grain of the science of means. Similarly, historians assume dependency in a series of sequential observations whereas some probabilistic approaches assume either independence or no linear correlation between sequential observations. The features that make a series "evolutive" or nonstationary are those that make it historical. Around the turn of the century, it was in the interests of both statisticians and social scientists to isolate and eliminate the secular or evolutive elements. In the early and mid-nineteenth century, Thomas Malthus, John Stuart Mill, Karl Marx, and William Roscher, among others, had pursued questions of secular change arising from a long-term perspective. Late nineteenth-century economic statisticians, however, were interested in the short-term irregular or periodic movements of economic variables. This may well be due to their attention to social and economic policy. As John Hicks (1979) has argued, economics is unique among the social sciences because it is specially concerned with the making of decisions and with the consequences that follow from decisions. As economics evolved into addressing the decisions of individuals, firms, and states, the relevant time frame became shorter.

The focus on the short-term and its relevance to decision making has been confining. Without that confinement, we could see secular change not as something we have to eliminate in our data but as something we should be focusing on. Steps in that direction have been taken by cliometricians investigating economic history and by statisticians using new methods to estimate the unobserved components of time series. An example of the former can be found in the lecture that Robert Fogel delivered upon his award of the 1993 Alfred Nobel Memorial Prize in Economic Sciences. Fogel used the terms "trend" or "secular change" eighteen times, and there is considerable measurement and innovative quantitative reasoning in his and other cliometricians' pursuit of long-term processes of economic growth. With regards to the statistical work on unobserved components, statisticians such as Andrew Harvey have used the Kalman filter and state space forms to model nonstationary phenomena such as stochastic trends, random walks, and seasonal patterns (see, e.g., Harvey 1989 or 1993), and advocates of cointegration acknowledge that long-run as well as short-run dynamics should be investigated (see, e.g., Perman 1991).

What is an average? The question, put to John Poynting in his 1884 Royal Statistical Society lecture on the use of moving averages, is rarely asked in our sophisticated statistical analyses of time series data. It is, however, an

helps students understand that the empirical measurement are indicative of, but not synonymous with, the causes (e.g., the hormonal changes in the case of the reproductive cycle).

important question in light of the fact that our tools of correlation, regression, and hypothesis testing rest on deviations from a meaningful average value. We usually seek as many observations as possible. The time intervals between observations are kept equal and our choice of interval duration is based on the exigencies of bookkeeping. The problems of time are perceived a posteriori – do empirical results indicate we have multicollinearity or autocorrelation of residuals? We should take more into consideration in our a priori approach and define statistical populations before constructing samples. With time series data this requires acknowledgment of the principle of complementarity, the potential inherent in relative time frameworks, and the conscious choice of interval duration. A series of observations united by a common name is not necessarily a sample from a singular statistical population. Also, the causes that influence a variable do not all act within the same time framework. There have been some recent attempts to replace the equal intervals of calendar time with historically determined data-based time scales (see, e.g., James Stock's 1988 essay on "time deformation"), but these are few and far between.

In addition to our typical approach of decomposing time series until the residual series is a tame, "normal" processes, there is another sense in which we engage measurement without history. We usually take our taming tools as given, assuming that the honing in academic discourse has left us with the best and sharpest of instruments. With the exception of a page or two of introductory text on the what and when of ivory tower discovery, our statistical manuals do not explore context of origin. Pursuing a history of the commercial and political practice and the scientific subject contexts that nurtured these algorithms is not only a scenic route to understanding time series analysis, it also makes us mindful of the capacities, and the lack thereof, of the tools that we use.

Appendix 1

Techniques of Time Series Analysis

The purpose of this appendix is to give a brief technical explanation of the concepts and techniques discussed in this history of time series analysis.

Data Manipulation Techniques Covered in Part I

First differences, index numbers, moving averages, and relative time frameworks are generally used on the raw time series before regression or spectral analysis is applied. These tools of data manipulation make time series more amenable to the statistical tools originally developed for cross section data or random trials; after manipulation the "residual" or "corrected" time series can often be assumed to be data generated from a stationary process. The first four techniques explained here and discussed in Part I are technical solutions to the contradictions involved in applying the analysis of logical, static comparison to the data emanating from temporal processes.

First Differences

With first differences, a new series is created by subtracting each value in a series from the previous value. For example, the series on the right are the first differences of the series on the left:

Date	Raw Data	First Differences
Month 1	$10,000	
Month 2	$12,000	$2,000
Month 3	$9,000	−$3,000
Month 4	$15,000	$6,000

Changes, or differences, are usually statistically more manageable than levels; they are more likely to oscillate about a constant mean with no trend component. The differenced series often satisfies the stationarity criteria empowering logical variation tools for the study of temporal processes. George

Box and Gwilym Jenkins (1970) suggested a model selection procedure based on the order of differencing needed to make a series stationary; this order of differencing, or of "integration," refers to the I in the ARIMA (autoregressive integrated moving averages) approach. Differencing is also a key procedure used in the modeling of short-run dynamics in cointegration models (see, e.g., Perman 1991 or Rao 1994). The development of this comparison by subtraction from the speculative method of financiers to the variate difference method of the econometricians is explored in Chapter 3. There is a further discussion of Oskar Anderson's study of the statistical properties of differenced series in Chapters 8 and 9.

Index Numbers

Similar to first differences, index numbers emphasize change. An indexed series is a scaled series used to make relative comparisons, usually percent difference from the base or from another location in the indexed series. The entries of the indexed series are not measured in any units and their absolute values are meaningless unless one knows the base standard of the index and/or compares one observation with another. In the example below the actual values are on the left and the indexed values, with the base being month 2 = 100, are on the right.

Date	Raw Data	Index
Month 1	$10,000	83
Month 2	$12,000	100
Month 3	$9,000	75
Month 4	$15,000	125

A key advantage of the indexed series is that simple comparison by subtraction can be used to get a sense of relative change from the base period. For example, if I wanted to determine the growth rate from the base of month 2 to month 4 with the raw data, I would have to use subtraction and division to calculate the percent change:

$$\frac{15000 - 12000}{12000} = 0.25$$

With the indexed series, however, all I have to do is subtract the base value of 100 from 125 to get the answer of 25%.

The earliest example of scaling time series to emphasize relative change that I have come across was the Bank of England's scaled series of bullion in 1797 (discussed in Chapter 4). The adaptation of this tool allowed investigators to aggregate or group changes in cases where aggregation of absolutes would be impossible. The focus on rates of change enabled William Stanley Jevons and others to treat percent changes in each year as a sample and to group and compare movement in one series with that of another. Most indices used nowadays are composite indices. For example, the October value for the consumer price index is formed by multiplying the September value by one plus a weighted average of the percent changes in prices from September to October. The weights, used in computing the composite weighted average of monthly price changes for a basket of goods, add up to one and are determined in occasional major surveys of consumer expenditure. With regards to the use of indices, statisticians often divide actual values of income or expenditure by the consumer price index to "deflate" the data and put it into a constant dollar form. Similarly, monthly or quarterly values of economic time series are often divided by indices of seasonal variation to seasonally adjust data (see Chapter 9).

Moving Averages

A moving average series is created by averaging over a sequence of observations then moving forward one step and averaging over the next sequence of the same length. For example, the raw data series to the left was used to construct a centered, three-period, equally weighted moving-average series, and the moving average was subtracted from the raw data to yield the series of deviations on the far right.

Date	Raw Data	Moving Average	Deviations from Moving Average
Month 1	$10,000		
Month 2	$12,000	$10,333	$1,667
Month 3	$9,000	$12,000	−$3,000
Month 4	$15,000	$12,000	$3,000
Month 5	$12,000	$14,666	−$2,666
Month 6	$17,000		

The moving average smoothes the data, and in the right circumstances can eliminate cycles in the data and yield a linear trend. The trend becomes the reference mean. A new series, formed by calculating the deviation of the actual value from the moving average, yields the cycle without the trend (note here an upward trend in the moving-average column of data and the alternating pattern in the deviations from the moving average). Moving averages have been used not only for smoothing and decomposition (see Chapters 4 and 9), but also for models of stochastic processes and forecasting tools. In 1927, Eugen Slutsky used a moving summation of randomly generated numbers to model cyclical processes. Building on this, Herman Wold suggested the moving average of random disturbances as one of the basic models inherent in all discrete stationary processes (see Chapter 10). This type of model forms a part of the ARIMA (autoregressive integrated moving average) method affiliated with the Box–Jenkins approach to time series analysis widely used since 1970.

In the 1950s, operational researchers, including C. C. Holt, suggested using an exponentially weighted moving average to smooth data or to forecast future values. As a forecasting tool, the EWMA gives the most weight to the most recent actual value and the weights on the previous values decline exponentially as one uses values further back in time. For example, the simple exponential smoothing done on months 2–6 of the series presented now will give us a prediction of $16,072 for month 7:

Date	Raw Data	Weights	Weights × Raw Data	Forecast Month 7
Month 1	$10,000			
Month 2	$12,000			
Month 3	$9,000	.008	$72	
Month 4	$15,000	.032	$480	
Month 5	$12,000	.160	$1,920	
Month 6	$17,000	.800	$13,600	
Month 7				$16,072

The EWMA is a simple and inexpensive means of forecasting. It has become such a commonly used forecasting tool that theorists advocating new models of time series have celebrated it as a reduced form of special cases of their approach. For example, forecasts from a first-order moving-average model of first differences, ARIMA (0,1,1), are identical to EWMA forecasts. Also, an important study in the development of the structural (unobserved components) approach to time series analysis was John Muth's demonstration in 1960 that the statistical properties of the EWMA were consistent with a structural model of a random walk plus white noise. The history of the moving average, rooted in the reporting of financial data, is discussed in Chapter 4.

Relative Time Frameworks

With absolute time, every data point is associated with a unique date. With relative time, every data point is associated with a place in a sequence. In statistics a sequence can be mapped in relative time by connecting the means or medians of cross-section groups at each stage of the sequence. An example of this is the growth curves used by family physicians to illustrate the development of the typical child. The 50th percentile curve for height is formed by connecting the median height for a large group of newborns with the median value for a cohort of six-month-old babies with the corresponding value for a sample of twelve-month old babies, and so on. The result is a curve in what I call "cycle time," the cycle in this case being the human life cycle.

The importance of the relative time frameworks used by European financiers and almanac makers in the nineteenth century lies in the restructuring of time series data into samples that could be treated as cross sections. An example of the transformation of a singular time series of quarterly observations spanning two years into sequenced means of cross sections connected to give a sense of quarterly variation in the annual cycle is given next. The original time series in absolute time is on the left; the series of the mean value of the respective quarterly cross sections sequenced in relative time is on the right.

Date	Raw Data	Mean	Sequence
1st Qtr Year 1	$31,000	$32,500	Typical 1st Qtr
2nd Qtr Year 1	$44,000	$46,500	Typical 2nd Qtr
3rd Qtr Year 1	$40,000	$42,000	Typical 3rd Qtr
4th Qtr Year 1	$36,000	$37,000	Typical 4th Qtr
1st Qtr Year 2	$34,000		
2nd Qtr Year 2	$49,000		
3rd Qtr Year 2	$44,000		
4th Qtr Year 2	$38,000		

This rearrangement of weekly time series data into cross sections in cycle time is evident in several nineteenth-century business journals and almanacs. Stanley Jevons, one of the early users of the cycle-time framework for empirical investigation, gave credit to the commercial roots of this practice and added calculations of means and deviations to form a statistical tool for revealing laws of seasonal variation. The use of cycle time frameworks in economics and meteorology is examined in Chapter 5.

Statistical Concepts Covered in Part II

Part II of this history of time series analysis focuses on the more sophisticated tools of logical variation used in empirical investigation and mathematical statistics. The normal frequency distribution, the Pearson product moment correlation coefficient, and ordinary least squares regression (OLS) lines are constructed within a context of deviation from a mean. The toughest question facing statisticians using these tools for time series analysis is, What is an average? If it makes little sense to summarize the series with the arithmetic mean, it makes little sense to use correlation coefficients and OLS to estimate relationships between the raw series.

The Normal Law (of Error, of Accidental Causes, of Deviation)

Several mathematicians and natural philosophers mentioned in this history equated "law" with mathematical curve. This applied to both deductive and inductive inquires. Carl Friedrich Gauss and Pierre Simon Laplace derived their law of error from a priori reasoning:

$$f(x;\ \mu,\ \sigma) = \frac{1}{\sqrt{2\pi}\sigma}\ e^{-\frac{1}{2}\left(\frac{x-\mu}{\sigma}\right)^2}$$

In this equation, μ is the arithmetic mean of the distribution, σ is the standard deviation, and x is the actual value (not a deviation). When plotted against possible values of the x variable, this equation maps out the likely frequency of measurements generated in attempts to observe the true value of x. The curve is the bell-shaped, "normal" frequency distribution (see Figure 1.6c). The law met criteria of common sense – small errors are more likely than large ones, overestimation is as likely as underestimation – and it was verified not only in empirical studies of errors of observation but also in such measurements as of heights of many people from the same regiment. So the Gaussian-Laplace law of error was also a law of accidental causes and a law of deviation. There are other laws of error, frequency, and deviation, but there were several advantages to assuming a "normal" law: measurements of central tendency – mean, median, mode – exactly coincide; the common measurement of dispersion – the standard deviation – gives us a measurement of probable error of occurrence (we know that 68 percent of the observations will be within one standard deviation above or below the mean); and, as illustrated in the equation, the values of the mean and standard deviation are alone sufficient for specifying a normal curve and calculating relative frequencies for any other specified value.

Correlation

Deviation from the mean is also the kernel of correlation coefficients. In quantifying the extent of a linear co-relationship between two variables, we are asking if in one year the value of one variable is greater than its average, is the value of the other variable likely to be above or below average or unrelated to the first variable. The most commonly used measurement of correlation is the Pearson product moment correlation coefficient:

$$ r = \frac{\Sigma \ (X - \mu_x)(Y - \mu_y)}{N\sigma_x\sigma_y} $$

A value of the Pearson product moment correlation coefficient close to $r = 1$ indicates a strong, positive linear relationship; a value close to $r = -1$ indicates a strong inverse linear relationship; and a value close to $r = 0$ indicates no linear relationship. One can see from the numerator that in the case of a higher than average X coincident with a lower than average Y a negative value will enter into the sum. If the deviations for Y are unrelated to deviations in X, then in the summing of the elements of the numerator over the sample size N, the positives and negatives will cancel out and the numerator will be close to zero. The history of correlation is discussed in Chapter 7.

Least Squares Regression

As explained in Chapter 6, the least squares algorithm was first used by Carl Friedrich Gauss and Adrian Legendre to reveal a true geometric relationship in the case where measurement error led to conflicting estimates. The criterion was to choose an estimate that minimized the sum of the squared errors. This criterion could be applied to one value – for example, the least squares criterion demonstrated that the arithmetic mean was the best estimate of the true value in the case of a normal distribution of values. There was initially an intimate relationship between the least squares algorithm and a normal distribution; Gauss first derived the latter as a by-product of his exploration of least squares. In 1897, Udny Yule suggested using the least squares algorithm to estimate a typical linear relationship between variables in the case where the relationship was not a fixed, physical or geometric one and in which the variables were not normally distributed. Ordinary least squares is now the most common means of performing linear regression.

Francis Galton never used the least squares algorithm in estimating regression coefficients, but his data and Pearson's diagram of Galton's experiment on sweet peas can be used to illustrate least squares regression. In Figure 5.12, prediction errors for the seven observed coordinates would be measured by the length of a line perpendicular to the horizontal axis and drawn from the observed Y to the Y predicted by the regression equation. So for a parent sweet pea seed of 15, the average observed offspring size was 15.3 and the predicted was 15.4 giving an error of -0.1. With OLS regression, we would choose the regression line that minimized the sum of the squared prediction errors. The general principle of least squares is discussed in Chapter 7 and least squares regression is discussed in Chapter 9.

Formal Time Series Analysis

Specific models of linear regression used to represent time series, such as autoregression and moving averages, are described in detail in the text. Wold's decomposition of stationary processes into a deterministic component of hidden periodicity (discussed in Chapters 9 and 10) and a nondeterministic component of autoregression and moving averages of random disturbances (discussed in Chapter 10) spurred further developments in spectral analysis and the use of ARMA models. Practitioners of both of these will find much that is familiar in part two of this history. There is less of a link with the structural approach to time series analysis that has blossomed since 1980. This is partly because the questions that drove me to write this book were connected with the contradictions involved in using least squares regression to analyze time series data. Andrew Harvey (1989, 22–23) gives a brief historical background of the structural approach in *Forecasting, Structural Time Series Models and the Kalman Filter*. Harvey's book along with Marc Nerlove's, David Grether's, and José Carvalho's *Analysis of Economic Time Series* and Terence Mills's *Time Series Techniques for Economists* (1990) and *The Econometric Modelling of Financial Time Series* (1994) are accessible texts on the current state of the art of time series analysis.

Frequency Analysis of Worldwide Studies in Time Series and Stochastic Processes: 1847–1938

In 1965 the International Statistical Institute published a *Bibliography on Time Series and Stochastic Processes*, edited by Herman Wold, that classified over 5,900 studies made worldwide before 1960. The international panel of collaborators who compiled the bibliography were from 30 different countries and included Wold, Kenneth Arrow, M. Bartlett, Harold Cramér, James Durbin, and Andrei Nikolaevich Kolmogorov. The following tables analyze the 991 entries included in this bibliography that date from Buys Ballot's work in 1847 to Herman Wold's treatise on stationary time series analysis in 1938.[1] The absolute frequencies, relative frequencies, and cross tabulations are based on the six-factor code assigned to each study.

Language

Time series plots of publications by language and cross tabulations with language revealed some interesting distinctions. It is important to note that language refers only to the publication and not the nationality of the author. For example, the 1938 treatise on time series analysis by the Swedish mathematician Herman Wold enters as an English publication. Oskar Anderson, the Russian statistician who was a professor in Bulgaria, has only German and English entries in the bibliography. In some of the analysis that follows, I excluded the thirty-nine studies that were in languages other than English, French, German, Italian, and Russian. Figure A2.1 shows the different temporal patterns of language publications from 1900 to 1938. The Russian graph is the most remarkable. Russian studies picked up considerably in the 1920s, but they plummeted from twenty-one studies in 1930 to zero in 1931, which was a year of widespread famine, purges, and harsh censorship under Stalin. The heights of the previous decade were not regained in the years that followed.

[1] Wold's "Graphic Introduction to Stochastic Processes," which precedes the bibliographic entries, serves as a useful summary of the state of the theory in the early 1960s. Although the bibliography is extensive with due considerations for a variety of books and journals from many countries, I did notice a few significant omissions. For example, although there is an entry for Arthur Schuster's work in 1897, his two studies in 1906 are not mentioned, and John Norton's 1902 time series study on the New York money market was not mentioned.

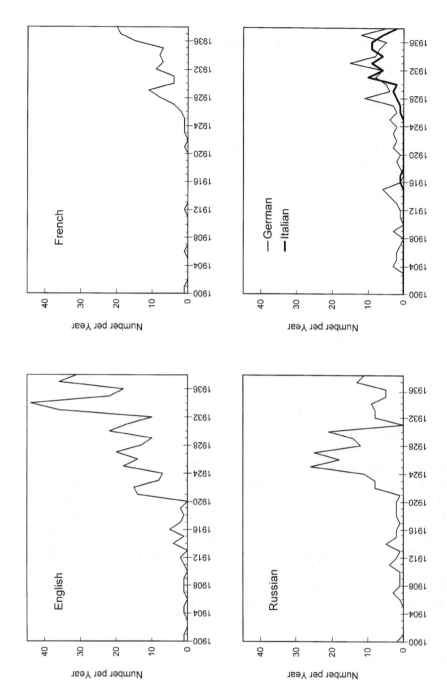

Figure A2.1   Annual frequency of time series studies by language of publication from 1900 to 1938. The data are based on the number of entries, by language, in the International Statistical Institute's *Bibliography on Time Series and Stochastic Processes* (1967).

Table A2.1 *Language of publication*

	Frequency	Percent
Bulgarian	3	.3
Czech	7	.7
Danish	8	.8
Dutch	3	.3
English	383	38.6
French	127	12.8
German	140	14.1
Hungarian	7	.7
Italian	67	6.8
Norwegian	1	.1
Polish	1	.1
Portuguese	1	.1
Russian	235	23.7
Romanian	2	.2
Swedish	2	.2
Ukrainian	4	.4
Total	991	100

The peak of English studies in 1934 is striking as well as the more than doubling of French studies from 1935 to 1937.

Table A2.9 is a cross tabulation of language and field of application. There was a close relationship between English language studies and economics: although 40% of all major language studies in this bibliography from 1847 to 1938 were in English, 59% of economics studies were in the English; similarly, although 36% of all studies pertained to economics, 52% of English studies were on economics. The Russian language publications also showed more economic applications than would be expected from the general pattern. The German language papers were more likely to be on the sciences, with few examples of economic applications. The French and Italian studies are distinguished by the high percentage that were not applied to any field.

Table A2.10 is a cross tabulation of language and type of problem. These contingencies are related to the correlations between language and field. For example, 90% of regression studies were in the field of economics (see Table A2.11), so it is not surprising to see that 69% of regression studies were in English, compared with 40% of total major language studies coded by group of problem. Similarly, relatively high percentages of correlation, trend, and seasonal variation/periodicity studies were in English or Russian. Also, 51% of diffusion studies were in English. With regards to French, although only 13% of studies coded by type of problem were in that language, 34% of diffusions studies, 35% of basic theory studies, and 46% of ergodic theory studies were in French. English works made up a very small proportion of studies dealing with classical limit theorem; these were more likely to be in

Table A2.2 *Year of publication*

Date	Frequency	Percent	Cumulative percent
1847	1	.1	.1
1879	1	.1	.2
1881	1	.1	.3
1889	1	.1	.4
1897	1	.1	.5
1898	1	.1	.6
1900	4	.4	1.0
1901	2	.2	1.2
1903	1	.1	1.3
1904	6	.6	1.9
1905	3	.3	2.2
1906	4	.4	2.6
1907	5	.5	3.1
1908	2	.2	3.3
1909	5	.5	3.8
1910	1	.1	3.9
1911	7	.7	4.6
1912	6	.6	5.2
1913	3	.3	5.5
1914	13	1.3	6.9
1915	9	.9	7.8
1916	9	.9	8.7
1917	6	.6	9.3
1918	5	.5	9.8
1919	6	.6	10.4
1920	3	.3	10.7
1921	19	1.9	12.6
1922	25	2.5	15.1
1923	20	2.0	17.2
1924	21	2.1	19.3
1925	50	5.0	24.3
1926	38	3.8	28.2
1927	57	5.8	33.9
1928	48	4.8	38.7
1929	43	4.3	43.1
1930	57	5.8	48.8
1931	39	3.9	52.8
1932	40	4.0	56.8
1933	77	7.8	64.6
1934	77	7.8	72.4
1935	55	5.5	77.9
1936	55	5.5	83.5
1937	90	9.1	92.5
1938	74	7.5	100
Total	991	100	

Table A2.3 *General type of process*

	Code	Frequency	Percent	Percent of nonmissing
General	1	116	11.7	12.0
Sums of independent variables	2	175	17.7	18.2
Markov processes	3	143	14.4	14.8
Stationary processes	4	64	6.5	6.6
Processes/discrete occurrences	5	42	4.2	4.4
Multivariable stochastic functions	6	9	.9	.9
Vacant class	7	7	.7	.7
Time series, no specification	8	316	31.9	32.8
Miscellaneous	9	92	9.3	9.5
Missing		27	2.7	
Total		991	100	100

Russian, German, or French. A relatively high percentage of studies of stochastic models of specific distributions were in Italian.

Field of Application

Cross tabulations of general field of application and type of problem are in Table A2.11. The natural and physical sciences were the subject for 22% of all time series published between 1847 and 1938, but they represented a much higher share of renewal, recurrence, passage time, diffusion, queuing, and storage problems and stochastic models for specific distributions. Economic studies comprised 36% of all studies, but a much higher percentage for investigations involving regression, correlation, trend, seasonal, and periodic analysis. Another cross tabulation revealed that empirical data were used in 57% of economic time series and in 31% of studies in the natural and physical sciences.

Temporal Patterns

Time series plots of the frequency of publications dealing with the analysis of trends and of periodicity are in Figure A2.2. It is important to note the small number of publications in most years and the fact that studies dealing with seasonal variation were grouped with general searches for strict periodicity (e.g., periodograms). Given that 88% of trend investigations and 73% of seasonal/periodic investigations were in the general area of economics, it is not surprising that these series follow a pattern similar to that of economic studies in Figure A2.3a. There was a downward trend in studies on trends during the economic depression of the thirties.

Figure A2.3a is an area graph of the total number of time series studies published in Europe and North America each year from 1900 to 1938 and the proportion accounted for by investigations applied to economics. The

Table A2.4 *Specific type of process*

	Frequency	Percent	Percent of nonmissing
General	4	.4	.4
Comprehensive, many processes	17	1.7	1.8
General theory of stochastic processes	72	7.3	7.5
Processes of order	2	.2	.2
Gaussian process	21	2.1	2.2
Sums of independent variables	12	1.2	1.3
Independent summands	135	13.6	14.0
Independent or orthogonal increments	29	2.9	3.0
Markov processes	10	1.0	1.0
Markov, discrete time	79	8.0	8.2
Markov, continuous time	11	1.1	1.1
Markov, discrete time/discrete space	5	.5	.5
Markov, discrete time/continuous space	9	.9	.9
Markov, continuous time/discrete space	4	.4	.4
Markov, continuous time/continuous space	25	2.5	2.6
Stationary processes	10	1.0	1.0
Stationary, discrete time	39	3.9	4.0
Stationary, continuous time	13	1.3	1.3
Stationary, Yule process	1	.1	.1
Processes w/ discrete occurrences	5	.5	.5
Poisson & other point processes	12	1.2	1.2
Branching processes	25	2.5	2.6
Stochastic functions of several variables	4	.4	.4
Sums of several variables	1	.1	.1
Stationary w/ other variables	4	.4	.4
Vacant class	7	.7	.7
Time series w/o stochastic specifications	316	31.9	32.8
Miscellaneous	93	9.4	9.6
Missing	27	2.7	
Total	991	100	100

effects of World War I (with European involvement from 1914 to 1918 and U.S. involvement from 1917 to 1918) and worldwide depression (beginning for many countries in 1929) are evident. Particularly striking is 1930 to 1932, when economic studies decreased by 94% from thirty-four studies to two, while noneconomic studies climbed 65%. The economy obviously affected economic studies far more than it affected studies in the natural and physical sciences or those with no application. The fluctuations in the total studies from year to year is considerable with most of that fluctuation being explained by the volatile economics component. We can see a more gentle upward movement from 1920 onward in the historical plot of noneconomic time series studies (Figure A2.3b). It's as if economic studies were primarily the

Table A2.5 *Group of problems*

	Frequency	Percent	Percent of economics
Process properties	3	.3	0.0
Basic theory	164	16.5	2.0
Classical Limit theorem	178	18.0	0.0
Renewal, recurrence	26	2.6	1.1
Diffusion, inc. random walk	67	6.8	.3
Ruin problems, theory of risk	17	1.7	0.0
Prediction problems	19	1.9	3.7
Queueing, storage problems	15	1.5	.6
Information theory	15	1.5	0.0
Ergodic theory	28	2.8	0.0
Stoch. models, specific distrib.	41	4.1	2.0
Methods of inference	3	.3	0.0
General theory of inference	46	4.6	9.7
Correlation methods	65	6.6	14.5
Regression methods	30	3.0	7.7
Trends, analysis, & elimination	85	8.6	21.3
Seasonal/periodicities	170	17.2	35.2
Surveying	3	.3	.6
General aids to computation	7	.7	.3
Random numbers, Monte Carlo	1	.1	0.0
Adaptation for computing machines	4	.4	1.1
Missing	4	.4	0.0
Total	991	100	100

Table A2.6 *Presence of empirical applications*

	Frequency	Percent
No applications	463	46.7
Indicated, not performed	203	20.5
Applied to empirical data	282	28.5
Applied to artificial data	31	3.1
Applied to emp. & art.	12	1.2
Total	991	100

erratic or cyclical component and the noneconomic studies were the informal trend component.

Confronted with these data for analysis, an econometrician would most likely decompose the series of total annual studies into the unobserved components of trend, cycle, and random elements, or she would difference the series until it was stationary and then model it as an autoregressive, moving-average

Table A2.7 *Field of application*

	Frequency	Percent	Percent of nonmissing
General or unspecified	1	.1	.2
Physics	59	6.0	9.8
Mechanics	10	1.0	1.7
Astronomy	8	.8	1.3
Geophysics	10	1.0	1.7
Meteorology	17	1.6	2.7
Engineering, electrical	17	1.7	2.9
Other technological	15	1.5	2.5
Chemistry	2	.2	.3
Biology	9	.9	1.5
Genetics	40	4.0	6.6
Medicine	8	.8	1.3
Miscellaneous	23	2.3	3.8
Economics, general	230	23.2	38.0
Consumer behavior	5	.5	.8
Inventory and invest.	6	.6	1.0
Economic growth, fluctuations	75	7.6	12.4
Complete economic model	23	2.3	3.8
Industry studies	9	.9	1.5
Distribution of income	4	.4	.7
Actuarial science	3	.3	.5
Demography	14	1.4	2.3
Mortality	10	1.0	1.7
Fertility	1	.1	.2
Psychology	1	.1	.2
Behavioral miscellaneous	2	.2	.3
Missing	386	39.0	
Total	991	100	100

Note: All economic applications comprised 35.5% of the total number of studies and 58.2% of those with some field of application.

Table A2.8 *Scientific nature of the entry*

	Frequency	Percent
Research paper	819	82.8
Expository paper	69	7.0
Monograph	66	6.7
Textbook	35	3.5
Total	989	100

Table A2.9 *Cross tabulation of language and field of application in time series studies, 1847–1938.*

Count Row Pct Col Pct	LANGUAGE					
	English En	French Fr	German Ge	Italian It	Russian Ru	Row Total
FIELD						
No Application	64 17.0 16.7	98 26.0 77.2	80 21.2 57.1	52 13.8 77.6	83 22.0 35.3	377 39.6
Science	109 51.9 28.5	21 10.0 16.5	52 24.8 37.1	12 5.7 17.9	16 7.6 6.8	210 22.1
Economics	198 58.6 51.7	6 1.8 4.7	4 1.2 2.9	2 .6 3.0	128 37.9 54.5	338 35.5
Demography & Sociol	12 44.4 3.1	2 7.4 1.6	4 14.8 2.9	1 3.7 1.5	8 29.6 3.4	27 2.8
Column Total	383 40.2	127 13.3	140 14.7	67 7.0	235 24.7	952 100.0

39 Missing Observations

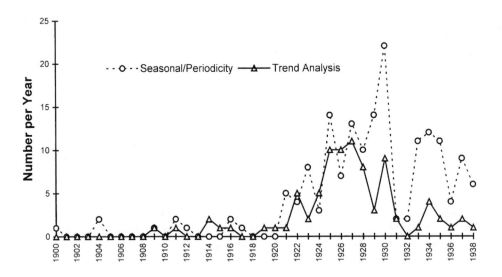

Figure A2.2   Annual frequency of studies in seasonal variation and periodicity and in trend analysis from 1900 to 1938. The data are based on the number of entries for these categories in the International Statistical Institute's *Bibliography on Time Series and Stochastic Processes* (1967).

process. Traditional analysis, however, yields little insight into this time series of time series studies. Decomposition of the series into the unobserved components of formal trend and deviations from the trend is less satisfactory than decomposition into the *observed* components of economic and noneconomic subjects. In addition to the problem of a trend, there is an alternating pattern from year to year. Udny Yule and Abraham Wald demonstrated the danger

Table A2.10 *Cross tabulation of language and type of problem in time series studies, 1847–1938.*

Count Row Pct TYPE OF PROBLEM	English	French	German	Italian	Russian	Row Total
Process properties		1 33.3	2 66.7			3 .3
Inference methods	2 66.7		1 33.3			3 .3
Basic theory	44 28.4	54 34.8	23 14.8	22 14.2	12 7.7	155 16.3
Classical Limit	10 5.7	41 23.4	45 25.7	19 10.9	60 34.3	175 18.5
Renewal, recurrence	18 69.2		1 3.8	5 19.2	2 7.7	26 2.7
Diffusion	34 50.7	3 4.5	23 34.3	3 4.5	4 6.0	67 7.0
Ruin problems	8 50.0	2 12.5	5 31.3		1 6.3	16 1.7
Prediction problem	7 43.8				9 56.3	16 1.7
Queueing,storage	3 25.0	1 8.3	4 33.3		4 33.3	12 1.3
Information,comm	14 93.3	1 6.7				15 1.6
Ergodic theory	5 17.9	13 46.4	6 21.4	1 3.6	3 10.7	28 2.9
Distribution models	16 39.0	2 4.9	9 22.0	14 34.1		41 4.3
General inference	25 58.1	1 2.3	3 7.0	2 4.7	12 27.9	43 4.5
Correlation	37 59.7	1 1.6	3 4.8		21 33.9	62 6.5
Regression	20 69.0	2 6.9			7 24.1	29 3.0
Trends	38 46.3	1 1.2	2 2.4		41 50.0	82 8.6
Season/periodicity	88 54.7	4 2.5	10 6.2		59 36.6	161 16.9
Surveying	1 50.0			1 50.0		2 .2
Computing methods	6 85.7		1 14.3			7 .7
Random #/Monte Car.	1 100.0					1 .1
Machine algorithms	4 100.0					4 .4
Column Total	381 40.2	127 13.4	138 14.6	67 7.1	235 24.8	948 100.0

43 Missing Observations

Table A2.11 *Cross tabulation of field of application and type of problem,*
1847–1938.

Count Row Pct	FIELD OF APPLICATION None	Science	Economics	Demography & Sociol.	Row Total
TYPE OF PROBLEM					
Process property	1 33.3	2 66.7			3 .3
Inference methods		2 66.7		1 33.3	3 .3
Basic theory	125 76.2	32 19.5	7 4.3		164 16.6
Classical Limit	168 94.4	8 4.5		2 1.1	178 18.0
Renewal, recurre	3 11.5	15 57.7	4 15.4	4 15.4	26 2.6
Diffusion	10 14.9	55 82.1	1 1.5	1 1.5	67 6.8
Ruin problems	12 70.6			5 29.4	17 1.7
Prediction probl	1 5.3	3 15.8	13 68.4	2 10.5	19 1.9
Queueing, storage	3 20.0	10 66.7	2 13.3		15 1.5
Information comm		15 100.0			15 1.5
Ergodic theory	20 71.4	8 28.6			28 2.8
Distribu. models	13 31.7	20 48.8	7 17.1	1 2.4	41 4.2
General inference	6 13.0	4 8.7	34 73.9	2 4.3	46 4.7
Correlation	3 4.6	10 15.4	51 78.5	1 1.5	65 6.6
Regression	1 3.3	1 3.3	27 90.0	1 3.3	30 3.0
Trends	4 4.7	3 3.5	75 88.2	3 3.5	85 8.6
Seasonal/periodic	13 7.6	28 16.5	124 72.9	5 2.9	170 17.2
Surveying			2 66.7	1 33.3	3 .3
Computing methods	2 28.6	4 57.1	1 14.3		7 .7
Random no./Monte C		1 100.0			1 .1
Machine algorithms			4 100.0		4 .4
Column Total	385 39.0	221 22.4	352 35.7	29 2.9	987 100.0

4 Missing Observations

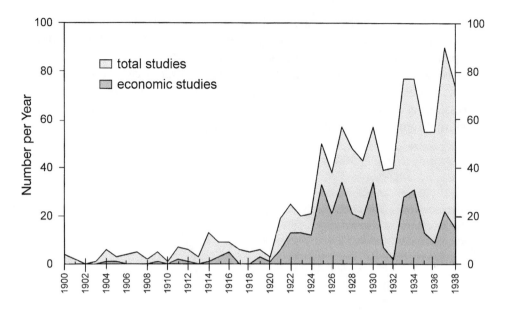

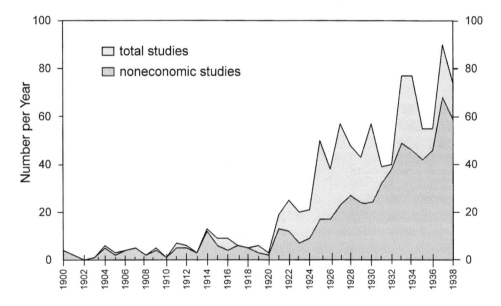

Figure A2.3   The number of studies published per year in time series analysis from 1900 to 1938. The top chart (a) illustrates the number of economic studies published annually in comparison with the total and the bottom chart (b) shows the annual frequency of noneconomic studies (applications in other social and natural sciences or those with no application). The data are based on the number of entries in the International Statistical Institute's *Bibliography on Time Series and Stochastic Processes* (1967).

of differencing such series that cycled within short intervals. Oskar Anderson was compelled to classify these *zackig* or zigzag series as ones not amenable to repeated differencing. Freezing history with our usual tool kit is ineffective in helping us to understand the development of time series analysis in the early twentieth century. Indeed, this time series is punctuated by war, political repression, economic depression, and a dynamic of academic discourse that defies mathematical reduction.

References

Alborn, Timothy. (1994) Economic Man, Economic Machine: Images of Circulation in the Victorian Money Market. In *Markets Read in Tooth and Claw*, ed. Philip Mirowski, pp. 173–196. Cambridge: Cambridge University Press.

Aldrich, John. (1987) Jevons As Statistician: The Role of Probability. *Manchester School*, 40, 233–253.

(1992) Probability and Depreciation: A History of the Stochastic Approach to Index Numbers. *History of Political Economy*, 24, 657–687.

Allardyce, Alexander. (1798) *An Address to the Proprietors of the Bank of England*, 3rd ed. London: W. J. and J. Richardson.

Anderson, Oskar. (1914) Nochmals über "The Elimination of Spurious Correlation Due to Position in Time or Space." *Biometrika*, 10, 269–279.

(1927) On the Logic of the Decomposition of Statistical Series into Separate Components. *Journal of the Royal Statistical Society*, 90, 548–569.

(1929) *Die Korrelationsrechnung in der Konjunkturforschung; ein Beitrag zur Analyse von Zeitreihn.* Bonn: K. Schroder.

Arnold, Barry C. (1983) *Pareto Distributions*. Fairland, MD: International Co-operative Publishing House.

Babbage, Charles. (1856) An Analysis of the Statistics of the Clearing House during the Year 1839. *Journal of the Royal Statistical Society*, 19, 28–48.

Bachelier, Louis. ([1900] 1964) Theory of Speculation. Trans. James Boness. In *The Random Character of Stock Market Prices*, ed. Paul Cootner, pp. 17–78. Cambridge, MA: MIT Press.

Bank of England. (1794–1802) *General Ledger*. No. 17, began 1 March 1794, ended 28 February 1802. London: Bank of England Archives, ADM 7 32.

(1819–1843) *Memorials, Contracts, Accounts for Parliament*. Vol. 1. London: Bank of England Archives, C66/1.

(1890) *Statistics Illustrating the Workings of the Accounts of the Bank of England.* London: Bank of England Archives No. ACC/B254.

Bateson, William. (1901) Heredity Differentiation, and Other Conceptions of Biology: a Consideration of Professor Karl Pearson's Paper "On the Principles of Homotyposis." *Proceedings of the Royal Society*, 69, 193–205.

([1913] 1930) *Mendel's Principles of Heredity*. Cambridge: Cambridge University Press.

Baxandall, Michael. (1988) *Painting and Experience in Fifteenth-Century Italy*. Oxford: Oxford University Press.

Bell, G. M. (1842) *The Country Banks and the Currency; an Examination of the Evidence on Banks of Issue, Given before a Select Committee of the House of Commons in 1841.* London: Longman, Brown, Green and Longmans.

Bell, John. (1665) *London's Remembrancer: A True Accompt of Every Particular Weeks Christening and Mortality in All the Years of Pestilence.* London: E. Cotes.

Bernoulli, Daniel. ([1778] 1961) The Most Probable Choice between Several Discrepant Observations and the Formation Therefrom of the most Likely Induction. Trans. C. G. Allen. *Biometrika*, 48, 1–18. Reprinted in *Studies in the History of Statistics and Probability*, ed. E. S. Pearson, Maurice G. Kendall, & R. L. Plackett, vol. 1, pp. 155–172. London: Charles Griffin, 1970–1977.

Bernoulli, James. ([1713] 1966) *Ars Conjectandi: Translations from James Bernoulli.* Trans. Bing Sung. Technical Report No. 2. Cambridge, MA: Harvard University, Department of Statistics.

Beveridge, William H. (1812) *Unemployment: A problem of industry.* London: Longmans, Green.

(1922) Wheat Prices and Rainfall in Western Europe. *Journal of the Royal Statistical Society*, 85, 412–459.

Block, Maurice. (1878) *Traité théorique et pratique de statistique.* Paris: Guillaumin et Cie.

Boag, Peter, & Grant, Peter. (1981) Intense Natural Selection in a Population of Darwin's Finches (Geospizinae) in the Galápagos. *Science*, 214, 82–85.

Bohr, Niels, & Henrik, David. ([1932] 1958) Light and Life. In *Atomic Physics and Human Knowledge*, pp. 3–12. New York: John Wiley & Sons.

Boltzmann, Ludwig. ([1872] 1909) Weitere Studien über das Wärmegleichgewicht unter Gasmolekülen. In *Wissenschaftliche Abhandlungen*, ed. Fritz Hasenöhrl, pp. 316–402. Leipzig: J. A. Barth. English translation in *Kinetic Theory*, vol. 2, ed. Stephen G. Brush, pp. 88–175. Oxford: Pergamon Press, 1966.

Bonar James. ([1929] 1966) *Theories of Population from Raleigh to Arthur Young.* London: Frank Cass.

Bourne, Stephen. (1894) Arithmetic, Political. In *Dictionary of Political Economy*, vol. 1, ed. R. H. Inglis Palgrave, p. 56. London: Macmillan.

Bouvard, A. (1827) Mémoire sur les observations météorologiques, faites à l'observatoire Royal de Paris. *Mémoires de l'Académie Royale des Sciences de l'Institute de France*, 7, 267–341.

Bowditch, Henry Pickering. (1877) The Growth of Children. In *8th Annual Report to the Massachusetts State Board of Health*. Boston: A. J. Wright.

(1891) The Growth of Children, Studied by Galton's Method of Percentile Grades. In *22nd Annual Report to the Massachusetts State Board of Health*. Boston: A. J. Wright.

(1894) Are Composite Photographs Typical Pictures? *McClures Magazine*, 3, 331–342.

(1980) *The Life and Writings of Henry Pickering Bowditch*, ed. Walter B. Cannon. New York: Arno Press.

Bowley, Arthur. L. (1895) Changes in Average Wage (Nominal and Real) in the United Kingdom between 1860 and 1901. *Journal of the Royal Statistical Society*, 58, 223–285.

(1901) *Elements of Statistics.* London: P. S. King and Son.

(1928) *F. Y. Edgeworth's Contributions to Mathematical Statistics.* London: Royal Statistical Society.

Box, George E. P., & Jenkins, Gwilym M. (1970) *Time-Series Analysis: Forecasting and Control.* San Francisco: Holden Day.

Brown, Robert. (1828) A Brief Account of Microscopical Observations Made in the Months of June, July and August 1827, on the Particles Contained in Pollen of Plants; and on the General Existence of Active Molecules in Organic and Inorganic Bodies. *Edinburgh New Philosophical Journal*, 5, 358–371.

Brush, Stephen G. (1968) A History of Random Processes. I. Brownian movement from Brown to Perrin. *Archive for the History of the Exact Sciences*, 5, 1–36. Reprinted in *Studies in the History of Statistics and Probability*, ed. E. S. Pearson, Maurice G. Kendall, & R. L. Plackett, vol. 2, pp. 347–382. London: Charles Griffin, 1970–1977.

  (1976) *The Kind of Motion We Call Heat: A History of the Kinetic Theory of Gases in the 19th Century*. 2 vols. Amsterdam: North Holland.

Burns, Arthur, & Mitchell, Wesley. (1946) *Measuring Business Cycles*. New York: National Bureau of Economic Research.

Burns, Eveline. (1927) Resume of Remarks at the Conference on Quantitative Economics. Oscar Morgenstern Papers, Box 3. Special Collections Library, Duke University.

Buys Ballot, Christoph Hendrik Diedrik. (1847) *Les changements périodiques de température, dépendants de la nature du soleil de la lune, mis en rapport avec le pronostic du temps, deduits d'observations Neerlandaises de 1729 à 1846*. Utrecht: Kemink & Fils.

  (1857) Note sur le rapport de l'intensité et de la direction du ven avec les écarts simultanés du baromètre. *Comptes Rendus Hebdomadaires des Séances de l'Académie des Sciences*, 45, 765–768. Paris: Mallet-Bachelier.

The Cambridge Encyclopedia of Astronomy (1977) Ed. Simon Mitton. New York: Crown.

Camerini, Jane R. (1993) Evolution, Biogeography, and Maps: An Early History of Wallace's Line. *Isis*, 84, 700–727.

Cargill, Thomas F. (1974) Early Applications of Spectral Methods to Economic Time Series. *History of Political Economy*, 6, 1–16.

Cartwright, Nancy. (1989) *Nature's Capacities and Their Measurement*. Oxford: Clarendon Press.

Cave, Beatrice, & Pearson, Karl. (1914) Numerical Illustrations of the Variate Difference Correlation Method. *Biometrika*, 10, 340–355.

Cave-Browne-Cave, F. E. (1905) On the Influence of the Time Factor on the Correlation between the Barometric Heights at Stations More Than 1000 Miles Apart. *Proceedings of the Royal Society of London*, 74, 403–413.

Cave-Browne-Cave, F. E., & Pearson, Karl. (1902) On the Correlation between the Barometric Height at Stations on the Eastern Side of the Atlantic. *Proceedings of the Royal Society of London*, 70, 465–470.

Chebyshev, Pafnuty Lvovich. (1867) On Mean Values. *Journal de Mathématiques Pures et Appliqées*, 12, 177–184.

Cheysson, M. Émile. (1887) *La statistique géométrique: Méthode pour la solution des problèmes commerciaux et industriels*. Paris: Publications du Journal Le Génie Civil.

  (1890) *Les méthodes de la statistique*. Paris: Librairie Guillaumin.

Cirillo, R. (1979) *The Economics of Vifredo Pareto*. London: Frank Case.

Clapham, Sir John. ([1944] 1966) *The Bank of England: A History*. 2 vols. Cambridge: Cambridge University Press.

Clarke, Hyde. (1847) Physical economy: A Preliminary Inquiry into the Physical Laws Governing the Periods of Famines and Panics. Cat. No. 34987.8. Kress Room, Harvard University, Cambridge MA.

Clayton, H. Helm. (1917) Effect of Short Period Variations of Solar Radiation on the Earth's Atmosphere. *Smithsonian Miscellaneous Collections*, 68(3), 1–18.

A Collection of the Yearly Bills of Mortality from 1657 to 1758 Inclusive ([1758] 1759) Ed. W. Heberden. London: A. Millar.

Cootner, Paul, ed. (1964) *The Random Character of Stock Market Prices*. Cambridge, MA: MIT Press.

The Correspondence between A. A. Markov and A. A.Chuprov on the Theory of Probability and Mathematical Statistics (1981) Ed. Kh. O. Ondar. Trans. Charles and Margaret Stein. New York: Springer-Verlag.

Cournot, Augustin. ([1838] 1927) *Researches into the Mathematical Principles of the Theory of Wealth*. New York: Macmillan.

Creighton, Charles. ([1891] 1965) *A History of Epidemics in Britain*. New York: Barnes and Noble.

Crum, W. L. (1923) Cycles of Rates on Commercial Paper. *Review of Economics and Statistics*, 5, 17–29.

Cunynghame, Henry. (1904) *A Geometrical Political Economy*. Oxford: Clarendon Press.

Darwin, Charles R. ([1845] 1960) *The Voyage of the Beagle*. London: J. M. Dent & Sons.

([1858] 1958) On the Variation of Organic Beings in a State of Nature; On the Natural Means of Selection; On the Comparison of Domestic Races and True Species. In *Evolution by Natural Selection*, pp. 259–267. Cambridge: Cambridge University Press.

([1859] 1928) *The Origin of Species*. London: J. M. Dent & Sons.

(1911) *The Life and Letters of Charles Darwin*, ed. Francis Darwin. New York: D. Appleton.

Dasgupta, Amiya K. (1985) *Epochs of Economic Theory*. Oxford: Basil Blackwell.

Daston, Lorraine. (1988) *Classical Probability in the Enlightenment*. Princeton, NJ: Princeton University Press.

David, Florence. (1962) *Games, Gods and Gambling. The Origins and History of Probability and Statistical Ideas from the Earliest times to the Newtonian Era*. London: Charles Griffen.

Davis, Harold T. (1941) *The Analysis of Economic Time Series*. Bloomington, IN: Principia Press.

Day, Richard. (1977) The Theory of the Long Cycle, Kondratiev, Trotsky, Mandel. *New Left Review*, 18, 66–82.

Defoe, Daniel. ([1722] 1968) *A Journal of the Plague Year*, ed. James Sutherland. New York: The Heritage Press.

Demidov, S. S. (1991) The Moscow School of the Theory of Functions in the 1930s. In *Golden Years of Moscow Mathematics*, ed. Smilka Zdravkovska & Peter L. Duren, pp. 35–54. Providence, RI: American Mathematical Society.

de Marchi, Neil, & Gilbert, Christopher, eds. (1990) *The History and Methodology of Econometrics*. Oxford: Oxford University Press.

De Moivre, Abraham. ([1718] 1756) *The Doctrine of Chances: or, A Method of Calculating the Probabilities of Events in Play*, 3rd ed. London: A. Millar.

Du Pont de Nemours, Pierre Samuel. ([1792] 1955) *On Economic Curves*. Trans. Henry W. Spiegel. Baltimore: Johns Hopkins Press.

The Economist, 1843–1943: A Centenary Volume (1943). London: Economist Newspaper.

Edgeworth, Francis Ysidro. (1885) Method of Statistics. *Journal of the Royal Statistical Society*, 50, 181–217.

(1887) Observations and Statistics: An Essay on the Theory of Errors of Observation and the First Principles of Statistics. *Transactions of the Cambridge Philosophical Society*, 14 (Part II), 138–169.

(1889) *Natural Inheritance* by Francis Galton. Book review. *Nature*, 39, 603–604.

([1891] 1925) Book Review of Alfred Marshall's *Principles of Economics*, vol. 1, 2nd ed. In *Papers Relating to Political Economy*, vol. 3, pp. 7–15. New York: Burt Franklin.

(1905) Law of Error. *Transactions of the Cambridge Philosophical Society*, 20, 36–65, 113–141.

(1908) On the probable errors of frequency constants. *Journal of the Royal Statistical Society*, 71, 381–387, 499–512, 651–678.

(1911) Probability. In *Encyclopedia Britannica*, 11th ed., pp. 376–403. Cambridge: Cambridge University Press.

(1925) *Papers Relating to Political Economy*. New York: Burt Franklin.

(1994) *Edgeworth on Chance, Economic Hazard, and Statistics*, ed. Philip Mirowski. Lanham, MD: Rowman & Littlefield.

Edwards, Ruth Dudley. (1993) *The Pursuit of Reason*. London: Hamish Hamilton.

Eisenhart, Churchill. (1961) Boscovich and the Combination of Observations. In *Roger Joseph Boscovich*, ed. L. L. Whyte, pp. 200–212. London: Allen & Unwin. Reprinted in *Studies in the History of Statistics and Probability*, ed. E. S. Pearson, Maurice G. Kendall, & R. L. Plackett, vol. 2, pp. 88–100. London: Charles Griffin, 1970–1977.

(1964) The Meaning of "Least" in Least Squares. *Journal of the Washington Academy of Sciences*, 54, 24–33.

(1983) Laws of Error I: Development of the Concept. In *Encyclopedia of Statistical Science*, vol. 4, pp. 530–547. New York: John Wiley & Sons.

Eldredge, Niles. (1985) *Time Frames: The Evolution of Punctuated Equilibria*. Princeton, NJ: Princeton University Press.

Epstein, Roy J. (1987) *A History of Econometrics*. Amsterdam: North Holland.

Evelyn, George Shuckburgh. (1798) An Account of Some Endeavours to Ascertain a Standard of Weight and Measure. *Philosophical Transactions*, 113, 133–182.

Falkner, Helen D. (1924) The measurement of seasonal variation. *Journal of the American Statistical Association*, 19, 167–179.

Farr, William. (1885) *Vital Statistics*. London: Sanitary Institute.

Feldman, Theodore S. (1990) Late Enlightenment Meteorology. In *The Quantifying Spirit in the 18th Century*, ed. Tore Frängsmyr, J. L. Heilbron, & Tobin E. Rider. Berkeley: University of California Press.

Ferber, Marianne A., & Nelson, Julie A. (1993) *Beyond Economic Man: Feminist Theory and Economics*. Chicago: University of Chicago Press.

Fermat, Pierre de. ([1654] 1962) Correspondence. Trans. M. Merrington. In *Games, Gods and Gambling: The Origins and History of Probability and Statistical Ideas from the Earliest Times to the Newtonian Era*, ed. Florence David, pp. 229–253. London: Charles Griffen.

Fetter, Frank Whiston. (1965) *Development of British Monetary Orthodoxy, 1797–1875*. Cambridge, MA: Harvard University Press.

Fienberg, Stephen E. (1979) Graphical Methods in Statistics. *American Statistician*, 33, 165–178.

Fisher, Irving. (1922) *The Making of Index Numbers: A Study of Their Varieties, Tests, and Reliability*. Boston: Houghton and Mifflin.

(1925) Our Unstable Dollar and the So-called Business Cycle. *Journal of the American Statistical Association*, 20, 179–202.

Fisher, Willard C. (1913) The Tabular Standard in Massachusetts History. *Quarterly Journal of Economics*, 27, 417–451.

Fogel, Robert. (1994) Economic Growth, Population Theory, and Physiology: The Bearing of Long-term Processes on the Making of Economic Policy. *American Economic Review*, 84, 369–395.

Foundations of Econometric Analysis. (1995) Ed. David F. Hendry & Mary S. Morgan. Cambridge: Cambridge University Press.

Frickey, Edwin. (1934) The Problem of Secular Trend. *Review of Economics and Statistics*, 16, 199–206.

Frisch, Ragnar. (1931) A Method of Decomposing an Empirical Series into its Cyclical and Progressive Components. *Journal of the American Statistical Association*, 26, 73–78.

(1933) Propagation Problems and Impulse Problems in Dynamic Economics. In *Economic Essays in Honour of Gustav Cassel*, pp. 171–205. London: George Allen & Unwin.

(1936) Annual Survey of General Economic Theory: The Problem of Index Numbers. *Econometrica*, 4, 1–38.

Gabaglio, Antonio. (1880) *Storia e teoria della statistica*. Milan: U. Hoepli.

Galilei, Galileo. ([1632] 1967) *Dialogue Concerning the Two Chief World Systems*. Trans. Stillman Drake. Berkeley: University of California Press.

([1642] 1962) Sopra le scoperte dei Dadi. Trans. E. H. Thorne. In *Games, Gods and Gambling*, ed. Florence David, pp. 192–195. London: Charles Griffin.

Galton, Francis. (1869) *Hereditary Genius: An Inquiry into Its Laws and Consequences*. London: Macmillan.

(1877) Typical Laws of Heredity. *Proceedings of the Royal Institution*, 8, 282–301.

(1886) Regression towards Mediocrity in Hereditary Stature. *Journal of the Anthropological Institute*, 15, 246–263.

(1889) *Natural Inheritance*. London: Macmillan.

(1901) Biometry. *Biometrika*, 1, 7–10.

(1909) *Essays on Eugenics*. London: Eugenics Education Society.

Gauss, Carl Friedrich. (1809) *Theoria motus corporum celestium*. Hamburg: Perthes et Besser.

([1821] 1957) Theory of the Combination of Observations Which Leads to the Smallest Errors. Trans. Hale F. Trotter. In *Gauss's Work (1803–1826) on the Theory of Least Squares*, pp. 1–46. Princeton, NJ. Mimeograph.

([1823] 1957) Application of Calculus of Probabilities to a Problem in Practical Geometry. Trans. Hale F. Trotter. In *Gauss's Work (1803–1826) on the Theory of Least Squares*, pp. 168–174. Princeton, NJ. Mimeograph.

Gauss, Carl Friedrich, & Weber, Wilhelm. ([1837] 1841) Results of the Observations made by the Magnetic Association in the Year 1836. Göttingen. In *Scientific Memoirs, Selected Transactions of Foreign Academies of Science and Learned Societies, and from Foreign Journals*, ed. Richard Taylor, pp. 20–97. London: Richard and John E. Taylor.

Georgescu-Roegen, Nicholas. (1971) *The Entropy Law and the Economic Process*. Cambridge, MA: Harvard University Press.

(1976) *Energy and Economic Myths: Institutional and Analytical Economic Essays*. New York: Pergamon Press.

Giffen, Robert. (1904) *Economic Inquiries and Studies*. London: George Bell and Sons.

(1913) *Statistics*, ed. Henry Higgs and G. Udny Yule. London: Macmillan.

Gigerenzer, Gerd, Swijtink, Zeno, Porter, Theodore, Daston, Lorraine, Beatty, John, & Krüger, Lorenz. (1989) *The Empire of Chance: How Probability Changed Science and Everyday Life*. Cambridge: Cambridge University Press.

Gilbart, James. (1854) The Laws of Currency As Exemplified in the Circulation of Country Bank Notes in England since the Passing of the Act of 1844. *Journal of the Royal Statistical Society*, 17, 289–321.

Gillispie, Charles. (1963) Intellectual Factors in the Background of Analysis of Probabilities. In *Scientific Change*, ed. A. C. Crombie, pp. 431–453. New York: Basic Books.

Gini, Corrado. (1926) The Contributions of Italy to Modern Statistical Methods. *Journal of the Royal Statistical Society*, 89, 703–724.

Gnedenko, Boris Vladimirovich, & Khinchin, Aleksandr Yakovlevich. (1962) *An Elementary Introduction to the Theory of Probability*. Trans. Leo Boron. New York: Dover Publications.

Gnedenko, Boris Vladimirovich, & Kolmogorov, Andrei Nikolaevich. ([1949] 1968) *Limit Distributions for Sums of Independent Random Variables*. Trans. K. L. Chung. Reading, MA: Addison-Wesley.

Gordon, H. Scott. (1955) The London *Economist* and the High Tide of Laissez Faire. *Journal of Political Economy*, 63, 461–488.

(1973) Alfred Marshall and the Development of Economics As a Science. In *Foundation of Scientific Method: the Nineteenth Century*, ed. T. Giere & R. Westfall, pp. 234–258. Bloomington: Indiana University Press.

Gottfried, Robert S. (1978) *Epidemic Disease in Fifteenth Century England: The Medical Response and the Demographic Consequences*. New Brunswick, NJ: Rutgers University Press.

Gould, Stephen Jay. (1981) *The Mismeasure of Man*. New York: W. W. Norton.

Graunt, John. ([1662] 1665) *Natural and Political Observations Made Upon the Bills of Mortality*. London: John Martin and James Allestry.

([1662] 1975) *Natural and Political Observations Made Upon the Bills of Mortality*. Salem, NH: Arno River Press.

([1662][1676] 1899) Natural and Political Observations Upon the Bills of Mortality, 5th ed. In *The Economic Writings of Sir William Petty Together with the Observations upon the Bills of Mortality More Probably by Captain John Graunt*, ed. C. H. Hull, pp. 318–346. Cambridge: Cambridge University Press. Reprinted in one volume by Augustus M. Kelly, 1986.

Great Britain, Parliament. (1832) *Report of the Committee on the Bank of England Charter 1832*. House of Commons Paper 722.

(1833) An Act for Giving to the Corporation of the Governor and Company of the Bank of England Certain Privileges for a Limited Period, under Certain Conditions, 3&4 WMIV cap.98.

Greenwood, Major. (1926) Professor Tschuprow of the Theory of Correlation. *Journal of the Royal Statistical Society*, 89, 320–325.

Hacking, Ian. (1975) *The Emergence of Probability*. Cambridge: Cambridge University Press.

(1990) *The Taming of Chance*. Cambridge: Cambridge University Press.

Hald, Anders. (1990) *A History of Probability and Statistics and Their Applications before 1750*. New York: John Wiley & Sons.

Hall, Lincoln W. (1924) Seasonal Variation As a Relative of Secular Trend. *Journal of the American Statistical Association*, 19, 156–166.

Hankins, Frank. (1908) *Adolphe Quetelet As Statistician*. New York: Longmans.

Harvey, Andrew C. (1989) *Forecasting, Structural Time Series Models and the Kalman Filter*. Cambridge: Cambridge University Press.

(1993) *Time Series Models*. Cambridge, MA: MIT Press.

Harvey, Andrew C., & Jaeger, Albert. (1993) Detrending, Stylized Facts and the Business Cycle. *Journal of Applied Econometrics*, 8, 231–247.

Heberden, William. ([1801] 1973) Observations on the Increase and Decrease of Different Diseases and Particularly of the Plague. In *Population and Disease in Early Industrial England*, ed. B. Benjamin. Farnborough: Gregg International Publishers.

Henderson, James P. (1985) The Whewell Group of Mathematical Economists. *Manchester School of Economic and Social Studies*, 53, 404–431.

   (1986) Sir John William Lubbock's *On Currency* – "an interesting book by a still more interesting man." *History of Political Economy*, 18, 383–404.

   (1994) The Place of Economics in the Hierarchy of Sciences: Section F from Whewell to Edgeworth. In *Markets Read in Tooth and Claw*, ed. Philip Mirowski, pp. 484–535. Cambridge: Cambridge University Press.

   (1996) *Early Mathematical Economics: William Whewell and the British Case*. Lanham, MD: Rowman & Littlefield.

Hendry, David F., & Morgan, Mary S. (1994) The ET interview – Professor Herman Wold. *Econometric Theory*, 10, 419–433.

Herschel, John Frederick. ([1850] 1857) Quetelet on probabilities. In *Essays from the Edinburgh and Quarterly Reviews*, pp. 365–465. London: Longman, Brown, Green, Longmans & Roberts.

   (1867) On the Estimation of Skill in Target-Shooting. London: Alexander Strahan.

Hicks, John. (1979) *Causality in Economics*. Oxford: Basil Blackwell.

Hilts, Victor L. (1973) Statistics and Social Science. In *Foundations of Scientific Method: The Nineteenth Century*, ed. Ronald Giere & Richard S. Westfall, pp. 206–233. Bloomington: Indiana University Press.

Holt, C. C. (1957) *Forecasting Seasonals and Trends by Exponentially Weighted Moving Averages*. ONR Research Memorandum, vol. 52. Pittsburgh, PA: Carnegie Institute of Technology.

Hooker, Reginald. (1898) Is the birth rate still falling? *Transactions of the Manchester Statistical Society*, 101–126.

   (1901) Correlation of the Marriage Rate with Trade. *Journal of the Royal Statistical Society*, 64, 485–703.

   (1905) On the Correlation of Successive Observations; Illustrated by Corn Prices. *Journal of the Royal Statistical Society*, 68, 696–703.

Hooper, Wynnard. (1881) The Method of Statistical Analysis. *Journal of the Royal Statistical Society*, 44, 31–48.

Hotelling, Harold. (1927) Differential equations subject to error, and population estimates. *Journal of the American Statistical Association*, 22, 283–314.

Hull, Charles H., editor. [(1899) 1986] *The Economic Writings of Sir William Petty Together with the Observations Upon the Bills of Mortality More Probably by Captain John Graunt*. Cambridge: Cambrige University Press. Reprinted in one volume by Augustus M. Kelly.

Hurd, Holliston Hill. (1993) Congestion Phase Analysis with Candlesticks. *Technical Analysis of Stocks & Commodities*, February, 37–44.

Huygens, Christian. (1657) Ratiociniis in aleae ludo. In *Exercitionum Mathematicarum*, ed. Francis van Schooten, pp. 517–534. Leiden: Johannis Elsevirii.

Ingrao, Bruna, & Israel, Giorgio. ([1987] 1990) *The Invisible Hand: Economic Equilibrium in the History of Science*. Trans. Ian McGilvray. Cambridge, MA: MIT Press.

International Statistical Institute. (1965) *Bibliography on Time Series and Stochastic Processes*, ed. Herman Wold. Cambridge, MA: MIT Press.

Jevons, William Stanley. (1857) On the cirrous form of cloud. *London, Edinburgh and Dublin Philosophical Magazine and Journal of Science*, 14, 22–35.

(1858) On the form of clouds. *London, Edinburgh and Dublin Philosophical Magazine and Journal of Science*, 15, 241–255.

([1862] 1884) On the Study of Periodic Commercial Fluctuations. In *Investigations in Currency and Finance*, ed. H. S. Foxwell, pp. 1–12. London: Macmillan.

(1863a) On the Study of Periodic Commercial Fluctuations. *British Association, Notes & Abstracts*, Report of 32nd Meeting (Oct. 1862), 157–158.

([1863b] 1884) A Serious Fall in the Value of Gold Ascertained and Its Social Effects Set Forth. In *Investigations in Currency and Finance*, ed. H. S. Foxwell, pp. 13–118. London: Macmillan.

([1866] 1884) On the Frequent Autumnal Pressure in the Money Market, and the Action of the Bank of England. In *Investigations in Currency and Finance*, ed. H. S. Foxwell. London: Macmillan.

(1869) The Depreciation of Gold. *The Economist*, 27, 530–532.

([1871] 1970) *The Theory of Political Economy*. London: Macmillan.

([1875] 1977) Letter to Alfred Marshall on 7 January, 1875. In *Papers and Correspondence of William Stanley Jevons*, vol. 4, ed. R. D. Collison Black, pp. 95–96. London: Macmillan.

([1877] 1958) *The Principles of Science: A Treatise on Logic and Scientific Method*, 2nd ed. New York: Dover Publications.

(1878a) On the Movement of Microscopic Particles Suspended in Liquids. London: Pamphlet of the *Quarterly Journal of Science*.

([1878b] 1884) The Periodicity of Commercial Crises and Its Physical Explanation. In *Investigations in Currency and Finance*, ed. H. S. Foxwell, pp. 206–219. London: Macmillan.

([1882] 1977) Married Women in Factories. Letter to the editor of the *Manchester Guardian*. In *Papers and Correspondence of William Stanley Jevons*, vol. 5, ed. R. D. Collison Black, pp. 163–167. London: Macmillan.

(1884) *Investigations in Currency and Finance*, ed. H. S. Foxwell. London: Macmillan.

(1972–1973) *Papers and Correspondence of W. S. Jevons*, ed. R. D. Collison Black. Clifton, NJ: Augustus Kelly.

Jordan, Karl. (1929) Sur la determination de la tendance séculaire des grandeurs statistiques par la méthode des moindres carrés. *Journal de la Societé Hongroise de Statistique*, 7, 567–599.

Kay, Geoffrey, & Mott, J. (1982) *Political Order and the Law of Labour*. London: Macmillan.

Kendall, Maurice G. (1945) On the Analysis of Oscillatory Times-Series. *Journal of the Royal Statistical Society*, 108, 93–141.

(1952) George Udny Yule, 1871–1951. *Journal of the Royal Statistical Society*, 115A, 156–161. Reprinted in *Studies in the History of Statistics and Probability*, ed. E. S. Pearson, Maurice G. Kendall, & R. L. Plackett, vol. 1, pp. 418–426. London: Charles Griffin, 1970–1977.

(1953) The Analysis of Economic Time Series – Part 1: Prices. *Journal of the Royal Statistical Society*, 96, 11–25.

(1956) The Beginnings of a Probability Calculus. *Biometrika*, 43, 1–14. Reprinted in *Studies in the History of Statistics and Probability*, ed. E. S. Pearson, Maurice G. Kendall, & R. L. Plackett, vol. 1, pp. 19–34. London: Charles Griffin, 1970–1977.

(1960) Where Shall the History of Statistics Begin? *Biometrika*, 47, 1–47. Reprinted in *Studies in the History of Statistics and Probability*, ed. E. S. Pearson, Maurice G. Kendall, & R. L. Plackett, vol. 1, pp. 45–46. London: Charles Griffin, 1970–1977.

(1961) Daniel Bernoulli on Maximum Likelihood. *Biometrika*, 48, 1–2. Reprinted in *Studies in the History of Statistics and Probability*, ed. E. S. Pearson, Maurice G. Kendall, & R. L. Plackett. London: Charles Griffin (1970–1977), 1:155–156.

(1969) The Early History of Index Numbers. *Review of the International Statistical Institute*, 37, 1–12. Reprinted in *Studies in the History of Statistics and Probability*, ed. E. S. Pearson, Maurice G. Kendall, & R. L. Plackett, vol. 2, pp. 51–62. London: Charles Griffin, 1970–1977.

Keynes, John Maynard. (1921) *A Treatise on Probability*. London: Macmillan.

(1925) Alfred Marshall, 1842–1924. In *Memorials of Alfred Marshall*, ed. A. C. Pigou, pp. 1–65. London: Macmillan.

(1936) William Stanley Jevons, 1835–1882. *Journal of the Royal Statistical Society*, 99, 523–524.

Khinchin, Aleksandr Yakovlevich. (1932) Sulle successioni stazionarie di eventi. *Giornale Institute Italian Attuari*, 3, 267–373.

(1934) Korrleationstheorie der Stationären Stochastischen Prozesse. *Mathematische Annalen*, 109, 604–615.

Kinetic Theory. (1966) Vol. 2, ed. Stephen G. Brush. Oxford: Pergamon Press.

King, George. (1909) On a New Method of Constructing and of Graduating Mortality and other Tables. *Journal of the Institute of Actuaries*, 43, 109–118.

King, Wilford I. (1912) *The Elements of Statistical Method*. London: Macmillan.

Klein, Judy L. (1986) The Conceptual Development of Population and Variation As Foundations of Econometric Analysis. Ph.D. Dissertation. London: London Guildhall University.

(1992) Mystical Scales – An Eighteenth Century Brainteaser. *Off the Record: A Bi-Annual Bulletin from the Bank of England Archive*, 1 (Winter), 1–2.

(1993) Mystical Scales and Cabalistical Numbers. *Off the Record: A Bi-Annual Bulletin from the Bank of England Archive*, 2 (Summer), 2, 6.

(1995a) The Ghosts of Octobers Past. *Wall Street Journal*, September 28, A20.

(1995b) The Method of Diagrams and the Black Arts of Inductive Economics. In *Measurement, Quantification and Economic Analysis*, ed. Ingrid Rima, pp. 98–139. London: Routledge.

Klein, Lawerence R. (1977) Comments on Sargent and Sims' "Business Cycle Modeling without Pretending to Have Too Much *a Priori* Economic Theory." In *New Methods in Business Cycle Research, Proceedings from a Conference*, ed. C. A. Sims, pp. 203–208. Minneapolis: Federal Bank of Minneapolis.

(1985) *Economic Theory and Econometrics*, ed. Jaime Marquez. Philadelphia: University of Pennsylvania Press.

Kolomogorov, Andrei Nikolaevich. ([1933] 1950) *Foundations of the Theory of Probability*. Trans. Nathan Morrison. New York: Chelsea.

Kondratieff, Nikolai Dmitrievich. (1922) *Mirovoe Khoziastvo i Ego Kon'iunktury vo Vremia i Posle Voiny*. Vologda: Oblastnoe Otdelenie Gosudartsvennogo Izdatelstva.

([1928] 1984) *The Long Wave Cycle*. New York: Richard and Snyder.

Krüger, Lorenz. (1990) Method, Theory and Statistics: The Lesson of Physics. In *Statistics in Science: the Foundations of Statistical Methods in Biology, Physics, and Economics*, ed. Roger Cooke & Domenico Costantini, pp. 1–14. Dordrecht: Kluwer.

Kreager, Philip. (1988) New Light on Graunt. *Population Studies*, 42, 129–140.

Kuznets, Simon. (1929) Random Events and Cyclical Oscillations. *Journal of the American Statistical Association*, 24, 258–274.

Kydland, Finn E., & Prescott, Edward C. (1996) The Computational Experiment: An Econometric Tool. *Journal of Economic Perspectives*, 10, 69–86.

Lambert, Johann Heinrich. (1760) *Photometria, sive di mensura et gradibus luminis colorum et umbrae*. Berlin: Augustae Vindelicorum.

(1779) *Pyrometrie*. Berlin: Bey Haude und Spencer.

Lancaster, H. O. (1972) Development of the Notion of Statistical Dependence. In *Mathematical Chronical*, 1970, pp. 1–16. Reprinted in *Studies in the History of Statistics and Probability*, ed. E. S. Pearson, Maurice G. Kendall, & R. L. Plackett, vol. 2, pp. 293–309. London: Charles Griffin, 1970–1977.

Laplace, Pierre Simon. (1810) Mémoire sur les approximations des formules qui sont fonctions de trés grands nombres et su leur application aux probabilités. *Mémoires de la Académie des Sciences de Paris*, 1809, 353–415, 559–565.

(1823) De l'action de la lune sur l'atmoshpere. *Annales de Chimie et de Physique*, 24, 280–294.

([1827] 1854) Mémoire sur le flux et reflux lunaire atmosphérique. In *Oeuvres complétes de Laplace publiees sous les auspices de l'Academie des sciences*, vol. 13, pp. 342–358. Paris: Gauthier-Villars.

Lardner, Dionysius. (1850) *Railway Economy: A Treatise on the New Art of Transport*, 2nd ed. New York: Harper & Brothers. Reprinted by Augustus Kelly in 1968.

Larson, Henrietta. (1948) *Guide to Business History*. Boston: J. S. Cramer.

Legendre, Adrien Marie. (1805) *Nouvelles méthodes pour la détermination des orbites des comètes*. Paris: Courcier.

Leibnitz, Gottfried W. F. ([1885] 1966) *Leibnizens Mathematische Shiften Herauspegeben von C. I. Gerhardt*. Trans. Bing Sung. Technical Report, no. 1966. Cambridge, MA: Harvard University Department of Statistics.

Lexis, Wilhelm. ([1879] 1942) *The Theory of the Stability of Statistical Series*. WPA No. 165-1-71-124. Trans. Eugen Altschul & W. C. Waite. Minneapolis: University of Minnesota, U.S. Works Projects Administration.

(1895) The Concluding Volume of Marx's *Capital*. *Quarterly Journal of Economics*, 10, 1–33.

Lorenz, Paul. (1935) Annual Survey of Statistical Technique: Trends and Seasonal Variations. *Econometrica*, 3, 456–471.

Lowe, Joseph. (1822) *The Present State of England in Regard to Agriculture, Trade & Finance; with a Comparison of the Prospects of England and France*. London: Longman, Hurst, Rees, Orme, and Brown. Reprinted by Augustus Kelly in 1967.

Lubbock, John William. (1830) The Tides. In *The British Almanac 1830: The Companion to the Almanac*, Society for the Diffusion of Economic Knowledge, pp. 49–67. London: Charles Knight.

(1833) Note on the Tides. *Philosophical Transactions*, 123, 19–22.

(1840) *On Currency*. London: Charles Knight.

Lyapunov, Aleksandr Mikhailovich. (1900) Sur une proposition de la théorie des probabilités. *Bulletin de l'Académie des Sciences de St. Pétersbourg*, 13, 359–386.

(1901) Nouvelle forme du théorème sur la limite de probabilités. *Mémoires de la Académie des Sciences de St.Pétersbourg*, 12, 1–24.

Lyell, Charles. (1853) *Principles of Geology or the Modern Changes of the Earth and Its Inhabitants Considered As Illustrative of Geology*, 9th ed. Boston: Little Brown.

Macaulay, Frederick. (1931) *The Smoothing of Time Series*. New York: National Bureau of Economic Research.

MacKenzie, Donald A. (1981) *Statistics in Britain, 1865–1930: The Social Construction of Scientific Knowledge.* Edinburgh: Edinburgh University Press.

MacKenzie, George. (1829) *Manual of the Weather for the Year MDCCCXXX: Including a Brief Account of the Cycles of the Winds and Weather, and of the Circle of the Prices of Wheat.* Edinburgh: William Blackwood and T. Cadell.

Maistrov, L. E. (1974) *Probability Theory: An Historical Sketch.* Trans. Samuel Kotz. New York: Academic Press.

Makridakis, Spyros. (1974) A Survey of Time Series. INSEAD Research Paper Series, No. 131. Fontainebleau, France: European Institute of Business Administration (INSEAD).

Malthus, Thomas. ([1798] 1926) *Essay on the Principle of Population As It Affects the Future Improvement of Society.* London: Royal Economic Society.

March, Lucien. (1905) Comparison numérique de courbes statistiques. *Journal de la Société de Statistique de Paris,* 46, 255–311.

Marey, Étienne Jules. (1878) *La méthode graphique dans les sciences expérimentales et principalement en physiologie et en médecine.* Paris: Libraire de l'Académie de Médecine.

Markov, Andrei Andreevich. (1899) The Law of Large Numbers and the Method of Least Squares (in Russian). *Izvestija Fiziko-Mathematicheskoe Obshchestva pri Kazanskom Universitet,* 8, 110–128.

(1906) Extension of the Law of Large Numbers to Interdependent Quantities (in Russian). *Izvestija Fiziko-Mathematiceskogo Obcestva pri Kazanskom Universitete,* 15, 135–156.

Marshall, Alfred. ([1885] 1925) The Present Position of Economics. In *Memorials of Alfred Marshall,* ed. A. C. Pigou, pp. 152–174. London: Macmillan.

(1898) Distribution and Exchange. *Economic Journal,* 8, 37–59.

([1920] 1961) *Principles of Economics,* 9th ed. London: Macmillan.

Marshall, Alfred, & Marshall, Mary Paley. (1881) *The Economics of Industry.* London: Macmillan.

Marx, Karl. ([1867] 1976) *Capital,* vol. 1. Trans. Ben Fowkes. Middlesex: Penguin Books.

Mathias, Peter. (1983) *The First Industrial Nation: An Economic History of Britain, 1700–1914,* 2nd ed. New York: Methuen.

Maxwell, James Clerk. ([1859] 1965) Illustrations of the Dynamical Theory of Gases. In *The Scientific Papers of James Clerk Maxwell,* vol. 1, ed. W. D. Niven, pp. 377–409. New York: Dover Publications.

([1870] 1965) Address to the Mathematical and Physical Sections of the British Association. In *The Scientific Papers of James Clerk Maxwell,* vol. 2, ed. W. D. Niven, pp. 215–229. New York: Dover Publications.

([1871] 1965) Introductory Lecture on Experimental Physics. In *The Scientific Papers of James Clerk Maxwell,* vol. 2, ed. W. D. Niven, pp. 241–255. New York: Dover Publications.

([1873] 1965) Molecules. In *The Scientific Papers of James Clerk Maxwell,* vol. 2, ed. W. D. Niven, pp. 361–378. New York: Dover Publications.

([1878] 1965) Diffusion. In *The Scientific Papers of James Clerk Maxwell.* vol. 2, ed. W. D. Niven, pp. 625–646. New York: Dover Publications.

Mayr, Ernst. (1982) *The Growth of Biological Thought: Diversity, Evolution, and Inheritance.* Cambridge, MA: Harvard University Press.

Mayr, Georg. (1877) *Die Gesetzmässigkeit im Gesellschaftsleben: Statistische Studien.* Munich: R. Oldenbourg.

McCulloch, J.R. (1856) *Dictionary, Practical, Theoretical, and Historical, of Commerce and Commerical Navigation.* London: Longman, Brown, Green, and Longmans.

Mean Looking. (1990) *The Economist,* May 5, 100.

Memorials of Alfred Marshall. (1925) Ed. A. C. Pigou. London: Macmillan.

Miller, Dennis. (1990) Economies of Scale. *Challenge,* May–June, 58–61.

Mills, Frederick Cecil. (1924) *Statistical Methods Applied to Economics and Business.* New York: Henry Holt.

Mills, Terence C. (1990) *Time Series Techniques for Economists.* Cambridge: Cambridge University Press.

(1993) *The Econometric Modelling of Financial Time Series.* Cambridge: Cambridge University Press.

Mirowski, Philip. (1984) Macroeconomic Fluctuations and "Natural" Processes in Early Neoclassical Economics. *Journal of Economic History,* 44, 345–354.

(1988) *More Heat Than Light: Economics As Social Physics, Physics As Nature's Economics.* Cambridge: Cambridge University Press.

(1989) "Tis a Pity Econometrics Isn't an Empirical Endeavor": Mandelbrot, Chaos, and the Noah and Joseph Effects. *Richerche Economisti,* 16, 111–129.

(1990) Problems in the Paternity of Econometrics. *History of Political Economy,* 22, 587–609.

Mitchell, Wesley C. (1909) The decline in the ratio of Banking Capital to Liabilities. *Quarterly Journal of Economics,* 23, 697–713.

(1927) *Business Cycles: The Problem and Its Setting.* New York: National Bureau of Economic Research.

(1929) A Review. In *Recent Economic Changes in the United States,* vol. 2, pp. 841–910. New York: McGraw-Hill.

Moore, Henry Ludwell. (1914) *Economic Cycles: Their Law and Cause.* New York: Macmillan.

(1917) *Forecasting the Yield and the Price of Cotton.* New York: Macmillan.

(1923) *Generating Economic Cycles.* New York: Macmillan.

Moore, Raymond C., Lalicker, Cecil G., & Fischer, Alfred G. (1952) *Invertebrate Fossils.* New York: McGraw-Hill.

Morgan, Mary S. (1987) Statistics without Probability and Haavelmo's Revolution in Econometrics. In *The Probabilistic Revolution,* vol. 2, ed. Lorraine Datson, Lorenz Krüger, & Michael Heidelberger, pp. 171–200. Cambridge, MA: MIT Press.

(1990) *The History of Econometric Ideas.* Cambridge: Cambridge University Press.

Morris, Corbyn. ([1758] 1759) Observations on the Past Growth and Present State of the City of London. In *A Collection of the Yearly Bills of Mortality from 1657 to 1758 Inclusive,* ed. William Heberden, pp. 77–86. London: A. Millar.

Mukerjee, Madhusree. (1995) About Face. *Scientific American,* December, 25.

Muth, John. (1960) Optimal Properties of Exponentially Weighted Forecasts. *Journal of the American Statistical Association,* 55, 299–306.

Nelson, Charles R., & Plosser, Charles I. (1982) Trends and Random Walks in Macroeconomic Time Series: Some Evidence and Implications. *Journal of Monetary Economics,* 10, 139–162.

Nerlove, Marc, Grether, David, & Carvalho, José. (1995) *Analysis of Economic Time Series: A Synthesis.* San Diego, CA: Academic Press.

Nison, Steve. (1991) *Japanese Candlestick Charting Techniques.* New York: Simon & Schuster.

Norton, John. (1902) *Statistical Studies in the New York Money Market.* New York: Macmillan.

Ogborn, Maurice Edward. (1962) *Equitable Assurances*. London: George Allen & Unwin.

Ogle, William. (1890) On Marriage Rates and Marriage Ages, with Special Reference to the Growth of Population. *Journal of the Royal Statistical Society*, 53, 253–280.

On the Finances of the Bank. (1797) *Monthly Magazine and Register*, 4, 248–251. Signed M.N., author believed to be William Morgan.

The Oxford Book of Money. (1995) Ed. Kevin Jackson. Oxford: Oxford University Press.

Palgrave, Inglis. (1873) Notes on Banking in Great Britain and Ireland, Sweden, Denmark and Hamburg. *Journal of the Royal Statistical Society*, 36, 27–158.

Pearson, Egon, ed. (1938) *Karl Pearson: An Appreciation of Some Aspects of His Life and Work*. Cambridge: Cambridge University Press.

(1965) Some Incidents in the Early History of Biometry and Statistics 1890–94. *Biometrika*, 52, 3–18. Reprinted in *Studies in the History of Statistics and Probability*, ed. E. S. Pearson, Maurice G. Kendall, & R. L. Plackett, vol. 1, pp. 323–338. London: Charles Griffin, 1970–1977.

Pearson, Egon S., Maurice G. Kendall, & R. L. Plackett, eds. (1970, 1977) *Studies in the History of Statistics and Probability*, 2 vols. London: Charles Griffin.

Pearson, Karl. (1891) The Geometry of Statistics. Lecture given at Gresham College. Pearson Papers, Box 49, The Library, University College, London.

([1892] 1969) *The Grammar of Science*. London: Walter Scott.

(1894a) Contributions to the Mathematical Theory of Evolution – I. *Philosophical Transactions*, 185, 71–110. London.

(1894b) The Geometry of Chance. Gresham College lecture notes. Pearson Papers, Box 49, The Library, University College London.

(1896) Mathematical Contributions to the Theory of Evolution – III. Regression, Heredity and Panmixia. *Philosophical Transactions*, 187, 253–318.

(1897) The Chances of Death. In *The Chances of Death and Other Studies in Evolution*, pp. 1–41. London: Edward Arnold.

(1898) Mathematical Contributions to the Theory of Evolution: On the Law of Ancestral Heredity. *Proceedings of the Royal Society of London*.

(1901a) Editorial. *Biometrika*, 1, 1–6.

(1901b) Mathematical Contributions to the Theory of Evolution. IX. On the Principle of Homotyposis and its Relation to Heredity, and to the Variability of the Individual and to That of Race. Part I. Homotyposis in the Vegetable Kingdom. *Philosophical Transactions*, 197, 285–379.

(1901c) On the Fundamental Conceptions of Biology. *Biometrika*, 1, 320–344.

(1904) On the Laws of Inheritance in Man. II. On the Inheritance of the Mental and Moral Characters in Man, and its Comparison with the Inheritance of the Physical Characters. *Biometrika*, 3, 109–112.

(1905) The Problem of the Random Walk. *Nature*, 72, 294, 342.

(1906a) Mathematical Contributions to the Theory of Evolution. – XV. A Mathematical Theory of Random Migration. Draper's Company Research Memoirs Biometric Series. Cambridge: Cambridge University Press.

(1906b) Walter Frank Raphael Weldon, 1860–1906. *Biometrika*, 5, 1–52. Reprinted in *Studies in the History of Statistics and Probability*, ed. E. S. Pearson, Maurice G. Kendall, & R. L. Plackett, vol. 1, pp. 265–322. London: Charles Griffin, 1970–1977.

(1914–1930) *The Life, Letters and Labours of Francis Galton*, 3 vols. in 4 parts. Cambridge: Cambridge University Press.

(1920) Notes on the History of Correlation. *Biometrika,* 13, 25–45. Reprinted in *Studies in the History of Statistics and Probability,* ed. E. S. Pearson, Maurice G. Kendall, & R. L. Plackett, vol. 1, pp. 185–206. London: Charles Griffin, 1970–1977.

(1923) Historical Note on the Origin of the Normal Curve of Errors. *Biometrika,* 16, 402–404.

(1978) *The History of Statistics in the 17th and 18th Centuries against the Changing Background of Intellectual, Scientific and Religious Thought: Lectures by Karl Pearson Given at University College London during the Academic Sessions, 1921–1933,* ed. Egon S. Pearson. London: Macmillan.

Pearson, Karl, & Elderton, Ethel. (1923) On the Variate Difference Method. *Biometrika,* 14, 281–309.

Pearson, Karl, & Lee, Alice. (1897) On the Distibrution of Frequency (Variation and Correlation) of the Barometric Height of Divers Stations. *Philosophical Transactions,* 190, 423–469.

Peart, Sandra. (1991) Sunspots and Expectations: W. S. Jevons's Theory of Economic Fluctuations. *Journal of the History of Economic Thought,* 13, 243–265.

(1993) W. S. Jevons's Methodology of Economics: Some Implications of the Procedures for "Inductive Quantification." *History of Political Economy,* 25, 435–460.

Penrose, Roger. (1989) *The Emperor's New Mind: Concerning Computers, Minds, and the Laws of Physics.* Oxford: Oxford University Press.

Perman, Roger. (1991) Cointegration: An Introduction to the Literature. *Journal of Economic Studies,* 18, 3–30.

Persons, Warren M. (1917) On the Variate Difference Correlation Method and Curve-Fitting. *Quarterly Publications of the American Statistical Association,* 16, 949–952.

(1923) Correlation of Time Series. *Journal of the American Statistical Association,* 18, 713–726.

(1924) Correlation of Time Series. In *Handbook of Mathematical Statistics,* ed. H. L. Rietz, pp. 150–165. Boston: Houghton Mifflin.

(1925) Statistics and Economic Theory. *Review of Economics and Statistics,* 7, 179–197.

Petty, William. ([1662]1986) Treatise on Taxes and Contributions. In *The Economic Writings of Sir William Petty,* ed. Charles H. Hull, pp. 1–97. Fairfield, NJ: Augustus M. Kelley.

([1676] 1899) Political Arithmetick. In *The Economic Writings of Sir William Petty,* ed. H. C. Hull, pp. 233–313. Cambridge: Cambridge University Press.

Plackett, R. L. (1958) The Principles of the Arithmetic Mean. *Biometrika,* 45, 130–135. Reprinted in *Studies in the History of Statistics and Probability,* ed. E. S. Pearson, Maurice G. Kendall, & R. L. Plackett, vol. 1, pp. 121–130. London: Charles Griffin, 1970–1977.

(1972) The Discovery of the Method of Least Squares. *Biometrika,* 59, 239–251. Reprinted in *Studies in the History of Statistics and Probability,* ed. E. S. Pearson, Maurice G. Kendall, & R. L. Plackett, vol. 2, pp. 279–292. London: Charles Griffin, 1970–1977.

Poincaré, Henri. ([1908] 1913) Science and Hypothesis. Trans. George Bruce Halsted. In *The Foundations of Science,* pp. 9–196. Lancaster PA: Science Press.

([1909] 1913) Science and Method. Trans. George Bruce Halsted. In *The Foundations of Science,* pp. 359–546. Lancaster PA: Science Press.

Poisson, Siméon-Denis. (1837) *Recherches sur la probabilité des jugements en matière criminell et en matière civile.* Paris: Bachelier.

Porter, Theodore M. (1985) The Mathematics of Society: Variation and Error in Quetelet's Statistics. *British Journal for the History of Science*, 18, 51–69.

(1986) *The Rise of Statistical Thinking, 1820–1900*. Princeton, NJ: Princeton University Press.

(1991) Objectivity and Authority: How French Engineers Reduced Public Utility to Numbers. *Poetics Today*, 12, 245–265.

Poynting, John Henry. ([1877] 1920) The Drunkenness Statistics of the Large Towns in England and Wales. In *Collected Scientific Papers*, pp. 497–503. Cambridge: Cambridge University Press.

(1884) A Comparison of the Fluctuations in the Price of Wheat and in Cotton and Silk Imports into Great Britain. *Journal of the Royal Statistical Society*, 47, 34–74.

Quetelet, L. Adolphe, J. (1827) Recherches sur la population, les naissances, les décès, les prison, les dépôts de mendicité, etc., dans le royaume des Pays-Bas. *Nouvaux Mémoires de l'Académie Royale des Sciences et Belles-Lettres de Bruxelles*, 4, 117–192.

(1835) *Sur l'homme et le development de se facultes, ou Essai de physique sociale*. Paris: Bachelier.

([1835] 1842) *A Treatise on Man and the Development of his Faculties*. Eng. Trans. of 1835 study. Edinburgh: William and Robert Chambers.

([1846] 1849) *Letters Addressed to H.R.H. the Grand Duke of Saxe Coburg and Gotha, on the Theory of Probabilites, As Applied to the Moral and Political Sciences*, Trans. O. G. Downes. London: Charles and Edwin Layton.

Quick, Rebecca. (1995) Betty Crocker Plans To Mix Ethnic Looks for Her New Face: General Mills Wants to Blend Features of 75 Women to Make One Perfect Cook. *Wall Street Journal*, September 11, A1, A6.

Rao, B. Bhaskara, editor. (1994) *Cointegration for the Applied Economist*. New York: St. Martin's Press.

Reid, Constance. (1982) *Neyman – from Life*. New York: Springer-Verlag.

Ricardo, David. (1962) *The Works and Correspondence of David Ricardo*, vol. 4, ed. Piero Sraffa. Cambridge: Cambridge University Press.

Richards, Joan L. (1988) *Mathematical Visions: The Pursuit of Geometry in Victorian England*. Boston: Academic Press.

Roberts, Harry. (1959) Stock-Market "Patterns" and Financial Analysis: Methodological Suggestions. *Journal of Finance*, 14, 1–10.

Robinson, Joan. (1980) Time in Economic Theory. *Kyklos*, 33, 219–229.

Roos, Charles F. (1934) *Dynamic Economics: Theoretical and Statistical Studies of Demand, Production and Prices*. Bloomington, IN: Principia Press.

Roscher, William. ([1877] 1878) *Principles of Political Economy*, 13th ed. Trans. J. Taylor. Chicago: Callaghan.

Ross, Dorothy. (1991) *The Origins of American Social Science*. Cambridge: Cambridge University Press.

Rutherford, Ernest. (1904) The Succession of Changes in Radioactive Bodies. *Philosophical Transactions*, 204, 169–219.

Rutherford, Ernest, & Soddy, Frederick. (1903) Radioactive Change. *Philosophical Magazine*, 5.

Samuelson, Paul A. (1947) *Foundations of Economic Analysis*. Cambridge MA: Harvard University Press.

Schabas, Margaret. (1990) *A World Ruled by Number: William Stanley Jevons and the Rise of Mathematical Economics*. Princeton, NJ: Princeton University Press.

Schlözer, August Ludwig. (1804) *Theorie der Statistik*. Göttingen: Vandenhoek und Ruprecht.

Schumpeter, Joseph. A. (1930) Book Review of Wesley Mitchell's *Business Cycles*. *Quarterly Journal of Economics*, 45, 150–172.

(1954) *History of Economic Analysis*. New York: Oxford University Press.

Schuster, Arthur. (1898) On Hidden Periodicities. *Terrestrial Magnetism*, 3, 13–41.

(1906) On the Periodicities of Sunspots. *Philosophical Transactions*, 206A, 69–100.

Seal, Hillary. (1967) The Historical Development of the Gauss Linear Model. *Biometrika*, 54, 1–24. Reprinted in *Studies in the History of Statistics and Probability*, ed. E. S. Pearson, Maurice G. Kendall, & R. L. Plackett, vol. 1, pp. 207–230. London: Charles Griffin, 1970–1977.

Shackle, G. L. S. (1965) *A Scheme of Economic Theory*. Cambridge: Cambridge University Press.

Sherman, Howard. (1991) *The Business Cycle: Growth and Crisis under Capitalism*. Princeton, NJ: Princeton University Press.

Sheynin, Oscar B. (1966) Origin of the Theory of Errors. *Nature*, 211, 1003–1004.

(1971) J. H. Lambert's Work on Probability. *Archive for the History of the Exact Sciences*, 7, 244–255.

(1984–1985) On the History of the Statistical Method in Meteorology. *Archive for the History of the Exact Sciences*, 31, 53–95.

(1989) A. A. Markov's Work on Probability. *Archive for the History of the Exact Sciences*, 39, 338–377.

(1994) Chebyshev's Lectures on the Theory of Probability. *Archive for the History of the Exact Sciences*, 46, 321–340.

Siberling, Norman. (1919) British Financial Experience, 1790–1830. *Review of Economic Statistics*, 1, 282–297.

Simpson, Thomas. (1755) A Letter to the Right Honorable George Earl of Marclesfield, President of the Royal Society, on the Advantage of Taking the Mean of a Number of Observations in Practical Astronomy. *Philosophical Transactions*, 49, 82–93.

(1757) An Attempt to Show the Advantage Arising by Taking the Mean of a Number of Observations, in Practical Astronomy. In *Miscellaneous Tracts on some Curious and very Interesting Subjects in Mechanics, Physical Astronomy and Speculative Mathematics*, p. 49. London: J. Nourse.

Sims, Christopher A. (1996) Macroeconomics and Methodology. *Journal of Economic Perspectives*, 10, 105–120.

Slutsky, Eugen E. (1927) Slojenie Sluchainih Prichin, Kakistochnik Ziklizeskih Prozessov. *Voprosy Konunktury*, 3, 1–61.

([1927] 1937) The Summation of Random Causes As the Source of Cyclic Processes. *Econometrica*, 5, 105–146.

Smith, Adam. ([1776] 1910) *An Inquiry into the Nature and Causes of the Wealth of Nations*. London: J. M. Dent & Sons.

Smith, Bradford B. (1926) Combining the Advantages of First-difference and Deviation-from-trend methods of Correlating Time Series. *Journal of the American Statistical Association*, 21, 55–59.

Snyder, Carl. (1933) The Concepts of Momentum and Inertia in Economics. In *Stabilization of Employment*, ed. Charles F. Roos, pp. 70–84. Bloomington, IN: Principia Press.

Society for the Diffusion of Useful Knowledge. (1830) *British Almanac*. London: Charles Knight.

Spearman, Charles E. (1906) "Footrule" for Measuring Correlation. *British Journal of Psychology*, 2, 89–108.

Speeches Delivered at a Dinner Held in University College, London, in Honour of Professor Karl Pearson, 23 April 1934 (1934). Cambridge: Cambridge University Press.

Sprat, Thomas. (1667) *The History of the Royal Society of London for the Improving of Natural Knowledge*. London: J. Martin.

Stewart, Balfour. ([1883] 1889) Meteorology: Terrestrial Magnetism. In *Encyclopedia Britannica*, 9th ed., pp. 159–184. New York: Charles Scribner's Sons.

Stigler, George. (1962) Henry L. Moore and Statistical Economics. *Econometrica*, 30, 1–21.

Stigler, Stephen M. (1982) Jevons As Statistician. *Manchester School*, 50, 354–365.

(1986) *The History of Statistics: The Measurement of Uncertainty before 1900*. Cambridge, MA: Belknap Press of Harvard University Press.

Stock, James H. (1988) Estimating Continuous-Time Processes Subject to Time Deformation. *Journal of the American Statistical Association*, 83, 77–85.

Stokes, George Gabriel. (1879) Note on the Above Paper. *Proceedings of the Royal Society*, 29, 122–123.

Strutt, John W. (1871) On a Correction Sometimes Required in Curves Professing to Represent the Connection between Two Physical Magnitudes. *London, Edinburgh and Dublin Philosophical Magazine and Journal of Science*, 42, 441–444.

Student (William Gosset). (1914) The Elimination of Spurious Correlation Due to Position in Time or Space. *Biometrika*, 10, 179–180.

Studies in the History of Statistics and Probability. (1970–1977) Ed. E. S. Pearson, Maurice G. Kendall, & R. L. Plackett. London: Charles Griffin

Swetz, Frank J. (1987) *Capitalism and Arithmetic: The New Math of the 15th Century*. La Salle, IL: Open Court.

Taylor, E. G. R. ([1954] 1968) *The Mathematical Practitioners of Tudor and Stuart England*. Cambridge: Cambridge University Press.

Thomas, Dorothy Swaine. (1925) *Social Aspects of the Business Cycle*. London: George Routledge and Sons.

Thompson, D'Arcy Wentworth. (1942) *On Growth and Form*. Cambridge: Cambridge University Press.

Tikhomirov, V. M. (1991) A. N. Kolmogorov. In *Golden Years of Moscow Mathematics*, ed. Peter Duren Smilka Zdravkovska, pp. 101–128. Providence, RI: American Mathematical Society.

Tilling, Laura. (1973) *The Interpretation of Observational Errors in the Eighteenth and Early Nineteenth Centuries*. Ph.D. Dissertation. University of London.

(1975) Early Experimental Graphs. *British Journal for the History of Science*, 8, 193–213.

Tinter, Gerhard. (1940) *The Variate Difference Method*. Bloomington, IN: Principia Press.

Todhunter, Issac. (1865) *History of the Theory of Probability*. London: Macmillan.

Tooke, Thomas. (1826) *Considerations on the State of the Currency*. London: John Murray.

(1829) *A Letter to Lord Grenville on the Effects Ascribed to the Resumption of Cash Payments on the Value of Currency*. London: John Murray.

Turner, H.H. (1913) On the Expression of Sun-Spot Periodicity As a Fourier Sequence, and on the General Use of a Fourier Sequence in Similar Problems. *Monthly Notices of the Royal Astronomical Society*, 73, Suppl., 714–732.

U.S. National Center for Health Statistics. (1995) *Vital Statistics of the United States, 1991: Life Tables*. Washington, DC: Public Health Service.

Veblen, Thorstein. (1919) *The Industrial System and the Captains of Industry*. New York: Oriole Chapbooks.

Viner, Jacob. (1937) *Studies in the Theory of International Trade*. New York: Harper & Brother Publishers.

von Thunen, Johann H. ([1842] 1966) *The Isolated State*, ed. P. Hall. Trans. C. M. Wartenberg. Oxford: Pergamon Press.

Wagner, Aldolpe. (1886) Wagner on the Present State of Political Economy. Trans. C. F. Dunbar. *Quarterly Journal of Economics*, 1, 113–133.

Wald, Abraham. (1936) *Berechnung und Ausschaltung von Saisonschwankungen*. Vienna: Verlag von J. Springer.

Walker, Gilbert. (1931) On Periodicity in Series of Related Terms. *Proceedings of the Royal Society*, 131, 518–532.

Walker, Helen. (1929) *Studies in the History of Statistical Method*. Baltimore: Williams & Wilkins.

Wallace, Alfred Russel. ([1858] 1958) On the tendency of varieties to depart indefinitely from the original type. In *Evolution by Natural Selection*, XV International Congress of Zoology and the Linnean Society of London, pp. 268–279. Cambridge: Cambridge University Press.

   (1916) *Alfred Russel Wallace Letters and Reminiscences*, ed. James Marchant. New York: Harper Bros.

Walras, Léon. ([1900] 1969) *Elements of Pure Economics or the Theory of Social Wealth*. Trans. William Jaffé. New York: Augustus Kelley.

Walsh, C.M. (1901) *The Measurement of General Exchange Value*. New York: Macmillan.

Weiner, Jonathan. (1994) *The Beak of the Finch*. New York: Alfred Knopf.

Weintraub, Roy. (1991) *Stabilizing Dynamics*. Cambridge: Cambridge University Press.

Weiss, George. (1986) Random Walks. In *Encyclopedia of Statistical Sciences*, vol. 7, pp. 574–580. New York: John Wiley & Sons.

Weldon, Walter Frank Rapheal. (1890) The Variation Occuring in Certain Decapod Crustacea I. Crangon Vulgaris. *Royal Society Proceedings*, 47, 445–453.

   (1892) Certain Correlated Variations in Crangon Vulgaris. *Royal Society Proceedings*, 51, 2–21.

   (1893) On Certain Correlated Variation in Carcinus Monas. *Royal Society Proceedings*, 54, 318–329.

Whitaker, John K. (1975) The Evolution of Alfred Marshall's Economic Thought and Writings over the Years 1867–90. In *The Early Economic Writings of Alfred Marshall, 1867–1890*, pp. 3–113. New York: Macmillan.

White, Lawrence H. (1984) *Free Banking in Britain*. Cambridge: Cambridge University Press.

Whittaker, E. T. (1924) *The Calculus of Observations: A Treatise on Numerical Mathematics*. London: Blackie and Son.

Whittaker, E. T., & G. Robinson. (1944) *The Calculus of Observations: A Treatise on Numerical Mathematics*, 4 ed. London: Blackie & Son.

Wiener, Norbert. (1964) *Selected Papers of Norbert Wiener*. Cambridge, MA: MIT Press.

Wilcox, Donald J. (1987) *The Measure of Times Past: Pre-Newtonian Chronologies and the Rhetoric of Relative Time*. Chicago: University of Chicago Press.

Wilson, James. (1840) *Fluctuations of Currency, Commerce and Manufactures Referable to the Corn Laws*. London: Longman, Orme, Brown, Greenard & Longmans.

   (1843) Editorial. *The Economist*, September 2, 15.

   (1844) Editorial. *The Economist*, May 11, 771.

Wise, Norton, & Smith, Crosbie. (1989) Work and Waste: Political Economy and Natural Philosophy in Nineteenth Century Britain. *History of Science*, 27, 263–301, 391–449.

Wold, Herman. ([1938] 1954) *A Study in the Analysis of Stationary Time Series*. Stockholm: Almqvist and Wiksell.

Working, Holbrook. (1934) A random-difference series for use in the analysis of time series. *Journal of the American Statistical Association*, 29, 11–24.

Wright, Sewall. (1967) Comments on the Preliminary Working Papers of Eden and Waddington. In *Mathematical Challenges to the Neo-Darwinian Interpretation of Evolution*, ed. P. S. Moorhead & M. M. Kaplan, pp. 117–120. Philadelphia: Wistar Insititute Press.

Young, Arthur. (1812) *An Inquiry into the Progressive Value of Money in England As Marked by the Price of Agricultural Products*. London: Macmillan.

Young, Warren L. (1982) Time and Concept Formation in Economics: A Suggested Approach. *Journal of Economic Issues*, 26, 161–179.

Yule, G. Udny. (1895) On the Correlation of Total Pauperism with Proportion of Out-Relief. *Economic Journal*, 5, 603–611.

(1896a) On the Correlation of Total Pauperism with Proportion of Out-Relief. *Economic Journal*, 6, 613–623.

(1896b) Notes on the History of Pauperism in England and Wales from 1850, Treated by the Method of Frequency-Curves; with an Introduction on the Method. *Journal of the Royal Statistical Society*, 59, 318–357.

(1897) On the Theory of Correlation. *Journal of the Royal Statistical Society*, 60, 812–854.

(1899) An Investigation into the Causes of Changes in Pauperism in England, Chiefly during the Last Two Intercensal Decades (Part I.). *Journal of the Royal Statistical Society*, 62, 249–295.

(1901a) The Applications of the Method of Correlation to Social and Economic Statistics. *Journal of the Royal Statistical Society*, 72, 721–730.

(1901b) Letter to Karl Pearson, July 1928. Pearson Papers, Box 905, The Library, University College, London.

(1906) On changes in the marriage- and birth-rates in England and Wales during the past half Century. *Journal of the Royal Statistical Society*, 69, 88–132.

(1911) *An Introduction to the Theory of Statistics*. London: Charles Griffin.

(1915) Review of *Economic Cycles: Their Law and Cause*. *Journal of the Royal Statistical Society*, 78, 302–305.

(1920) A Note on Mr. King's Method of Graduation and Its Relation to Graphic Method. *Journal of the Institute of Actuaries*, 52, 135–140.

(1921) On the Time-Correlation Problem with Especial Reference to the Variate-Difference Correlation Method. *Journal of the Royal Statistical Society*, 84, 497–526.

(1926) Why Do We Sometimes Get Nonsense-Correlations between Time-Series? – A Study in Sampling and the Nature of Time-Series. *Journal of the Royal Statistical Society*, 89, 1–65.

(1927) On a Method of Investigating Periodicities in Disturbed Series with Special Reference to Wolfer's Sunspot Numbers. *Philosophical Transactions*, 226, 267–298.

(1944) Obituary: Reginald Hawthorn Hooker, M.A. *Journal of the Royal Statistical Society*, 107, 74–77.

Index